BERTOLT BRECHT

Collected Plays: One

Baal
translated by Peter Tegel

Drums in the Night
translated by John Willett

In the Jungle of Cities
translated by Gerhard Nellhaus

The Life of Edward II of England
translated by Jean Benedetti

A Respectable Wedding
translated by Jean Benedetti

The Beggar or The Dead Dog
translated by Michael Hamburger

Driving Out a Devil
translated by Richard Grunberger

Lux in Tenebris
translated by Eva Geisel and Ernest Borneman

The Catch
translated by John Willett

Edited and introduced by
John Willett and Ralph Manheim

Methuen Drama

METHUEN WORLD CLASSICS

This edition first published in Great Britain in 1994 by Methuen Drama
an imprint of Reed Consumer Books Ltd
Michelin House, 81 Fulham Road, London SW3 6RB
and Auckland, Melbourne, Singapore and Toronto
by arrangement with Suhrkamp Verlag, Frankfurt am Main

This collection first published in Great Britain in 1970 by Methuen & Co. Ltd

A CIP Catalogue record for this book is available from the British Library

ISBN 0 413 68570 5

Printed and bound in Great Britain by Cox & Wyman Ltd, Reading, Berkshire

Contents

Introduction

I

This volume contains the plays which Brecht wrote in Bavaria before moving to Berlin in the autumn of 1924. In spring 1918, when he began work on the first of them, he was just twenty and a new student at Munich university. Six and a half years later he was a recognized, if controversial writer and the winner of a major literary prize. The best directors and actors of the day were performing his plays; he had also written many poems and short stories and directed one remarkable production. He had just been on the staff of the Munich Kammerspiele, one of the most enterprising small theatres in Germany, where his first and so far most successful play had been performed. Now he was about to go as a 'dramaturg', or literary adviser, to Max Reinhardt's Deutsches Theater in Berlin, at that time one of the world's three or four leading theatres.

Born on 10 February 1898, Brecht had been brought up in Augsburg, about forty miles west of Munich. His father, a native of the Black Forest, was sales director of the Haindl paper works there; his mother died in May 1920. *Baal*, whose first version was finished by July 1918, reflects much of the imaginary world of himself and his group of Augsburg friends, as well as the taverns and physical surroundings of the old city. For a few months just before and after the armistice of November 1918 he served as a medical orderly in a local army hospital, but had returned to Munich by February 1919, the early days of the Bavarian Soviet, during which he dashed off the first version of *Drums in the Night*. There he showed both plays to Lion Feuchtwanger, the author of *Jew Süss*, who was then living in Munich and had recently met him for the first time. His own drama professor Artur Kutscher was always bitterly critical of his work, but Feuchtwanger was encouraging, so that he began to make contact with publishers and, at the end of the summer vacation, to write theatre criticisms for the Augsburg Socialist paper. The one-act plays are also thought to have been mainly written that year, as well as a wealth of lost or unfinished works.

Baal was accepted by Feuchtwanger's own publisher Georg Müller, who had also published Wedekind's collected plays, but was withdrawn when already in proof for fear of the censorship. *Drums in the Night* was shown by Feuchtwanger to the Kammerspiele 'dramaturg' Rudolf Frank, who at some point in the summer of 1920 accepted it for production. Neither publication nor production in fact materialized for another two years, but the encouragement to Brecht was obvious. He left the university in the summer of 1921 and in November set out to try his luck in Berlin, a much more important city from the theatrical point of view.

The expedition was less successful than he had hoped. Neither the Deutsches Theater nor the State Theatre under Leopold Jessner would make any promises, and although Brecht was asked to direct Arnolt Bronnen's play *Vatermord* for the experimental Junge Bühne, it ended disastrously with a walk-out of the actors. He himself was taken to hospital suffering from undernourishment, due no doubt in part to the galloping currency inflation. But at least he made many connections or friendships which were to be important for his work: notably Bronnen (with whom he began collaborating on film treatments and various joint theatrical projects), Herbert Ihering the critic of the *Berliner Börsen-Courier* (a lifelong supporter, whose paper was later to serve as a launching-platform for many of his ideas), and Moritz Seeler the organizer of the Junge Bühne (who was to produce *Life Story of the Man Baal* in 1926). By the time of his return to Augsburg at Easter he had also completed the first version of *In the Jungle*.

In Bavaria 1922 was a Brecht year. Soon after his return the Munich Residenztheater accepted *In the Jungle*, thanks to the recommendations of its artistic adviser Jacob Geis and of its new chief director Erich Engel, who had arrived a few months earlier from his native Hamburg. *Baal* was at last published (by Gustav Kiepenheuer of Potsdam), while 29 September saw the première of *Drums in the Night*. Clearly this was very different from later Brecht productions, for Otto Falckenberg, the head of the Kammerspiele, staged it in expressionist style with angular poses and sets to match by his own staff designer Otto Reigbert. But Ihering came from Berlin to review it, and in the *Berliner Börsen-Courier* of 5 October he wrote that 'At 24 the writer Bert Brecht has changed Germany's literary complexion overnight. Bert Brecht has given our time a new tone, a new melody, a new vision.' Here too was 'a physical sense of chaos and decay':

Hence the unparallelled creative force of his language. It is a language you can feel on your tongue, in your gums, your ear, your spinal column.

Ihering was known to be the judge for that year's award of the Kleist Prize. This had been founded in 1911 by a group of Kleist enthusiasts to celebrate the centenary of the poet's death, and was intended for writers who had yet to establish themselves. Up to its abolition in 1932 it was probably the most significant literary award in Germany, having previously been given to the playwrights Sorge, Unruh, Hasenclever and Jahnn, while in 1923–5 it went to Musil, Barlach and Zuckmayer. On 13 November the *Berliner Börsen-Courier* announced that it had gone to Brecht, and not for *Drums in the Night* only but for all three of his completed plays. 'Brecht's linguistic power,' said Ihering's citation,

> is even more richly developed in *Baal* and *In the Jungle*. His language is vivid without being deliberately poetic, symbolical without being over literary. Brecht is a dramatist because his language is felt physically and in the round.

Because *Drums in the Night* was generally regarded as the prize-winning play it was widely performed all over Germany, notably in Berlin immediately before Christmas, when Falckenberg again directed it for the Deutsches Theater with a first-rate cast. Brecht always claimed that he had only written it to make money, and certainly it differs in several ways from his other works. Alone of those in this volume it seems to contain no anticipations of his later plays.

In Munich for two nights after the première it was followed by a midnight show called *The Red Grape* (*Die rote Zibebe*, a name at one time given to the tavern in Act 4, and also used of the moon which hangs so conspicuously over the action). This was described as an 'improvisation in two scenes by Bert Brecht and Karl Valentin', the latter being a famous Munich music-hall comedian. In the first scene Max Schreck, the actor who played Glubb, was the Freakshow Landlord who opened a series of curtained cabins, each containing a performer who stepped out to do a solo turn. The programme shows that these included the sailor-poet Joachim Ringelnatz, the reciter Ludwig Hardt, Brecht himself singing songs, and the dancer Valeska Gert, though for the second performance Brecht seems to have been replaced by his fellow-poet Klabund. The second scene was a sketch called 'Christmas Evening' by Valentin, whom a short programme note by Brecht compared with

Chaplin, among other things for his 'virtually complete rejection of mimicry and cheap psychology'. Valentin's influence has sometimes been seen in Brecht's farcical one-acters, though Brecht himself acknowledged it rather as affecting his work as a director, particularly his use of grouping.

That October Brecht was appointed to the Kammerspiele's dramaturgical and directing staff, where his main task was the adaptation and production of Marlowe's *Edward II*. The actual writing of this play, which is very largely an original work, must have taken place mainly in the winter of 1922–3, since the Berlin State Theatre started showing an interest in it early in the new year. It was done in collaboration with Feuchtwanger, whom Brecht saw frequently throughout 1923 and who is said to have inspired the speech characteristics of Shlink in *In the Jungle*. It was not however performed till the next year, and although there were two more Brecht premières in 1923, neither was at the Kammerspiele itself. First *In the Jungle* was staged at the Residenztheater on 9 May by Engel, with settings by Brecht's school-friend Caspar Neher: the beginning of a lifelong collaboration between the three men. Jessner of the State Theatre came from Berlin, as did Ihering, who again wrote enthusiastically, though not without observing that to anyone insensitive to its language the play must appear a muddle. This the local critics bore out; the three-hour performance was poorly received; it ran for only six evenings, and altogether was a disastrous enough flop to occasion the sacking of the theatre's artistic adviser. Nor was *Baal* in Leipzig at the end of the year any more successful. Alvin Kronacher's production at the Old Theatre on 8 December was taken off by order of the city council within a week, and the director reprimanded. It brought an interesting press controversy between Ihering and his rival Alfred Kerr as to the relative originality of Brecht and Toller, but Kerr was undoubtedly right when he wrote that 'The only hope for a Baalade like this is as a posthumous fragment . . .'. For the text as we have it was not performed again for another forty years.

The rehearsals for *Edward II* began that autumn under Brecht's own direction. Brecht also supplied the music; the sets were again by Neher, and as in the two previous Munich Brecht productions the actor Erwin Faber played the lead. The première on 19 March 1924 was somewhat thrown out by the drunkenness of one of the principal actors, but the local critics appreciated Brecht's success in conveying his ballad-like conception of the story (he apparently had the scene titles and dates announced before each episode), while Ihering was impressed by his handling of the ensemble scenes and the careful dissection of the long speeches. Knowing something of Brecht's as yet unformulated theoretical ideas, he realized that the audience with which he most sympathized was that for boxing matches, sporting events and incidents in the street, and attributed to this novel orientation part of the success of the production. Looking back two years later he saw it as something more: a major turning-point in the German theatre's understanding of the classics. For here had been an attempt at demonumentalization, an appeal for 'not so much plaster . . .' (the title of one of Brecht's subsequent essays), in which

> He did not analyse the characters; he set them at a distance . . .
> He called for a report on the events.

Viewed from 1926 it seemed like an early example of the 'epic' style.

Brecht's Munich period came to an end with the 1923–4 theatrical season, for once established in Berlin he remained based there until he went into exile in 1933. Only the one-acters had not been performed by the time of his move. *Baal, Drums in the Night* and *Edward* were all in print, while the *Hauspostille*, his first book of poems, was enjoying something of an underground reputation, having been announced as early as 1922, five years before its actual publication. That first winter in Berlin he was to have the rare distinction (for a young author) of two productions in the major theatres: *Edward II* directed by Jürgen Fehling (this gifted director's only Brecht production) at the State Theatre, with Werner Krauss as Mortimer and Faber once more as Edward, and *Jungle* at the Deutsches Theater directed by Engel, who had been lured to Berlin by Max Reinhardt a few months before Brecht. The outstanding young actor Fritz Kortner turned down a part in Reinhardt's *St Joan* in order to play Shlink: another indication of the interest already stimulated by Brecht's early work.

II

If the Bavarian years made Brecht's name they also established the main lines of argument for and against his work, with Kerr and Ihering respectively as counsel for the prosecution and the defence. Already the point at issue was his literary borrowings, and a number of later attacks on him (including that dealt with in the notes to *In the Jungle of Cities*) were foreshadowed in Kerr's *Baal* critique, with its dismissal of the play as second-hand Büchner and Grabbe. 'The gifted Brecht,' he wrote, 'is a frothing plagiarist.' To which Ihering countered:

> A writer's productivity can be seen in his relationship with old themes. In *Schweiger* Werfel invented a 'hitherto unheard of story' and was none the less imitative in every respect. Brecht was fired by Marlowe's *Edward II* and was creative through and through.

At the same time Brecht had been able to build the nucleus of his subsequent team of supporters and collaborators: first and foremost Neher, then Engel, the rather older Feuchtwanger, Kortner, Homolka, Klabund's actress wife Carola Neher and the playwright Marieluise Fleisser, all of them people who have left their individual marks on the German theatre. Here Brecht's personal magnetism clearly played a part: something to which there have been many tributes, starting with Feuchtwanger's fictional picture of him as the engineer Pröckl in his novel *Success* (1931). The first three plays all bore dedications: to his school-friend George Pfanzelt (the 'Orge' of the poems), to Bie Banholzer who bore his illegitimate son Frank (killed in the war) and to Marianne his first wife, whom he married in 1922. With *Edward II* this practice came to an end.

These were Brecht's pre-collectivist, indeed in a sense his pre-political years. He undoubtedly had opinions, many of them progressive and even revolutionary, but they were far from systematic, and politics and economics were wholly absent from what we know of his reading. On the other hand it was an extraordinarily tense and eventful time for Germany in general and Bavaria in particular, and Brecht was much too sensitive a writer not to reflect this in his work. A good deal has been made of his supposed pacifism in the First World War – though his schoolboy writings show that in fact he set out from a conventionally patriotic attitude and hardly developed beyond concern at the casualties – and of the impact made on him by his military service, which in fact was done on his own doorstep and in a hospital for venereal diseases, and started only a month or two before the end of the war. Several of the *Hauspostille* poems which are held to express his post-war sense of release had in fact already been written by then. Nor is there any evidence that he was more than a spectator of the revolutionary movements of November 1918, when the monarchy fell, and the first months of 1919, when Munich and Augsburg were governed by Soviets following Kurt Eisner's murder and the short-lived Spartacist revolt in Berlin.

Yet the 'Legend of the Dead Soldier' which he wrote in 1918 and took into *Drums in the Night* (see pp. 101 and 391) is always supposed to have earned him a place on the Munich Nazis' black list, while the play itself, though their paper the *Völkischer Beobachter* thought that it 'at any rate showed something of the idiocy of the November Revolution', struck none of the liberal critics as an unfair picture. It was certainly a very confused one, as the muddle over the dating of the action will confirm, and Brecht himself came to judge it in the severest terms, very nearly suppressing the play altogether. The revolutionary setting, however, was only a background to the real drama, and it had an instinctive poetic power which was not to be found in Brecht's later amendments.

The element of revolt in his writing of this time was largely directed against his own middle-class background: the satirical first scene of *Baal*, for instance, and the first two acts of *Drums in the Night*. Much of his reading, too, was exotic-escapist, as can be seen from the allusions in this volume to Gauguin and *Treasure Island* and Rudyard Kipling, and certainly this partly explains Brecht's interest in Rimbaud, whose elevated prose underlies Garga's 'psalmodizing' in *In the Jungle* (cf. Brecht's own semi-prose 'Psalms') and whose relationship with Verlaine was surely the model for that of Baal and Ekart. 'How boring Germany is!' says a note of 18 June 1920. 'It's a good average country, its pale colours and its surfaces are beautiful, but what inhabitants!' 'What's left?' he concluded: 'America!' That year he read two novels about Chicago, J. V. Jensen's *The Wheel* (which has never appeared in English) and Upton Sinclair's *The Jungle*, and when he began work on his own *In the Jungle* it was under their influence, intensified no doubt by his first experience of 'the crushing impact of cities' (about which he wrote an early poem) in the hard winter of 1921–2.

By the time of its first performance the French occupation of the Ruhr had given a great stimulus to nationalism throughout Germany, and not least to the Nazis in Bavaria. The *Völkischer Beobachter* particularly detested this play, claiming that the audience was full of Jews and that the Chinese characters spoke Yiddish. A month later Brecht and Bronnen heard Adolf Hitler addressing a meeting in a Munich circus, and were inspired (according to Bronnen) to work out what sort of a political show they could put on in a circus themselves. In November the Beer-Cellar Putsch interrupted the rehearsals of *Edward II* for a day. Brecht, with his colleague Bernhard Reich, went to call on Feuchtwanger, who saw this as the sign that they must leave Bavaria (and did in fact leave in 1924). But Reich recalls no particular concern with the Nazis on Brecht's part, and indeed not only was the putsch quite firmly suppressed – and Hitler jailed – but the stabilization of the currency by the central government set the Nazi movement back for a number of years.

The period covered by this volume saw not only a certain element of political restoration throughout central and eastern Europe but also the end of Expressionism in the arts. To the poet-playwright Iwan Goll, who in 1921 published an essay called 'Expressionism is Dying', the two phenomena were connected. 'Expressionism was a fine, good, grand thing . . .' he wrote. 'But the result is, alas, and through no fault of the Expressionists, the German Republic of 1920.' Dadaism likewise was breaking up by 1922; at the Bauhaus the semi-mystical Itten was about to be succeeded by the technologically minded Moholy-Nagy; while artists like Grosz, Dix, Beckmann and Schlichter were evolving the coolly representational, socially conscious style which in 1924 became known as *Neue Sachlichkeit*. Brecht was always much too conscious of his own aims to care to be labelled as part of a movement; none the less his works of these years very clearly reflect the decline of Expressionism and the rise of the new style. He defined his position admirably in a note of 27 June 1920:

> I can compete with the ultra-modernists in hunting for new forms and experimenting with my feelings. But I keep realizing that the essence of art is simplicity, grandeur and sensitivity, and that the essence of its form is coolness.

Baal was written as a kind of counter-play to the Expressionists' invocations of Humanity with a capital H, yet the wandering poet remains a romantic-expressionist figure, while the influence of Georg Büchner is one that is also noticeable in a number of Expressionist plays. *Drums in the Night* too, with its symbolic use of the moon, its cinematic third act and its hero's slightly mad rhetoric, can reasonably be termed an Expressionist play. *In the Jungle*, however, was written at the turning-point, the watershed between the two movements. The Rimbaud allusions, the colour references before each scene in the 1922 version, the attic-cum-undergrowth setting, the use of spotlights referred to in Brecht's note of 1954: all this is expressionistic, whereas the American milieu, the pre-occupation with the big cities and the very notion of the 'fight' were to become characteristic concerns of the mid-1920s. A further note of 10 February 1922 even suggests that Brecht was looking forward to his own 1930s doctrine of 'alienation':

> I hope in *Baal* and *Jungle* I've avoided one common artistic bloomer, that of trying to carry people away. Instinctively, I've kept my distance and ensured that the realization of my (poetical and philosophical) effects remains within bounds. The spectator's 'splendid isolation' is left intact; it is not *sua res quae agitur*; he is not fobbed off with an invitation to feel sympathetically, to fuse with the hero and seem significant and indestructible as he watches himself in two different versions. A higher type of interest can be got from making comparisons, from whatever is different, amazing, impossible to overlook.

Thus though *In the Jungle* is still wildly romantic it already foreshadows the detached impersonalities of the machine age. And those supporters who, like Ihering and Engel and Geis, thought that Brecht would help lead the theatre out of the Expressionist undergrowth can now be seen to have been absolutely right.

III

The final texts of these plays often make Brecht's evolution difficult to follow. He was a restless amender and modifier of his own work, so that any one of them may consist of layer upon layer of elements from different periods. 'He is more interested in the job than in the finished work,' wrote Feuchtwanger in an article of 1928 called 'Portrait of Brecht for the English',

> in the problem than in its solution, in the journey than in its goal. He rewrites his works an untold number of times, twenty or thirty times, with a new revision for every minor provincial production. He is not in the least interested in seeing a work completed. . . .

Thus between 1922 and its publication in 1927 *In the Jungle* became *In the Jungle of Cities*. The city allusions were strengthened, the boxing foreword was added and various boxing allusions worked into the text, the colour references at the start of each scene gave way to mock-precise ('objective') data of time and place, the whole flavour of the play was changed. The same was done still more drastically with *Baal* in 1926, though in this case Brecht later decided to scrap the more 'objective', technologically flavoured version and go back (more or less) to the 1922-3 text. *Drums in the Night* he seems to have left alone after 1922, perhaps because it was not performed again after the first, largely topical wave of interest had subsided – though the discussion on p. 401 ff. suggests that Piscator was considering it. Then for his Collected Plays in the 1950s he largely rewrote the last two acts.

All this means that each play as we now have it reflects the views and to some extent the spirit of a number of different periods. The performances which have gone into theatrical history were not based on these particular texts. Even Brecht's own notes are difficult to understand without knowing to which version each of them relates.

It is an impossible problem editorially, and our policy has been to print the final text but to provide all the variant material from other versions published in Brecht's lifetime, together with extensive notes on the main unpublished scripts. This is so that the reader should not get false ideas of Brecht's evolution and of his ideas and achievements at any given time. Brecht was a profound believer in change, whom it would be wrong to present statically in a final 'authoritative' mould. Indeed opinions might well differ as to whether any such mould is the right one: not only are there fine things in many of the rejected versions, which it would be cruel not to publish, but informed judgement often disagrees with Brecht's last choices. Thus the chief German expert on *Baal* and the author of much the best book on Brecht's early years both prefer the 1919 script of *Baal*; an outstanding West German theatre critic wants the 1922 *Drums in the Night*; while Ihering wrote of the (final) published version of *In the Jungle of Cities* in 1927:

> I love the fullness and colour of the old *Jungle*. There seemed to be no better evidence of Brecht's richness and gifts than those crackling, exotically pulsating scenes as they shot to and fro. . . . The new *Jungle*, the *Jungle of Cities*, has lost in colour and atmosphere. It has gained in clarity and concentration.

Not that there is much chance that Brecht himself would have accepted his own choices as final if he had lived longer, or seen them staged, or looked again at some of the earlier texts which for one reason or another he did not have before him when preparing the collected plays. It is characteristic that he already wanted the 1926 version of *Baal* printed as an appendix. For he was always a man in motion, who progressed best by disagreeing with what had already been said. Often it had been said by himself.

As for the translations, they are as good as translators and editors can make them, but they make no claim to be definitive.

Better translations may well appear with time – quite apart from the obvious fact that each time must make its own translations. In all the poetry Brecht's rules of punctuation are followed; that is to say there are no commas at the ends of lines, the line break being considered sufficient pause for anything short of a colon. Our aim is that the poetry should so far as possible fit any settings by the main composers with whom Brecht collaborated. A note will normally indicate where this is not the case, though there may be some tunes, particularly of Brecht's own, which we have failed to track down.

All translation in the notes is by the responsible editor, as is the selection of material printed. The aim here has been to include anything of relevance to the understanding or production of the play in question, leaving those notes which comprise more general statements of Brecht's theatrical ideas to be published in the volumes devoted to his theoretical writings. The essay 'On Looking Through my First Plays', which he wrote as a foreword to the first two volumes of his collected *Stücke* in 1954 (too late for the first printing) has been split into its component sections, of which that on *Man equals Man* will follow in the next volume. It can be reconstituted by reading it in the order indicated, starting with (i), the section on *Drums in the Night*.

The German text used throughout, unless otherwise stated, is that of the *Gesammelte Werke* (or Collected Works) edited by Elisabeth Hauptmann and a team comprising Werner Hecht, Rosemarie Hill, Herta Ramthun and Klaus Völker, and published by Suhrkamp-Verlag, Frankfurt-am-Main, in 1967. This is referred to as GW, plus the appropriate subdivision: *Stücke* (plays), *Schriften zum Theater* (writings on the theatre), and so on. When the same terms (*Stücke*, for instance, as above) are used without the prefix GW they refer to the earlier collected edition issued by the same publisher from 1953 on. Particulars of other sources are given in full where reference is made to them. We would like to thank the editors and publisher for the help which they have given with various queries. The Brecht Archive in East Berlin has been generous in supplying material, and we are grateful for the support given us from the outset by Stefan S. Brecht.

THE EDITORS

Chronology

1898   10 February: Eugen Berthold Friedrich Brecht born in Augsburg.

BAVARIA

1914   17 August: first contribution to *Augsburger Neueste Nachrichten*.

1919   21 October: first theatre criticism for *Augsburger Volkswille*.

1921   6 September: first short story in *Der neue Merkur* (Munich).

1922   5 September: first contribution to *Berliner Börsen-Courier*. 30 September: *Trommeln in der Nacht (Drums in the Night)* première, Munich. Publication of plays *Baal* and *Trommeln in der Nacht*. December: *Trommeln in der Nacht* at Deutsches Theater, Berlin.

1923   9 May: *Im Dickicht (der Städte) (In the Jungle of Cities)* première, Munich. 8 December: *Baal* première, Leipzig.

1924   18 March: *Edward II* première, Munich, Brecht's first production.

BERLIN

1924   29 October: *Im Dickicht* at Deutsches Theater, Berlin. October: *Edward II* at Staatstheater, Berlin.

1926   14 February: *Baal* at Deutsches Theater, produced by Homolka and Brecht. 25 September: *Mann ist Mann (Man equals Man)* première, Darmstadt. December: *Die Hochzeit (A Respectable Wedding)* première, Frankfurt.

1927   First book of poems: *Die Hauspostille* (*Sermons for the Home*).
23 March: *Mann ist Mann* broadcast, Berlin, with Helene
Weigel. 17 July: *Mahagonny* ('Songspiel') première, Baden-
Baden. First collaboration with Kurt Weill. Produced by
Brecht. 14 October: radio adaptation of *Macbeth* broadcast, Berlin. 27 November: article in the *Frankfurter Zeitung*
on the 'Epic Theatre'. December: *Im Dickicht der Städte*
(revised version) at Darmstadt.

1928   5 January: *Mann ist Mann* at the Volksbühne, Berlin.
31 August: *Threepenny Opera* première, Theater am
Schiffbauerdamm, Berlin.

1929   July: *Lindberghflug* (*Flight over the Ocean*) and *Badener
Lehrstück* (*The Baden-Baden Cantata*) premières, at Baden-
Baden. Both produced by Brecht. First 'Lehrstücke' (or
didactic pieces). September: *Happy End* première, Theater
am Schiffbauerdamm, Berlin, produced by Brecht. *Berliner
Requiem* with Weill broadcast during summer.

1930   First three issues of Brecht's *Versuche*, or miscellaneous
collected writings, including first notes on the plays.
9 March: *Aufstieg und Fall der Stadt Mahagonny* (*The Rise
and Fall of the City of Mahagonny*) première, Leipzig Opera.
23 June: *Der Jasager* (*He Who Said Yes*) première, Berlin.
10 December: *Die Massnahme* (*The Decision*) première,
Berlin. First collaboration with Hanns Eisler. First out-
spokenly Communist work.

1931   Release of *Threepenny Opera* film. 16 January: first contribution to *Die Rote Fahne* (Berlin). 30 January: radio adaptation of *Hamlet* broadcast, Berlin. 6 February: *Mann ist
Mann* (revised version) at Staatstheater, Berlin. Produced
by Brecht. 21 December: *Aufstieg und Fall der Stadt Mahagonny*
at Kurfürstendamm-Theater, Berlin. Produced by Brecht
and Caspar Neher.

1932   Release of *Kuhle Wampe* film. 17 January: *Die Mutter*
(*The Mother*) première, Berlin. 11 April: *St Joan of the
Stockyards* broadcast, Berlin.

1933   All publications and productions in Germany interrupted.

SCANDINAVIA

1933   June: *Anna-Anna ou les Sept Péchés Capitaux* première at
Théâtre des Champs-Elysées, Paris. Brecht's only ballet.
His last major work with Kurt Weill, *Die Sieben Todsünden*
(*The Seven Deadly Sins*).

1934   First (and only completed) novel: *Der Dreigroschenroman*
(*Threepenny Novel*). Second book of poems: *Lieder Gedichte
Chöre* (*Songs Poems Choruses*) (with Eisler). Writing of
Die Horatier und die Kuriatier (*The Horatii and the Curiatii*),
Brecht's last 'Lehrstück'.

1935   June: speech to International Writers' Congress in Defence
of Culture, Paris. 19 November: *Die Mutter* in English,
New York.

1936   July: first number of *Das Wort* (Moscow) edited by Brecht,
Feuchtwanger and Bredel. 4 November: *Die Rundköpfe
und die Spitzköpfe* (*Round Heads and Pointed Heads*) première,
Copenhagen. (The notes on this play contain the first
known mention of 'Verfremdung', or alienation.)

1937   16 October: *Senora Carrar's Rifles* première, Paris.

1938   First (and only) two volumes of *Malik* edition of Collected Plays. May: *Furcht und Elend des Dritten Reiches* (*Fear
and Misery in the Third Reich*) première, Paris, produced
by Dudow.

1939   March: final number of *Das Wort*. Third book of poems:
Svendborger Gedichte (*Svendborg Poems*).

1940   12 May: *Das Verhör des Lukullus* (*The Trial of Lucullus*)
broadcast, Beromünster.

1941   19 April: *Mother Courage* première, Zurich Schauspielhaus.

USA

1942   Release of film *Hangmen also Die*.

1943   4 February: *The Good Person of Szechwan* première, Zurich
Schauspielhaus. 9 September: *Galileo* première, Zurich
Schauspielhaus.

1945   June: *Private Life of the Master Race* (adaptation of *Furcht
und Elend*) in English, San Francisco and New York.

1946   15 October: *The Duchess of Malfi* is staged on Broadway.

1947   August: *Galileo* (second version; translated by Brecht and Laughton) in Hollywood.

ZURICH

1948   First: (and only) volume of short stories: *Kalendergeschichten* (*Tales from the Calendar*). February: *Antigone* première, Chur (Switzerland); produced by Brecht and Neher; Helene Weigel's first professional appearance since 1933. 4 May: student production of *The Caucasian Chalk Circle* in English, Northfield (Minnesota). 5 June: *Herr Puntila und sein Knecht* (*Mr Puntila and his Man Matti*) première, Zurich Schauspielhaus.

BERLIN

1949   11 January: *Mother Courage* at Deutsches Theater, East Berlin; produced by Brecht and Engel, with Helene Weigel. 12 November: *Herr Puntila und sein Knecht* at Deutsches Theater, produced by Brecht and Engel; first production of the Berliner Ensemble. Publication of the *Versuche* resumed. 'Kleines Organon für das Theater' ('Short Organum for the Theatre'), Brecht's chief theoretical work, appears in a special number of *Sinn und Form* (Potsdam).

1950   15 April: Lenz's *Der Hofmeister* (*The Tutor*) in Brecht's adaptation, at Deutsches Theater; produced by Brecht, with Berliner Ensemble. 8 October: *Mother Courage* in Munich Kammerspiele, produced by Brecht.

1951   First selected poems: *Hundert Gedichte* (*A Hundred Poems*). 10 January: *Die Mutter* at Deutsches Theater; produced by Brecht, with Berliner Ensemble. 17 March: *Das Verhör des Lukullus*, opera version by Paul Dessau, given trial performance in East Berlin State Opera. August: *Herrnburger Bericht* (*Report from Herrnburg*) première at World Youth Festival in East Berlin. 12 October: *Die Verurteilung des Lukullus* (*The Condemnation of Lucullus*) put into State Opera's repertoire after changes to title, score and text.

1952   16 November: *Senora Carrar's Rifles* at Deutsches Theater,
with Berliner Ensemble.

1953   First two volumes of *Stücke*, or Complete Dramatic Works.
17 May: Erwin Strittmatter's *Katzgraben* at Deutsches
Theater, produced by Brecht, with Berliner Ensemble.

1954   March: first performance by Berliner Ensemble in Theater
am Schiffbauerdamm as an independent State Theatre.
March: *The Threepenny Opera* (English adaptation by
Marc Blitzstein) begins a long run in New York. 15 June:
Caucasian Chalk Circle German première at Theater am
Schiffbauerdamm; produced by Brecht, with Berliner En-
semble. July: International Theatre Festival, Paris. Berliner
Ensemble production of *Mother Courage*.

1955   Illustrated war verses: *Kriegsfibel* (*War Primer*). 12 January:
J. R. Becher's *Winterschlacht* produced by Brecht and
Wekwerth, with Berliner Ensemble. June: Second International Theatre Festival, Paris, Berliner Ensemble production
of *Caucasian Chalk Circle*.

1956   14 August: Brecht dies in East Berlin, of a heart infarct.

The Resistible Rise of Arturo Ui, *The Visions of Simone
Machard* and *Schweyk in the Second World War* were
neither published nor produced during Brecht's lifetime.
They were published in the *Stücke* edition in 1957 and
produced in Stuttgart, Frankfurt and Warsaw respectively
the same year.

Baal

To my friend George Pfanzelt

Translator: PETER TEGEL

Characters

Baal, poet · Mech, merchant and publisher · Emilie, his wife ·
Dr Piller, critic · Johannes Schmidt · Pschierer, director of the
water rates · a young man · a young woman · Johanna · Ekart ·
Luise, a waitress · the two sisters · the landlady · Sophie
Barger · the tramp · Lupu · Mjurk · the nightclub singer · a
pianist · the parson · Bolleboll · Gougou · the old beggar ·
Maja, the beggarwoman · the young woman · Watzmann · a
waitress · two policemen · drivers · peasants · woodcutters

HYMN OF BAAL THE GREAT

Baal grew up within the whiteness of the womb
With the sky already large and pale and calm
Naked, young, endlessly marvellous
As Baal loved it when he came to us.

And that sky remained with him through joy and care
Even when Baal slept, blissful and unaware.
Nights meant violet sky and drunken Baal
Dawns, Baal good, sky apricottish-pale.

So through hospital, cathedral, bar
Baal trots coolly on, and learns to let them go.
When Baal's tired, boys, Baal will not fall far:
Baal will drag his whole sky down below.

Where the sinners herd in shame together
Baal lies naked, soaking up the calm.
Just the sky, but sky to last for *ever*
Hides his nakedness with its strong arm.

And that lusty girl, the world, who laughs when yielding
To the man who'll stand the pressure of her thighs
Gives him instants of a sweet ecstatic feeling.
Baal survives it; he just looks and sees.

And when Baal sees corpses all around
Then a double pleasure comes to him.
Lots of space, says Baal; they're not enough to count.
Lots of space inside this woman's womb.

Once a woman, Baal says, gives her all
She'll have nothing more, so let her go!
Other men would represent no risk at all.
Even Baal is scared of babies, though.

Vice, says Baal, is bound to help a bit
And so are the men who practise it.
Vices leave their mark on all they touch.
Stick to two, for one will be too much.

Slackness, softness – that's what you should shun.
Nothing's tougher than pursuing fun.
Powerful limbs are needed, and experience too
Swollen bellies may discourage you.

Baal watches the vultures in the star-shot sky
Hovering patiently to see when Baal will die.
Sometimes Baal shams dead. The vultures swoop.
Baal, without a word, will dine on vulture soup.

Under mournful stars in our sad vale of trouble
Munching, Baal can graze broad pastures down to stubble.
When they're cropped, into the forest deep
Baal trots, singing, to enjoy his sleep.

And when Baal's dragged down to be the dark womb's
    prize
What's the world to Baal? Baal has been fed.
Sky enough still lurks behind Baal's eyes
To make just enough sky when he's dead.

Baal decayed within the darkness of the womb
With the sky once more as large and pale and calm
Naked, young, endlessly marvellous
As Baal loved it when he came to us.

Dining Room

Mech, Emilie Mech, Pschierer, Johannes Schmidt, Dr Piller, Baal and other guests enter through the revolving door.

MECH *to Baal:* Would you like some wine, Mr Baal? *All take seats, Baal in the place of honour.* Do you like crab? That's a dead eel.

PILLER *to Mech:* I'm very glad that the immortal poems of Mr Baal, which I had the honour of reading to you, have earned your approval. *To Baal:* You must publish your poetry. Mr Mech pays like a real patron of the arts. You'll be able to leave your attic.

MECH: I buy cinnamon wood. Whole forests of cinnamon float down the rivers of Brazil for my benefit. But I'll also publish your poetry.

EMILIE: You live in an attic?

BAAL *eating and drinking:* 64 Klauckestrasse.

MECH: I'm really too fat for poetry. But you've got the same-shaped head as a man in the Malayan Archipelago, who used to have himself driven to work with a whip. If he wasn't grinding his teeth he couldn't work.

PSCHIERER: Ladies and gentlemen. I admit it frankly: I was shattered to find a man like him in such modest circumstances. As you know, I discovered our dear poet in my office, a simple clerk. I have no hesitation in calling it a disgrace to our city that personalities of his calibre should be allowed to work for a daily wage. May I congratulate you, Mr Mech! Your salon will be famous as the cradle of this genius's, yes genius's, worldwide reputation. Your health, Mr Baal!

Baal wards off the speech with a gesture; he eats.

PILLER: I shall write an essay about you. Have you any manuscripts? I have the backing of the press.

A YOUNG MAN: How, my friend, do you get that accursed naïve effect? It's positively homeric. I consider Homer one, or rather one of several, highly civilized adapters with a penetrating delight in the naïveté of the original folk sagas.

A YOUNG LADY: You remind me more of Walt Whitman. But you're more significant. That's what I think.

ANOTHER MAN: I'd say he had something rather more of Verhaeren.

PILLER: Verlaine! Verlaine! Even in physiognomy. Don't forget our Lombroso.

BAAL: Some more of the eel, please.

THE YOUNG LADY: But you have the advantage of greater indecency.

JOHANNES: Mr Baal sings his songs to the lorry-drivers. In a café down by the river.

THE YOUNG MAN: Good God, none of those poets are even in the same category. My friend, you're streets ahead of any living poet.

THE OTHER MAN: At any rate he's promising.

BAAL: Some more wine please.

THE YOUNG MAN: I consider you a precursor of the great Messiah of European literature whom we can undoubtedly expect within the very near future.

THE YOUNG LADY: Dear poet, ladies, and gentlemen. Permit me to read you a poem from the periodical 'Revolution' which will also be of interest to you. *She rises and reads:*

The poet shuns shining harmonies.
He blows trombones, shrilly whips the drum.
He incites the people with chopped sentences.

The new world
Exterminating the world of pain,
Island of rapturous humanity.
Speeches. Manifestos.
Songs from grandstands.
Let there be preached the new,
The holy state, inoculated into the blood of the people,
Blood of their blood.

Paradise sets in.
– Let us spread a stormy climate!
Learn! Prepare! Practise!

Applause.

THE YOUNG LADY *quickly:* Permit me! I shall turn to another
poem in the same issue. *She reads:*

Sun had made him shrivel
And wind had blown him dry.
By every tree rejected
He simply fell away.

Only a single rowan
With berries on every limb,
Red as flaming tongues, would
Receive and shelter him.

So there he hung suspended,
His feet lay on the grass.
The blood-red sunset splashed him
As through his ribs it passed.

It moved across the landscape
And struck all the olive groves.
God in his cloud-white raiment
Was manifest above.

Within the flowering forest
There sang a thousand snakes
While necks of purest silver
With slender murmurs shook.

And they were seized with trembling
All over that leafy domain
Obeying the hands of their Father
So light in their delicate veins.

Applause.

CRIES OF: Brilliant! Extreme but in good taste. Simply heavenly.

THE YOUNG LADY: In my opinion it comes closest to the Baalian conception of the world.

MECH: You should travel! The Abyssinian mountains. That's something for you.

BAAL: They won't come to me, though.

PILLER: Why? With your zest for life! Your poems had an enormous effect on me.

BAAL: The lorry-drivers pay if they like them.

MECH *drinking:* I'll publish your poems. I'll let the cinnamon logs float away, or do both.

EMILIE *to Mech:* You shouldn't drink so much.

BAAL: I haven't got any shirts. I could use some white shirts.

MECH: You're not interested in the publishing deal?

BAAL: But they'd have to be soft.

PILLER *ironic:* Oh, and what can I do for you?

EMILIE: You write such wonderful poems, Mr Baal. So sensitive.

BAAL *to Emilie:* Won't you play something on the harmonium?

Emilie plays.

MECH: I like eating to the harmonium.

EMILIE *to Baal:* Please don't drink so much, Mr Baal.

BAAL *looks at Emilie:* Do you have forests of cinnamon floating for you, Mech? Butchered forests?

EMILIE: You can drink as much as you like. I was only asking a favour.

PILLER: Even your drinking shows promise.

BAAL *to Emilie:* Play higher up! You've got lovely arms.

Emilie stops playing and approaches the table.

PILLER: Apparently you don't care for the music itself.

BAAL: I can't hear the music. You're talking too much.

PILLER: You're a queer fish, Baal. I gather you don't want to get published.

BAAL: Don't you trade in animals too, Mech?

MECH: Do you object?

BAAL *stroking Emilie's arm:* What's my poetry to you?

MECH: I wanted to do you a favour. Couldn't you be peeling some more apples, Emilie?

PILLER: He's afraid of being sucked dry. – Haven't you found a use for me yet?

BAAL: Do you always wear wide sleeves, Emilie?

PILLER: But now you really must stop drinking.

PSCHIERER: Perhaps you ought to go easy on the alcohol. Full many a genius —

MECH: Would you like to have a bath? Shall I have a bed made up for you? Have you forgotten anything?

PILLER: Your shirts are floating away, Baal. Your poetry has floated off already.

BAAL *drinks:* I'm against monopolies. Go to bed, Mech.

MECH *has risen:* I delight in all the animals on God's earth, but this is one animal you can't do business with. Come, Emilie! Shall we go, ladies and gentlemen?
All have risen indignantly.

CRIES: Sir! Astounding! That's the . . .!

PSCHIERER: I am shattered, Mr Mech . . .

PILLER: Your poetry has a malicious streak.

BAAL *to Johannes:* What is the gentleman's name?

JOHANNES: Piller.

BAAL: Well, Piller, *you* can send me some old newspapers.

PILLER *leaving:* You mean nothing to me. You mean nothing to literature.
All go.

SERVANT *entering:* Your coat, sir.

Baal's Attic

Starlit night. At the window Baal and the adolescent Johannes. They look at the sky.

BAAL: When you lie stretched out on the grass at night you

can feel in your bones that the earth is round and that we're flying, and that there are beasts on this star that devour its plants. It's one of the smaller stars.

JOHANNES: Do you know anything about astronomy?

BAAL: No.

Silence.

JOHANNES: I'm in love with a girl. She's the most innocent creature alive, but I saw her once in a dream being made love to by a juniper tree. That is to say, her white body lay stretched out on the juniper tree and the gnarled branches twisted about her. I haven't been able to sleep since.

BAAL: Have you ever seen her white body?

JOHANNES: No. She's innocent. Even her knees . . . There are degrees of innocence, don't you think? And yet, there are times when I hold her, just for a second, at night, and she trembles like a leaf, but only at night. But I haven't the strength to do it. She's seventeen.

BAAL: In your dream, did she like love?

JOHANNES: Yes.

BAAL: She wears clean linen, a snow-white petticoat between her knees? Bed her and she may turn into a heap of flesh without a face.

JOHANNES: You're saying what I always felt. I thought I was a coward. I can see now that you also think intercourse is unclean.

BAAL: That's the grunting of the swine who are no good at it. When you embrace her virginal loins, the joy and fear of created man turns you into a god. As the juniper tree's many roots are entwined within the earth, so are your limbs in bed. Blood flows and hearts beat.

JOHANNES: But it's punishable by law, and by one's parents.

BAAL: Your parents – *he reaches for his guitar* – they're a thing of the past. How dare they open their mouths, filled with rotten teeth, to speak against love, which anybody may die of? If you can't take love, there's nothing left but vomit. *He tunes the guitar*.

JOHANNES: Do you mean if I make her pregnant?

BAAL *striking chords on his guitar:* When the pale mild summer ebbs and they're swollen with love like sponges, they turn back into beasts, evil and childish, shapeless with their fat stomachs and hanging breasts, their damp arms clinging like slimy tentacles, and their bodies collapse and grow heavy unto death. And with hideous shrieks as if they were bringing a new world into being, they yield a small fruit. They spew out with pain what they once sucked in with pleasure. *He plucks the strings.* You have to have teeth for it, then love is like biting into an orange, with the juice squirting into your teeth.

JOHANNES: Your teeth are like an animal's. They're yellow and large, sinister.

BAAL: And love is like putting your naked arm into a pond and letting it float with weeds between your fingers, like the pain in which the drunken tree groans and sings as the wild wind rides it, like drowning in wine on a hot day, her body surging like a cool wine into every crease of your skin, limbs soft as plants in the wind, and the weight of the collision to which you yield is like flying against a storm, and her body tumbles over you like cool pebbles. But love is also like a coconut, good while it is fresh but when the juice is gone and only the bitter flesh remains you have to spit it out. *He throws the guitar aside.* I'm sick of this hymn.

JOHANNES: Then you think it's something I ought to do, if it's so wonderful?

BAAL: I think it's something for *you* to avoid, Johannes.

An Inn

Morning. Lorry-drivers. Ekart at the back with Luise, the waitress. White clouds can be seen through the window.

BAAL *talking to the lorry-drivers:* He threw me out of his nice clean room, because I threw up his wine. But his wife ran after me, and in the evening we celebrated. I'm lumbered with her and sick of it.

DRIVERS: She needs a good hiding . . . They're randy as cats but stupider. Tell her to go and eat figs! . . . I always beat mine before I give her what she wants.

JOHANNES *enters with Johanna:* This is Johanna.

BAAL *to the drivers, who go to the back:* I'll give you a song later.

JOHANNA: Johannes read me some of your poems.

BAAL: Ah. How old are you?

JOHANNES: She was seventeen in June.

JOHANNA: I'm jealous. He does nothing but talk about you.

BAAL: You're in love with your Johannes. It's spring. I'm waiting for Emilie . . . Better to love than make love.

JOHANNES: I can understand your winning a man's love, but how can you have any success with women?
Emilie enters quickly.

BAAL: Here she comes. And how are you, Emilie? Johannes is here with his fiancée. Sit down!

EMILIE: How could you ask me to come here! A cheap bar, only fit for drunken louts! Typical of your taste.

BAAL: Luise, a gin for the lady.

EMILIE: Do you want to make a laughing stock of me?

BAAL: No. You'll drink. We're all human.

EMILIE: But you're not.

BAAL: How do you know? *He holds the glass out to Luise.* Don't be so mean, Luise. *He takes hold of her.* You're devilishly soft today, like a plum.

EMILIE: How ill-bred you are!

BAAL: Tell the world, darling.

JOHANNES: It's interesting here, I must say. Ordinary people. Drinking and amusing themselves. And then, those clouds in the window!

EMILIE: He dragged you here too, I expect. For a view of the clouds.

JOHANNA: Wouldn't it be nicer to go for a walk in the meadows by the river, Johannes?

BAAL: Nothing doing! Stay here! *He drinks.* The sky is

purple, particularly if you happen to be drunk. Beds on the other hand are white. To begin with. That's where love is, between Heaven and Earth. *He drinks.* Why are you such cowards? The sky's free, you feeble shadows! Full of bodies! Pale with love!

EMILIE: You've had too much again and now you're babbling. And with that bloody wonderful babble he drags you to his sty.

BAAL: Sometimes – *drinks* – the sky is yellow. Full of vultures. Let's all get drunk. *He looks under the table.* Who's kicking my shins? Is it you, Luise? Ah, you, Emilie! Well, no matter. Drink up.

EMILIE *half rising:* I don't know what's wrong with you today. Perhaps I shouldn't have come here after all.

BAAL: Have you just noticed? You might as well stay now.

JOHANNA: Don't say things like that, Mr Baal.

BAAL: You've a good heart, Johanna. You'll never be unfaithful, will you?

DRIVER *winning:* Ace, you bastards! – Trumped!

SECOND DRIVER: Keep going, the tart said, the worst's over. *Laughter.* Tell her to go and eat figs.

THIRD DRIVER: How could you betray me, as the lady said to the butler when she found him in bed with the maid.

JOHANNES *to Baal:* Because of Johanna. She's a child.

JOHANNA *to Emilie:* Will you come with me? We can go together.

EMILIE *bursting into tears at the table:* I feel so ashamed now.

JOHANNA *putting her arm round Emilie:* I understand; it doesn't matter.

EMILIE: Don't look at me like that. You're still so young. You don't know anything yet.

BAAL *gets up forbiddingly:* Comedy, entitled Sisters in Hades! *He goes to the drivers, takes the guitar down from the wall and tunes it.*

JOHANNA: He's been drinking. He'll regret it tomorrow.

EMILIE: If only you knew. He's always like this. And I love
  him.
BAAL *sings:*

  Orge told me that:

In all the world the place he liked the best
Was not the grass mound where his loved ones rest

Was not the altar, nor some harlot's room
Nor yet the warm white comfort of the womb.

Orge thought the best place known to man
In this world was the lavatory pan.

That was a place to set the cheeks aglow
With stars above and excrement below.

A place of refuge where you had a right
To sit in private on your wedding night.

A place of truth, for there you must admit
You are a man; there's no concealing it.

A place of wisdom, where the gut turns out
To gird itself up for another bout.

Where you are always doing good by stealth
Exerting tactful pressure for your health.

At that you realize how far you've gone:
Using the lavatory – to eat on.

DRIVERS *clapping:* Bravo! . . . A good song! Give the gentleman a cherry brandy, if you'll accept the offer, sir! He made
it up all on his own . . . What a man!
LUISE *in the middle of the room:* You're a one, Mr Baal!

DRIVER: If *you* did a real job, you'd do all right for yourself. You could end up running a transport business.

SECOND DRIVER: Wish I had brains like that!

BAAL: That's nothing. You have to have a backside and the rest. Your very good health, Luise. *He goes back to his table.* And yours, Emmi. Come on, drink up. Even if you can't do anything else. Drink, I said.

Emilie, tears in her eyes, sips her drink.

BAAL: That's better. There'll be some life in you yet.

EKART *gets up and comes round slowly from the bar to Baal. He is lean, a powerful man:* Baal! Brother! Come with me! Give it up! Out to the hard dusty highroad: at night the air grows purple. To bars full of drunks: let the women you've stuffed fall into the black rivers. To cathedrals with small, pale ladies: you ask, dare a man breathe here? To cowsheds where you bed down with the beasts. It's dark there and the cows moo. And into the forests where axes ring out above and you forget the light of day: God has forgotten you. Do you still remember what the sky looks like? A fine tenor you've turned into! *He spreads his arms.* Come, brother! To dance, to sing, to drink! Rain to drench us! Sun to scorch us! Darkness and light! Dogs and women! Are you that degenerate?

BAAL: Luise! Luise! An anchor! Don't let me go with him. *Luise goes to him.* Help me, everyone.

JOHANNES: Don't let him lead you astray!

BAAL: My dear chap!

JOHANNES: Think of your mother, remember your art! Resist! *To Ekart:* You ought to be ashamed. You're evil.

EKART: Come, brother! We'll fly in the open sky as blissful as two white doves. Rivers in the morning light! Graveyards swept by the wind and the smell of endless unmown fields.

JOHANNA: Be strong, Mr Baal.

EMILIE *holding him:* I won't allow it! Do you hear? You can't throw yourself away!

BAAL: Not yet, Ekart! There's still another way. They won't play, brother.

EKART: Then go to the devil, you with your soft, fat, sentimental heart! *He goes.*

DRIVERS: Out with the ten ... Damn it! Add up ... Let's pack it in.

JOHANNA: You've won this time, Mr Baal.

BAAL: I'm sweating all over. Got any time today, Luise?

EMILIE: Don't talk like that, Baal! You don't know what you do to me when you talk like that.

LUISE: Stop upsetting the lady, Mr Baal. A child could see she's not herself.

BAAL: Don't worry, Luise! Horgauer!

DRIVER: What do you want?

BAAL: There's a lady being badly treated here, she wants love. Give her a kiss, Horgauer.

JOHANNES: Baal!

Johanna puts her arm round Emilie.

DRIVERS *laughing and hitting the table with their fists:* Press on, Andreas ... Have a go ... high class, blow your nose first ... You're a bastard, Mr Baal.

BAAL: Are you frigid, Emilie? Do you love me? He's shy, Emmi. Give him a kiss. If you make a fool of me in front of these people, it's the finish. One, two ...

The driver bends down. Emilie raises her tear-stained face. He kisses her vigorously. Loud laughter.

JOHANNES: That was evil, Baal. Drink brings out the evil in him, and then he feels good. He's too strong.

DRIVERS: Well done! What's she come to a place like this for? ... That's the way to treat them ... her kind break up families! ... Serves her right! *They get up from their card game.* Tell her to go and eat figs!

JOHANNA: How disgusting! You ought to be ashamed!

BAAL *going up to her:* Why are your knees shaking, Johanna?

JOHANNES: What do you want with her?

BAAL *a hand on his shoulder:* Must you also write poetry? While life's so decent? When you shoot down a racing

stream on your back, naked under an orange sky, and you
see nothing except the sky turning purple, then black like a
hole . . . when you trample your enemy underfoot . . . or
burst with joy at a funeral . . . or sobbing with love you eat
an apple . . . or bend a woman across a bed. *Johannes leads
Johanna away without saying a word.*

BAAL *leaning on the table:* It's all a bloody circus. Did you feel
it? Did it get under your skin? You have to lure the beast
from its cage! Get the beast into the sun! My bill! Let love
see the light of day! Naked in the sunshine! Under a clear
sky!

DRIVERS *shaking him by the hand:* Be seeing you, Mr Baal! . . .
At your service, sir! . . . For my part I always did say Mr
Baal had a screw loose. What with those songs and the
rest! But one thing's certain, his heart's in the right place! –
You have to treat women the way they deserve. – Well,
somebody exposed their precious white bottom here today.
– Good-bye, Mr Circus. *They go.*

BAAL: And good-bye to you, my friends! *Emilie has thrown
herself sobbing down on the bench. Baal touches her forehead with
the back of his hand.* Emmi! You can calm down now. The
worst is over. *He raises her head and brushes her hair from her
tear-stained face.* Just forget it! *He throws himself heavily on her
and kisses her.*

Baal's Attic

1 *Sunrise.*
Baal and Johanna sitting on the edge of the bed.

JOHANNA: Oh, what have I done! I'm wicked.
BAAL: Wash yourself instead.
JOHANNA: I still don't know how it happened.
BAAL: Johannes is to blame for everything. Drags you up
here and behaves like a clown when he sees why your
knees are shaking.

JOHANNA *gets up, lowers her voice:* When he comes back . . .

BAAL: Time for a bit of literature. *He lies down again.* First light over Mount Ararat.

JOHANNA: Shall I get up?

BAAL: After the flood. Stay in bed.

JOHANNA: Won't you open the window?

BAAL: I like the smell. – What about another helping? What's gone's gone.

JOHANNA: How can you be so vile?

BAAL *lazily on the bed:* White and washed clean by the flood, Baal lets his thoughts fly like doves over the dark waters.

JOHANNA: Where's my petticoat . . . I can't . . . like this . . .

BAAL *handing it to her:* Here! What can't you . . . like this, darling?

JOHANNA: Go home. *She drops it, but then she dresses.*

BAAL *whistling:* God, what a girl! I can feel every bone in my body. Give me a kiss!

JOHANNA *by the table in the middle of the room:* Say something! *Baal is silent.* Do you still love me? Say it. *Baal whistles.* Can't you say it?

BAAL *looking up at the ceiling:* I'm fed to the teeth!

JOHANNA: Then what was it last night? And before?

BAAL: Johannes could make things awkward. And Emilie's staggering around like a rammed schooner. I could die of starvation here! None of you would lift a finger for me. There's only one thing you're out for.

JOHANNA *confused, clearing the table:* And you – didn't you ever feel differently about me?

BAAL: Have you washed? Not an ounce of sense. Did you get nothing out of it? Go home! You can tell Johannes I took you home last night and spew gall at him. It's been raining. *Rolls himself up in his blanket.*

JOHANNA: Johannes? *She walks wearily to the door and goes.*

BAAL *suddenly turning:* Johanna! *Goes from his bed to the door.* Johanna! *At the window.* There she goes. There she goes.

2 *Noon.*
Baal lies on his bed.

BAAL *humming:*

The evening sky grows dark as pitch
With drink; or often fiery red.
Naked I'll have you in a ditch . . .

The two sisters come into the room arm in arm.

THE OLDER SISTER: You said we were to come and visit you
again.

BAAL *still humming:*

Or on a white and spacious bed.

THE OLDER SISTER: Well, we came, Mr Baal.

BAAL: Now they come fluttering in pairs to the dove-cot.
Take off your clothes.

THE OLDER SISTER: Mother heard the stairs creak last week.
She undoes her sister's blouse.

THE YOUNGER SISTER: It was getting light on the landing
when we got to our room.

BAAL: One day I'll be stuck with you.

THE YOUNGER SISTER: I'd drown myself, Mr Baal.

THE OLDER SISTER: We came together . . .

THE YOUNGER SISTER: I feel ashamed.

THE OLDER SISTER: It isn't the first time . . .

THE YOUNGER SISTER: But it was never so light. It's broad
daylight outside.

THE OLDER SISTER: And it isn't the second time.

THE YOUNGER SISTER: You get undressed as well.

THE OLDER SISTER: I will.   :

BAAL: When you've done, come on in! It'll be dark all right.

THE YOUNGER SISTER: You go first today.

THE OLDER SISTER: I was first last time . . .

THE YOUNGER SISTER: No, it was me . . .

BAAL: You'll both get it at once.

THE OLDER SISTER *standing with her arms round the younger one:* We're ready. It's so light in here!

BAAL: Is it warm outside?

THE OLDER SISTER: It's only April.

THE YOUNGER SISTER: But the sun's warm today.

BAAL: Did you enjoy yourselves last time?

The sisters do not answer.

THE OLDER SISTER: A girl threw herself into the river. Johanna Reiher.

THE YOUNGER SISTER: Into the Laach. I wouldn't go in there. The current's too strong.

BAAL: Into the river? Does anyone know why?

THE OLDER SISTER: There are rumours. People talk . . .

THE YOUNGER SISTER: She went off one afternoon and stayed out all night.

BAAL: Didn't she go home in the morning?

THE YOUNGER SISTER: No, then she went in the river. They haven't found her yet.

BAAL: Still afloat . . .

THE YOUNGER SISTER: What's the matter?

THE OLDER SISTER: Nothing. A chill perhaps.

BAAL: I'm too lazy today. You can go home.

THE OLDER SISTER: You can't do that, Mr Baal. You shouldn't do that to her.

Knocking at the door.

THE YOUNGER SISTER: Somebody's knocking. It's mother.

THE OLDER SISTER: For God's sake, don't open!

THE YOUNGER SISTER: I'm frightened.

THE OLDER SISTER: Here's your blouse.

Loud knocking.

BAAL: If it's your mother you're in for it.

THE OLDER SISTER *dressing quickly:* Wait a minute, don't open yet. Bolt the door, please, for God's sake!

LANDLADY *fat, enters:* Ah ha! I thought as much. Two at a time now! Aren't you ashamed of yourselves? A pair of you in his fishpond? Night and day, that fellow's bed never gets cold. Now I'm going to have my say. My attic isn't a brothel.

Baal turns to the wall.

LANDLADY: You're sleepy, are you? My word, don't you ever get enough of it? I can see the daylight through you. You look like a ghost. You're nothing but a bag of bones.

BAAL *moving his arms:* Like swans they fly to my wood.

LANDLADY *clapping her hands:* Nice swans! The way you put things! You could be a poet, you! If your knees don't rot first.

BAAL: I indulge in white bodies.

LANDLADY: White bodies! You're a poet, you really are! Don't know what else you are though. And the poor young things! You're sisters, are you? And snivelling because you're poor orphans, I suppose. How about a good hiding? For your white bodies? *Baal laughs.* And he laughs. You ruin poor girls by the hundredweight, poor girls you drag here. You disgusting pig! I'm giving you notice. As for you, look sharp and back to your mother! I'm coming with you.

The younger sister sobs loudly.

THE OLDER SISTER: It isn't her fault.

LANDLADY *taking both by the hand:* Now for the waterworks! These girls! Oh well, you're not the only ones. That one's up to his neck in swans. There's plenty besides you he's made happy, then dumped on the rubbish heap. Off with you now, into the fresh air! There's no need for tears. *She puts her arms round them both.* I know what he's like. I know the make. Stop snivelling, else it'll show in your eyes. Go home to your mother like good girls and don't do it again. *She pushes them out.* And you, you've had your notice. You can set up your swan-sty somewhere else. *She pushes the girls out of the room and goes out herself.*

BAAL *gets up, stretches:* A bitch with a heart! . . . I'm dead lazy today anyway. *He throws paper down on the table and sits down.* I'll make the new Adam. *He sketches big letters on the paper.* I'll have a go at the inner man. I'm hollowed out, but

hungry as a vulture. Nothing but a bag of bones. The bitch!
He leans back and stretches his arms and legs with emphasis. I'll
make summer. Red. Scarlet red. Greedy. *He hums again.*

3 *Evening.*
Baal sits at his table.

BAAL *picks up the bottle. The following speech to be delivered with
pauses:* I've covered the paper with red summer for four
days now: wild, pale, greedy; and fought the bottle. There
have been defeats, but the bodies on the wall are beginning
to retreat into the dark, into the Egyptian night. I nail them
to the wall, but I must stop drinking. *He murmurs:* This
white liquor is my rod and staff. It reflects my paper and has
remained untouched since the snow began to drip from the
gutter. But now my hands are shaking. As if the bodies
were still in them. *He listens.* My heart's pounding like a
horse's hoof. *With enthusiasm:* Oh Johanna, one more
night in your aquarium, and I would have rotted among the
fish. But now I smell the warm May nights. I'm a lover
with no one to love. I give in. *He drinks and gets up.* I must
move. First I'll get myself a woman. To move out alone is
sad. *He looks out of the window.* No matter who. One with a
face like a woman. *Humming, he goes out. Tristan is being
played down below on the hurdy gurdy.*
*Johannes enters, wretched and pale. He riffles the papers on the
table, picks up the bottle and goes shyly to the door.*
He waits there.
Noise on the landing. Whistling.
BAAL *pulling Sophie Barger into the room. Whistles:* Be nice to
me, darling. That is my room. *He sits down, sees Johannes.*
What are you doing here?
JOHANNES: I only wanted to . . .
BAAL: So you wanted to? What are you standing there for?
A tombstone for my Johanna, who's been washed away?
The ghost of Johannes from another world, is that it? I'll
throw you out! Leave this room at once! *Runs round him.* It's

an impertinence! I'll knock you down. It's spring, anyway. Get out!

Johannes looks at him and goes.

Baal whistles.

SOPHIE: What did the poor boy do to you? Let me go!

BAAL *opens the door wide:* When you get to the first floor, turn to the right.

SOPHIE: They followed us after you picked me up in front of the door. They'll find me.

BAAL: No one will find you here.

SOPHIE: I don't even know you. What do you want from me?

BAAL: If you mean that, you may as well go.

SOPHIE: You rushed up to me in the street. I thought it was an orangutan.

BAAL: It's spring, isn't it? I need something white in this damned hole, a cloud. *He opens the door and listens.* Those idiots, they've lost their way.

SOPHIE: I'll get thrown out if I come home late.

BAAL: Especially —

SOPHIE: Especially what?

BAAL: The way a woman looks when I've made love to her.

SOPHIE: I don't know why I'm still here.

BAAL: I can give you the information.

SOPHIE: You needn't think the worst of me, please!

BAAL: Why not? You're a woman like any other. The faces vary, the knees are always weak.

Sophie is half prepared to go; at the door she looks round.

Baal looks at her, astride a chair.

SOPHIE: Good-bye!

BAAL *indifferently:* Do you feel faint?

SOPHIE *leans against the wall:* I don't know. I feel so weak.

BAAL: I know. It's April. It's growing dark, and you smell me. That's how it is with animals. *Gets up.* Now you belong to the wind, white cloud. *He goes to her quickly, slams the door, and takes Sophie Barger into his arms.*

SOPHIE *breathlessly:* Let me go!

BAAL: My name's Baal.

SOPHIE: Let me go!

BAAL: You must console me. The winter left me weak. And you look like a woman.

SOPHIE *looks up at him:* Your name's Baal?

BAAL: That makes you want to stay?

SOPHIE *looking up at him:* You're so ugly, so ugly, it's frightening. – But then —

BAAL: Mm?

SOPHIE: Then it doesn't matter.

BAAL *kisses her:* Are your knees steady, mm?

SOPHIE: You don't even know my name. I'm Sophie Barger.

BAAL: Forget your name. *Kisses her.*

SOPHIE: Don't – don't – it's the first time anybody's ever . . .

BAAL: Untouched? Come! *He leads her to the bed. They sit down.* You see! Bodies have poured through this room like water. But now I want a face. We'll go out tonight. We'll lie down in the fields. You're a woman. I've become unclean. You must love me, for a while.

SOPHIE: Is that what you're like? . . . I love you.

BAAL *rests his head on her breasts:* Now the sky's above us, and we're alone.

SOPHIE: But you must lie still.

BAAL: Like a child.

SOPHIE *sitting up:* My mother's at home. I have to go home.

BAAL: Is she old?

SOPHIE: She's seventy.

BAAL: Then she's used to wickedness.

SOPHIE: What if the earth swallowed me up? What if I'm carried off at night and never return?

BAAL: Never? *Silence.* Have you any brothers or sisters?

SOPHIE: Yes, they need me.

BAAL: The air here is like milk. *Goes to the window.* The willows down by the river are soaking wet, and unkempt from the rain. *Takes hold of her.* Your thighs must be pale.

Whitewashed Houses with Brown Tree Trunks

Sombre ringing of bells. Baal. The tramp, a pale drunk individual.

BAAL *striding in a half circle round the tramp, who sits on a stone, his pale face turned to the sky:* Who nailed the tree corpses to the wall?

TRAMP: The pale ivory wind around the corpses of trees. Corpus Christi.

BAAL: Not to mention ringing the bells when plants die!

TRAMP: Bells give me a moral uplift.

BAAL: Don't the trees depress you?

TRAMP: Pff! Tree carcasses! *Drinks from a bottle.*

BAAL: Women's bodies aren't any better!

TRAMP: What have women's bodies to do with a religious procession?

BAAL: They're both obscene. There's no love in you.

TRAMP: There's love in me for the white body of Jesus. *Passes him the bottle.*

BAAL *calmer:* I wrote songs down on paper. They get hung up in lavatories these days.

TRAMP *transfigured:* To serve the Lord Jesus! I see the white body of Jesus. Jesus loves sinners.

BAAL *drinking:* Like me.

TRAMP: Do you know the story about him and the dead dog? They all said, it's a stinking mess. Fetch the police! It's unbearable! But, he said, it has nice white teeth.

BAAL: Perhaps I'll turn Catholic.

TRAMP: He didn't. *Takes the bottle from him.*

BAAL *runs about enraged:* But the women's bodies he nails to the wall. I wouldn't do that.

TRAMP: Nailed to the wall! They never floated down the river. They were slaughtered for him, for the white body of Jesus.

BAAL *takes the bottle from him, turns away:* There's too much religion or too much gin in your blood. *Walks away with the bottle.*

TRAMP *beside himself, shouting after him:* So you won't defend your ideals, sir! You won't join the procession? You love plants and won't do anything for them?

BAAL: I'm going down to the river to wash myself. I can't be bothered with corpses. *Goes.*

TRAMP: But I'm full of drink, I can't bear it. I can't bear the damned dead plants. If I had more gin in me, perhaps I could bear it.

Spring Night Beneath Trees

Baal. Sophie.

BAAL *lazily:* It's stopped raining. The grass must still be wet . . . it never came through the leaves of our tree. The young leaves are dripping wet, but here among the roots it's dry! *Angrily.* Why can't a man make love to a plant?

SOPHIE: Listen!

BAAL: The wild roaring of the wind through the damp, black foliage. Can you hear the rain drip from the leaves?

SOPHIE: I can feel a drop on my neck . . . Oh, let me go!

BAAL: Love rips the clothes from a man like a whirlpool and buries him naked among the corpses of leaves, after he's seen the sky.

SOPHIE: I should like to hide in you, Baal, because I'm naked.

BAAL: I'm drunk and you're staggering. The sky is black and we're on a swing with love in our bodies and the sky is black. I love you.

SOPHIE: Oh, Baal, my mother'll be weeping over my dead body, she'll think I drowned myself. How many weeks is it now? It wasn't even May then. It must be nearly three weeks.

BAAL: It must be nearly three weeks, said the beloved among the roots of the tree, after thirty years had passed and she was half rotted by then.

SOPHIE: It's good to lie here like a captive, with the sky above, and never be alone again.

BAAL: I'm going to take your petticoat off again.

A Club Called 'The Night Cloud'

A small, swinish café; whitewashed dressing-room; at the back on the left a dark brown curtain; to the side on the right a whitewashed door made of boards leading to the lavatory. At the back on the right a door. When it is open blue night sky is seen. A woman entertainer sings at the back of the café.

Baal walks around, chest and shoulders bare, drinking and humming. Lupu, a fat, pale boy with black glossy hair gummed down in two strips on to his sweaty, pale face and a prominent back to his head, stands in the doorway right.

LUPU: The lamp has been knocked down again.

BAAL: Only pigs come here. Where's my gin ration?

LUPU: You've drunk it all.

BAAL: You watch your step!

LUPU: Mjurk said something about a sponge.

BAAL: Does that mean I don't get a drink?

LUPU: No more gin for you until you've done your number, Mjurk said. I'm sorry for you.

MJURK *by the curtain:* Make yourself scarce, Lupu!

BAAL: No drink, no song.

MJURK: You shouldn't drink so much, or one of these days you won't be able to sing at all.

BAAL: Why else do I sing?

MJURK: Next to Savettka, you're the 'Night Cloud's' most brilliant attraction. You're my personal discovery. Was there ever such a delicate talent in such a fat lump? The fat lump makes the success, not the songs. Your drinking'll ruin me.

BAAL: I'm sick of haggling every night for gin that's my con-tractual right. I'm clearing out.

MJURK: I've got police backing. You should try sleeping one of these nights, you crawl around as if you'd been hamstrung. Tell your sweetheart to go to hell! *Applause in the café.* You're on now, anyway.

BAAL: I'm fed to the teeth.

Savettka with the pianist, a pale apathetic individual, coming from behind the curtain:

SAVETTKA: That's my lot. I'm off now.

MJURK *forcing a tail-coat on Baal:* You don't go half naked on to the stage in my club.

BAAL: Moron! *He throws down the tail-coat and goes off behind the curtain, dragging the guitar.*

SAVETTKA *sits down and drinks:* He only works for that woman he's living with. He's a genius. Lupu imitates him shamelessly. He has taken his tone as well as his girl.

PIANIST *leaning on the lavatory door:* His songs are divine but he's been haggling with Lupu for his drink for the last ten days.

SAVETTKA *drinking:* Life's hell!

BAAL *from behind the curtain:* Small am I, pure am I, a jolly little boy am I. *Applause. Baal continues, accompanying himself on the guitar:*

Through the room the wild wind comes.
What's the child been eating? Plums.
Soft and white its body lay
Helping pass the time away.

Applause and whistles. Baal goes on singing, and the noise gets rowdier as the song gets more and more shameless. Finally, uproar in the café.

PIANIST *phlegmatically:* My God, he's packing up. Call a doctor! Now Mjurk's talking, they'll tear him to pieces. No one censored that!

Baal comes from behind the curtain, dragging his guitar.

MJURK *following him:* You bastard! I'll have the hide off you!

You are going to sing! As stated in the contract! Or I'll get the police. *He goes back behind the curtain.*

PIANIST: You'll ruin us, Baal.

Baal raises a hand to his throat and goes to the lavatory door.

PIANIST *not letting him pass:* Where are you off to?

Baal pushes him aside and goes through the door, dragging his guitar after him.

SAVETTKA: Taking your guitar to the lavatory? Lovely!

GUESTS *peering in:* Where's that bastard? Go on with the song – don't stop now! The filthy bastard! *They return to the room.*

MJURK: I spoke like a Salvation Army general. We can rely on the police. But they're shouting for him again. Where is he? He'll have to go on.

PIANIST: The main attraction's sitting on the lavatory.

Cry from behind the scenes: Baal!

MJURK *drumming on the door:* You. Answer me! Damn it, I forbid you to lock yourself in! While I'm paying you! I've got it in writing. You swindler! *Thumps wildly.*

LUPU *in the door on the right. Blue night sky outside:* The lavatory window's open. The bird has flown. No drink, no song!

MJURK: Empty! Gone? Out through the lavatory? The cut-throat! Police! I want the police! *He rushes out. Calls in rhythm from behind the curtain: Baal! Baal! Baal!*

Green Fields. Blue Plum Trees

Baal. Ekart.

BAAL *slowly coming through the fields:* Since the sky turned green and pregnant, summertime, wind, no shirt in my trousers. *Back to Ekart.* They rub my backside, my skull's blown up with the wind, and the smell of the fields hangs in the hair of my armpits. The air trembles as if it were drunk.

EKART *behind him:* Why are you running away from the plum trees like an elephant?

BAAL: Put your hand on my head. It swells with every pulse-beat and goes down like a balloon. Can't you feel it?

EKART: No.

BAAL: You don't understand my soul.

EKART: Let's go and lie in the river.

BAAL: My soul, brother, is the groaning of the cornfields as they bend in the wind, and the gleam in the eyes of two insects who want to devour each other.

EKART: A mad summer boy with immortal intestines, that's what you are! A dumpling, who'll leave a grease spot on the sky.

BAAL: Only words. But it doesn't matter.

EKART: My body's light as a little plum in the wind.

BAAL: That's because of the pale summer sky, brother. Shall we soak up the warm water of a blue pond? Otherwise the white roads that lead across the land will draw us like angels' ropes up to heaven.

Village Inn

Evening. Farmers. Baal. Ekart on his own in a corner.

BAAL: I'm glad I've got you all here together. My brother will be here tomorrow evening. The bulls have to be here by then.

FARMER *gaping:* How can we see if a bull's the right sort for your brother?

BAAL: Only my brother can see. They all have to be strong, fine beasts. Or they're no use. Another gin!

SECOND FARMER: Will you buy the bull on the spot?

BAAL: The one with the strongest legs.

THIRD FARMER: For your price they'll bring them from eleven villages.

FIRST FARMER: Come and have a look at *my* bull.

BAAL: A gin!

FARMERS: My bull is the best! Tomorrow evening, you said? *They separate.* – Are you staying the night here?

BAAL: Yes, in a bed.

The farmers go.

EKART: What are you trying to do? Have you gone mad?

BAAL: Wasn't it wonderful, the way they gawped and gaped, and then they got the idea and began to add up.

EKART: It brought in a few gins! But now we'd better get out quickly.

BAAL: Go now? Are you mad?

EKART: You're crazy! Think of the bulls!

BAAL: And just why did I jockey the boys?

EKART: Well – for the drinks?

BAAL: Wake up! I wanted to give you a treat, Ekart. *He opens the window behind him. It grows dark. He sits down again.*

EKART: You're drunk on six gins. You should be ashamed.

BAAL: It's going to be tremendous. I love these simple people. You're going to see an impressive sight, Ekart. Your health!

EKART: You love pretending to be more naïve than you are. Those poor fellows will beat me up – and you.

BAAL: It'll be part of their education. I'm thinking about them now on this warm evening with a certain tenderness. They come, in their own simple way, to swindle, and that pleases me.

EKART: All right, the bulls or me! I'm going, before the land-lord catches on.

BAAL: The evening is so warm. Stay another hour. Then I'll go with you. You know I love you. One can even smell the dung on the fields from here. Do you think the landlord would stand the promoters of the bull business another gin?

EKART: There's someone coming!

PARSON *enters:* Good evening! Are you the man with the bulls?

BAAL: I am.

PARSON: What is the object of this hoax?

BAAL: Because we have nothing else in the world! How strong the smell of the hay is! Is it always like this in the evenings?

D

PARSON: Your world seems to be very impoverished, my friend.

BAAL: My heaven is full of trees and naked bodies.

PARSON: Don't talk like that. The world isn't a circus for your entertainment.

BAAL: What is the world, then?

PARSON: Just clear out. I'm a very good-natured person, you know. I don't want to make things difficult for you. I've dealt with the matter.

BAAL: The man of God has no sense of humour, Ekart.

PARSON: Don't you realize how childish your plan was? *To Ekart:* What does your friend want?

BAAL *leaning back:* In the evening when it gets dark – of course, it has to be evening and of course the sky must be cloudy – when the air is warm and the wind gentle, the bulls come. They come trotting from every direction, an impressive sight. And the poor farmers stand in the middle and don't know what to do with the bulls, and they've miscalculated: all they get is an impressive sight. I like people who miscalculate. And where else can you see so many animals together?

PARSON: And just for this you wanted to mobilize seven villages?

BAAL: What are seven villages compared with an impressive sight?

PARSON: Now I understand. You're just a poor fellow. With a particular liking for bulls, I suppose?

BAAL: Come, Ekart, he's spoilt it all. Christians don't love animals any more.

PARSON *laughs, then seriously:* I can't agree with you there. Be off now, and don't make yourselves conspicuous. I think I'm rendering you a considerable service.

BAAL: Let's go, Ekart. You've missed your treat, brother. *He slowly leaves with Ekart.*

PARSON: Good evening! I'll settle the gentlemen's bill.

LANDLORD *behind the table:* Eleven gins, your reverence.

Trees in the Evening

Six or seven woodcutters are sitting on the ground leaning against a tree, among them Baal. A corpse in the grass.

FIRST WOODCUTTER: It was an oak tree. It didn't kill him at once. He suffered.

SECOND WOODCUTTER: Only this morning he said the weather seemed to be getting better. This is how he liked it, green and a bit of rain. And the wood not too dry.

THIRD WOODCUTTER: He was a good lad, Teddy. He used to keep a small shop somewhere. In the old days. Used to be as fat as a priest. He ruined his business on account of a woman, and he came up here. Lost a bit of his paunch every year.

ANOTHER WOODCUTTER: Didn't he ever say anything about the woman?

THIRD WOODCUTTER: No. And I don't know that he wanted to go back. He saved quite a bit, but maybe that was because he was abstemious. Nobody tells the truth up here. It's better that way.

A WOODCUTTER: Last week he said he was going north this winter. It seems he had a cabin somewhere up there. Didn't he tell you where, elephant? *To Baal:* You were talking about it, weren't you?

BAAL: Leave me alone. I don't know anything.

THE PREVIOUS ONE: You wouldn't be thinking of moving in yourself, eh?

SECOND WOODCUTTER: You can't trust that one. Remember how he put our boots in the water that night, so we couldn't go to the forest the next day. Only because he was lazy as usual.

ANOTHER WOODCUTTER: He does nothing for his money.

BAAL: It's not a day for wrangling. Can't you spare a thought for poor Teddy?

A WOODCUTTER: Where were you when he packed in?
Baal gets up, sways over the grass to Teddy. He sits there.

THE PREVIOUS ONE: Look, he can't walk straight!

ANOTHER: Leave him alone! The elephant had a shock!

THE THIRD: Can't you keep it quiet just for today while he's
lying there.

THE OTHER: What are you doing to Teddy, elephant?

BAAL *by the corpse:* Teddy is at peace, and we are the opposite.
Both are good. The sky is black. The trees shudder. Somewhere clouds gather. That is the setting. One eats. After
sleep one wakes. Not him. Us. And that's doubly good.

THE OTHER: What did you say the sky was like?

BAAL: The sky is black.

THE OTHER: You're not all there. The good ones always cop
it first.

BAAL: How right you are, my dear chap!

A WOODCUTTER: It couldn't happen to Baal. He's never
around where there's work.

BAAL: But Teddy, he was a hard worker. Teddy was generous. Teddy was friendly. One thing's certain: Teddy *was*.

THE SECOND: Wonder where he is now?

BAAL *points to the dead man:* There he is.

THE THIRD: I always get the feeling that the wind is made of
dead souls, especially on spring evenings. But I get the
feeling in autumn too.

BAAL: And in summer, in the sun, over the cornfields.

THE THIRD: That doesn't fit. It has to be dark.

BAAL: It has to be dark, Teddy.
Silence.

FOURTH WOODCUTTER: What are we going to do with
him?

THE THIRD: He's got nobody who wants him.

THE OTHER: He was just on his own in the world.

A WOODCUTTER: What about his things?

THE THIRD: There isn't much. He carried his money off
somewhere, to a bank. It'll stay there even if he doesn't
turn up. Got any idea, Baal?

BAAL: He doesn't stink yet.

A WOODCUTTER: I've just had a good idea.

THE OTHER: Out with it!

THE MAN WITH THE IDEA: The elephant's not the only one with ideas, mate. What about drinking Teddy's good health?

BAAL: That's indecent, Bergmeier.

THE OTHERS: Rot, indecent. What shall we drink? Water? What a lousy idea!

THE MAN WITH THE IDEA: Gin!

BAAL: I vote in favour. Gin is decent. Whose gin?

THE MAN WITH THE IDEA: Teddy's gin.

THE OTHERS: Teddy's! – Sounds all right. – Teddy's ration! – Teddy was careful. – Not a bad idea for an idiot.

THE MAN WITH THE IDEA: A brainwave, what! Something for you blockheads! Teddy's gin at Teddy's funeral! Cheap and fitting! Anybody made a speech yet? Isn't that the proper thing to do?

BAAL: I did.

SOME: When?

BAAL: Earlier. Before you began to talk rubbish. It began with 'Teddy is at peace' . . . You don't notice anything until it's over.

THE OTHERS: Blockhead! Let's get the gin!

BAAL: It's a disgrace!

THE OTHERS: Oho! – Why, you big elephant.

BAAL: It's Teddy's property. The bottles must not be opened. Teddy's got a wife and five poor orphans.

A WOODCUTTER: Four! Four orphans!

ANOTHER: It's all coming out now.

BAAL: Do you want to drink the gin that belongs to Teddy's five poor orphans? Is that Christian?

THE PREVIOUS ONE: Four! Four orphans!

BAAL: Taking gin out of the mouths of Teddy's four orphans.

A WOODCUTTER: Teddy hasn't any family at all.

BAAL: But orphans, my friend, orphans.

ANOTHER: Do you think these orphans the elephant keeps

kidding you about are going to drink Teddy's gin? All right, it's Teddy's property . . .

BAAL *interrupts:* It was . . .

THE OTHER: What are you getting at?

A WOODCUTTER: He's jabbering. He's not all there.

THE OTHER: As I said, it was Teddy's property and so we'll pay for it. In cash. That'll fix the orphans.

EVERYBODY: A good suggestion. So much for the elephant. He must be mad, not to want any gin. Let's leave him and get Teddy's drink!

BAAL *calls after them:* Come back, you bloody scavengers! *To Teddy:* Poor Teddy! And the trees are pretty strong today and the air is good and soft, and I feel fortified within. Poor Teddy, don't you feel a tickle? You're through, I'm telling you, soon you'll stink, and everything will go on as before, the wind will blow, and I know where your cabin is, and your property will be taken over by the living, and you abandoned it and only wanted peace. Your body wasn't so bad, Teddy, it isn't so bad now, only a little damaged on one side and the legs . . . it would have finished you with women, you can't put that on top of a woman. *He lifts the dead man's leg.* With a bit more luck you could have gone on living, though, in that body, but your soul was too bloody choosy, the building was condemned, and the rats left the sinking ship. You were just a victim of your own habits, Teddy.

THE OTHERS *returning:* Hey, elephant! You're in for it! Where's the gin Teddy kept under his old bed? – Where were you when we were looking after Teddy? Teddy wasn't even dead then. – Where were you then, you son of a bitch, robbing the dead, protecting Teddy's poor orphans, eh?

BAAL: You've got no proof, my friends!

THE OTHERS: Where's the gin, then? In your esteemed opinion, did the bottle drink it? – This is a serious matter, old chap! – Stand up, you, get up! Walk in a straight line and then try and tell us it's the shock, it's because you're completely rotten, body and soul, you swine! – Get him on his legs! Liven him up, boys. Besmirching Teddy's poor old name! *They put Baal on his feet.*

BAAL: Bastards! Don't trample on poor Teddy! *He sits down and takes the arm of the corpse under his arm.* If you do anything to me, Teddy'll fall flat on his face. Is that piety? Anything I do will be in self-defence. There are seven of you, seven, and sober. And I'm on my own and drunk. Is that right, is that honourable? Seven against one! Calm down! Teddy's calmed down.

SOME *sad and indignant:* Nothing's sacred to him. – God forgive his drunken soul! – He's the blackest sinner on God's earth.

BAAL: Sit down, I don't like this preacher's cant. There are some with brains and some without. It makes for a better division of labour. Now you've seen for yourselves. I work with my brains. *He smokes.* You've always been too irreverent, friends! And what effect would it have if you sank that good gin? Me, I make discoveries, let me say. I was telling Teddy some most important things. *He takes papers from Teddy's jacket and looks at them.* But you had to run after that wretched gin. Sit down. Look at the sky growing dark between the trees. Is that nothing? There's no religion in your blood!

A Hut

You can hear the rain. Baal. Ekart.

BAAL: This is the winter sleep of white bodies in the black mud.

EKART: You still haven't been to fetch the meat?

BAAL: You're working on your mass, I suppose?

EKART: Why worry about my mass? Worry about your woman! Where have you driven her to this time, in the rain?

BAAL: She runs after us like a mad woman and hangs round my neck.

EKART: You're sinking lower and lower.

BAAL: I'm too heavy.

EKART: You're not reckoning to peg out, I suppose?

BAAL: I'll fight it to the last ditch. I'll live without a skin. I'll retreat into my toes. I'll fall like a bull. On the grass, where it's softest. I'll swallow death and know nothing.

EKART: You've got fatter while we've been lying here.

BAAL *putting his right hand under his left armpit:* My shirt has got bigger. The dirtier it gets the bigger it gets. There's room for someone else, but no one fat. What are you lolling about for, you lazy bag of bones?

EKART: There's a kind of sky in my head, very green and vast, where my thoughts drift like featherweight clouds in the wind. They're completely undecided in their course. All that's inside me.

BAAL: It's delirium. You're an alcoholic. You see, it gets you in the end.

EKART: When I'm delirious I can feel it by my face.

BAAL: Your face has room for the four winds. Concave! *He looks at him.* You haven't a face. You're nothing. You're transparent.

EKART: I'm growing more and more mathematical.

BAAL: Nobody knows your history. Why don't you ever talk about yourself?

EKART: I shan't ever have one. Who's that outside?

BAAL: You've got a good ear! There's something in you that you hide. You're a bad man, like me, a devil. But one day you'll see rats. Then you'll be a good man again.
Sophie at the door.

EKART: Is that you, Sophie?

BAAL: What do you want this time?

SOPHIE: May I come in now, Baal?

A Plain. Sky

Evening. Baal, Ekart, Sophie.

SOPHIE: My knees are giving way. Why are you running like a mad man?

BAAL: Because you're hanging round my neck like a millstone.

EKART: How can you treat her like this? You made her pregnant.

SOPHIE: I wanted it, Ekart.

BAAL: She wanted it, and now she's hanging round my neck.

EKART: You behave like an animal! Sit down, Sophie.

SOPHIE *sits down heavily:* Let him go.

EKART: If you throw her out I'll stay with her.

BAAL: She won't stay with you. But you'd desert me! Because of her? That's like you.

EKART: Twice you took my place in bed. You didn't want my women. They left you cold, but you stole them from me although I loved them.

BAAL: Because you loved them. Twice I defiled corpses to keep you clean. I need that. God knows, it gave me no pleasure.

EKART *to Sophie:* Are you still in love with this depraved animal?

SOPHIE: I can't help it, Ekart. I'd love his corpse. I even love his fists. I can't help it, Ekart.

BAAL: Don't ever tell me what you two were up to while I was inside!

SOPHIE: We stood together in front of the white prison wall and looked up at your window.

BAAL: You were together.

SOPHIE: Beat me for it.

EKART *shouts:* Didn't you throw her at me?

BAAL: You might have been stolen from me.

EKART: I haven't got your elephant's hide.

BAAL: I love you for it.

EKART: Keep your damned mouth shut about it while she's still with us!

BAAL: Tell her to get lost! She's turning into a bitch! *He puts his hands up to his throat.* She's washing her dirty laundry in your tears. Can you still not see that she's running naked between us? I have the patience of a lamb, but I can't change my skin.

EKART *sits down beside Sophie:* Go home to your mother.

SOPHIE: I can't.

BAAL: She can't, Ekart.

SOPHIE: Beat me if you want, Baal. I won't ask you to walk slowly again. I didn't mean to. Let me keep up with you, as long as I can. Then I'll lie down in the bushes and you needn't look. Don't drive me away, Baal.

BAAL: Throw your fat body into the river. I'm sick of you, and it's your own doing.

SOPHIE: Do you want to leave me here or don't you? You're still uncertain, Baal. You're like a child, to talk like that.

BAAL: I'm fed to the teeth with you.

SOPHIE: But not at night, Baal, not at night! I'm afraid alone. I'm afraid of the dark. I'm frightened of it.

BAAL: In your condition? No one will touch you.

SOPHIE: But tonight! Just wait both of you tonight.

BAAL: Go to the bargemen! It's midsummer night. They'll be drunk.

SOPHIE: A few minutes!

BAAL: Come on, Ekart!

SOPHIE: Where shall I go?

BAAL: To heaven, darling!

SOPHIE: With my child?

BAAL: Bury it.

SOPHIE: I pray that you'll never have cause to remember what you've just said to me, under this beautiful sky you love. I pray for it on my knees.

EKART: I'll stay with you. And then I'll take you to your mother, if you say you'll stop loving this swine.

BAAL: She loves me.

SOPHIE: I love him.

EKART: Are you still on your feet, you swine! Haven't you
    got knees? Are you besotted with drink or poetry?
    Depraved swine! Depraved swine!

BAAL: Simpleton.

Ekart attacks him, they fight.

SOPHIE: Mother of God! They're like wild animals!

EKART *fighting:* Did you hear what she said? Back there! And
    it's getting dark now. Depraved animal! Depraved animal!

BAAL *against him, pressing Ekart to himself:* Now you're close to
    me. Can you smell me? Now I'm holding you. There's
    more than the closeness of women. *He stops.* Look, you
    can see the stars above the trees now, Ekart.

EKART *looks hard at Baal, who gazes up into the sky:* I can't strike
    this thing!

BAAL *his arm round Ekart:* It's getting dark. We must find a
    place for the night. There are hollows in the wood where
    the wind never penetrates. Come, I'll tell you about the
    animals. *He draws him away.*

SOPHIE *alone in the dark, screams:* Baal!

Brown Wooden Bar

*Night. Wind. At tables, Gougou, Bolleboll. The old beggar and
Maja with a child in a box.*

BOLLEBOLL *playing cards with Gougou:* I've no more money.
    Let's play for our souls.

THE BEGGAR: Brother wind wants to come in. But we don't
    know our cold brother wind. Heh, heh, heh!
    The child cries.

MAJA *the beggar woman:* Listen! Something's prowling round
    the house. Pray God it's no wild beast!

BOLLEBOLL: Why? Are you feeling randy again?
    Knocking at the door.

MAJA: Listen! I won't open.

THE BEGGAR: You will open.

MAJA: No, no, Mother of God, no!

THE BEGGAR: Bouque la Madonne! Open up!

MAJA *crawls to the door:* Who's outside?
The child cries. Maja opens the door.

BAAL *enters with Ekart, soaked to the skin:* Is this where they look after the sick?

MAJA: Yes, but there's no bed free. *More insolently:* And I'm ill.

BAAL: We've brought champagne. *Ekart has gone to warm himself by the stove.*

BOLLEBOLL: Come here! The man who knows what champagne is, is good enough for us.

THE BEGGAR: There's high society here today, my boy!

BAAL *goes up to the table and pulls two bottles from his pocket:* Mmm?

THE BEGGAR: That's fishy.

BOLLEBOLL: I know where you got that champagne. But I won't give you away.

BAAL: Here, Ekart! Any glasses?

MAJA: Cups, kind gentlemen. Cups. *She brings some.*

GOUGOU: I need a cup of my own.

BAAL *doubtful:* Are you allowed to drink champagne?

GOUGOU: Please! *Baal pours him some.*

BAAL: What's wrong with you?

GOUGOU: Bronchitis. Nothing bad. A little inflammation. Nothing serious.

BAAL *to Bolleboll:* And you?

BOLLEBOLL: Stomach ulcers. Won't kill me!

BAAL *to the beggar:* There's something wrong with you too, I trust?

THE BEGGAR: I'm mad.

BAAL: Here's to you! We understand each other. I'm healthy.

THE BEGGAR: I knew a man who said he was healthy too. He believed it. He came from the forest and one day he went back there as there was something he had to think over. He found the forest very strange and no longer familiar, he walked for many days. Always deeper into the forest, because he wanted to see how independent he was and how much endurance there was left in him. But there wasn't much. *He drinks.*

BAAL *uneasy:* What a wind! We have to move on tonight, Ekart.

THE BEGGAR: Yes, the wind. One evening, at sunset, when he was no longer alone, he went through the great stillness between the trees and stood beneath one of the highest. *Drinks.*

BOLLEBOLL: That was the ape in him.

THE BEGGAR: Yes, perhaps it was the ape. He leant against it, very closely, and felt the life in it, or thought so. And he said, you are higher than I am and stand firm and you know the earth beneath you, and it holds you. I can run and move better, but I do not stand firm and I do not reach into the depths of the earth and nothing holds me up. Nor do I know the quiet of the endless sky above the still tree-tops. *He drinks.*

GOUGOU: What did the tree say?

THE BEGGAR: Yes. And the wind blew. A shudder ran through the tree. And the man felt it. He threw himself down on the ground and he clutched the wild, hard roots and cried bitterly. But he did it to many trees.

EKART: Did it cure him?

THE BEGGAR: No. He had an easier death, though.

MAJA: I don't understand that.

THE BEGGAR: Nothing is understood. But some things are felt. If one understands a story it's just that it's been told badly.

BOLLEBOLL: Do you believe in God?

BAAL *with an effort:* I've always believed in myself. But a man *could* turn atheist.

BOLLEBOLL *laughs loudly:* Now I feel happy. God! Champagne! Love! Wind and rain! *He reaches for Maja.*

MAJA: Leave me alone. Your breath stinks.

BOLLEBOLL: And I suppose you haven't got the pox? *He takes her on his lap.*

THE BEGGAR: Watch it! *To Bolleboll:* I'm getting drunker and drunker. If I get completely drunk you can't go out in the rain tonight.

GOUGOU *to Ekart:* He used to be better looking, that's how he got her.

EKART: What about your intellectual superiority? Your psychic ascendancy?

GOUGOU: She wasn't like that. She was completely innocent.

EKART: And what did you do?

GOUGOU: I was ashamed.

BOLLEBOLL: Listen! The wind. It's asking God for peace.

MAJA *sings:*

Lullaby baby, away from the storm
Here we are sheltered and drunken and warm.

BAAL: Whose child is that?

MAJA: My daughter, sir.

THE BEGGAR: A virgo dolorosa.

BAAL *drinks:* That's how it used to be, Ekart. And it was all right too.

EKART: What?

BOLLEBOLL: He's forgotten what.

BAAL: Used to be! That's a strange phrase!

GOUGOU *to Ekart:* The best of all is nothingness.

BOLLEBOLL: Pst! We're going to have Gougou's aria. A song from the old bag of worms.

GOUGOU: It's as if the air was quivering on a summer evening. Sunshine. But it isn't quivering. Nothing. Nothing at all. You just stop. The wind blows, and you don't feel cold. It rains, and you don't get wet. Funny things happen, and you don't laugh with the others. You rot, and you don't need to wait. General strike.

THE BEGGAR: That's Hell's Paradise.

GOUGOU: Yes, that's paradise. No wish unfulfilled. You have none left. You learn to abandon all your habits. Even wishing. That's how you become free.

MAJA: What happened in the end?

GOUGOU *grins:* Nothing. Nothing at all. There is no end. Nothingness lasts for ever.

BOLLEBOLL: Amen.

BAAL *gets up, to Ekart:* Ekart, get up. We've fallen among murderers. *He supports himself by putting his arm round Ekart's shoulders.* The vermin multiply. The rot sets in. The maggots sing and show off.

EKART: It's the second time that's happened to you. I wonder if it's just the drink.

BAAL: My guts are hanging out . . . this is no mud bath.

EKART: Sit down. Get drunk. Warm yourself.

MAJA *drunk, sings:*

Summer and winter and snowstorms and rain
If we aren't sober we won't feel the pain.

BOLLEBOLL *takes hold of Maja and pummels her:* Your aria tickles me, little Gougou. Itsiwitsi, little Maja.
The child cries.

BAAL *drinks:* Who are you? *Amused, to Gougou:* Your name's bag of worms. Are you a candidate for the mortuary? Your health! *He sits down.*

THE BEGGAR: Watch out, Bolleboll! Champagne doesn't agree with me.

MAJA *hanging on to Bolleboll, sings:*

Seeing is suffering, keep your eyes shut
All go to sleep now, and nothing will hurt.

BAAL *brutally:*

Float down the river with rats in your hair
Everything's lovely, the sky is still there.

He gets up, glass in hand. The sky is black! Did that scare you? *Drums on the table.* You have to stand the roundabout. It's wonderful. *He sways.* I want to be an elephant in a circus and pee when things go wrong . . . *He begins to dance and sing.* Dance with the wind, poor corpse! Sleep with a cloud, you degenerate God! *He goes up to the table, swaying.*

EKART *gets up, drunk:* I'm not going with you any farther. I've got a soul too. You corrupted my soul. You corrupt everything. And then I shall start on my Mass again.

BAAL: Your health! I love you.

EKART: But I'm not going with you any farther. *He sits down.*

THE BEGGAR *to Bolleboll:* Hands off, you pig!

MAJA: What's it got to do with you?

THE BEGGAR: Shut up, you poor thing!

MAJA: You're raving!

BOLLEBOLL *venomously:* He's a fraud. There's nothing wrong with him. That's right. It's all a fraud!

THE BEGGAR: And you've got cancer.

BOLLEBOLL *uncannily quiet:* I've got cancer?

THE BEGGAR *turning coward:* I didn't say anything. Leave her alone! *Maja laughs.*

BAAL: Why's it crying? *Sways to the box.*

THE BEGGAR *angry:* What do you want?

BAAL *leans over the box:* Why are you crying? Have you never seen them at it before? Or do you cry every time?

THE BEGGAR: Leave it alone, you! *He throws his glass at Baal.*

MAJA: You pig!

BOLLEBOLL: He's only having a peep under her skirt!

BAAL *gets up slowly:* Oh you swine! You don't know what's human any more. Come on, Ekart! We'll wash ourselves in the river. *He leaves with Ekart.*

Green Thicket. River Beyond

Baal. Ekart.

BAAL *sitting in the thicket:* The water's warm. You can lie like
a crab on the sand. And the shrubs and white clouds in the
sky. Ekart!

EKART *concealed:* What do you want?

BAAL: I love you.

EKART: I'm too comfortable here.

BAAL: Did you see the clouds earlier?

EKART: Yes, they're shameless. *Silence.* A while ago a woman
went by on the other side.

BAAL: I don't care for women any longer . . .

Country Road. Willows

*Wind. Night. Ekart asleep in the grass. Baal comes across the fields
as if drunk, his clothes open, like a sleepwalker.*

BAAL: Ekart! Ekart! I've got it! Wake up!

EKART: What's the matter? Are you talking in your sleep
again?

BAAL *sits down by him:* This:

When she had drowned, and started her slow descent
Down the streams to where the rivers broaden
The opal sky shone most magnificent
As if it had to be her body's guardian.

Wrack and seaweed cling to her as she swims
Slowly their burden adds to her weight.
Coolly fishes play about her limbs
Creatures and growths encumber her in her final state.

And in the evening the sky grew dark as smoke
And at night the stars kept the light still soaring.
But soon it cleared as dawn again broke
To preserve her sequence of evening and morning.

As her pale body decayed in the water there
It happened (very slowly) that God gradually forgot it
First her face, then the hands, and right at the last her hair
Then she rotted in rivers where much else rotted.

The wind.

EKART: Has the ghost risen? It's not as wicked as you. Now sleep's gone to the devil and the wind is groaning in the willows like an organ. Nothing left but the white breast of philosophy, darkness, cold, and rain right up to our blessed end, and even for old women nothing left but their second sight.

BAAL: You don't need gin to be drunk in this wind. I see the world in a soft light: it is the excrement of the Almighty.

EKART: The Almighty, who made himself known once and for all through the association of the urinary passage with the sexual organ.

BAAL *lying down:* It's all so beautiful.

Wind.

EKART: The willows are like rotten teeth in the black mouth of the sky. I shall start work on my Mass soon.

BAAL: Is the quartet finished?

EKART: When did I have the time?

Wind.

BAAL: It's that redhead, the pale one, that you drag everywhere.

EKART: She has a soft white body, and at noon she brings it with her under the willows. They've drooping branches like hair, behind which we fuck like squirrels.

BAAL: Is she more beautiful than me?

Darkness. The wind blows on.

Young Hazel Shrubs

Long red switches hanging down. In the middle of them, Baal, sitting.
Noon.

BAAL: I'll satisfy her, the white dove . . . *He looks at the place.*
You get a good view of the clouds here through the willow
. . . when he comes there'll only be skin left. I'm sick of his
love affairs. Be calm!
A young woman comes out of the thicket. Red hair, a full figure.
BAAL *without looking round:* Is that you?
THE YOUNG WOMAN: Where's your friend?
BAAL: He's doing a Mass in E flat minor.
THE YOUNG WOMAN: Tell him I was here.
BAAL: He's too thin. He's transparent. He defiles himself.
He's regressing into zoology. Do sit down! *He looks round.*
THE YOUNG WOMAN: I prefer to stand.
BAAL: He's been eating too many eggs lately. *He pulls himself*
up by the red switches.
THE YOUNG WOMAN: I love him.
BAAL: You're no concern of mine. *He takes her in his arms.*
THE YOUNG WOMAN: Don't touch me! You're too dirty!
BAAL *slowly reaches for her throat:* Is that your throat? Do you
know how they put down pigeons, or wild ducks in the
wood?
THE YOUNG WOMAN: Mother of God! Leave me alone! *She*
struggles.
BAAL: With your weak knees? You're falling over already.
You want to be laid in the willows. A man's a man, in this
respect most of them are equal. *He takes her in his arms.*
THE YOUNG WOMAN *shaking:* Please, let me go!
BAAL: A shameless bird! I'll have it. Act of rescue by
desperate man! *He takes her by both arms and drags her into the*
thicket.

Maple Trees in the Wind

Clouded sky. Baal and Ekart, sitting among the roots.

BAAL: Drink's needed, Ekart. Any money left?

EKART: No. Look at the maple in the wind!

BAAL: It's trembling.

EKART: Where's that girl you used to go around the bars with?

BAAL: Turn into a fish and look for her.

EKART: You overeat, Baal. You'll burst.

BAAL: I'd like to hear the bang.

EKART: Do you ever look into water when it's black and deep and got no fish in it? Don't ever fall in. Watch out for yourself. You're so very heavy, Baal.

BAAL: I'll watch out for somebody else. I've written a song. Do you want to hear it?

EKART: Read it, then I'll know you.

BAAL: It's called Death in the Forest.

And a man died deep in the primaeval woods
While the storm blew in torrents around him —
Died like an animal scrabbling for roots
Stared up through the trees, as the wind skimmed the woods
And the roar of the thunderclap drowned him.

Several of them stood to watch him go
And they strove to make his passage smoother
Telling him: We'll take you home now, brother.
But he forced them from him with a blow
Spat, and cried: and where's my home, d'you know?
That was home, and he had got no other.

Is your toothless mouth choking with pus?
How's the rest of you: can you still tell?
Must you die so slowly and with so much fuss?
We've just had your horse chopped into steaks for us.
Hurry up! They're waiting down in hell.

Then the forest roared above their head
And they watched him clasp a tree and stagger
And they heard his screams and what he said.
Each man felt an overwhelming dread
Clenched his fist or, trembling, drew his dagger:
So like them, and yet so nearly dead!

You're foul, useless, mad, you mangy bear!
You're a sore, a chancre, filthy creature!
Selfish beast, you're breathing up our air!
So they said. And he, the cancer there:
Let me live! Your sun was never sweeter!
– Ride off in the light without a care!

That's what none of them could understand:
How the horror numbed and made them shiver.
There's the earth holding his naked hand.
In the breeze from sea to sea lies land:
Here I lie in solitude for ever.

Yes, mere life, with its abundant weight
Pinned him so that even half-decayed
He pressed his dead body ever deeper.
At dawn he fell dead in the grassy shade.
Numb with shock, they buried him, and cold with hate
Covered him with undergrowth and creeper.

Then they rode in silence from that place
Turning round to see the tree again
Under which his body once had lain
Who felt dying was too sharp a pain:
The tree stood in the sun ablaze.
Each made the mark of the cross on his face
And rode off swiftly over the plain.

EKART: Well, well! I suppose it's come to that now.
BAAL: When I can't sleep at night I look up at the stars. It's
just as good.

EKART: Is it?

BAAL *suspiciously:* But I don't do it often. It makes you weak.

EKART *after a pause:* You've made up a lot of poetry recently. You haven't had a woman for a long time, have you?

BAAL: Why?

EKART: I was thinking. Say no.

Baal gets up, stretches, looks at the top of the maple and laughs.

Inn

Evening. Ekart. The waitress. Watzmann. Johannes, in a shabby coat with a turned-up collar, hopelessly gone to seed. The waitress has the features of Sophie.

EKART: It's been eight years.

They drink. Wind.

JOHANNES: They say life only begins at twenty-five. That's when they get broader and have children.

Silence.

WATZMANN: His mother died yesterday. So he runs around trying to borrow money for the funeral. When he gets it he comes here. Then we can pay for the drinks. The landlord's a good man. He gives credit on a corpse which was a mother. *Drinks.*

JOHANNES: Baal! There's no wind left in his sails.

WATZMANN *to Ekart:* You must have to put up with a lot from him?

EKART: One can't spit in his face. The man's done for.

WATZMANN *to Johannes:* Does it distress you? Do you think about it?

JOHANNES: It's a waste of a man, I tell you. *Drinks.*
Silence.

WATZMANN: He's getting more and more disgusting.

EKART: Don't say that. I don't want to hear it. I love him. I don't resent him, because I love him. He's a child.

WATZMANN: He only does what he has to. Because he's so lazy.

EKART *goes to the door:* It's a mild night. The wind's warm. Like milk. I love all this. One should never drink. Or not so much. *Back to the table.* It's a mild night. Now and for another three weeks into the autumn a man can live on the road all right. *He sits down.*

WATZMANN: Do you want to leave tonight? You'd like to get rid of him, I suppose? He's a burden.

JOHANNES: You'd better be careful.

Baal enters slowly.

WATZMANN: Is that you, Baal?

EKART *hard:* What do you want now?

BAAL *enters, sits down:* What a miserable hole this place has turned into! *The waitress brings drink.*

WATZMANN: Nothing's changed here. Only you, it would appear, have got more refined.

BAAL: Is that still you, Luise?

Silence.

JOHANNES: Yes, it's agreeable here. – I have to drink, you see, drink a lot. It makes one strong. Even then one makes one's way to hell along a path of razors. But not in the same way. As if your legs were giving way under you, yielding, you know. So that you don't feel the razors at all. With springy loose joints. Besides, I never used to have ideas of this sort, really peculiar ones. Not while everything went well, when I lived a good bourgeois life. But now I have ideas, now that I've turned into a genius. Hm.

EKART *bursting out:* I'd like to be back in the forest, at dawn! The light between the trees is the colour of lemons! I want to go back up into the forest.

JOHANNES: That's something I don't understand, you must buy me another drink, Baal. It's really agreeable here.

BAAL: A gin for —

JOHANNES: No names! We know each other. I have such fearful dreams at night, you know, now and then. But only now and then. It really is agreeable here.

The wind. They drink.

WATZMANN *hums:*

The trees come in avalanches
Each very conveniently made.
You can hang yourself from their branches
Or loll underneath in their shade.

BAAL: Where was it like that? It was like that once.

JOHANNES: She's still afloat, you see. Nobody's found her.
But sometimes I get a feeling she's being washed down my
throat with all the drink, a very small corpse, half rotted.
And she was already seventeen. Now there are rats and
weed in her green hair, rather becoming . . . a little swollen
and whitish, and filled with the stinking ooze from the
river, completely black. She was always so clean. That's
why she went into the river and began to stink.

WATZMANN: What is flesh? It decays just like the spirit.
Gentlemen, I am completely drunk. Twice two is four.
Therefore I am not drunk. But I have intimations of a
higher world. Bow! . . . be hup! . . . humble! Put the old
Adam aside! *Drinks heavily and shakily.* I've not reached
rock bottom yet, not while I have my intimations, not
while I can add up properly that twice two . . . What is this
thing called two? Two – oo, curious word! Two! *Sits down.*
Baal reaches for his guitar and smashes the light with it.

BAAL: Now I'll sing. *Sings:*

Sick from the sun, and eaten raw by the weather
A looted wreath crowning his tangled head
He called back the dreams of a childhood he had lost al-
together
Forgot the roof, but never the sky overhead.

Then speaks: My voice is not entirely clear as a bell. *Tunes*
the guitar.

EKART: Go on singing, Baal.

BAAL *goes on singing:*

O you whose life it has been always to suffer
You murderers they threw out from heaven and hell
Why did you not stay in the arms of your mother
Where it was quiet, and you slept, and all was well?

Speaks. The guitar's not in tune either.

WATZMANN: A good song. Very apt in my case. Romantic.

BAAL *goes on singing:*

Still he explores and scans the absinthe-green ocean
Though his mother give him up for lost
Grinning and cursing, or weeping at times with contrition
Always in search of that land where life is best.

WATZMANN: I can't find my glass. The table's rocking stupidly. Put the light on. How's a man to find his mouth?

EKART: Idiot! Can you see anything, Baal?

BAAL: No. I don't want to. It's good in the dark. With champagne in the blood and homesickness without memory. Are you my friend Ekart?

EKART *with an effort:* Yes, but sing!

BAAL *sings:*

Loafing through hells and flogged through paradises
Calm and grinning, with expressionless stare
Sometimes he dreams of a small field he recognizes
With blue sky overhead and nothing more.

JOHANNES: I'll always stay with you. You could take me with you. I hardly ever eat.

WATZMANN *has lit the lamp, with an effort:* Let there be light. Heh heh heh heh.

BAAL: It's blinding. *Gets up.*
Ekart, with the waitress on his lap, gets up with an effort and tries to take her arm from his neck.

EKART: What's the matter? This is nothing. It's ridiculous.
Baal gets ready to leap.

EKART: You're not jealous of her?

Baal gropes, a glass falls to the floor.

EKART: Why shouldn't I have women?

Baal looks at him.

EKART: Am I your lover?

Baal throws himself at him, chokes him.

The light goes out. Watzmann laughs drunkenly, the waitress screams. Other guests from the adjoining room enter with a lamp.

WATZMANN: He's got a knife.

THE WAITRESS: He's killing him. Oh God!

TWO MEN *hurl themselves on the wrestlers:* Blast you, man! Let go! – He's stabbed him! God Almighty!

Baal gets up. Sunset suddenly bursts into the room. The lamp goes out.

BAAL: Ekart!

10° E. of Greenwich

Forest. Baal with guitar, his hands in his pockets, walks off into the distance.

BAAL: The pale wind in the black trees! They're like Lupu's wet hair. At eleven the moon'll rise. It'll be light enough then. This is a small wood. I'll go where there are forests. I can move now that I'm on my own again. I must bear north. Follow the ribbed side of the leaves. I'll have to shrug off that little matter. Forward! *Sings:*

Baal will watch the vultures in the star-shot sky
Hovering patiently to see when Baal will die.

Disappearing.

Sometimes Baal shams dead. The vultures swoop.
Baal, without a word, will dine on vulture soup.

Gust of wind.

A Country Road

Evening. Wind. Rain. Two policemen struggle against the wind.

FIRST POLICEMAN: The black rain and this wailing wind! The bloody tramp!

SECOND POLICEMAN: It seems to me he keeps moving northwards towards the forests. It'll be impossible to find him there.

FIRST POLICEMAN: What is he?

SECOND POLICEMAN: Above all, a murderer. Before that, revue actor and poet. Then roundabout proprietor, woodsman, lover of a millionairess, convict and pimp. When he did the murder they caught him, but he's got the strength of an elephant. It was because of a waitress, a registered whore. He knifed his best and oldest friend because of her.

FIRST POLICEMAN: A man like that has no soul. He belongs to the beasts.

SECOND POLICEMAN: And he's childish too. He carries wood for old women, and nearly gets caught. He never had anything. Except for the waitress. That must have been why he killed his friend, another dubious character.

FIRST POLICEMAN: If only we could get some gin somewhere or a woman! Let's go! It's eerie. And there's something moving over there. *Both go.*

BAAL *comes out of the undergrowth with rucksack and guitar. He whistles through his teeth:* So he's dead? Poor little animal! Getting in my way. Now things are getting interesting. *He follows the men.*

Wind.

Hut in the Forest

Night. Wind. Baal on a dirty bed. Men at cards and drink.

A MAN *by Baal:* What do you want? You're at your last gasp.
A child could see that. And who's going to look after you?
Have you got anyone? That's it! That's it! Grit your teeth!
Got any teeth left? Now and then it even gets the ones that
could go on enjoying themselves, millionaires! But you
don't even have any papers. Don't you be afraid, the
world'll keep rolling, round as a ball, tomorrow morning
the wind'll whistle. See the situation in a more reasonable
light. Tell yourself it's a rat that's on the way out. That's it!
Don't move! You've no teeth left.

THE MEN: Is it still pissing? We'll have to spend the night
with the corpse. – Shut your mouth! Trumped! – Got any
breath left, fatty? Sing us a song! 'Baal grew up within
the . . .' – Let him be! He'll be a cold man before the black
rain's stopped. On with the game! – He drank like a sieve
but there's something about that pale hunk that makes you
think about yourself. That's something he didn't have
crooned over his cradle. – Ten of clubs! Keep your cards
up, please! That's no way to play; if you're not going to be
serious, you can't get a good game going.

Silence, except for a few curses.

BAAL: What's the time?

ONE OF THE MEN: Eleven. Are you going?

BAAL: Soon. Are the roads bad?

THE MAN: Rain.

THE MEN *getting up:* It's stopped raining. Time to go. –
Everything'll be soaking wet. – Another excuse for him to
do nothing.

They pick up the axes.

A MAN *stops in front of Baal and spits:* Good night and good-
bye. Have you had it?

ANOTHER MAN: Are you on the way out? Incognito?

A THIRD MAN: Arrange your smelly periods better tomorrow, if you don't mind. We'll be working till twelve and then we want to eat.

BAAL: Can't you stay a little longer?

ALL *amid loud laughter*: Do you want us to play mother? – Do you want to sing us your swan song? – Do you want to confess, you old soak? – Can't you throw up on your own?

BAAL: If you could stay half an hour.

ALL *amid loud laughter*: You know what? Snuff out on your own! – Let's get moving! The wind's died down. – What's the matter?

THE MAN: I'll follow.

BAAL: It can't last much longer, gentlemen. *Laughter*. You won't like dying on your own, gentlemen! *Laughter*.

ANOTHER MAN: Old woman! Here's a souvenir! *Spits in his face.*
  They go.

BAAL: Twenty minutes.
  The men leave by the open door.

THE MAN *in the door:* Stars.

BAAL: Wipe the spit away!

THE MAN *to him:* Where?

BAAL: On my forehead.

THE MAN: Done! What are you laughing at?

BAAL: I like the taste.

THE MAN *indignant:* You're done for. Good-bye! *With his axe to the door.*

BAAL: Thanks.

THE MAN: Is there anything else . . . but I have to go to work. Jesus. Corpses!

BAAL: You! Come closer! *The man bends down.* It was very beautiful . . .

THE MAN: What was, you crazy hen? I nearly said capon.

BAAL: Everything.

THE MAN: Snob! *Laughs loudly, goes, the door remains open, one sees the blue night.*

BAAL *uneasy:* You! You there!

THE MAN *at the window :* Mmmm?

BAAL: Are you going?

THE MAN: To work.

BAAL: Where?

THE MAN: What's that got to do with you?

BAAL: What's the time?

THE MAN: A quarter past eleven. *Goes.*

BAAL: He's gone.

Silence.

Mother! Tell Ekart to go away, the sky's so damned near too, you can touch it, everything's soaking wet again. Sleep. One. Two. Three. Four. It's suffocating in here. It must be light outside. I want to go out. *Raises himself.* I will go out. Dear Baal. *Sharply.* I'm not a rat. It must be light outside. Dear Baal. You can get to the door. You've still got knees, it's better in the door. Damn it! Dear Baal! *He crawls on all fours to the threshold.* Stars ... mmm. *He crawls out.*

Early Morning in the Forest

Woodcutters.

A WOODCUTTER: Give me the bottle! Listen to the birds!

ANOTHER: It'll be a hot day.

A THIRD: There's plenty of trees left standing that'll have to be down before nightfall.

A FOURTH: He'll be cold by now.

THE THIRD: Yes. Yes. He'll be cold by now.

THE SECOND: Yes. Yes.

THE THIRD: We could have had the eggs now if he hadn't eaten them all. There's a man for you, stealing eggs on his deathbed. First he kept moaning at me, I got sick of that. He never got a whiff of the bottle in all three days, thank God. It's inconsiderate. Eggs in a corpse.

THE FIRST: He had a way of laying himself down in the dirt,

and then he never got up again, and he knew it. It was like a ready-made bed to him. He lay down carefully. Did anybody know him? What's his name? What did he do?

THE FOURTH: We'll have to bury him, anyway. Give me the bottle!

THE THIRD: I asked him, as the death-rattle was in his throat, what are you thinking about? I always want to know what goes on in a man's head then. I'm still listening to the rain, he said. I went cold all over. I'm still listening to the rain, he said.

Drums in the Night
a play

Translator: JOHN WILLETT

Characters

Andreas Kragler · Anna Balicke · Karl Balicke, her father · Amalie Balicke, her mother · Friedrich Murk, her fiancé · Babusch, journalist · Two men · Manke, waiter at the Piccadilly Bar · His brother, waiter at Glubb's bar · Glubb, schnaps distiller · A drunk man · Bulltrotter, a newspaper seller · A worker · Laar, a peasant · Augusta, Marie – prostitutes · A maid · A woman selling newspapers

The Manke brothers are played by the same actor.

[Annotations refer to passages from the 1922 version, printed in the Notes, p. 409 ff.]

ACT ONE (AFRICA) — *KRAGLERS IN AFRICA*

At the Balickes'

Dark room with muslin curtains. Evening.

BALICKE *shaving at the window :* It's now four years since they posted him missing. He'll never come back now. Times are damned uncertain. <u>Any man's worth his weight in gold.</u> I'd have given my blessing two years ago. Your bloody sentimentality stopped me. Nothing'll stop me now.

FRAU BALICKE *by the <u>framed photograph of Kragler as a gunner</u> :* He was such a good man. A man just like a child.

EVER PRESENT

BALICKE: He's dead and buried by now.

FRAU BALICKE: Suppose he comes back.

BALICKE: People don't come back from heaven.

FRAU BALICKE: Anna would drown herself, as heaven's my witness!

BALICKE: If that's what she says she's an ass, and I've never seen an ass drown itself.

ANNA PREGNANT

FRAU BALICKE: <u>As it is she can't keep anything down.</u>

BALICKE: <u>She shouldn't keep stuffing with blackberries and Bismarck herring.</u> Murk's a fine chap, and we ought to go down on our knees and thank God for him.

FRAU BALICKE: He's making money all right. But compared with *him* . . . It makes me want to cry.

BALICKE: Compared with that corpse? I tell you straight: it's now or never. Is she waiting for the Pope? <u>Has it got to be a nigger?</u> I'm fed up with the whole silly story.

KRAGLER

FRAU BALICKE: And suppose he *does* come – the corpse you say is dead and buried – back from heaven or hell? 'The name is Kragler' – who's going to tell him that he's a corpse and his girl is lying in someone else's bed?

BALICKE: I'll tell him. And now *you* tell that creature that I'm fed up and we've ordered the wedding march and it's to be Murk. If *I* tell her she'll flood us out. So kindly put the light on, will you?

FRAU BALICKE: I'll get the sticking plaster. You always cut yourself when there's no light.

BALICKE: Cuts cost nothing, but light . . . *Calls:* Anna!

ANNA *in the doorway:* What is it, Father?

BALICKE: Kindly listen to what your mother's got to say to you and no blubbering on your big day!

FRAU BALICKE: Come over here, Anna. Father thinks you're so pale you can't be sleeping at all.

ANNA: I am sleeping.

FRAU BALICKE: It can't go on like this for ever, don't you see? He'll definitely not come back now. *Lights candles.*

BALICKE: She's making those crocodile eyes again.

FRAU BALICKE: It hasn't been easy for you, and he was such a good man, but he's dead now.

BALICKE: Dead, buried and decayed.

FRAU BALICKE: Karl! And here's Murk, a good hard worker who's sure to get on.

BALICKE: So there you are.

FRAU BALICKE: And you're to say yes, for God's sake.

BALICKE: Without making a song and dance about it.

FRAU BALICKE: You're to accept him, for God's sake.

BALICKE *furiously occupied with his sticking plaster:* Hell and damnation, do you imagine fellows are going to stand being kicked around like footballs? Yes or no! It's rubbish rolling your eyes up to heaven like that.

ANNA: Yes, Father.

BALICKE *huffily:* Blub away, then, the floodgates are open. I'm just off to get my life-jacket.

FRAU BALICKE: Aren't you in love with Murk at all, then?

BALICKE: Well, I call that simply immoral!

FRAU BALICKE: Karl! Well, what about you and Friedrich, Anna?

ANNA: Of course. But of course you know, and I feel so horribly sick.

BALICKE: I know nothing at all! I tell you, the fellow's dead, buried and rotten; all his bones have come apart. Four years! And not a sign of life! And his whole battery blown up! in the air! to smithereens! missing! Not so difficult to say where he has got to, eh? You're too damned scared of ghosts, that's what it is. Get yourself a man, and you won't have to be scared of ghosts any more, *Going up to Anna, expansively.* Are you a brave little woman, or aren't you? Get on with it, then.

Bell rings.

ANNA *frightened:* That's him!

BALICKE: Catch him before he comes in, and put him wise.

FRAU BALICKE *in the door, with the dirty clothes basket:* Haven't you got anything for the laundry?

ANNA: Yes. No. No, I don't think I've got anything . .

FRAU BALICKE: But today's the eighth.

ANNA: The eighth?

FRAU BALICKE: The eighth, of course.

ANNA: And what if it was the eighteenth?

BALICKE: What's all that chatter in the doorway? Come inside.

FRAU BALICKE: Well, you'd better see you have got something for the laundry. *Exit.*

BALICKE *sits down, takes Anna on his knee:* Now look, a woman without a husband, that's a blasphemous business. You've been missing that fellow they sent to a better world, right. But would you know him now? Not a bit of it, my dear. Death has turned him into something fit for a freak show. Three years he's been improving his looks; if he weren't dead as mutton he'd look very different from what you think. Anyway, he's dead and buried and not very pretty. He's got no nose now. But you miss him. So get yourself another man. It's nature, you see. You'll wake up like a dog with two tails. You've got stout limbs and strong appetites, haven't you? That's really not blasphemous, that isn't.

ANNA: But I *can't* forget him. Never. You keep on talking at me, but I *can't*.

BALICKE: You take Murk, he'll help you get over him.

ANNA: <u>I do love him</u> all the same, and <u>one day I'll love him only</u>, but not yet.

BALICKE: He'll bring you round, girl; all he needs is certain prerogatives, the kind of thing that comes best with marriage. I can't explain now, I'll tell you when you're older. *Tickles her*. Well: is that settled?

[margin note: SHUTS OUT THINGS HE DOESN'T WANT TO SEE]

ANNA *laughs salaciously:* I really don't know if Friedrich wants to.

BALICKE: Mrs, stick your head in.

FRAU BALICKE: Come into the lounge, won't you, Herr Murk, it's an honour.

BALICKE: Evening, Murk. Looking like something out of the morgue, eh?

MURK: Miss Anna!

BALICKE: What's the matter? Bottom fallen out of the market? <u>You're white as a sheet</u>, man. Is it the sound of shooting in the evening air? *Silence*. Come on, Anna, jolly him up.

Exit expansively with his wife.

ANNA: What is it, Friedrich? You really are pale.

MURK *nosing around:* I suppose the red wine's for our engagement? *Silence*. Someone been here? *Going up to Anna*. Anybody been here? Why have you gone so white now? Who's been here?

ANNA: Nobody! No one's been here. What's wrong with you?

MURK: What's the hurry about, then? Don't kid me. Oh, who cares? But I'm not celebrating my engagement in this dump.

ANNA: Who said anything about engagement?

MURK: The old girl. The eye of the Lord maketh the cattle fat. *Walking round restlessly*. Oh well, what about it?

ANNA: You keep acting as if it mattered to my parents. God knows it doesn't matter to my parents. Not the least little bit.

MURK: And when did you leave Sunday school?

ANNA: I just mean you're taking a good deal for granted.

MURK: Really? The other fellow?

ANNA: I wasn't saying anything about the other fellow.

MURK: But there he is, and there he hangs, and there he walks.

ANNA: That was something absolutely different. That was something you'll never understand, because it was spiritual.

MURK: And between you and me, that's carnal?

ANNA: Between you and me, that's nothing.

MURK: What about now? It's something now all right.

ANNA: You don't know anything about it.

MURK: Ha, it'll be a different tune before long.

ANNA: Think what you like.

MURK: I'm asking for your hand.

ANNA: Is that your way of saying you love me?

MURK: That'll come presently.

ANNA: After all, it's a box factory.

MURK: You little tart, you! Didn't they hear anything last night either?

ANNA: Oh, Friedrich! They sleep like dormice! *Snuggles up to him.*

MURK: Not like us.

ANNA: Gangster!

MURK *pulls her to him but kisses her coolly:* Tart!

ANNA: Quiet a moment. That's a train passing in the night. Hear it? Sometimes I'm frightened he's going to turn up. I get shivers all down my back.

MURK: That Egyptian mummy? Leave him to me. Here, let me tell you something: he's got to get out. No stiffs in bed between you and me. I'm not standing for another man in my bed.

ANNA: Don't get annoyed. Will you forgive me, Friedrich?

MURK: Saint Andrew Kragler? Imagination! He'll last as long after our wedding as after his own funeral. Bet on it? *Laughs.* I bet – a baby.

ANNA *hiding her face against him:* Oh, don't say such things, Friedrich.

MURK *stoutly:* Trust me! *To the door.* Come in, Mother. Evening, Father.

FRAU BALICKE *immediately behind the door:* Oh, children! *Bursts into tears.* What a wonderful surprise! — FALSE

BALICKE: Difficult birth, what? *Mutual embraces and emotion.*

MURK: Triplets! When shall we have the wedding? Time's money. UNAWARE OF PREGNANCY

BALICKE: Three weeks would suit me. The twin beds are in good shape. Supper, Mother!

FRAU BALICKE: In a moment, in a moment, just let me get my breath. *Hurrying out.* What a wonderful surprise!

MURK: May I have the pleasure of inviting you to split a bottle with me at the Piccadilly Bar tonight? I'm for celebrating our engagement right away, aren't you, Anna?

ANNA: If we must. RELUCTANT

BALICKE: Here, though. Why the Piccadilly Bar? Are you in your right mind?

MURK *uneasily:* Not here. Definitely not here. — SCARED OF KRAGLER RETURNING

BALICKE: Well, what next?

ANNA: He's funny. So come along to the Piccadilly Bar, then.

BALICKE: Tonight of all nights! At the risk of one's life!

FRAU BALICKE *enters with the maid, bringing supper:* Here you are, children. Everything comes to him who waits. Take your places, gentlemen. ORDERS WIFE
They stuff.

BALICKE *raises his glass:* To the happy pair! *Clinking glasses.* Times are uncertain. The war's over. This pork is too fatty, Amalie. Now the demobilization's washing greed, disorder and swinish inhumanity into the still backwaters of peaceful labour. — IRONIC BEER MAKING BACILLI WEAPONS SENDING SOLDIERS HOME

MURK: Where we turn out ammunition boxes, cheers! Cheers, Anna!

BALICKE: Doubtful characters appearing on the scene, shady gentlemen. The government's being far too soft with

those scavengers of the revolution. *Opens a newspaper.* The masses are all worked up and without any ideals. And worst of all – I can say it here – the troops back from the front, shabby, half-savage adventurers who've lost the habit of working and hold nothing sacred. Truly a difficult time, Anna, a man's worth his weight in gold. Hold on to him. It'll be up to you two to win through, but always as a couple, mind you, always winning through, cheers!
He winds up a gramophone.

MURK *wiping away perspiration:* Bravo! You've got to be a man to come through. You want a pair of elbows and nails in your boots, and the right looks and no backward glances. What's to stop us, Anna? I'm from the bottom myself. Errand boy, shop floor, a turn of the hand here and there, picked up a thing or two. The whole of Germany's worked its way up like that. Not with kid gloves on always, but hard work the whole time, God knows! Now on top! Cheers, Anna! *The gramophone plays 'Ich bete an die Macht der Liebe'.*

BALICKE: Bravo! Well, what's wrong, Anna?

ANNA *has got up, stands half turned away:* I don't know. It's all happening so quickly. Perhaps that isn't a good thing, eh, Mother?

FRAU BALICKE: What's the matter, child? So silly! Go on, enjoy yourself. Not a good thing, indeed!

BALICKE: Sit! Or wind the gramophone, as you're up.
Anna sits down.
Pause.

MURK: So cheers, then! *Clinks glasses with Anna.* What's wrong?

BALICKE: Then about the business, Fritz, ammunition boxes, that'll soon be a dead duck. A few more weeks of civil war, that's the best you can hope for, then finish. I know the ideal answer, I'm not joking: children's prams. The factory's tip-top all along the line. *He takes Murk's arm and draws him upstage. Pulls back the curtains.* New buildings Three and Four. All modern and permanent. Anna, wind up the gramophone. I always find that moving. *The gramophone plays 'Deutschland, Deutschland über alles'.*

MURK: Hey, there's a man in the factory yard. What's going on?

ANNA: Oh, how creepy! I think he's looking up here.

BALICKE: Probably the night-watchman. Why are you laughing, Fritz! Cough it up. The ladies look quite pale.

MURK: A funny idea came into my head: the Spartacists, don't you know . . .

BALICKE: Rubbish. None of that round here. *Turns away all the same, disagreeably disturbed.* So that's the factory. *Approaches the table. Anna draws the curtain.* The war put me in the proverbial clover. The stuff was lying around for anybody to pick up, why not, it would have been too stupid. Someone else would have had it. Can't make omelettes without breaking eggs. Looked at the right way the war was a godsend to us. We've got our pile, round, fat, and snug. We can sit back and make prams. No special hurry. Am I right?

MURK: Absolutely, Dad. Cheers!

BALICKE: The same way you can sit back and make children. Hahahaha.

MAID: Herr Babusch, Herr Balicke.

BABUSCH *trots in:* Hey, hey, you folks are well dug in against the red terror. Spartacus has mobilized. Negotiations been broken off. Artillery fire over Berlin in another twenty-four hours.

BALICKE *has his napkin round his neck:* To hell with it, can't those fellows be satisfied?

FRAU BALICKE: Artillery? O godogodogodogod! What a night! What a night! Balicke, I'm going to the cellar.

BABUSCH: It's all quiet so far in the central districts.[1] But the story is that they want to seize the newspaper offices.

BALICKE: What! We're celebrating an engagement! And this is the day we choose! Quite mad!

MURK: They should execute the lot.

BALICKE: A firing squad for all grumblers.

BABUSCH: Is it *your* engagement, Balicke?

MURK: Babusch: my fiancée.

FRAU BALICKE: A wonderful surprise. But when'll the shooting start?

BABUSCH *shakes Anna's and Murk's hands:* Spartacus have been hoarding weapons for all they're worth. Lowdown secretive lot. Anna, Anna! Don't let them put you off. Nothing'll touch you here. Here's a peaceful retreat. The family. The German family. My home is my castle.

FRAU BALICKE: What times these are! What times these are! And on your big day! Anna!

BABUSCH: It's damned interesting all the same, folks.

BALICKE: Not to me it isn't. Not one little bit. *Wipes his mouth with the napkin.*

MURK: You know what? Come to the Piccadilly Bar with us. We're celebrating.

BABUSCH: And Spartacus?

BALICKE: Can wait, Babusch. Shoot some other fellow in the guts, Babusch. Come to the Piccadilly Bar with us. Get your fineries on, girls!

FRAU BALICKE: Piccadilly Bar? Tonight? *Sits on a chair.*

BALICKE: Piccadilly Bar it used to be called. It's the Café Vaterland now. Friedrich's taking us out. What's wrong with tonight? What are cabs for? Gee up; get your togs on, old girl!

FRAU BALICKE: I'm not moving a foot outside these four walls. What's got into you, Fritzi?

ANNA: It's a free country. Friedrich seems to want it. *All look at Murk.*

MURK: Not here. Definitely not here. Me, I want music, lights. It's a classy place. Here it's all dark. I put my decent outfit on on purpose. So how about it, Mother?

FRAU BALICKE: It's all beyond me. *Leaves the room.*

ANNA: Wait for me, Friedrich, I'll be ready in a minute.

BABUSCH: Lots happening, boys. The whole bag of tricks is going up. Babes in arms, get yourselves organized! By the way, apricots, soft as butter, flesh-coloured, juicy, are five marks the pound. Loafers, don't let them provoke you! Everywhere shady gangs are sticking their fingers in their mouths and whistling into the brightly lit cafés. Their emblem, the idle loaf. And the dance-halls full of the so-called upper crust. Well, here's to your wedding-day!

MURK: The ladies aren't changing. We're all equal now. Too much dazzle only makes you conspicuous.

BALICKE: Hear hear. Critical time like this. Any old outfit's good enough for this shower. Come down at once, Anna.

MURK: We're going straight on. Don't change.

ANNA: Roughneck! *Exit.*

BALICKE: Gee up . . . Sound the trumpets, next stop paradise. I must change my shirt.

MURK: You'll follow on with Mother, eh? And Babusch can come with us, and be our chaperone, eh? *Sings.* Babusch, Babusch, Babusch, trotting to and fro.

BABUSCH: That miserable third-rate, crazy schoolboy doggerel, can't you forget it? *Exit, taking his arm.*

MURK *still singing off:* Pull your finger out, my lads, and make the party go. Anna!

BALICKE *alone, lights a cigar:* Thank God for that. All snug as a bug. What a damn grind! You have to drive her to bed. Calf love for that corpse! My clean shirt's soaked with sweat. Now I can take them all on. Pram's the word. *Exit.* Mrs, a shirt!

ANNA *off:* Friedrich! Friedrich! *Enter quickly.* Friedrich!

MURK *in the doorway:* Anna! *Dry, uneasy, with hanging arms like an orang-outang.* Do you want to come along?

ANNA: What's the matter? What are you looking like that for?

MURK: Do you want to come? I know what I'm asking. Don't play-act. Straight answer!

ANNA: I should think I do. Odd, isn't it?

MURK: Fine, then. I'm not so sure. Twenty years I lodged in attics, frozen to the marrow; now I wear buttoned boots, look for yourself! I sweated in the darkness, by gaslight, it ran into my eyes; now I go to a tailor. But I'm still unsteady, the wind blows down there, there's an icy draught down there, one's feet get chilled down there. *Goes up to Anna without touching her, stands swaying in front of her.* At last the superfluous flesh is increasing. At last the red wine is flowing. At last I've got there! Bathed in sweat, eyes shut, fists clenched till the fingernails cut into the flesh. It's over! Security! Warmth! Off with the overalls! A bed, white, broad, soft! *As he passes the window he glances fleetingly out.* Come to me: I'll unclench my fists, I'll sit in the sun in my shirtsleeves, I've got you.

ANNA *flies to him:* Darling!

MURK: Sex kitten!

ANNA: At last you've got me.

MURK: Isn't she there yet?

BABUSCH *off:* Come on, come on! I'm the bridesmaid, folks.

MURK *winds the gramophone once more. It again starts 'Ich bete an die Macht der Liebe':* I'm the best possible fellow if only they'll give me my head. *Exeunt both, in close contact with each other.*

COMMUNISTS

FRAU BALICKE *swishes in, in black, arranges her bonnet in front of the glass:* Such a huge moon and so red . . . And the children, dear God! Yes, yes . . . we've much to be thankful for in our prayers tonight.

At this point a man with a muddy dark blue artillery uniform and a stumpy pipe appears in the door.

THE MAN: The name is Kragler.

FRAU BALICKE *supports herself, with trembling knees, against the table the mirror is on:* Good heav . . .

KRAGLER: Well, no need to look so supernatural. Did *you* chuck away good money on a wreath too? Pity. Beg to report: set up shop as a ghost in Algiers. But now the corpse is most horribly hungry. I could eat worms. What's the matter, Ma Balicke? Idiotic song! *Stops the gramophone. Frau Balicke continues to say nothing and simply stares at him.*

KRAGLER: Don't faint all at once. Here's a chair. There ought to be a glass of water about. *Goes humming to the cupboard.* Still know my way around pretty well. *Pours wine.*

Wine! Nierensteiner! Plenty of life in the old ghost, eh?
Sees to Frau Balicke.

BALICKE *off:* Come along, old girl! On the move! How
beautiful you are, my angel! *Comes in, stands taken aback.*
Well?

KRAGLER: Evening, Herr Balicke. Your wife's not feeling
well. *Tries to make her drink some wine, but she turns away in
horror.*

Balicke looks on uncomfortably for a moment.

KRAGLER: Won't you have some? You won't? It'll pass in a
moment. No idea I was so fresh in the memory. Just back
from Africa, you see. Spain, fiddle with passports, and all
the rest of it. But where's Anna?

BALICKE: Leave my wife alone, for God's sake. You're
drowning her.

KRAGLER: As you say.

FRAU BALICKE *takes refuge with Balicke, who stands upright:*
Karl!

BALICKE *severely:* Herr Kragler, if you are the person you
claim to be, would you mind telling me what you are doing
here?

KRAGLER *shocked:* You realize I was a prisoner of war in
Africa?

BALICKE: Hell! *Goes to a small cupboard, drinks a schnaps.*
That's fine. You would be. A damned disgusting business!
What d'you want? My daughter announced her engage-
ment less than half an hour ago.

KRAGLER *staggers, a bit unsure:* What do you mean?

BALICKE: You've been away four years. She's waited four
years. We've waited four years. Now time's up and you've
had your chance.

Kragler sits down.

BALICKE *not quite firmly, unsure but making an effort to preserve
his dignity:* Herr Kragler, I have commitments this evening.

KRAGLER *looking up:* Commitments . . .? *Distractedly.* Yes . . .
Slumps back.

FRAU BALICKE: Don't take it too hard, Herr Kragler. There

are lots of other girls. That's the way it is. You must grin and bear it.

KRAGLER: Anna!

BALICKE *curtly:* Mrs! *She goes hesitantly to him, he suddenly firm:* Bah! Sentimental stuff, let's go. *Exit with his wife. The maid appears in the door.*

KRAGLER: Hm! . . . *Shakes his head.*

MAID: Herr and Frau Balicke have gone out.
Silence.
Herr and Frau Balicke have gone to the Piccadilly Bar for the engagement party.
Silence. Wind. — SYMBOLIC

KRAGLER *looking up at her:* Hm! *He gets up slowly and laboriously, looks round the room. Walks around silently, with bent head, looks through the window, turns round, slowly takes himself off, whistling, without his cap.*

MAID: Here! Your cap! You've left your cap behind!

ACT TWO (PEPPER)

Piccadilly Bar

Big window at the back. Music. In the window a <u>red moon</u>. When the door opens, <u>wind</u>.

BABUSCH: This way to the <u>menagerie</u>, folks! There's plenty of moonlight. Up Spartacus! Bullshit! Red wine!

MURK *enters with Anna on his arm, they take off their things:* <u>A night like in a story-book.</u> Shouting round the newspaper offices. The coach bearing the happy couple.

ANNA: It's no good, I feel horrible today. I can't control my arms and legs.

BABUSCH: Cheers to that, Friedrich!

MURK: This is where I'm at home. Damned uncomfortable in the long run but absolutely slap-up. Look after the older generation, will you, Babusch?

BABUSCH: Right. *Drinks.* You look after the next. *Goes out.*

ANNA: Kiss me.

MURK: Nonsense. Half Berlin's looking.

ANNA: Doesn't matter. Nothing matters when I want something. Don't you find that?

MURK: Not for a minute. Nor do you.

ANNA: You're common.

MURK: That's right.

ANNA: Coward! *Murk rings, enter a waiter.*

MURK: Atten . . . shun! *He leans across the table, knocking glasses over, and forcibly kisses Anna.*

ANNA: You!

MURK: Dis . . . miss! *Exit waiter.* Am I a coward? *Looks under the table.* And you needn't push your feet at me now.

ANNA: What's got into you?

MURK: Honour and obey, that's it.

BALICKE *enters with Babusch and Frau Balicke:* There they are.
Service!

ANNA: Where've you been?

FRAU BALICKE: There's such a red moon tonight. I'm quite
upset because it's so red. And more shouting round the
newspaper offices.

BABUSCH: Pack of wolves.

FRAU BALICKE: See that you two get together.

BALICKE: In bed, Friedrich, eh?

ANNA: Mother, are you all right?

FRAU BALICKE: When do you think of getting married?

MURK: In three weeks, Mamma.

FRAU BALICKE: Shouldn't we have asked more people to
come and celebrate? This way nobody knows. But they
ought to know.

BALICKE: Rubbish, I say, rubbish. Because the wolves are
howling? Let them howl. Till their tongue hangs red
between their knees. I'll shoot them down, no question.

BABUSCH: Murk, help me get the cork out. *Quietly to him:*
He's there. Arrived with the moon. The wolf with the
moon. From Africa.

MURK: Andy Kragler?

BABUSCH: The wolf. Not funny, is it?

MURK: He's in his grave, that's all. Pull the curtains.

FRAU BALICKE: Every other doorway your father found a
boozer to tumble into. He's got a monkey on his back all
right. There's a man for you! What a man! He'll drink
himself to death for his children, that man will.

ANNA: Yes, but what makes him do it?

FRAU BALICKE: Don't ask, child. Don't ask me. Everything's upside down. The world's coming to an end. I must
have a kirsch at once, child.

BALICKE: That's only the red moon, Mother. Draw the curtains! *Waiter does so.*

BABUSCH: You had a hunch?

MURK: I'm ready down to the last button. Has he been to
their place?

BABUSCH: Yes, just now.

MURK: Then he'll come here.

BALICKE: What are you two cooking behind the bottles? Park yourselves here! Engagement party! *All sit around the table.* Get cracking! I haven't time to feel tired.

ANNA: Ha, the horse! Wasn't that funny? The middle of the road, and he just stopped. Friedrich, get out, the horse has packed up. And then in the middle of the road the horse standing. And trembling. It had eyeballs like gooseberries, though, all white, and Friedrich prodded its eyes with a stick and made it hop. It was like a circus.

BALICKE: Time's money. It's damned hot here. I'm sweating again. I've sweated one shirt through today already.

FRAU BALICKE: You'll land us in the workhouse with the laundry bills, the way things are going.

BABUSCH *munching prunes from his pocket:* Apricots are ten marks a pound now. Well, well. I shall write an article about prices. Then I'll be able to buy apricots. Suppose the world does come to an end, I'll write about it. But what are the others to do? If the whole Zoo district blows up I'll be sitting pretty. But the people . . .!

MURK: Shirts, apricots, the Zoo. When's the wedding?

BALICKE: In three weeks. Wedding in three weeks' time. I have spoken. Heaven has heard it. We all agreed? All agreed about the wedding? Right, then ready, steady, go, the happy couple! *They clink glasses. The door has opened. Kragler stands in the doorway. The wind makes the candles flicker and dim.*

BALICKE: Now, now, why so shaky with the glass? Like your mother, Anna?

Anna, who is sitting opposite the door, has seen Kragler. She sits hunched up and looks fixedly at him.

FRAU BALICKE: Good heavens, what's made you fold up like that, child?

MURK: What's that wind?

KRAGLER *hoarsely:* Anna!

Anna gives a subdued scream. All now look round, leap to their feet. Tumult. Speaking at once:

BALICKE: Hell! *Pours wine down his gullet.* The ghost, Mother!

FRAU BALICKE: God! Kra . . .

MURK: Throw him out! Throw him out!

Kragler has remained swaying in the doorway for a moment; he looks sinister. During the short tumult he comes quite quickly but clumsily up to Anna, who is now sitting alone holding her glass shakily before her face, takes the glass away from her, props himself on the table, and stares at her.

BALICKE: He's drunk.

MURK: Waiter! This is a disturbance of the peace. Throw him out! *Runs along the wall, pulls back the curtain in the process. Moon.*

BABUSCH: Be careful. He's got raw flesh under his shirt still. It's stinging him. Don't touch him. *Bangs the table with his stick.* No scenes here, please. Leave quietly. Pull yourselves together and leave.

ANNA *has meanwhile left the table and throws her arms round her mother:* Mother! Help!

Kragler goes round the table unsteadily after Anna.

FRAU BALICKE *all more or less simultaneously:* Spare my child's life! You'll end up in gaol! Oh God, he's killing her!

BALICKE *at a considerable distance, swelling up:* Are you drunk? Pauper! Anarchist! Ex-serviceman! You pirate! You moon ghost! Where's your white sheet?

BABUSCH: If you have a stroke now he'll marry her. Shut up, all of you! He's the one who's been wronged. Clear out! He must be allowed to have his say. He has a right to. *To Frau Balicke:* Haven't you any feeling? Four years he's been away. It's a matter of feeling.

FRAU BALICKE: She can hardly stand on her legs, she's as white as chalk.

BABUSCH *to Murk:* Have a look at his face. She's seen it already. It used to be like milk and blood. Now it's a rotten lemon. No need for you to be frightened. *Exeunt.*

MURK: If you're thinking about jealousy I'm not that sort. Ha!

BALICKE *is still standing between the door and the table, somewhat drunk, with crooked legs and a glass in his hand. During what follows he says:* That wog on wheels! Face like a, a collapsed elephant. Utterly broken down. A piece of impertinence. *Clears off so that there's now nobody left but the waiter by the door right, a tray in his hands. Gounod's 'Ave Maria'. The light goes down.*

KRAGLER *after a moment:* It's as if everything in my head had been wiped away, I've nothing but sweat left there, I find it hard to understand things.

ANNA *picks up a candle, stands helplessly, lights up his face:* Didn't the fishes eat you?

KRAGLER: I don't know what you mean.

ANNA: Weren't you blown to pieces?

KRAGLER: I can't understand you.

ANNA: Didn't they shoot your face away?

KRAGLER: Why are you looking at me like that? Is that what I look like? *Silence. He looks towards the window.* I've a skin like a shark's: black. *Silence.* And I used to be like milk and blood. *Silence.* And then I keep on bleeding, it just streams out of me.

ANNA: Andy.

KRAGLER: Yes.

ANNA *going hesitantly towards him:* Oh, Andy, why were you away so long? Did they bar your way with guns and swords? And now I can no longer get through to you.

KRAGLER: Was I away?

ANNA: You were with me a long while at the beginning, your voice hadn't yet died away. When I walked down the passage I brushed against you and in the fields I heard you calling from behind the sycamore. Even though they wrote that your face had been shot away and two days later you'd been buried. But the time came when it changed. When I walked down the passage, it was deserted, and the sycamore had nothing to say. When I straightened myself over the washtub I could still see your face, but when I spread the things on the grass I lost sight of it and all that long while

I had no idea what you looked like. But I ought to have
waited.

KRAGLER: You could have done with a photo.

ANNA: I was frightened. I ought to have waited all the same,
but I am no good. Don't touch my hand, nothing about
me's any good.

KRAGLER *looks towards the window:* I don't know what you're
talking about. Perhaps it's just the red moon. I must try
and think what it means. I've got swollen hands, they've
got webs on them, I've no manners and I break glasses
when I drink. I can't talk properly to you any longer. My
throat's full of nigger language.

ANNA: Yes.

KRAGLER: Give me your hand. Do you think I'm a ghost?
Come here, give me your hand. Don't you want to come to
me?

ANNA: Do you want it?

KRAGLER: Give it me. I've stopped being a ghost now. Can
you see my face again? Is it like crocodile hide? I can't see
properly. I've been in salty water. It's just the red moon.

ANNA: Yes.

KRAGLER: You take my hand too. – Why don't you press it?
Give me your face. Is it bad?

ANNA: No, no.

KRAGLER *takes hold of her:* Anna! A wog on wheels, that's
me. Throat full of crap. Four years! Will you have me?
Anna! *Pulls her round and catches sight of the waiter, whom he
stares at with a grin while bending forward.*

WAITER *disconcerted, drops his tray, stammers:* The point is . . .
her lily . . . has she still got her lily?

KRAGLER *with his hands round Anna, gives a horse-laugh:* What
did he say? Lily? *The waiter hurries off.* Here, wait a moment,
you with the taste for cheap novels. That's something he
didn't mean to say. Lily! Something that's happened to
him. Lily! Did you hear it? He felt it as deeply as that.

ANNA: Andy!

KRAGLER *looks at her, stooping, having let go of her:* Say that again, that's your voice. *Hurries off right.* Waiter! Come here, man.

BABUSCH *in the doorway:* What a fleshly laugh you have. You laugh velly fleshly. How's it going?

FRAU BALICKE *behind him:* Anna, my child! What a worry you are to us! *Next door 'The Lady from Peru' has been playing for a while.*

BALICKE *sobered up somewhat, hurries in:* Sit down. *He draws the curtain, there is a metallic sound.* They've got the red moon with them and rifles behind them in Babusch's newspaper district. They're a serious proposition. *He relights all the candles.* Sit down.

FRAU BALICKE: What a look on your face! My legs are starting to shake again. Waiter! Waiter!

BALICKE: Where's Murk?

BABUSCH: Friedrich Murk's shuffling round the dance floor.

BALICKE *softly:* Just get him to sit down. Once he's sitting we can get him where we want him. Nobody can make a drama sitting down. *Aloud.* Sit down, everybody. Quiet! Pull yourself together, Amalie. *To Kragler:* You sit down too, for God's sake.

FRAU BALICKE *takes a bottle of kirsch from the waiter's tray:* I've got to have kirsch or I'll die. *She returns to the table with it.*
The following are seated: Frau Balicke, Balicke, Anna. Babusch has leapt around and got them to sit down. He now pushes Kragler, who was standing looking lost, into a chair.

BABUSCH: Sit down, your knees aren't too firm. Would you like some kirsch? Why do you laugh like that? *Kragler gets up again. Babusch pushes him down. He remains seated.*

BALICKE: Andreas Kragler, what do you want?

FRAU BALICKE: Herr Kragler! Our Kaiser said, 'You must grin and bear it.'

ANNA: Stay in your chair.

BALICKE: Shut up! Let him speak. What do you want?

BABUSCH *rises:* Would you like a nip of kirsch perhaps? Speak up!

ANNA: Think, Andy. Before you say anything.

FRAU BALICKE: You'll have me in my grave. Hold your tongue! You don't understand a thing.

KRAGLER *wants to get up, but is pushed back by Babusch. With extreme seriousness:* If you're asking me it's not at all simple. And I don't want to drink any kirsch. There's too much involved.

BALICKE: Get a move on. Say what you want. Then I'll chuck you out.

ANNA: No, no!

BABUSCH: You'd better have a drink, you know. You're so dried up. It'll make it easier, believe me. *At this point Friedrich Murk shuffles in left with a prostitute called Marie.*

FRAU BALICKE: Murk!

BABUSCH: Genius has its limits. Sit down.

BALICKE: Bravo, Fritz! Show the man what a man's made of! Fritz isn't scared. Fritz is having fun. *Claps.*

MURK *sinister, he has been drinking, leaves Marie standing where she is and comes to the table:* Haven't you settled this third-rate farce yet?

BALICKE *pulls him down on to a chair:* Shut up!

BABUSCH: Go on, Kragler. Ignore interruptions.

KRAGLER: He's got misshapen ears.

ANNA: He used to be the look-out boy.

MURK: He's got an egg in his noddle.

KRAGLER: He must leave the room!

MURK: Then they hit him on it.

KRAGLER: I must be very careful what I say.

MURK: So he's got egg-nog in his noddle.

KRAGLER: Yes, they hit me on the head. I've been away four years. I couldn't write letters. There was no egg in my brain. *Silence.* Four years have passed, I must be very careful. You (*Anna*) haven't recognized me, you're still on a see-saw and can't feel it yet. But I'm talking too much.

FRAU BALICKE: His brains have dried up. *Shaking her head.*

BALICKE: Had a bad time did you? Fought for Kaiser and Country? I feel sorry for you. Anything you want?

FRAU BALICKE: And the Kaiser said, 'Be strong in your sorrow.' Have some of this. *Pushes the kirsch towards him.*

BALICKE *drinking, weightily:* You stood under a hail of bullets? Firm as a rock? Splendid. Our army can be proud of itself. It marched to a hero's death with a song on its lips. Have a drink. What do you want?

ANNA: Andy! Didn't they give you another uniform? Still got the old blue one on? Those aren't worn any more.

FRAU BALICKE: There are lots of other girls! Waiter, more kirsch! *Passes him the kirsch.*

BALICKE: We did our bit too. So what do you want? Not a penny to your name? No place of your own? Fatherland can only offer you a barrel-organ? We can't have that. That kind of thing can't be allowed to happen any longer. What do you want?

ANNA: 'Stormy the night and the sea runs high,' ha!

KRAGLER *has risen. To Anna:* Since I feel I've no rights here I beg you, from the bottom of my heart, to go with me at my side.

BALICKE: What kind of talk is that? What's he saying? Bottom of my heart. At my side. What an extraordinary way of speaking.

The others laugh.

KRAGLER: Because no one's got a right . . . Because I can't live without you . . . From the bottom of my heart.

Much laughter.

MURK *puts his feet up on the table. Cold, nasty, drunk:* Sunk right to the ocean bed. Fished up. Mouth full of slime. Look at my boots. They used to be the same sort as yours. Buy yourself a pair like mine. Come again. Do you know what you are?

MARIE *suddenly:* Were you in the army?

WAITER: Were you in the army?

MURK: Shut your trap! *To Kragler:* The steamroller squashed you, did it? The steamroller squashed a lot of people. All right. It wasn't us set it rolling. Got no face left? Eh? Want a new one for nothing? Are the three of us supposed to fit you out again? Was it because of us you went under? Do you still not know what you are?

BABUSCH: Oh, do be quiet.

WAITER *coming forward:* Were you in the army?

MURK: Nope. I'm one of the people who have to settle the bill for your heroism. The roller's gone bust.

BABUSCH: Oh, don't make a drama of this. It's too squalid. After all, you made a packet, didn't you? So leave your boots out of it.

BALICKE: There you are, that's the long and the short of it. That's where the shoe pinches. It isn't a drama. It's political realism. Something we Germans are short of. It's very simple. Have you got the means to support a wife? Or have you got webbed fingers?

FRAU BALICKE: Hear that, Anna? He hasn't a penny.

MURK: If he has I'll marry his mother. *Jumps up.* He's just a perfectly ordinary fortune-hunter.

WAITER *to Kragler:* Say something! Answer something!

KRAGLER *has risen, trembling, to Anna:* I don't know what to say. When we were just skin and bone, and we kept having to drink schnaps to be able to work on the roads, we'd often only the evening sky, that's extremely important, because that's when I lay in the bushes with you in April. I used to say the same thing to the others. But they went down like flies.

ANNA: Like horses, no?

KRAGLER: Because of the heat, and we kept boozing away. But why am I going on telling you about the evening sky, that's not what I meant to do, I don't know . . .

ANNA: Were you always thinking of me?

FRAU BALICKE: Listen to his way of speaking! Like a child. Makes you blush for him, to hear it.

MURK: Won't you sell me your boots? For the war museum. I'll offer forty marks.

BABUSCH: Go on speaking, Kragler. It's just what's needed.

KRAGLER: Then we didn't have any shirts left. That was the

worst of all, I can tell you. Can you conceive that that might be the worst of all?

ANNA: Andy, they're listening to you.

MURK: Then I offer sixty marks. You ought to sell.

KRAGLER: Beginning to be ashamed of me, are you? Because they're standing round the ring like in a circus and the elephant's pissing with fear. Yet they know absolutely nothing.

MURK: Eighty marks.

KRAGLER: I'm not a pirate. The red moon's no affair of mine. It's just that I can't get my eyes open. I'm flesh and blood and I've got a clean shirt on. So I'm not a ghost.

MURK *leaps up:* A hundred marks, then.

MARIE: You should be ashamed to the depths of your soul.

MURK: The swine, he won't let me have his old boots for a hundred marks.

KRAGLER: Something's speaking, Anna. What's that voice?

MURK: You've got sunstroke. Do you need help to leave?

KRAGLER: Anna, it thinks it shouldn't be squashed.

MURK: Are we seeing your face at last?

KRAGLER: Anna, it's one of God's creatures.

MURK: Is that you? What do you really want? You're just a corpse. You're getting smelly. *Holds his nose.* Have you no idea of hygiene? D'you want a monument put up to you because you've had a touch of the African sun? I've worked. I've sweated till the blood ran into my boots. Look at my hands. You get all the sympathy, because you got yourself shot up, it wasn't me did the shooting. You're a hero and I'm a worker. And that's my girl.

BABUSCH: That still holds good if you sit down, Murk. You're still a worker sitting down. Kragler, the history of humanity would be different if only people sat on their bottoms more.

KRAGLER: I can't see into him. He's like a lavatory wall. Covered with obscene scribbles. Not the wall's fault. Anna, is that the man you love? Is it?

Anna laughs and drinks.

BABUSCH: You're cutting off your nose to spite your face, Kragler.

KRAGLER: I'm cutting out a tumour. Is it him you love? With a green face like an unripe nut? Am I to be sent away for his sake? He's got an English suit and a chest padded out with paper and boots full of blood. And I have only my old suit, which has the moth in it. Say you can't marry me because of my suit, say it. I'd rather!

BABUSCH: Oh, do sit down. To hell with it. Now we're off.

MARIE: That's him! And the embarrassing way he danced with me, how he pushed his knees into my stomach.

MURK: Put a cork in it. They only have to look at you. Haven't you got a knife on you that you can cut my throat with, because you got bubbles in the brain in Africa? Get out your knife, I'm fed up to here, slit it through.

FRAU BALICKE: How can you listen, Anna?

BALICKE: Waiter, bring me four glasses of kirsch. I couldn't care less.

MURK: Mind you don't draw that knife. Pull yourself together, we don't want you playing the hero here. Here it means gaol.

MARIE: Were you in the army?

MURK *furious, chucks a glass at her:* Why weren't you?

KRAGLER: At last I've come.

MURK: Who asked you?

KRAGLER: At last I've got there.

MURK: Swine!

ANNA: Don't answer.

Kragler lets it pass.

MURK: Bandit!

KRAGLER *silently:* Thief!

MURK: Ghost!

KRAGLER: Look out.

MURK: You look out for that knife of yours. Feel it twitching? Ghost! Ghost! Ghost!

MARIE: You swine! You swine!

KRAGLER: Anna! Anna! What am I doing? Staggering over

the ocean full of corpses: it won't drown *me*. Rolling south in darkened cattle-trucks: nothing can happen to *me*. Burning in the fiery furnace: I myself burn hotter. Someone goes mad in the sun: not me, thank you. Two men fall down a water-hole: I sleep on. I shoot niggers. I eat grass. I'm a ghost. *At this point the waiter rushes to the window and pulls the curtain. The music stops abruptly, there are excited cries of They're coming! Quiet! The waiter blows out the candles.* 2> *Sound of the 'Internationale' from outside.* <2

A MAN *appears in the door left:* Ladies and gentlemen, please keep calm. You are requested not to leave the premises. Disturbances have broken out. They are fighting around the newspaper offices. The outcome is uncertain.

BALICKE *sits down heavily:* Spartacus! Your friends, Mr Andreas Kragler. Your murky companions. Your comrades who are now roaring round the newspaper offices.[3] Smelling of murder and arson. Animals! *Silence.* Animals! Animals! Animals! Want to know why you're animals: you eat flesh. You should be stamped out.

WAITER: By you! You who've eaten yourselves silly!

MURK: Where d'you keep your knife! Out with it!

MARIE *goes up to him with the waiter:* Will you shut up?

WAITER: It's inhuman. Animal, that's what it is.

MURK: Draw the curtains! Ghosts!

WAITER: Are we supposed to be put up against a wall we built with our own hands, while you people swill down kirsch behind it?

KRAGLER: There's my hand and there's my artery. Cut it. If I'm destroyed it'll bleed all right.

MURK: Ghost! Ghost! What are you really? Am I supposed to grovel because you've got an African skin on?[4] And go roaring round the newspaper offices? Is it my fault you were in Africa? Is it my fault I wasn't?

WAITER: He must get his girl back. It's inhuman.

FRAU BALICKE *in front of Anna, furiously:* The whole lot are sick. They've all got something. Syphilis! Syphilis! They've all got syphilis!

BABUSCH *bangs the table with his stick:* That's the last straw.

FRAU BALICKE: Kindly leave my child alone! Kindly leave her alone! You hyena! You're a swine, you are!

ANNA: Andy, I can't. You people are destroying me.

MARIE: You're the swine.

WAITER: It's not human. A man must have some rights.

FRAU BALICKE: Be quiet! You menial! You little bastard, I ordered kirsch, do you hear? You'll be sacked!

WAITER: It's the human element. It's all of our business. He must get . . .

KRAGLER: Oh, get out. I've had enough. Human and inhuman! What does that drunk cow think she wants? I've been on my own and I want my girl. What does that sodden archangel think he wants? D'you want to hawk her body as if it were a pound of coffee? Tear her away from me with grappling-hooks and you'll simply rip her apart.

WAITER: You'll rip her apart.

MARIE: Yes, like a pound of coffee.

BALICKE: A man absolutely without money!

BABUSCH: You kick his teeth in, he spits them back in your face.

MURK *to Anna:* You look like a baby's vomit, letting him lick you up with his eyes like that. With a face like you'd pissed in a bed of nettles.

BALICKE: Is that how you speak about your fiancée?

MURK: Fiancée! That what she is? My fiancée, is she? Isn't she cutting loose already? Back, is he? Do you love him? Is the unripe nut sinking to the bottom? Is it African thighs you've an urge for? Is that the way the wind lies?

BABUSCH: That's something you wouldn't have said if you'd been sitting down.

ANNA *continually getting closer to Kragler, regards Murk with disgust. Softly:* You're drunk.

MURK *pulls her to him:* Let's see your face! Show us your teeth! Whore!

KRAGLER *simply lifts Murk to his feet, the glasses rattle on the table, Marie keeps applauding:* You're not too steady on your feet. Go outside. Make yourself sick. You've drunk too much. You're falling over. *Gives him a push.*

MARIE: Let him have it! Do let him have it!

KRAGLER: Leave him be. Come to me, Anna. I want you now. He wanted to buy my boots off me, but I'm taking my coat off. The sleet cut through my skin so that it's red and splits in the sun. My bag's empty, I have no money whatever, I want you. I'm not beautiful. Up to now I've been frightened out of my wits, but now I'm drinking. *Drinks.* And then we'll go. Come!

MURK *completely collapsed, tipped towards Kragler, says almost calmly:* Don't drink. You don't know the half of it. Call it a day. I was drunk. But you don't know the half of it. Anna – *soberly* – you tell him. What are you going to do? In your state?

KRAGLER *doesn't hear him:* Don't be frightened, Anna! *With the kirsch.* Nothing will happen to you. No call to be scared. We'll get married. I've always got along all right.

WAITER: Bravo.

FRAU BALICKE: You bastard!

KRAGLER: If you've got a conscience, the birds'll shit on your roof. If you've got patience, you'll end up eaten by vultures. They've got it all fixed.

ANNA *suddenly sets off, falls across the table.* Andy! Help me! Help, Andy!

MARIE: What's the matter? What is it?

KRAGLER *looks at her astounded:* Well?

ANNA: Andy, I don't know, I'm so miserable, Andy. I can't tell you anything, you mustn't ask. *Looks up.* I can't belong to you. God knows it. *Kragler drops his glass.* And I'm asking you to go, Andy. *Silence. In the next room the Man can be heard asking 'What's happening?' The waiter answers him, talking through the door left.*

WAITER: The crocodile-hide suitor from Africa has been waiting for four years and the bride still has her lily in her hand. But the other suitor, a man with buttoned boots, won't give her up and the bride who still has her lily in her hand doesn't know which side to go off.

VOICE: Anything else?

WAITER: The revolution in the newspaper district is part of it all and then the bride has a secret, something the suitor from Africa who has been waiting for four years doesn't know about. It's still quite undecided.

VOICE: No decision one way or the other?

WAITER: It's still quite undecided.

BALICKE: Waiter! Who are that low-down crowd? Are we supposed to sit and drink surrounded by vermin? *To Kragler:* Have you heard enough now? Are you satisfied? Shut up! The sun was hot, was it? That's what Africa's for. That's in the geography books. And you were a hero? That'll be in the history books. But the cheque book's empty. Hence the hero will be going back to Africa. Period. Waiter, show that object out! *The waiter starts to tow away Kragler, who accompanies him slowly and with reluctance. But Marie the prostitute walks on his left side.*

BALICKE: Chimpanzees' tea-party! *Shouts after Kragler, because it's too quiet:* Wanted meat, did you? It isn't a meat auction. Pack your <u>red moon</u> up and sing your <u>monkeys</u> something. I'm not interested in your palm trees. The whole of you's come out of a novel. <u>Where do you keep your birth certificate?</u> *Kragler is off.*

FRAU BALICKE: You'll be better for a good cry. But what's that? Want to drink yourself senseless with all that kirsch?

BALICKE: What sort of a face is that, anyway? Paper-white!

FRAU BALICKE: No, just look at the child. What are you thinking of? You ought to lay off now.

Anna sits behind the table, motionless, almost up against the curtains, ill-naturedly, with a glass in front of her.

MURK *goes up to her, sniffs her glass:* Pepper! Hell's bells! *She takes it contemptuously away from him.* Oh really! – What the hell are you up to with that pepper? You'll be wanting a hot douche next, will you? Then have to be fixed up

manually, I suppose? Hell's bitches! *Spits and flings the glass to the floor.*
Anna smiles.
Machine-gun fire is heard.
BABUSCH *at the window:* It's starting. The masses are stirring. Spartacus is rising. The slaughter continues.
All stand rigid, listening to the noises outside.

ACT THREE (RIDE OF THE VALKYRIES)

[5>]Street Leading to the Newspaper District[<5]

Red-brick barrack wall from up left to down right. Behind it the city, in dim starlight. Night. Wind.

MARIE: Where are you off to?

KRAGLER *with no cap, collar turned up, hands in his trouser pockets, has entered, whistling:* What kind of a red fig is that?

MARIE: Don't run so.

KRAGLER: Can't you keep up?

MARIE: D'you think someone's after you?

KRAGLER: D'you want to go to bed? Where's your room?

MARIE: But that's no good.

KRAGLER: Yes. *Wants to go on.*

MARIE: It's in my lungs.

KRAGLER: Why tag along like a dog, then?

MARIE: But your[6] . . .

KRAGLER: Pooh, that's been scrubbed! Washed out! Cancelled!

MARIE: What'll you do till morning, then?

KRAGLER: [7]There's knives.

MARIE: Dear Jesus . . .

KRAGLER: Quiet, I don't like it when you scream like that, there's also [8>]schnaps[<8]. What d'you want? I can try laughing if you like. Tell me, did they lay you on the steps before you were confirmed? Scrub that! D'you smoke? *He laughs.* Let's go on.[9>]

MARIE: There's firing down by the newspaper offices.[<9]

KRAGLER: We might be useful. *Exeunt both.*

Wind. Two men in the same direction.

THE ONE: I think we'll do it here.

THE OTHER: Mightn't have a chance down there . . .
They make water.

10>THE ONE: Gunfire.

THE OTHER: Hell! In the Friedrichstrasse!<10

THE ONE: Where you watered the synthetic alcohol.

THE OTHER: That moon alone's enough to drive you crazy.

THE ONE: When you've been selling doctored tobacco.

THE OTHER: All right, I've sold doctored tobacco, but you've stuffed human beings into rat-holes.

THE ONE: That must be a comfort to you.

THE OTHER: I won't be the only one to hang.

11>THE ONE: You know what the Bolsheviks did? Show us your hands. No callouses? Bang bang. *The Other looks at his hands.* Bang bang. You're getting smelly already.<11

THE OTHER: O God.

THE ONE: Fine business if you turn up in your bowler hat.

THE OTHER: You've a bowler too.

THE ONE: Battered, my dear fellow.

THE OTHER: I can batter mine.

THE ONE: That stiff collar of yours is as good as a hangman's noose.

THE OTHER: I'll sweat till it's soft; you've got button boots, though.

THE ONE: Your waistline!

THE OTHER: Your voice!

THE ONE: Your look! Your way of walking! Your manner!

THE OTHER: Yes, they'll hang me for that, but you've a grammar school face.

THE ONE: I've a mangled ear with a bullet through it, my dear sir.

THE OTHER: The devil!

Exeunt both. Wind.

From the left now the entire Ride of the Valkyries: Anna, as if fleeing. Next her, wearing an evening coat but no hat, Manke, the waiter from the Piccadilly Bar, who behaves as if intoxicated. After them comes Babusch, dragging Murk, who is drunk, pale and bloated.

MANKE: Forget it. He's gone. Blown away. He may be swallowed up in the [12>]newspaper district[<12] already. They're shooting all over the place, all kinds of things are happening at the newspapers, this night of all nights and he might even be shot. *Speaking to Anna as if drunk:* One can run away when they shoot, but one can also choose not to. Anyhow: another hour and no one will be able to find him. He's dissolving like paper in water. He's got the moon in his head. He's running after every drum. Go! Save your beloved that was, no, is.

BABUSCH *flinging himself in Anna's path:* Halt, all you Valkyries! Where are you going? It's cold and there's a wind too and he's landed in some schnaps bar. *Aping the waiter.* He who waited four years. Nobody's going to find him now, though.

MURK: Nobody. Not a soul. *He sits on a stone.*

BABUSCH: And look at that, will you?[13]

MANKE: He's nothing to do with me. Give him a coat. Don't waste time. He who waited four years is now running quicker than those clouds are drifting. He's gone quicker than this wind is gone.

MURK *apathetic:* The punch had colouring matter in it. Just now when everything's set. The linen got together, the rooms rented. Come over here, Bab!

MANKE: What are you standing about like Lot's wife for? This is no Gomorrah. Does drunken misery impress you? Can you find a way round? Is it the linen?[14] Will the clouds hang back for that?

BABUSCH: What business is that of yours? How are the clouds your affair? You're a waiter, aren't you?

MANKE: My affair? The stars run clean off their rails if a man's left unmoved by unfairness. *Seizes his own throat.* It's driving me too. It's got me by the throat too. A man frightened out of his wits is nothing to be petty about.

BABUSCH: What's that? Out of his wits? Where did you see that? I'm telling you: something's going to be bellowing like a bull down at the newspapers before daybreak.

[15]> And that'll be the mob thinking here's a chance to settle old scores. <[15]

MURK *has stood up, whines:* Dragging a man round in this wind! I feel terrible. What are you running away for? What is it? I need you. It's not the linen.

ANNA: I can't.[16]

MURK: I can't stand on my feet.

MANKE: Sit down! You're not the only one. It's infectious. Father gets a stroke. The drunken kangaroo is in tears. But the daughter goes down to the slums. To her lover who has waited four years.[17]

ANNA: I can't do it.

MURK: You've got all the linen. And the furniture's already in the rooms.

MANKE: The linen is folded, but the bride is not coming.

ANNA: My linen has been bought, I laid it in the cupboard piece by piece, but now I need it no longer. The room has been rented and the curtains hang ready and the wallpaper is up. But he is come who has[18] no shoes and only one coat, and the moths are in that.

MANKE: And he is swallowed up by the [19]>newspaper district<[19]. Awaited by the schnaps saloons. The night! The misery! The dregs! Rescue him!

BABUSCH: All this is a drama called The Angel of the Dockland Boozers.

MANKE: Yes, the angel.

MURK: And you want to go down there [20]>to the Friedrichstrasse?<[20] And nothing's going to stop you?

ANNA: Nothing that I know of.

MURK: Nothing?[21] Won't you still be thinking of 'the other thing'?

ANNA: No. I don't want that any more.

MURK: You don't want 'the other thing'?

ANNA: That's the tie.

MURK: And it doesn't bind you?

ANNA: It's broken now.

MURK: Your child means nothing to you?

ANNA: It means nothing.

MURK: Because he is come who has no coat?

ANNA: I didn't recognize him.

MURK: It's no longer him. You didn't recognize him.

ANNA: He stood in the middle like some animal. 22>And you<22 beat him like an animal.

MURK: And he howled like an old woman.

ANNA: And he howled like a woman.

MURK: And cleared off and left you sitting there.

ANNA: And went away and left me sitting there.

MURK: Finished, he 23>is.

ANNA: And he's finished.<23

MURK: He has gone away . . .

ANNA: But when he was gone away and he was finished . . .

MURK: Nothing remained. Absolutely nothing.

ANNA: There was a turbulence behind him and a slight wind and it grew very strong and was stronger than anything else and now I am going away and now I am coming and now it's all finished for us, for me and for him. Because where is he gone? Does God know where he is? How big is the world and where is he? *She looks composedly at Manke and says softly:* Go to your bar, I'm grateful to you, and please see that he gets there.24 But Bab, you come with me! *And hurries off right.*

MURK *plaintively:* Where's she off to?25>

BABUSCH: That's the end of the Ride of the Valkyries, my boy.<25

MANKE: The lover has already vanished, but his beloved hastens after him on wings of love. The hero has been brought low, but his path to heaven is already prepared.

BABUSCH: But the lover's going to stuff his beloved down a sewer and take the path to hell instead. O you romantic institute, you!

MANKE: She is vanishing already as she hastens 26>down to the newspaper buildings<26. Like a white sail she can be seen still, like an idea, like a final cadence, like an intoxicated swan flying across the waters . . .

BABUSCH: What are we to do with this sodden clod?

MURK: I'm staying here. It's cold. If it gets any colder they'll come back. You know nothing about it. Because you don't know the other thing. Let her run. He won't want two. He left one behind and got two running after him. *Laughs*.

BABUSCH:²⁷ She's vanishing heavenwards like a final cadence. *Slogs after her*.

²⁸˃MANKE *calls after him:* Glubb's bar, Chausseestrasse! That whore with him hangs out in Glubb's bar. *Spreads both his arms widely once more:* The revolution is˂²⁸ swallowing them up. Will they find one another?

A Small Schnaps Distillery

Clad in white, Glubb, the proprietor, sings the 'Ballad of the Dead Soldier'[1] to guitar accompaniment. Laar and a sinister drunk man stare at his fingers. A small square man called Bulltrotter is reading the paper. Manke, the waiter, brother of the Manke from the Piccadilly Bar, is drinking with Augusta, a prostitute, and all are smoking.

BULLTROTTER: I want schnaps, not a dead soldier, I want to read the paper and I need schnaps for that or by God I won't understand it.

GLUBB *with a cold glassy voice:* Don't you feel at home?

BULLTROTTER: Yes, but there's a revolution on.

GLUBB: What for? This is my place where the scum feels at home and Lazarus sings.

THE DRUNK MAN: I'm scum, you're Lazarus.30>

A WORKER *enters and goes up to the bar:* Evening, Karl.

GLUBB: In a hurry?

THE WORKER: Hausvogteiplatz at eleven.

GLUBB: Plenty of rumours.

THE WORKER: There's been a guards division at the Anhalt station since six. All quiet at the 'Vorwärts' building. We could do with your boy Paul today, Karl.

MANKE: We don't talk about Paul here usually.

THE WORKER *paying:* Today's unusual. *Exit.*

MANKE *to Glubb:* Wasn't it unusual last November? You need a gun in your hand and a sticky feeling at the tips of the fingers.

GLUBB *chilly:* What can I do for you, sir?

BULLTROTTER: Freedom! <30 *He takes off his coat and collar.*

GLUBB: Drinking in shirtsleeves is against the law.

[1] See p. 391.

BULLTROTTER: Reactionaries.

MANKE: They're practising the [31]>Internationale<[31], in four parts with tremolo[32]. Freedom! Then I suppose a fellow with clean cuffs will be put to scrub the lavatories?

GLUBB: They'll make a mess of the false marble.

AUGUSTA:[33] So people with clean cuffs are not to scrub the lavatories, eh?

BULLTROTTER: You'll be put up against a wall, mate.

AUGUSTA: Then let them with the clean cuffs be so good as to strap up their arseholes.

MANKE: Augusta, you're crude.

AUGUSTA: O you swine, you ought to be ashamed, your bowels should be ripped out, you should be hanged too, and them with the clean cuffs be strung up a lamp-post. 'Can't you cut the price, ducky, now we've lost the war?' You've no business making love if you haven't got the money, and you've no business making war if you don't know how to. Take your feet down when there are ladies present. Why should I smell your stinking feet, you dirty bugger?

GLUBB: His cuffs aren't a bit clean.

THE DRUNK MAN: What's that rumbling?

MANKE: Guns.

THE DRUNK MAN *gives the others a pale grin:* What's that rattling?
Glubb goes to the window, throws it open, they hear guns racing down the street. All at the window.

[34]>BULLTROTTER: That's the regiment they call the Cock-chafers.<[34]

AUGUSTA: Jesus Christ, where are they going?

GLUBB: To the newspaper offices, girl. They're the readers. *He shuts the window.*[35]

AUGUSTA: Jesus Christ, who's coming in?
Kragler swaying in the doorway as if drunk, rocking on the soles of his feet.

[36]>MANKE: Are you laying an egg in that doorway?<[36]

AUGUSTA: Who are you[37]?

KRAGLER *grinning maliciously :* Nobody.

AUGUSTA *drying him :* The sweat's running down his collar.[38]
Been running hard, haven't you ?[39]

THE DRUNK MAN: Got squitters ?

KRAGLER: No, I've not got the squitters.[40>]

MANKE *goes across to him :* Well, what have you been up to, my
boy ? I know the type.

MARIE *appears behind him :* He hasn't been up to anything. I
invited him, Augusta; he hasn't got anywhere to go. He's
been in Africa. Sit down.

Kragler continues to stand in the doorway. [< 40]

MANKE: Prisoner of war ?

MARIE: And posted missing.

AUGUSTA: Missing too ?

MARIE: And a prisoner of war.[41>] And in the meantime they
pinched his fiancée.

AUGUSTA: Come to Mummy, then. Have a seat, gunner. *To
Glubb :* Five double kirsches, Karl.

Glubb pours out five glasses, which Manke puts on a small table.

GLUBB: Last week they pinched my bicycle.
Kragler goes to the table. [< 41]

AUGUSTA: Tell us about Africa.[42>]

Kragler drinks without answering.

BULLTROTTER: Cough it up. The landlord's a red.

GLUBB: What did you say I was ?

BULLTROTTER: A red.

MANKE: Mind yourself, sir; there's nothing red about this
place, if you don't mind.

BULLTROTTER: All right. Not red, then.

AUGUSTA: And what did you do out there ?

KRAGLER: Shot wogs in the belly. Made roads. – Is it your
lungs ?

AUGUSTA: How long for ?

KRAGLER *keeps addressing Marie :* Twenty-seven.

MARIE: Months.

AUGUSTA: And before that ?

KRAGLER: Before that ? I lay in a hole full of mud.

BULLTROTTER: And what were you doing there?

KRAGLER: Stinking.

GLUBB: Yes, you could lie around as much as you wanted.

BULLTROTTER: What were the tarts like in Africa?

Kragler is silent.

AUGUSTA: Don't be crude.

BULLTROTTER: And when you got back she wasn't at home, eh? I suppose you thought she'd go to the barracks every morning and wait around for you among the dogs?

KRAGLER *to Marie:* Shall I hit him?

GLUBB: No, not yet. Give us a tune on the nickelodeon, that's what you can do.

KRAGLER *stands up swaying, and salutes:* Sir! *He goes and starts up the nickelodeon.*

BULLTROTTER: Mush.

AUGUSTA: It's just that he feels he's a corpse. He's dead but he won't lie down.

GLUBB: Yes, yes. He's been the victim of a slight injustice. He'll get over it.

BULLTROTTER: Here, you're a red, aren't you? Glubb! Weren't they saying something about your nephew?

GLUBB: They were. Not in this house, though.

BULLTROTTER: No, not in this house. At the Siemens works.

GLUBB: For a short while.

BULLTROTTER: For a short while at Siemens's. He worked a lathe. He worked a lathe for a short while. Worked a lathe till last November, didn't he?

THE DRUNK MAN *who has done nothing but laugh so far, sings:*

My brothers are all dead
And I was nearly so.
November I was red
But January no.

GLUBB: Herr Manke, this gentleman doesn't want to be a nuisance to anybody. See that he isn't.

KRAGLER *has seized Augusta's waist and is dancing round with her:*

'A dog went to the kitchen
To get a bone to chew.
The cook picked up his chopper
And cut that dog in two.'

THE DRUNK MAN *convulsed with laughter:* Worked a lathe for a short while ...<42

GLUBB: You're not to smash my glasses, gunner.

MARIE: He's drunk now. It'll be a relief.43>

KRAGLER: A relief, is it? Console yourself, brother Schnaps-vat, just say: it's not possible.

AUGUSTA: Drink up, love.

THE DRUNK MAN: Weren't they saying something about a nephew?

KRAGLER: What is a swine in the eyes of the Lord, sister prostitute? He is nothing.

THE DRUNK MAN: Not in this house.

KRAGLER: And why? Can we do away with the army or God? Can you do away with torture, Red, with the torments the devil has learnt from the human race? No, you can't do away with them, but you can serve schnaps.<43 So drink up and shut the door and don't let the wind in, which is frozen too, but put wood between.44

BULLTROTTER: The landlord says you're the victim of a slight injustice; you'll get over it, he says.

45>KRAGLER: Will I? Did you say injustice, brother Red? What sort of a word is that? Injustice! A whole lot of little words like that they keep inventing, and blowing in the air, and then they can put their feet up and one gets over it. And big brother clouts his little brother on the jaw, and the cream of society takes the cream off the milk, and everyone gets over it nicely.

THE DRUNK MAN: Over that nephew. The one they say nothing about in this house.

KRAGLER:

    'The other dogs came running
    To dig that dog a grave
    And set him this inscription
    Upon the stone above:

    A dog went to the kitchen . . .'

Therefore make yourselves at home on our planet, it's cold here and rather dark, Red; the world's too old for the millennium and heaven has been let, my friends.

MARIE: What are we to do, then? He says he wants to <45 go to the newspaper offices. There they are, but what's happening there?

KRAGLER: A cab driving to the Piccadilly Bar.

AUGUSTA: Is she inside?

KRAGLER: With her inside. 46> My pulse is quite normal: feel. *Holds out his hand, while drinking with the other.*

MARIE: He's called Andy.

KRAGLER: Andy. Yes, I was called Andy. *He continues absent-mindedly to feel his pulse.* <46

LAAR: They were mainly fir trees, little fir trees . . .

GLUBB: The stone's starting to talk.[47]

BULLTROTTER: And you sold, you 48> idiot?

LAAR: Me?

BULLTROTTER: Oh, the bank? Interesting, Glubb, but not in this house.

GLUBB: Are you feeling offended? Well, control yourselves then. All right, then prepare to be controlled. <48 Keep calm when they pull the skin off you, gunner, or it may split; it's the only one you've got. 49> *Still busy with glasses:* Yes, you're a bit offended; <49 you've been killed off by guns and sabres, shat on a bit, and spat on a bit. 50> Well, what about it?

BULLTROTTER *referring to the glasses:* Aren't they clean yet?

THE DRUNK MAN: Wash me, Lord, that I may become white! Wash me that I may become white as snow! *Sings:*

My brothers all are dead, yes dead
And I was very nearly so.
November I was red, ah red
But January no . . .

GLUBB: That'll do.

AUGUSTA: You cowards!

NEWSPAPER WOMAN *enters:*[50] Spartacus threatens press
offices! Red Rosa speaks at Zoo![51] Mob rule for how long?
Where are the troops? Ten pfennigs, soldier? Where are
the troops: ten pfennigs. *>Exit, as there are no customers.*

AUGUSTA: And Paul not there.[<]

KRAGLER: That whistling again?[52>]

GLUBB *closes his cupboard, dries his hands:* We're closing.

MANKE: Let's go, Augusta. He's saying nothing against you,
but let's go. *To Bulltrotter:* Anything the matter, sir? Two
marks sixty.

BULLTROTTER:[<52] I was at Jutland; that was no picnic
either.

[53]THE DRUNK MAN *with his arm round Marie:*

The saintly slattern disappears
Swimming with him through floods of tears.[54>]

KRAGLER: Down to the papers, everyone!

'A dog went to the kitchen
To get a bone to chew.
The cook picked up his chopper
And cut that dog in two.'[<54]

LAAR *staggers to the nickelodeon, pulls the drum away and starts a
roll, swaying after the others.*

ACT FIVE (THE BED)

Wooden Bridge

Shouting, big red moon.

BABUSCH:[55] It's time for you to go home.

ANNA: I can't go back there.[56] What's the use, I waited four years with a photo and took another man. I was frightened at night.

BABUSCH: I've run out of cigars. Aren't you ever going home?[57] They're flinging torn-up papers in the puddles, screaming at machine-guns, shooting in each other's ears, imagining they're building a new world. Here's another group coming now.

ANNA: There he is!

As the group approaches there is a great disturbance in the street. Shooting breaks out in many directions.

ANNA:[58] I'm going to tell him.

BABUSCH: I'll stop you.

ANNA: I'm not an animal. I'll scream!

BABUSCH:[59] And I've run out of cigars.

From between the houses come Glubb, Laar, the drunk man, the two women, the waiter Manke from the Piccadilly Bar, and Andy Kragler.

KRAGLER: I'm hoarse. I've got Africa in the throat. I'm going to hang myself.

GLUBB: Why not hang yourself tomorrow and come with us to the newspaper buildings now?

KRAGLER *stares towards Anna:* Yes.

AUGUSTA: Seen an apparition?

MANKE: Hey, your hair's standing on end.

GLUBB: Is that her?

KRAGLER: What's the matter, then; are you stopping here? I'll have you shot. March, march, double march!

ANNA *goes to meet him:* Andy!

THE DRUNK MAN: Lift your leg, I spy love!

ANNA: Andy, stop a moment, it's me, I wanted to say something. *Silence.* I wanted to remind you of something; stop just a moment, I'm not drunk. *Silence.* [60]You've no cap, either; it's cold. I must say something to you privately.[61]

KRAGLER: Are you drunk?

AUGUSTA: His fiancée comes after him, and his fiancée's boozed.

ANNA: What do you think? *Walks a few steps.* I'm with child. *Augusta laughs shrilly.*
Kragler sways, squints towards the bridge, springs around as if trying out walking.

AUGUSTA: Are you a fish, gasping for air like that?

MANKE: You must think you're asleep.

KRAGLER *hands down his trouser seams:* Sir!

MANKE: She's with child. Having children's her business. Come on!

KRAGLER *stiffly:* Sir! Where to, sir?

MANKE: He's gone off his head.

GLUBB: Usedn't you to be in Africa?

KRAGLER: Morocco, Casablanca, Hut 10.

ANNA: Andy!

KRAGLER *listens:* Listen! My [62>]fiancée,[<62] the whore! She's come, she's there, she's got a bulge in her belly!

GLUBB: She's a bit anaemic, isn't she?

KRAGLER: Sh! It wasn't me, I didn't do it.

ANNA: Andy, there are people around.

KRAGLER: Is your body blown up with air or did you make a whore of yourself? I was away; I couldn't keep an eye on you. I was lying in the filth. Where did you lie while I was lying in the filth?

MARIE: You shouldn't speak like that. What do you know about it?

KRAGLER: And it was you I wanted to see. Otherwise I'd be lying where I belong, would have wind in my skull, dust in my mouth, and know nothing. But I wanted to see you first. I wouldn't settle for less. I ate husks. They were bitter. I crept on all fours from my hole in the mud. That was comic. Swine that I am. *Opens his eyes suddenly*. Have a good look, eh? Did you get free tickets?

He picks up lumps of earth and throws them about him.

AUGUSTA: Hold him down!

ANNA: Throw them, Andy! Throw them! Throw them at me!

MARIE: Get the woman away, he'll stone her to death.

KRAGLER: Go to the devil! You've everything you need! Open your mouths. There isn't anything else.

AUGUSTA: Down with his head! Rub it in the dirt!

The men hold him to the ground.[63]

AUGUSTA: Blow, will you, miss?

GLUBB *to Anna:* Yes, you go home, the early morning air's no good for the ovaries.

BABUSCH *crosses the battlefield to Kragler, and tells him while chewing his mangled cigar:* That'll teach you where the shoe pinches. You're God; you've thundered. As to the woman, she's pregnant, she can't go on sitting on that stone, the nights are chilly, perhaps you'll say something . . .

GLUBB: Yes, perhaps you'll say something.

The men allow Kragler to get up. There is silence, the wind is heard, two men pass by in a hurry.

[64>]THE ONE: They've got the Ullstein building.

THE OTHER: And artillery's getting into position outside the Mosse building.

THE ONE: We're far too few.

THE OTHER: Far more are on the way.

THE ONE: Far too late.

They have passed.[<64]

AUGUSTA: There you have it. Pack it in.

MANKE: Stuff the answer down his gullet, that bourgeois and his tart!

AUGUSTA *tries to drag Kragler along:* Come along to the newspaper buildings, love! You're beginning to wake up.

GLUBB: Let her stay on her stone if she wants. The underground starts at seven.

AUGUSTA: It won't be running today.[65]

THE DRUNK MAN: Forward, forward to alleluia!

Anna has risen to her feet again.

MARIE *looks her over:* White as a sheet.

GLUBB: A bit pale and a bit thin.

BABUSCH: She's on her way out.

GLUBB: It's just the unflattering light. *Looks at the sky.*

AUGUSTA: [66>]Here come the workers from Wedding.[<66]

GLUBB *rubbing his hands:* You came with the guns. Perhaps you belong with them. *Kragler is silent.* You don't say anything, that's sensible. *Walking round.* Your tunic's been slightly shot up, and [67]altogether you're a bit pallid, a bit worn down.[68] But it doesn't much matter. The only slightly displeasing thing is your shoes, they squeak. But you can put grease on them. *He sniffs the air.* [69]Of course, one or two star-spangled skies have gone under since eleven and a number of Redeemers have been gobbled up by the sparrows, but I'm glad you're still there. Just your digestion worries me. All the same you aren't transparent yet, at least one can see you.

KRAGLER: Come over here, Anna.

MANKE: 'Come over here, Anna'.[70]

ANNA: Where is the underground, does anyone know?

AUGUSTA: No underground today. No underground, no elevated, no local services, for the whole of today. Today there will be universal rest, on all tracks today the trains will be stopped, and we shall walk around like civilized people till evening, my dear.

KRAGLER: Come over here to me, Anna.

[71>]GLUBB: Won't you come along for a bit, brother gunner?[<71]

Kragler is silent.

GLUBB: One or two of us would like to have drunk another schnaps or so, but you were against it. One or two would like to have slept in a bed again, but you hadn't got a bed, [72>]so it was no good planning to go home either.

Kragler is silent. [<72]

ANNA: Won't you go, Andy? They're waiting for you.

MANKE: Fish your paw out of your pocket, mate, anyhow.[73]

KRAGLER: Fling stones at me, here I am: I can rip the shirt off my back for you, but bare my throat to the knife, I will not.

THE DRUNK MAN: Heaven, arseholes and little bits of string.

AUGUSTA: And and and the newspapers?[74]

KRAGLER: It's no use. I won't let myself be dragged down to the newspapers in my shirtsleeves. I'm not a lamb any more. I don't want to die.[75] *Takes his pipe once more from his trouser pocket.*[76]

GLUBB: A bit pathetic, isn't it?

KRAGLER: Look, they'll riddle your chest like a sieve. [77>]Anna! What the devil are you looking at me like that for? Have I got to defend myself to you too? *To Glubb:* They shot your nephew, but I've got my wife back. Anna, come.

GLUBB: It looks as though we'd better go on without him.[<77]

AUGUSTA: Then was all that lies, Africa and so on?

KRAGLER: No, it was true. Anna!

MANKE: The gentleman was bellowing like a stockbroker and now he wants his bed.

KRAGLER: Now I've got my wife.

MANKE: Have you got her?

KRAGLER: Here, Anna. She is not untarnished, nor is she innocent; have you been an honest woman or have you got a brat in your body?

ANNA: A brat, yes, I've got one.

KRAGLER: You've got one.

ANNA: Here he is, inside here, the pepper didn't do any good and my figure has gone for ever.

KRAGLER: Yes, that's her.

MANKE: And us? Soaked to the heart in schnaps and filled to the navel with talk, and with knives in our paws, and who did they come from?

KRAGLER: They came from me. *To Anna:* Yes, that's the sort you are.

ANNA: Yes, that's the sort I am.

GLUBB: You didn't yell 'To the newspaper buildings!' I suppose?

KRAGLER: Yes, I did that. *To Anna:* Walk over here.

MANKE: Yes, you did that, it'll be the end of you, mate, you yelled 'To the newspaper buildings!' all right.

KRAGLER: And I'm going home. *To Anna:* 78>Get moving<78.

AUGUSTA: You swine.

ANNA: Let me alone. I pretended to Father and Mother, and I lay in bed with a bachelor.

AUGUSTA: Swine too.

KRAGLER: What's the matter?

ANNA: I bought the curtains with him. And I slept with him in the bed.

KRAGLER: Stop it!

MANKE: Look, mate, I shall hang myself if you change your mind.

A distant shouting off.

AUGUSTA: 79>They're attacking the Mosse building.<79

ANNA: And despite the photo I forgot everything about you.

KRAGLER: Stop it.

ANNA: Forgot! Forgot!

KRAGLER: 80>And I don't give a damn.<80 Am I to fetch you with my knife?

ANNA: Yes, fetch me. Yes, with the knife.

MANKE: 81Into the water with that lump of rotten flesh!

They fling themselves on Anna.

AUGUSTA: Yes, let's get rid of his tart!

MANKE: Get a hand on her neck!

AUGUSTA: Under water, that profiteer's tart!

ANNA: Andy!

KRAGLER: Hands off!

No sound but panting.

In the distance dull gunfire is heard irregularly.

MANKE: What's that?

AUGUSTA: Artillery.

MANKE: Guns.

AUGUSTA: God have mercy now on all of them down there. They're bursting open like fishes.

KRAGLER: Anna!

Augusta runs upstage, bent double.

BULLTROTTER *appears on the bridge upstage:* For God's sake, where are you all?

GLUBB: He's going to the lavatory.

MANKE: Louse. *Making his way off.*

KRAGLER: I'm going home now, dear man.

GLUBB *has reached the bridge:* Yes, [82]you've got your balls intact.

KRAGLER *to Anna:* It's whistling again, hold on to me, Anna.

ANNA: I'll make myself very thin.

GLUBB: You'll hang yourself all the same, tomorrow morning in the lavatory.

Augusta and the others have already gone.

KRAGLER: You're heading for the wall, man.

GLUBB: Yes, my boy, the morning will see quite a lot of things.[83] Some people will manage to get away safely, of course. *He disappears.*

KRAGLER: They almost drowned with weeping over me and I simply washed my shirt in their tears. Is my flesh to rot in the gutter so that their idea should get into heaven? Are they drunk?

ANNA: Andy! None of it matters.

KRAGLER *doesn't look her in the eyes, wanders around, grips himself by the throat:* I'm fed up to here. *He laughs irritably.* It's just play-acting. Boards and a paper moon and the butchery off-stage, which is the only real part of it. *He walks round again, his arms dangling, and in this way he fishes up the drum from the schnaps bar.* They've left their drum. *He bangs on it.* [84>]Half a Spartacist[<84] or The Power of Love; Bloodbath round the Newspaper Offices, or [85>]Everybody is Top Man in His Own Skin.[<85] *Looks up, blinks.* To do or to die. *He drums.*

The bagpipes play, the poor people die around the newspaper buildings, the houses fall on top of them, the dawn breaks, they lie like drowned kittens in the roadway, I am a swine and the swine's going home. *He draws breath.* I'll put on a clean shirt, my skin's intact, my jacket I'll take off, my boots I'll put grease on. *Laughs unpleasantly.* The shouting'll all be over tomorrow morning, but tomorrow morning I shall lie in bed and reproduce myself so I don't die out. *Drum.* Stop that romantic staring! You racketeers! *Drum.* You bloodsuckers! *Laughing full-throatedly, almost choking.* You cowardly cannibals, you! *His laughter sticks in his throat, he cannot continue, he staggers around, throws the drum at the moon, which was a lantern, and drum and moon together fall into the river, which is without water.*[86] Very drunken and infantile. Now comes bed, the great, white, wide bed, come!

ANNA: Oh, Andy!

KRAGLER *leads her off:* Are you warm?

ANNA: But you've got no coat on. *She helps him on with it.*

KRAGLER: [87]>It's cold.<[87] *He wraps her scarf round her neck.* Come now.

[88]*The two walk side by side, without touching one another, Anna slightly behind him. In the air, high up, a long way off, a white, wild screaming: it comes from the newspaper buildings.*

KRAGLER *stops, listens, puts his arm round Anna:* It's now four years.

As the screaming continues they walk away.

In the Jungle of Cities

*The fight between two men in the
great city of Chicago*

Translator: GERHARD NELLHAUS

Prologue

You are in Chicago in 1912. You are about to witness an inexplicable wrestling match between two men and observe the downfall of a family that has moved from the prairies to the jungle of the big city. Don't worry your heads about the motives for the fight, concentrate on the stakes. Judge impartially the technique of the contenders, and keep your eyes fixed on the finish.

Characters

Shlink the lumber dealer, a Malay · George Garga · John Garga, his father · Mae Garga, his mother · Mary Garga, his sister · Jane Larry, his girl friend · Skinny, a Chinese, Shlink's clerk · Collie Couch, known as Baboon, a pimp · J. Finnay, known as Worm, hotel owner · Pat Manky, a first mate · A Salvation Army preacher · Two Salvation Army girls · The pugnosed man · The barman · C. Maynes, owner of a lending library · Waiter · Railway workers

[*Numbers in the text refer to notes on p. 450 ff.*]

The Lending Library of C. Maynes in Chicago

The Morning of 8 August 1912
Garga behind the counter. The doorbell rings. Enter Shlink and Skinny.

SKINNY: If we read the sign right, this is a lending library. We'd like to borrow a book.

GARGA: What kind of a book?

SKINNY: A fat one.

GARGA: For yourself?

SKINNY *who looks at Shlink before each answer:* No, not for me; for this gentleman.

GARGA: Your name?

SKINNY: Shlink, lumber dealer, 6 Mulberry Street.

GARGA *taking down the name:* Five cents a week per book. Take your pick.

SKINNY: No, you choose one.

GARGA: This is a detective story, it's no good. Here's something better – a travel book.

SKINNY: Just like that you say the book is no good?

SHLINK *stepping up to him:* Is that your personal opinion? I'll buy your opinion. Is ten dollars enough?

GARGA: Take it as a gift.

SHLINK: You mean you've changed your opinion and now it's a good book?

GARGA: No.

SKINNY: Ten dollars will buy you some fresh linen.

GARGA: My job here is wrapping books, that's all.

SKINNY: It drives the customers away.

GARGA: What do you want of me? I don't know you. I've never seen you before.

SHLINK: I never heard of this book and it doesn't mean a thing to me. I'm offering you forty dollars for your opinion of it.

GARGA: I'll sell you the opinions of Mr J. V. Jensen and Mr Arthur Rimbaud, but I won't sell you my own opinion.

SHLINK: Your opinion is as worthless as theirs, but right now I want to buy it.

GARGA: I indulge in opinions.

SKINNY: Are your family millionaires?

GARGA: My family live on rotten fish.

SHLINK *obviously pleased:* A fighter! I'd have expected you to come across with the words that would give me pleasure and get your family something better than fish.

SKINNY: Forty bucks! That's a lot of linen for you and your family.

GARGA: I'm not a prostitute.

SHLINK *with humour:* I hardly think my fifty dollars would interfere with your inner life.

GARGA: Raising your offer is one more insult and you know it.

SHLINK *naïvely:* A man's got to know which is better, a pound of fish or an opinion. Or two pounds of fish or the opinion.

SKINNY: Dear sir, your stubbornness will get you into trouble.

GARGA: I'm going to have you thrown out.

SKINNY: Having opinions shows you don't know anything about life.

SHLINK: Miss Larry says you wanted to go to Tahiti!

GARGA: How do you know Jane Larry?

SHLINK: She's starving. She's not getting paid for the shirts she sews. You haven't been to see her in three weeks. *Garga drops a pile of books.*

SKINNY: Watch your step! You're only an employee.

GARGA: You're molesting me. But there's nothing I can do about it.

SHLINK: You're poor.

GARGA: I live on fish and rice. You know that as well as I do.

SHLINK: Sell!

SKINNY: Are you an oil king?

SHLINK: The people in your neighbourhood feel sorry for you.

GARGA: I can't shoot down the whole neighbourhood.

SHLINK: Your family that came from the prairies . . .

GARGA: Sleep three in a bed by a broken drainpipe. I smoke at night, it's the only way I can get to sleep. The windows are closed because Chicago is cold. Are you enjoying this?

SHLINK: Of course your sweetheart . . .

GARGA: Sews shirts for two dollars a piece. Net profit: twelve cents. I recommend her shirts. We spend Sundays together. A bottle of whisky costs us eighty cents, exactly eighty cents. Does this amuse you?

SHLINK: You're not coughing up your secret thoughts.

GARGA: No.

SHLINK: Nobody can live on twelve cents profit.

GARGA: Each man to his taste. Some people like Tahiti, if you don't mind.

SHLINK: You're well informed. That's the simple life. On Cape Hay there are storms. But farther south you've got the Tobacco Isles, and green rustling fields. You live like a lizard.

GARGA *looking out of the window, dryly:* 94 degrees in the shade. Noise from the Milwaukee Bridge. Traffic. A morning like every other morning.

SHLINK: But this morning is different; I'm starting my fight with you. I'm going to start by rocking the ground you stand on. *The bell rings, Maynes enters.* Your man has gone on strike.

MAYNES: Why aren't you taking care of these gentlemen, George?

SKINNY *bitingly:* His relations with us are strained.

MAYNES: What do you mean by that?

SKINNY: We don't care for his greasy shirt.

MAYNES: How dare you come to work like that, George? Is this a hash house? It won't happen again, gentlemen.

SKINNY: He's saying something. He's cursing up his sleeve! Speak up, man, use the voice God gave you!

GARGA: I must ask you for new shirts, Mr Maynes. You can't be a gigolo on five dollars a week.

SHLINK: Go to Tahiti. Nobody washes there.

GARGA: Thanks. Your concern is touching. I'll send my sister to pray for you in church.

SHLINK: Please do. She has nothing else to do anyhow. Manky's the right man for her. He runs himself ragged for her. Your parents are starving and she doesn't bat an eyelash.

GARGA: Are you running a detective agency? Your interest in us is flattering, I hope.

SHLINK: You're just shutting your eyes. Your family is headed for disaster. You're the only one who's making any money, and you indulge in opinions! When you could be on your way to Tahiti. *Shows him a sea chart that he has with him.*

GARGA: I've never seen you before in all my life.

SHLINK: There are two passenger lines.

GARGA: You just bought this map, didn't you? It's brand-new.

SKINNY: Think it over, the Pacific!

GARGA *to Maynes:* Please ask these gentlemen to leave. They didn't come to buy anything. They're driving the customers away. They've been spying on me. I don't even know them.

J. Finnay, called Worm, enters. Shlink and Skinny step back, pretending not to know him.

WORM: Is this C. Maynes's lending library?

MAYNES: In person.

WORM: Shady establishment, if you ask me.

MAYNES: Are you looking for books, magazines, stamps?

WORM: So there are books? Filthy business. What's the point of it? Aren't there enough lies? 'The sky was blue, the clouds flew east.' Why not south? What people won't swallow!

MAYNES: Let me wrap this book for you, sir.

SKINNY: Why not let him catch his breath? And I ask you, does this gentleman look like a bookworm?

GARGA: It's a plot.

WORM: You don't say! Listen to this. She says, 'When you kiss me I always see your beautiful teeth.' How can you see when you're kissing? But that's the way she is. Posterity will find out. The lewd bitch! *He grinds his heels on the books.*

MAYNES: Look here, sir, you've ruined those books, you'll have to pay for them.

WORM: Books! What good are they? Did libraries stop the San Francisco earthquake?

MAYNES: George, get a policeman.

WORM: I've got a liquor store. That's an honourable business.

GARGA: He isn't even drunk.

WORM: The sight of such loafers makes me tremble like a leaf.

GARGA: It's a put-up job. They're out to get me.
Couch, called Baboon,[1] *enters with Jane Larry. Worm steps back pretending not to know them.*

BABOON: Come on in, my little white chick. This is Maynes's rental library.

GARGA: You'd better close the shop, Mr Maynes. Strange vermin are crawling into your papers, moths are eating your magazines.

WORM: I always say: Look life straight in the eye.

BABOON: Get your face out of my way! I can't stand paper, especially newspaper.

GARGA: Get the gun!

SHLINK *steps forward:* I ask you again, will you sell?

GARGA *noticing Jane:* No!

JANE: George, is this your shop? Why are you staring at me? I was just going for a little walk with this gentleman.

GARGA: Keep walking.

BABOON: Say, let's not get rough. Don't you trust her? If I get excited, this book will end up in a thousand pieces. You still don't trust her?

MAYNES: I'll fire you if you won't trust her. My books are being ruined.

GARGA: Go home, Jane, please. You're drunk.

JANE: What's wrong with you, George? These gentlemen are being nice to me. *She drinks out of Baboon's bottle.* They've bought me drinks. It's hot today – 94. You know, George, it rips through you like lightning.

GARGA: Go on home now. I'll come tonight.

JANE: You haven't shown up for three weeks. I'm not going home any more. I'm fed up sitting around with those shirts.

BABOON *pulling Jane on to his lap:* That's all over now.

JANE: Oh, you're tickling me. Stop that! George doesn't like it.

BABOON: In brief, she's got a body that's worth a few bucks. Can you afford it, sir? It's a question of love and a question of drinks.

WORM: Maybe you'd like to keep her a virgin? What do you want her to do? Scrub floors? Wash clothes?

SKINNY: You expect a nice little pigeon like her to be an angel?

GARGA *to Shlink:* Are you trying to turn this place into the Wild West? Knives? Guns? Cocktails?

WORM: Hold on! You can't leave your job here. Maybe somebody will fall by the wayside. Sell!

GARGA: Strange. Everybody knows what's going on except me. – Jane!

BABOON: Tell him!

JANE: Don't look at me that way, George! This may be my only chance. Can you buy me drinks? Oh, it's not for the drinks! It's like this, George: every morning I look in the mirror. It's been two years now. You always go off and work for four weeks. When you were sick of it and needed liquor, you thought of me. I can't take it any more! The nights, George! That doesn't make me bad, not me. Don't look at me that way, it's not fair!

BABOON: That's smart. Have another drink and you'll be even smarter.

GARGA: Whisky's rotting your brain. Can you hear what I'm saying? Let's go away! Together! To Frisco! Anywhere you want. I don't know if a man can love for ever, but I can tell you this much: I'll stick by you.

JANE: You can't, Georgie.

GARGA: I can do anything. I can even make money if that's it. I've got a special feeling for you. There are no words for it! But we'll get together again. I'll come tonight. This very evening!

JANE: I hear every word; you don't need to shout and you don't need to tell these gentlemen here you didn't love me. You're only saying the bitterest things you know, and naturally I've got to listen. You know it as well as I do.

WORM: Cut the comedy! Just tell him you were in bed with this gentleman from nine to ten-thirty.

JANE: That might not be so good. But now at least you know, George, it's not the whisky or the heat!

SHLINK: Sell! I'll double the price again. This is so unpleasant.

GARGA: That doesn't count. What's nine to eleven against two years?

SHLINK: I assure you two hundred dollars means nothing to me. I hardly dare make such an offer.

GARGA: Would you be kind enough to send your friends away.

SHLINK: As you wish. Consider the ways of this planet and sell.

MAYNES: You're a fool and a dishrag and a lazy coolie; just think of . . .

SKINNY: Your innocent careworn parents!

WORM: Your sister!

BABOON: Your sweetheart! This lovely young girl.

GARGA: No, no, no!

SHLINK: Tahiti!

GARGA: I refuse.

MAYNES: You're fired!

SHLINK: Your economic existence! The ground you stand on! It's shaking!

GARGA: This is freedom! Here, take my coat! *Takes it off.* Give it away! *Takes a book from the shelf and reads:* 'Idolatry! Lies! Lechery! I'm a beast, a black. But I can be saved. You're phony niggers, maniacs, savages, misers! Merchant, you are a black and, Judge, you are a black, Emperor, you old leper, you're a nigger, you drink untaxed liquor from Satan's still. This people inspired by fever and cancer!' *Drinks.* 'I'm unversed in metaphysics. I understand no laws. I have no moral sense, I'm a brute; you are mistaken!'[2] *Shlink, Skinny, Worm, and Baboon have gathered round Garga and applaud as at a theatrical performance.*

SHLINK *smoking:* Why get so excited? Nobody's doing anything to you.

JANE *her arms round his neck:* Is it that bad, George?

GARGA: Here are my shoes! Are you smoking your little black cigar, sir? It might make you dribble. Here, my handkerchief. Yes, yes, I'll auction off this woman! I'm throwing these papers in your face. I want the tobacco fields of Virginia and a ticket to the Islands. I want, I want my freedom. *He runs out in his trousers and shirt.*

SHLINK *calls after him:* My name's Shlink, Shlink the lumber-dealer! Six Mulberry Street!

SKINNY: He'll toe the line . . . What's all this paper cost?

WORM: You're really going to pay?

MAYNES: The books are worth ten dollars.

SKINNY: Here's twenty.

BABOON *to Jane, who is crying:* Aha, now comes the awakening! Go weep in the gutter.

WORM: You've got to look life straight in the eye.

SHLINK: How much is this stuff?

MAYNES: The clothes? Jacket? Tie? Shoes? They're not really for sale. Ten dollars.

SKINNY: We finally drove him out of his skin. Let's take it with us.
Shlink goes out slowly towards the back, Skinny follows him with the bundle of clothes.

2

Chicago. The Office of C. Shlink, lumber dealer

22 August, shortly before 7 p.m.
Shlink at his little table.

SKINNY *voice from left rear:* Seven carloads of Kentucky.
WORM *in the rear:* Right.
SKINNY: Two carloads of stripped logs.
WORM: There's a man asking to see Mr Shlink.
SHLINK: Send him in.
WORM: Here's Mr Shlink!
   Garga enters.
SHLINK *please:* So here you are! Here are your clothes. Put them on.
GARGA: You've been waiting for me? You've brought my clothes here? Filthy rags. *Kicks the bundle of clothes away.*
   Shlink strikes a small gong.
MARY *enters:* George!
GARGA: You here, Mary?
MARY: Where've you been, George? They were worried about you. And the way you look!
GARGA: Just what are you doing here?
MARY: I take care of the linen. We can live on that. Why are you looking at me like that? You look as if you'd been having a hard time. I'm doing fine here. They said they'd fired you.
GARGA: Mary, pack your things and go home. *Pacing around.* I don't know what they want of me. They've harpooned me and pulled me in. I can feel the ropes. I'll have to depend on you, sir. But leave my sister out of it!
SHLINK: As you wish. *To Mary:* But first get him a clean shirt, and a suit. If you don't mind.
MARY: I can't understand my brother. He wants me to leave you.

SHLINK: And when you've finished, please go home too. I don't know anything about linen.

Mary leaves.

SHLINK: Have you been drinking?

GARGA: Kindly tell me if that doesn't fit in with your plans.

SHLINK: I only have saki. But I'll get you anything you like. You prefer cocktails?

GARGA: I do everything in one fell swoop. I'm in the habit of doing nothing for weeks but drink, make love, and smoke, all at the same time.

SHLINK: And leaf through the Britannica . . .

GARGA: You know everything.

SHLINK: When I heard about your habits, I thought to myself: There's a good fighter.

GARGA: What's the hold-up with those clothes?

SHLINK: Excuse me . . . *He stands up and strikes the little gong.*

MARY *enters:* Here's your linen, George, and your suit.

GARGA: Wait and we'll leave together. *He changes clothes behind a screen.*

MARY: I have to say good-bye, Mr Shlink. I couldn't quite finish the linen. Thanks for letting me stay at your house.

GARGA *from behind the screen:* This suit has no pockets.

Shlink whistles.

GARGA *coming out:* Who are you whistling for? In the last few weeks you've got left, I want you to stop whistling for people.

SHLINK: I accept your orders.

GARGA: You opened up this western. I'll accept the challenge. You skinned me alive for the fun of it. You won't make amends by giving me a new skin. I'm going to wipe you out. *Pulls a gun.* An eye for an eye, a tooth for a tooth.

SHLINK: Then the fight's on?

GARGA: Yes! Without obligation, of course.

SHLINK: And no question why?

GARGA: No question why. I don't want to know why you need a fight. If you've got a reason, I'm sure it's rotten. For me it's enough that you think you're the better man.

SHLINK: Well, let's think it over. Owning a house and a lumber business, for instance, puts me in a position to sick the dogs on you. Money is everything. Right? But my house is yours now, and so is the lumber business. From now on, Mr Garga, my fate's in your hands. I don't know you! From now on I'm going to be your slave. Every look that comes into your eyes will trouble me. Every one of your wishes, known or unknown, will find me willing. Your cares will be my cares, my strength will be yours. My feelings will be dedicated to you alone, and you will be an evil master.

GARGA: I accept your challenge. I hope you'll have nothing to laugh about.

Baboon, Skinny, and Worm enter silently. Garga notices with a grin that their suits are the same as his.

SHLINK: This house and this lumber business, carried on the Chicago Register of Deeds as the property of Shlink, are being transferred this day to Mr George Garga of Chicago.

GARGA *to Shlink:* That's me. All right. How many stripped logs have you in stock?

SHLINK: Maybe four hundred. I don't know exactly.

SKINNY: They belong to Broost and Company of Virginia.

GARGA: Who sold them?

WORM: I, known as Worm, owner of the Chinese Hotel in the coal district.

GARGA: Sell them again.

WORM: Sell them twice! That's fraud.

GARGA: Right.

WORM: And who'll be responsible for this order?

GARGA: Sell those logs in Frisco under the name of Shlink. Turn the money over to Mr Shlink, who'll hold it for me until I ask him for it. Any objections, Mr Shlink? *Shlink shakes his head.*

WORM: That's barefaced fraud. We'll have the law on us in no time.

GARGA: How soon?

SHLINK: Six months at the most. *He brings Garga the ledger.*

BABOON: This is a bog.

GARGA: Storks thrive on bogs.

BABOON: It's better to work with a switchblade than with phony papers. Can you forget that Chicago is cold?

GARGA: You meant your actual lumber business, didn't you, Shlink? The house, the logs, the whole inventory?

SHLINK: Of course. Here's the ledger.

GARGA: Pour ink over the ledger. You!

SKINNY: Me?

Shlink hands him a bottle of ink.

SKINNY *over the ledger:* All these entries! All our transactions!

GARGA: Go ahead, pour!

Skinny pours carefully.

BABOON: That's that.

WORM: What an ending after twenty years! Some joke! I don't get it. This used to be a lumber business.

GARGA: And now turn off the saws and that will be the end of this lumber business.

BABOON: Anything you say, boss! *Goes out.*

The sound of the saws outside stops. Shlink's cronies put on their coats and stand against the wall. Garga laughs loudly.

MARY: What are you doing, George?

GARGA: Shut up! Fire that man, Mr Shlink!

SHLINK: You may leave.,

SKINNY: Leave? After working in this place for twenty years come April?

SHLINK: You're fired.

MARY: I don't think you're doing right, George.

GARGA: I want you to go home, Mary.

MARY: And I want you to come with me. You'll only come to grief around here. Let him go, Mr Shlink.

SHLINK: Give me your orders, Garga.

GARGA: Certainly. As long as there's nothing left for you to do around here, my orders are to set up a little poker game with your former staff.

Shlink and his cronies sit down to play poker.

MARY: You're coming home with me, George. This whole thing is a joke, can't you see that?

GARGA: We grew up on the prairies, Mary. Here we're being sold out.

MARY: We? What do they want of us?

GARGA: You're of no consequence in all this. They're only trying to rope you in. Two weeks ago a man spat a small cherry pit into my eye. I come to see him. With a gun in my pocket. And he only bows and scrapes and offers me his lumber business. I don't understand a thing, but I accept. I'm alone on the prairie, and, Mary, I can't help you.

WORM *addressing Garga and Mary from behind:* He plays like a paper god. I swear he cheats.

GARGA *to Shlink:* I don't understand a thing, sir, I'm like a nigger in all this. I came with a white flag, but now I'm attacking. Give me the papers that are your fortune and hand over your personal assets. I'll put them in my pocket.

SHLINK: Paltry things, I beg you not to despise them. *Shlink and Garga go out.*

SKINNY: Things were bad around here and the rain came in on us, but being fired is always an injustice.

WORM: Don't talk like a fool. *Mocking him.* He thinks we've been talking about the mildew in the floor.

SKINNY: I love you, lady. You have a way of holding out your hand . . .

WORM: Christ! He's lost his bed, and he wants a woman to share it.

SKINNY: Come with me. I'll work for you. Come with me.

BABOON *also comes forward:* Pitiful! There are all sorts of women, black and golden yellow and white like apples! Black women. Straight as a die from hip to foot! Full thighs, by God, not chicken legs like this! Oh Papua! Forty dollars for Papua!

SHLINK *appears in the doorway and turns to call offstage:* Yes, that's all.

WORM *to the Baboon:* You're a barbarian. Ungrateful! The lady's innocent. Does she smoke a pipe? She's inexperienced, but who's to say she has no fire? Forty dollars, and all for the lady.

SKINNY: As much as you want for her!

BABOON: Without make-up, naturally, uncooked, the naked flesh. Ah, the tropics! Seventy dollars for the chick!

MARY: Protect me, Mr Shlink.

SHLINK: I'm ready to protect you.

MARY: Do you think I should go with him?

SHLINK: Here nobody loves you. He loves you.

GARGA *has entered:* Do you like being for sale? There's a lot of lumber here, and now they've put a few pounds of flesh up for auction! And isn't jiu-jitsu known as the gay and easy art?

SHLINK *walks up to Garga, troubled:* But aren't you making things too easy for yourself?

MARY *to Garga:* You should have helped me. Come with me, George, this minute. Something terrible has happened. Even if I go away now, this thing may not be over. You must be blind not to see that you're losing.

In the background, the sound of two guitars and a drum. Salvation Army girls sing: 'Christ receiveth sinful men.'

GARGA: I can see you're ready to lose yourself. It's the bog that's sucking you in. Here's something for you, Mary. The Salvation Army! Marching in here for you. *He gets up from the table and goes to the rear.* Hey! Salvation Army! This way!

WORM *to Mary:* A river has drained off here, and at night the place is haunted by the ghosts of drowned rats. Go home to your parents!

GARGA *coming back:* Clean this joint up. Get rid of that whisky! *Shlink starts to do so, but Mary does it for him.* Come in, you people.

Shlink, bowing low, opens the wooden gate. A young Salvation Army preacher enters, followed by two girls with guitars and an old sinner with a drum.

PREACHER: Did you want me?

WORM: Hallelujah! The Salvation Army!

GARGA: I don't think much of what you people are doing. You could use a house though. Here, take this one.

PREACHER: The Lord will bless you.

GARGA: Maybe. *To Shlink:* Did you inherit this house and these papers?

SHLINK: No.

GARGA: You worked forty years for them?

SHLINK: Worked my fingers to the bone. I never slept more than four hours.

GARGA: Were you poor when you came over?

SHLINK: I was seven. I've worked ever since.

GARGA: You don't own anything else?

SHLINK: Not a thing.

GARGA *to the preacher:* I'll give you this man's property on one condition. For the sake of the orphans and drunks whose shelter this will be, you must let me spit in your insufferable face.

PREACHER: I'm a man of God.

GARGA: Then take the consequences.

PREACHER: I have no right.

GARGA: Snow falls on the orphans, the drunks die like flies, and you take care of your face.

PREACHER: I'm ready. I've kept my face clean; I'm twenty-one. You must have your reasons I beg you to understand me: please ask the lady to turn around.

MARY: I'll despise you if you accept.

PREACHER: I expect that. There are better faces than mine. But none too good for this.

GARGA: Spit in his face, Shlink, if you please.

MARY: This isn't right, George. I don't like it.

GARGA: A tooth for a tooth, if you please.

Shlink steps coolly up to the Preacher and spits in his face. Worm bleats like a goat. The reformed sinner plays a drum roll.

PREACHER *shaking his fists, in tears:* Excuse me.

GARGA *throws the papers at him:* Here is the deed of gift. For the Salvation Army. And this is for you. *Gives him his gun.* Now get out, you swine!

PREACHER: I thank you in the name of my mission. *He leaves, bowing awkwardly. The hymn singing fades with striking speed.*

GARGA: You spoiled my fun. Your brutality has no equal.

I'll keep some of the money. But I'm not staying here, because this is the point of the whole thing, Mr Shlink from Yokohama: I'm going to Tahiti.

MARY: You're yellow, George. When the preacher left, you winced. I saw you. How desperate you are!

GARGA: I came here peeled to the bones. Trembling from the spiritual debauches of the last two weeks. I spat in his face many times. Each time he swallowed it. I despise him. It's all over.

MARY: Disgusting!

GARGA: You left me in the lurch. A tooth for a tooth.

MARY: And now you're going to carry on the fight with me? You never knew where to stop. God will punish you. I want nothing from you, only my peace.

GARGA: And to find bread for your parents in a whore's bed. And to offer your horse's smell for sale and say: It's not me! That you may prosper in bed and dwell long upon the earth. *He exits with the others.*

MARY: I don't really understand you, Mr Shlink. But you can go in all four directions, while others have only one. A man has many possibilities, hasn't he? I can see that a man has many possibilities. *Shlink shrugs his shoulders, turns around and leaves. Mary follows him.*

3

Living-room of the Garga Family

22 August, after 7 p.m.
A filthy attic. In the rear a curtain hangs in front of a small balcony. John Garga and his wife Mae. Manky is singing a song.

JOHN: Something has happened here that's hard to talk about.

MANKY: They say your son George is mixed up in the kind of

deal that never ends. They say he's mixed up with a yellow man. The yellow man has done something to him.

MAE: We can't interfere.

JOHN: If he's been fired, we can eat grass.

MAE: Ever since he was a little boy, he's had to have things his way.

MANKY: They say you shouldn't have hired out your daughter, Mary, to this yellow man.

MAE: Yes, Mary's been gone two weeks now too.

MANKY: People must be beginning to see that it all hangs together.

MAE: When our daughter left, she told us she'd been offered a job in a lumber business. Ten dollars a week and only linen to attend to.

MANKY: Linen for a yellow man!

JOHN: In cities like this nobody can see the next house. When people read a newspaper, they never know what it means.

MANKY: Or when they buy a ticket.

JOHN: When they ride in these electric trolleys, it probably gives them . . .

MANKY: Stomach cancer.

JOHN: Nobody knows. Here in the States wheat grows summer and winter.

MANKY: But suddenly, without any warning, there's no dinner for you. You walk in the street with your children, observing the fourth commandment to the letter, and suddenly you've only got your son's or daughter's hand in your hand, and your son and daughter themselves have sunk into a sudden gravel pit.

JOHN: Hello, who's there?

Garga stands in the doorway.

GARGA: Still chewing the fat?

JOHN: Have you finally got the money for the two weeks?

GARGA: Yes.

JOHN: Have you still got your job or not? A new jacket! Looks like you've been well paid for something? Huh?

There's your mother, George. *To Mae:* Why are you standing there like Lot's wife? Your son's here. Our son has come to take us out to dinner at the Metropolitan Bar. Your darling son looks pale, doesn't he? Slightly drunk maybe. Come on, Manky, let's go. We'll smoke our pipes on the stairs!

Both go out.

MAE: Tell me, George, are you mixed up with somebody?

GARGA: Has somebody been here?

MAE: No.

GARGA: I've got to go away.

MAE: Where?

GARGA: Any place. You always get scared at once.

MAE: Don't go away.

GARGA: I've got to. One man insults another. That's disagreeable for the man who gets insulted. But under certain circumstances the first man is willing to give up a whole lumber business for the pleasure of insulting the other. That's even more disagreeable for the second man. Maybe when he's been insulted like that, he'd better leave town. But since that might be too pleasant for him, even that may no longer be possible. In any case, he's got to be free.

MAE: Aren't you free?

GARGA: No. *Pause.* We're none of us free. It starts in the morning with our coffee, and we're beaten if we play the fool. A mother salts her children's food with her tears and washes their shirts with her sweat. And their future is secure until the Ice Age, and the root sits in their heart. And when you grow up and want to do something, body and soul, they pay you, brainwash you, label you, and sell you at a high price, and you're not even free to fail.

MAE: But tell me what's getting you down.

GARGA: You can't help me.

MAE: I can help you. Don't run away from your father. How are we going to live?

GARGA *giving her money:* I've been fired. But here's enough money for six months.

MAE: We're worried about not hearing from your sister. We hope she's still got her job.

GARGA: I don't know. I advised her to leave the yellow man.

MAE: I know you won't let me talk to you the way other mothers do.

GARGA: Oh, all those other people, the many good people, all the many other good people who stand at their lathes and earn their bread and make all the good tables for all the many good bread eaters; all the many good table makers and bread eaters with their many good families, so many, whole armies of them, and nobody spits in their soup, and nobody sends them into the next world with a good kick in the pants, and no flood comes over them to the tune of 'Stormy the night and the sea runs high'.[3]

MAE: Oh, George!

GARGA: No! Don't Oh, George me! I don't like it, and I don't want to hear it any more.

MAE: You don't want to hear it any more? But what about me? How am I to live? With these filthy walls and a stove that won't last through the winter.

GARGA: It's plain as day, Mother. Nothing can last long now, neither the stove nor the walls.

MAE: How can you say that? Are you blind?

GARGA: And neither will the bread in the cupboard or the dress on your back, and neither will your daughter for that matter.

MAE: Sure, go ahead and shout, so everybody can hear. How everything is useless and anything that takes an effort is too much and wears you down. But how am I to live? And I've still got so much time ahead of me.

GARGA: If it's as bad as all that, speak up. What makes it so bad?

MAE: You know.

GARGA: Yes, I know.

MAE: But the way you say that! What do you think I said? I won't have you looking at me like that. I gave you birth and fed you milk, I gave you bread and beat you, so don't look at me like that. A husband is what he wants to be, I won't say a word to him. He has worked for us.

GARGA: I want you to come with me.

MAE: What's that?

GARGA: Come south with me. I'll work, I can cut down trees. We'll build a log cabin and you'll cook for me. I need you terribly.

MAE: Who are you saying that to? The wind? When you come back, you can come by and see where we spent our last days. *Pause.* When are you leaving?

GARGA: Now.

MAE: Don't say anything to them. I'll get your things together and put your bundle under the stairs.

GARGA: Thank you.

MAE: Don't mention it.

Both go out.

Worm enters cautiously and sniffs around the room.

MANKY: Hey, who's there? *Comes in with John.*

WORM: Me, a gentleman. Mr Garga, I presume? Mr John Garga?

MANKY: What do you want?

WORM: Me? Nothing. Could I speak to your son – I mean, if he's had his bath?

JOHN: What's it all about?

WORM *sadly shaking his head:* What inhospitality! If it's not too much of an effort, could you tell me where your excellent son is taking his nap?

JOHN: He's gone away. Go to the devil. This isn't an information bureau.

Mae enters.

WORM: Too bad! Too bad! We miss your son terribly, sir. And it's about your daughter, too, in case you're interested.

MAE: Where is she?

WORM: In a Chinese hotel, milady, in a Chinese hotel.

JOHN: What?

MAE: Holy Mary!

MANKY: What's the meaning of this? What's she doing there?

WORM: Nothing, just eating. Mr Shlink wants me to tell you and your son that he should come and get her. She's too expensive, it's running into money, the lady's got a healthy appetite. She doesn't lift a finger. But she pursues us with immoral propositions. She's demoralizing the hotel. She'll have the police after us.

MAE: John!

WORM *shouting:* We're sick of her.

MAE: Christ!

MANKY: Where is she? I'll get her right away.

WORM: Sure, you'll get her. Are you a bird dog? How do you know where the hotel is? You young fool! It's not so simple. You should have kept an eye on the lady. It's all your son's fault. Tell him to call for the bitch and kindly look after her. Or tomorrow night we'll get the police on the move.

MAE: Good God. Just tell us where she is. I don't know where my son is. He's gone away. Don't be hard-hearted. Oh, Mary! John, plead with him. What's happened to Mary? What's happening to me? Oh, George! John, what a city this is! What people! *Goes out.*

Shlink appears in the doorway.

WORM *mutters in a fright:* Yes, I . . . this place has two entrances . . . *Sneaks out.*

SHLINK *simply:* My name is Shlink. I used to be a lumber dealer, now I catch flies. I'm all alone in the world. Can you rent me a place to sleep? I'll pay board. On the door plate downstairs I recognized the name of a man I know.

MANKY: Your name is Shlink? You're the man who's been holding these people's daughter.

SHLINK: Who's that?

JOHN: Mary Garga, sir. My daughter, Mary Garga.

SHLINK: Don't know her. I don't know your daughter.

JOHN: The gentleman who was just here . . .

MANKY: Sent by you, I presume.

JOHN: Who slipped away the moment you came in.

SHLINK: I don't know the gentleman.

JOHN: But you and my son . . .

SHLINK: You're making fun of a poor man. Of course there's no danger in insulting me. I've gambled away my fortune; often you don't know how these things happen.

MANKY: What I say is, when I steer my ship into port, I know my channel.

JOHN: You can't trust anybody.

SHLINK: Lonely through sheer bungling at an age when the ground must close if snow is not to fall into the crevices, I see you deserted by your breadwinner. I'm not without compassion; and if you'll keep me, my work will have a purpose.

JOHN: Reasons won't fill anybody's stomach. We're not beggars. We can't eat fish heads. But our hearts aren't made of stone, we feel for your loneliness. Your elbows want to rest on a family table. We're poor people.

SHLINK: I like everything, I can digest gravel.

JOHN: It's a small room. We're already packed in like sardines.

SHLINK: I can sleep on the floor, and a space half my length is good enough for me. I'm as happy as a child as long as my back's protected from the wind. I'll pay half the rent.

JOHN: All right, I understand. You don't want to wait out in the wind. You may share our roof.

MAE *comes in:* I've got to hurry downtown before dark.

JOHN: You're always gone when I need you. I'm taking this man in. He's lonely. There's room now that your son has run away. Shake hands with him.

MAE: Our home was on the prairies.

SHLINK: I know.

JOHN: What are you doing in the corner?

MAE: I'm making up my bed under the stairs.

JOHN: Where's your bundle?

SHLINK: I have nothing. I'll sleep on the stairs, ma'am. I won't intrude. My hand will never touch you. I know the skin on it is yellow.

MAE *coldly:* I'll give you mine.

SHLINK: I don't deserve it. I meant what I said. I know you didn't mean your skin. Forgive me.

MAE: I open the window over the stairs at night. *Goes out*.

JOHN: She's a good soul under that skin.

SHLINK: God bless her. I'm a simple man, don't expect words from my mouth. I've only teeth in it.

4

Chinese Hotel

The Morning of 24 August
Skinny, Baboon and Jane.

SKINNY *in the doorway:* Aren't you even thinking of starting a new business?

BABOON *lying in a hammock, shakes his head:* All the boss does is walk along the waterfront, checking the passengers on the ships bound for Tahiti. Some fellow has run off with his soul and his entire fortune, maybe to Tahiti. It's him he's looking for. He's brought what was left of his belongings for safekeeping, down to the last cigar butt. *Referring to Jane:* And he's been feeding this here free of charge for the last three weeks. He's even taken the fellow's sister in. What he means to do with her is a mystery to me. He often sits up all night, talking to her.

SKINNY: You've let him put you out in the street, and now you feed him and his hangers-on too?

BABOON: He makes a few dollars hauling coal, but he gives them to the fellow's family; he's taken up lodging with them, but he can't live there, they don't like having him around. That fellow really took him for a ride. He got himself a cheap trip to Tahiti and hung a tree trunk over the boss's head that's likely to come crashing down any minute;

because in five months at the most they're going to drag him into court for selling the same lumber twice.

SKINNY: And you bother to feed a wreck like that?

BABOON: He had to have his little joke. A man like him can always get credit. If that fellow stays lost, the boss will be back at the top of the lumber business in three months.

JANE *half dressed, making up:* I've always thought I'd end up like this: in a Chinese flophouse.

BABOON: You've no idea what's in store for you.

Two voices are heard from behind a screen.

MARY: Why don't you ever touch me? Why are you always wearing that smoky sack? I've got a suit for you, like other men wear. I can't sleep; I love you.

JANE: Pst! Listen! You can hear them again.

SHLINK: I am unworthy. I don't know anything about virgins. And I've been conscious of the smell of my race for years.

MARY: Yes, it's a bad smell. Yes, it's bad.

SHLINK: Why cut yourself in pieces like that? Look: My body is numb, it even affects my skin. Man's skin in its natural state is too thin for this world, that's why people do their best to make it thicker.[4] The method would be satisfactory if the growth could be stopped. A piece of leather, for instance, stays the way it is, but a man's skin grows, it gets thicker and thicker.

MARY: Is it because you can't find an opponent?

SHLINK: In the first stage a table has edges; later on, and that's the nasty part of it, the same table is like rubber, but in the thick-skinned stage there's neither table nor rubber.

MARY: How long have you had this disease?

SHLINK: Since I was a boy on the rowboats on the Yangtze Kiang. The Yangtze tortured the junks and the junks tortured us. There was a man who trampled our faces every time he stepped into the boat. At night we were too lazy to move our faces away. Somehow the man was never too lazy. We in turn had a cat to torture. She was drowned

while learning to swim, though she'd eaten the rats that
were all over us. All those people had the disease.

MARY: When were you on the Yangtze Kiang?

SHLINK: We lay in the reeds in the early morning and felt the
disease growing.

WORM *enters:* The wind has swallowed the fellow. There's
neither hide nor hair of him in all Chicago.

SHLINK: You'd better get some sleep. *Steps out.* Still no
news?

*Shlink goes out; through the open door the sound of Chicago waking
is heard, the shouts of the milkmen, the rumbling of meat waggons.*

MARY: Chicago is waking up. The shouting of milkmen, the
rumbling of meat waggons, the newspapers and the fresh
morning air. It would be good to go away, it's good to
wash in water, there's something good about the prairie
and the asphalt.⁵ Right now, for instance, there's surely a
cool wind in the prairies where we used to live.

BABOON: Do you still know your shorter catechism, Jane?

JANE *droning:* Things are getting worse, things are getting
worse, things are getting worse.

*They begin to straighten the room, pull up the blinds, and stand the
sleeping mats up.*

MARY: For my part, I'm a little out of breath. I want to sleep
with a man and I don't know how. Some women are like
dogs, yellow and black ones. But I can't do it. I'm all torn
apart. These walls are like paper. You can't breathe.
You've got to set it all on fire. Where are the matches, a
black box, to make the water come in. Oh, if I swim away,
I'll be in two parts, swimming in two different directions.

JANE: Where has he gone?

BABOON: He's looking into the faces of all the people who
are leaving town because Chicago's too cruel.

JANE: There's an east wind. The Tahiti-bound ships are
weighing anchor.

5

Same Hotel

A month later, 19 or 20 September
A filthy bedroom. A hall. A glass-enclosed bar. Worm, George Garga, Manky and Baboon.

WORM *from the hall towards the bar:* He never sailed after all. The harpoon is in deeper than we thought. We thought the earth had swallowed him up. But now he's in Shlink's room, licking his wounds.

GARGA *in the bedroom:* That dog Shlink. 'In my dreams I call him my infernal bridegroom.[6] We are parted from bed and board, he has no room any more. His little bride smokes stogies, and tucks money away in her stocking.' That's me! *Laughs.*

MANKY *in the bar behind the glass partition:* Life is strange. I knew a man who was really tops, but he loved a woman. Her family was starving. He had two thousand dollars, but he let them starve before his eyes. Because with those two thousand dollars he loved the woman, without them he couldn't get her. That was infamous, but he can't be held responsible.

GARGA: 'Behold, I am a sinner. I loved deserts, burnt orchards, run-down shops, and hot drinks.[7] You are mistaken. I am a little man.' I'm through with Mr Shlink from Yokohama.

BABOON: Take that lumber dealer. He never had any heart. But one day a passion made him wreck his whole lumber business. And now he's hauling coal down there. He had the whole neighbourhood by the throat.

WORM: We took him in the way you might take in an exhausted pedigree dog. But now by some stroke of luck his lost bone has turned up again, and if he won't let it go our patience will be at an end.

GARGA: 'One day I'll be his widow. That day, I know, has already been marked on the calendar. And I in clean underwear shall walk behind his corpse, swinging my legs lustily in the warm sun.'[8]

MARY *enters with a lunch basket:* George.

GARGA: Who's that? *Recognizing her.* Good God! You look like a soiled rag!

MARY: I know.

WORM *in the direction of the bar:* He's dead drunk. And now his sister has come to see him. He's told her that she's soiled. Where's the old man?

BABOON: He's coming today. I've brought Jane. For bait, I suppose. There won't be any punches pulled in this fight.

JANE *shakes her head:* I don't understand you. Give me a drink. Gin.

MARY: I'm glad to see you had a better opinion of me. Or you wouldn't be surprised to see me here now. Besides, I remind you of the days when you were the pride of women, dancing the shimmy and ragtime with a crease in your pants on Saturday night, when your only vices were tobacco, whisky and the love of women, the legitimate vices of men. I wish you'd think of that, George. *Pause.* How do you live?

GARGA *lightly:* It gets cold here at night. Do you need anything? Are you hungry?

MARY *lightly, shaking her head and looking at him:* Oh, George, we've had vultures over our heads for some time now.

GARGA *lightly:* When were you home last? *Mary is silent.* I heard you were spending your time around here.

MARY: Is that so? I wonder who's looking after them at home.

GARGA *coldly:* You needn't worry. I've heard that somebody's taking care of them. And I know what you've been doing. And I know something about a certain Chinese hotel too.

MARY: Does it make you feel good to be so cold-hearted, George?

Garga looks at her.

MARY: Don't look at me like that. I know you expect a confession.

GARGA: Go ahead!

MARY: I love him. Why don't you say something?

GARGA: Go ahead and love him. That will weaken him.

MARY: For God's sake, stop looking at the ceiling. I can't win him.

GARGA: That's disgraceful.

MARY: I know. – Oh, George, I'm torn in two. Because I can't win him. I tremble under my dress when I see him and I say the wrong thing.

GARGA: I can't tell you the right thing. A rejected woman! I had one once who wasn't worth a bottle of rum, but she knew how to attract men. She got paid for it too. And she knew her power.

MARY: You say such biting things. They swim in my head like gin. But are they good? You ought to know if they're good. But I understand you now.

Shlink enters the hall.

WORM: I can tell you from experience: humanity has fallen fists over calluses for a lot of paper dreams. And nothing is so much like paper as real life. *Mary Garga turns round and bumps into Shlink.*

SHLINK: You here, Miss Garga?

MARY: It's considered wrong for a woman to tell a man she loves him. But I'd like to tell you that my love for you doesn't prove a thing. I don't want anything from you. It's not easy for me to tell you that. Maybe you knew it all along.

GARGA *comes out of the bedroom:* Stay here, Mary. We've got the prairies written on our faces, and here we've been tossed into the city. Don't hold back. Do what you want to do.

MARY: Yes, George.

GARGA: He works like a horse, and I lie lazily in a pool of absinthe.

SHLINK: The men who conquer the world like to lie on their backs.

GARGA: And those who own it work.

SHLINK: Are you worried?

GARGA *to Shlink:* Every time I look at you, you're sizing me up. Have you backed the wrong horse? Your face has grown old.

SHLINK: Thank you for not forgetting me. I was beginning to think you had gone south. Forgive me. I have taken the liberty of supporting your unfortunate family with the work of my hands.

GARGA: Is that true, Mary? I didn't know that. You've wormed your way in? You're vile enough to support my family, and you enjoy it? You hand me a laugh. *Goes left into the bedroom, lies down, and laughs.*

SHLINK *follows him:* Go ahead and laugh, I like to hear you laugh. Your laughter is my sunshine, it was misery here. It's been dismal without you. It's been three weeks, Garga.

GARGA: I've been satisfied, all in all.

SHLINK: Of course. You've been rolling in clover.

GARGA: Only my back is getting thin as a rail from lying on it.

SHLINK: How pitiful life is! You're rolling in clover and the clover's not sweet enough.

GARGA: I expect more out of life than to wear my shoes out kicking you.

SHLINK: Kindly take no notice of my insignificant person or my intentions. But I'm still here. If you have to quit, you won't leave the ring in innocence.

GARGA: I'm quitting, though. I'm going on strike. I throw in the towel. Have I sunk my teeth so deep into you? You're a small hard betel nut, I ought to spit it out, I know it's harder than my teeth and that it's only a shell.

SHLINK *pleased:* I'm doing my best to give you all the light you need. I show myself in every possible light, Mr Garga. *Goes under the lamp.*

GARGA: You want to auction off your pock-marked soul? Are you hardened to all suffering? Utterly callous?

SHLINK: Crack the nut.

GARGA: You're withdrawing into my corner. You're staging a metaphysical fight, but leaving a slaughterhouse behind you.

SHLINK: You mean this business with your sister? I haven't butchered anything your hands protected.

GARGA: I have only two hands. Whatever is human to me you devour like a chunk of meat. You open my eyes to possible sources of help by choking them off. You use my family to help yourself. You live on my reserves. I'm getting thinner and thinner. I'm getting metaphysical. And on top of everything, you vomit all this in my face.

MARY: Please, George, can't I go now? *She retreats towards the rear.*

GARGA *pulling her forward:* No, certainly not! We've just started talking about you. I've just noticed you.

SHLINK: It's my misfortune to tread on delicate ground. I'll retreat. You're never aware of your affections until their objects are in the morgue, and I feel the need of acquainting you with your affections. But please proceed, I understand you perfectly.

GARGA: But I am making sacrifices. Have I refused?

MARY: Let me go. I'm afraid.

GARGA: This way, sir. *Runs into the hall.* Let's start a family!

MARY: George!

GARGA: Stay here! *In the direction of the bedroom.* I demand a little human involvement on your part, sir.

SHLINK: I wouldn't say no for a minute.

GARGA: You love this man? And he's indifferent? *Mary weeps.*

SHLINK: I hope you're not overestimating your power. *Runs back to the bedroom.*

GARGA: Don't worry. This will be a step forward. Let's see

now, this is Thursday night. This is the Chinese hotel and this is my sister, Mary Garga. *Runs out.* Come here, Mary. My sister. This is Mr Shlink from Yokohama. He has something to tell you.

MARY: George!

GARGA *goes out to get drinks:* 'I fled into the outskirts of the city, where women with crooked orange mouths cower white in glowing thorn bushes.'

MARY: It's dark in the window and I want to go home now.

SHLINK: I'll go with you if you like.

GARGA: 'Their hair was black-lacquered shells, ever so thin, their eyes were dulled by the winds of debauch in the drunken night and by sacrifices in the open fields.'

MARY *softly:* Please don't ask me that.

GARGA: 'Their thin dresses, like iridescent snake skins drenched with never-ending rain slapped against their for ever excited limbs.'

SHLINK: I meant it when I asked you. I have no secrets from anyone.

GARGA: 'They cover their legs to the very toenails, which are incrusted with molten copper; the madonna in the clouds turns pale at the sight of her sisters.' *Comes back, hands Shlink a glass.* Won't you drink? I find it necessary.

SHLINK: Why do you drink? Drinkers lie.[9]

GARGA: It's fun talking with you. When I drink, half my thoughts float downward. I guide them to the ground and then they seem lighter. Drink!

SHLINK: I'd rather not. But if you insist.

GARGA: I'm inviting you to drink with me and you refuse.

SHLINK: I don't refuse, but my brain is all I've got.

GARGA *after a moment:* Forgive me, let's go halves: You'll turn off your brain. When you've drunk, you'll make love.

SHLINK *drinks as in a ritual:* When I have drunk, I'll make love.

GARGA *calls from the bedroom:* Won't you have a drink, Mary? No? Why don't you sit down?

BABOON: Shut up. I could hear them talking before. Now they're not saying anything.

GARGA *to Mary:* This is the Black Pit. Forty years are passing. I don't say no. The ground is giving way, the water of the sewers rises to the surface, but the tide of their lusts is too weak. For four hundred years I have dreamed of mornings on the ocean, I had the salt wind in my eyes. How smooth it was! *He drinks.*

SHLINK *submissively:* I ask you for your hand, Miss Garga. Shall I throw myself humbly at your feet? Please come with me. I love you.

MARY *runs into the bar:* Help! They're selling me!

MANKY: Here I am, beautiful!

MARY: I knew you'd be wherever I am.

GARGA: 'Like at the opera, a breeze opens gaps in the partitions.'[10]

SHLINK *bellowing:* Will you kindly come out of the bar, Mary Garga! *Mary comes out of the bar.* I beg you, don't throw yourself away, Miss Garga.

MARY: All I want is a little room with nothing in it. I've stopped wanting very much, Pat, I promise you that I never will again.

GARGA: Fight for your chance, Shlink.

SHLINK: Think of the years that won't pass, Mary Garga, and think how sleepy you are.

MANKY: Come with me, I've got four hundred pounds, that means a roof in the winter and no more ghosts except in the morgues.

SHLINK: I implore you, Mary Garga, come with me. I shall treat you like my wife and wait on you and hang myself without any fuss if ever I hurt you.

GARGA: He's not lying. I promise you that. That's what you'll get if you go with him. Down to the last cent. *Goes into the bar.*

MARY: Tell me, Pat, even if I don't love you, do you love me?

MANKY: I think so, beautiful. And it's not written anywhere between heaven and earth that you don't love me.

GARGA: Is that you, Jane? Polishing off the cocktails? You don't look exactly yourself. Have you sold everything?

JANE: Get rid of him, Baboon. I can't stand his face. He's molesting me. Even if I'm not living in milk and honey these days, I don't have to put up with ridicule.

BABOON: I'll crack the nose of any man who says you're an old shoe.

GARGA: Did they feed you too? Your face looks like a lemon ice that's been left standing. Damn it all, you used to wear glad rags like an opera singer, and now you look as if they'd sprinkled you with black powder. But I'll say this much: you didn't come of your own accord when only the flies made spots on you, my drunken chick.

MARY: Let's go, then. I'd have gladly obliged you, Shlink, but I can't. It's not pride.

SHLINK: Stay if you like. I won't repeat my offer if it displeases you. But don't let the pit swallow you up. There are many places to get away from a man.

GARGA: Not for a woman. Forget it, Shlink. Don't you see what she's driving at? If you'd preferred a roof in the winter, Jane, you'd still be sewing shirts.

SHLINK: Drink before you make love, Mary Garga.

MARY: Come, Pat. This isn't a good place. Is this your woman, George? Is she? I'm glad I had a chance to see her. *Out with Manky.*

SHLINK *calls after her:* I won't forsake you. Come back when you've found out.

BABOON: An old shoe, gentlemen, well worn. *He laughs.*

GARGA *shining a candle in Shlink's face:* Your face is in good shape. But where does your good will get me?

SHLINK: The sacrifices on both sides have been considerable. How many ships do you need to get to Tahiti? Do you want me to hoist my shirt for a sail, or your sister's? I hold you responsible for your sister's fate. You showed her that men would always treat her as an object. I haven't spoiled anything for you, I hope. I almost got her as a virgin, but you wanted me to have left-overs. And don't forget your family

that you're abandoning. Now you've seen what you are
sacrificing.

GARGA: I want to slaughter them all now. I know that. I
think I'll get the jump on you. And now I understand why
you've fattened them on what you earn hauling coal. I
won't let you do me out of my fun. And now I'm taking
delivery of this little animal that you've been keeping for
me.

JANE: I refuse to be insulted. I stand on my own feet, I
support myself.

GARGA: And now I request you to hand over the money you
made selling that lumber twice. I hope you've been keeping
it for me. The time has come.

Shlink takes out the money and gives it to Garga.

GARGA: I'm dead drunk. But drunk or sober, I've got a good
idea, Shlink, a very good idea. *Goes out with Jane.*

BABOON: That was your last money, sir. And where did it
come from? They'll be asking you about it. Broost & Co.
have demanded delivery of the lumber they paid for.

SHLINK *not listening to him:* A chair. *They have occupied the
chairs and do not stand up.* My rice and water.

WORM: There's no more rice for you, sir. Your account is
overdrawn.

6

Lake Michigan

The end of September
Woods: Shlink and Mary.

MARY: The trees look draped in human dung, the sky is
close enough to touch, but what is it to me? I'm cold. I'm
like a half-frozen quail. I can't help myself.

SHLINK: If it will do you any good, I love you.

MARY: I've thrown myself away. Why has my love turned to bitter fruit? Others have their summer when they love, but I'm withering away and tormenting myself. My body is soiled.

SHLINK: Tell me how low you feel. It will relieve you.

MARY: I lay in bed with a man who was like an animal. My whole body was numb, but I gave myself to him, many times, and I couldn't get warm. He smoked stogies in between, a seaman. I loved you every hour I spent between those papered walls, I was so obsessed that he thought it was love and wanted to stop me. I slept into the black darkness. I don't owe you anything, but my conscience cries out to me that I've soiled my body, which is yours even if you scorned it.

SHLINK: I'm sorry you're cold. I thought the air was warm and dark. I don't know what the men of this country say to the women they love. If it will do you any good: I love you.

MARY: I'm such a coward, my courage has gone with my innocence.

SHLINK: You'll wash yourself clean.

MARY: Maybe I ought to go down to the water, but I can't. I'm not ready yet. Oh, this despair! This heart that won't be appeased! I'm never anything more than half, I can't even love, it's only vanity. I hear what you say, I have ears and I'm not deaf, but what does it mean? Maybe I'm asleep, they'll come and wake me, and maybe it's just that I'd do the most shameful things to get a roof over my head, that I lie to myself and close my eyes.

SHLINK: Come, it's getting cold.

MARY: But the leaves are warm and shelter us from the sky that's too close. *They go out.*

MANKY *enters:* Her tracks point this way. You need a good sense of humour in a September like this. The crayfish are mating, the rutting cry of the deer is heard in the thicket, and the badger season is open. But my flippers are cold and

I've wrapped my black stumps in newspaper. Where can she be living? That's the worst of it. If she's lying around like a fishbone in that greasy saloon, she'll never have a clean petticoat again. Only stains. Oh, Pat Mankyboddle, I'm going to court-martial you. Too weak to defend myself, I'd better attack. I'll devour the no-good with skin and bones, I'll speed up my digestion with prayers, the vultures will be shot at sunrise and hung up in the Mankyboddle Museum. Brrr! Words! Toothless phrases! *He takes a revolver from his pocket.* This is the coldest answer! Stalk through the jungle looking for a woman, will you, you old swine! Down on all fours! Damn, this underbrush is suicide. Watch yourself, Paddy. Where can a woman go when it's all up with her? Let her go, Paddy boy, have a smoke, take a bite to eat, put that thing away. Forward, march! *Goes out.*

MARY *coming back with Shlink:* It's loathsome before God and man. I won't go with you.

SHLINK: Mouldy sentiments. Air out your soul.

MARY: I can't. You're making a sacrifice of me.

SHLINK: You've always got to have your head in some man's armpits, no matter whose.

MARY: I'm nothing to you.

SHLINK: You can't live alone.

MARY: You took me so quickly, as if you were afraid I'd get away. Like a sacrifice.

SHLINK: You ran into the bushes like a rabid bitch and now you're running out again like a rabid bitch.

MARY: Am I what you say? I'm always what you say. I love you. Never forget that, I love you. I love you like a bitch in heat. That's what you said. But now pay me. Yes, I'm in the mood to get paid. Give me your money, I'll live on it. I'm a whore.

SHLINK: Something wet is running down your face. What kind of a whore is that?

MARY: Don't make fun of me, just give me the money. Don't look at me. It's not tears that make my face wet, it's the fog.

Shlink gives her paper money. I won't thank you, Mr Shlink from Yokohama. It's a straight business deal, no need for thanks.

SHLINK: You'd better be going. You won't make money here. *Goes out.*

7

The Garga Family's Living-room

29 September 1912
The room is full of new furniture. John Garga, Mae, George, Jane, Manky, all dressed in new clothes for the wedding dinner.

JOHN: Ever since that man we don't like to speak of, who has a different skin but who goes down to the coal yards to work night and day for a family he knows; ever since the man in the coal yards with the different skin has been watching over us, things have been getting better for us every day, in every way. Today, without knowing of the wedding, he's made it possible for our son George to have a wedding worthy of the director of a big business. New ties, black suits, the breath of whisky on our lips – amid new furniture.

MAE: Isn't it strange that the man in the coal yards should make so much hauling coal?

GARGA: I make the money.

MAE: From one day to the next you decided to get married. Wasn't it a little sudden, Jane?

JANE: The snow melts, and where is it then? And you can pick the wrong man, it often happens.

MAE: Right man, wrong man, that's not the question. The question is whether you stick to him.

JOHN: Nonsense! Eat your steak and give the bride your hand.

GARGA *takes Jane by the wrist:* It's a good hand. I'm all right here. Let the wallpaper peel, I've got new clothes, I eat steak, I can taste the plaster, I've got half an inch of mortar all over me, I see a piano. Hang a wreath on the picture of our dear sister, Mary Garga, born twenty years ago on the prairies. Put everlastings under glass. It's good to sit here, good to lie here, the black wind doesn't come in here.

JANE *stands up:* What's the matter, George? Have you a fever?

GARGA: I feel fine in my fever, Jane.

JANE: I keep wondering what your plans are for me, George.

GARGA: Why are you so pale, mother? Isn't your prodigal son back again under your roof? Why are you all standing against the wall like plaster statues?

MAE: Perhaps because of the fight you keep talking about.

GARGA: It's only flies in my brain. I can shoo them away. *Shlink enters.* Mother, get a steak and a glass of whisky for our welcome guest. I was married this morning. My dear wife, tell him!

JANE: Fresh out of bed this morning, my husband and I went to the sheriff and said: Can we be married here? He said: I know you, Jane – will you always stay with your husband? But I saw that he was a good man with a beard, he had nothing against me, so I said: Life isn't exactly the way you think.

SHLINK: Congratulations, Garga. You're a vindictive man.

GARGA: There's a hideous fear in your smile! For good reason. Don't eat too fast. You have plenty of time. Where's Mary? I hope she's being taken care of. Your satisfaction must be complete. Unfortunately there's no chair for you at the moment, Shlink. We're one chair short. Otherwise our furnishings are new and complete. Look at the piano. A delightful place. I mean to spend my evenings here with my family. I've started a new life. Tomorrow I'm going back to C. Maynes's lending library.

MAE: Oh, George, aren't you talking too much?

GARGA: Do you hear that? My family doesn't want me to

have anything more to do with you. Our acquaintance is at an end, Mr Shlink. It has been most profitable. The furniture speaks for itself. My family's wardrobe speaks loud and clear. There's plenty of cash. I thank you.

Silence.

SHLINK: May I ask just one favour of you? A personal matter. I have a letter here from the firm of Broost & Co. It bears the seal of the Attorney-General of the State of Virginia. I haven't opened it yet. You would oblige me by doing so. Any news, even the worst, would be more acceptable to me from your lips. *Garga reads the letter.* Of course this is my own private affair, but a hint from you would make things much easier for me.

MAE: Why don't you say something, George? What are you planning to do, George? You look as if you were planning something. There's nothing that frightens me more. You men hide behind your unknown thoughts as if they were smoke. And we wait like cattle before slaughter. You say: wait a while, you go away, you come back, and you're unrecognizable. And we don't know what you've done to yourselves. Tell me your plan, and if you don't know what it is, admit it, so I'll know what to do. I've got to plan my life too. Four years in this city of steel and dirt! Oh, George!

GARGA: You see, the bad years were the best, and now they're over. Don't say anything to me. You, my parents, and you, Jane, my wife, I've decided to go to jail.

JOHN: What are you saying? Is that where your money comes from? It was written on your face when you were five years old that you'd end up in jail. I never asked what went on between the two of you, I knew it was rotten. You've both lost the ground from under your feet. Buying pianos and going to jail, dragging in whole armloads of steak and robbing a family of its livelihood is all the same to you. Where's Mary, your sister? *He tears off his jacket and throws it on the floor.* There's my jacket, I never wanted to put it on. But I'm used to the kind of humiliations this city still has in store for me.

JANE: How long will it be, George?

SHLINK *to John:* Some lumber was sold twice. Naturally that means jail, because the sheriff isn't interested in the circumstances. I, your friend, could explain certain things to the sheriff as neatly and simply as Standard Oil explains its tax returns. I am prepared to listen to your son, Mrs Garga.

JANE: Don't let them talk you into anything, George, do what you see fit, regardless. I, your wife, will keep the house running while you're gone.

JOHN *laughing loudly:* She's going to keep the house running! A girl who was picked off the streets only yesterday. We're to be fed by the wages of sin!

SHLINK *to George:* You've given me to understand that your family means a great deal to you. You'd like to spend your evenings among this furniture. You'll have a thought or two for me, your friend, who is busy making things easier for you all. I am prepared to save you for your family's sake.

MAE: You can't go to jail, George.

GARGA: I know you don't understand, Mother. It's so hard to harm a man, to destroy him is utterly impossible. The world is too poor. We wear ourselves out cluttering it with things to fight about.

JANE *to Garga:* There you go philosophizing with the roof rotting over our heads.

GARGA *to Shlink:* Search the whole world, you'll find ten evil men and not one evil action. Only trifles can destroy a man. No, I'm through. I'll draw a line under the account, and then I'll go.

SHLINK: Your family would like to know if they mean anything to you. If you won't hold them up, they'll fall. One little word, Garga!

GARGA: I give you all your freedom.

SHLINK: They'll rot, and you'll be to blame. There aren't many of them left. They might take a notion, just like you, to make a clean sweep, to cut up the dirty tablecloth and shake the cigar butts out of their clothes. The whole lot of them might decide to imitate you, to be free and indecent, with slobber on their shirts.

MAE: Be still, George, everything he says is true.

GARGA: Now at last, if I half close my eyes, I see certain things in a cold light. Not your face, Mr Shlink, maybe you haven't got one.

SHLINK: Forty years have been written off as so much dirt, and now there will be a great freedom.

GARGA: That's how it is. The snow tried to fall, but it was too cold. My family will eat left-overs again, and again they'll be hungry. But I, I will strike down my enemy.

JOHN: All I see is weakness, nothing else. Since the day I first laid eyes on you. Go ahead and leave us. Why shouldn't they take the furniture away?

GARGA: I've read that feeble waters erode whole mountains. And I still want to see your face, Shlink, your damned invisible, frosted-glass face.

SHLINK: I have no desire to talk with you any further. Three years. For a young man that's no more than a swing of the door. But for me! I've drawn no profit from you if that's any comfort to you. But you're not leaving a trace of sadness in me, now that I'm going back into the noisy city to carry on my business as I did before we met. *Exit*.

GARGA: All that remains for me to do now is phone the police. *Exit*.

JANE: I'm going to the Chinese bar. I can do without the police. *Exit*.

MAE: Sometimes I think Mary will never come back either.

JOHN: She has only herself to blame. Can we be expected to help them when they live in vice?

MAE: Is there any better time to help them?

JOHN: Don't talk so much.

MAE *sits down next to him*: I wanted to ask you: what are you going to do now?

JOHN: Me? Nothing. This part of our life is over.

MAE: You understand, don't you, what George is going to do to himself?

JOHN: Yes. More or less. It won't help us any.

MAE: And what are you going to live on?

JOHN: On the money that's still left. And we'll sell the piano.

MAE: They'll take it away, it was come by dishonestly.

JOHN: Maybe we'll go back to Ohio. We'll do something.

MAE *stands up:* There's something else I wanted to tell you, John, but I can't. I've never believed that a man could suddenly be damned. It's decided in heaven. This is a day like any other, and nothing has changed, but from this day on you're damned.

JOHN: What are you going to do?

MAE: I'm going to do a certain thing, John, something I want very much to do. Don't imagine I have any special reason. But first I'll put some coal on the fire, you'll find your supper in the kitchen. *Goes out.*

JOHN: Take care that the ghost of a shark doesn't eat you on the stairs.

WAITER *enters:* Mrs Garga has ordered you a grog. Do you wish to drink it in the dark, or should I put the light on?

JOHN: What do you think? Give us some light. *The waiter goes out.*

MARY *enters:* Don't make any speeches. I've brought money.

JOHN: You dare to set foot here? A fine family. And look at you!

MARY: I look fine. But where did you get all this new furniture? Have you taken in some money? I've taken in some money too.

JOHN: Where did you get the money?

MARY: Do you really want to know?

JOHN: Give it here. You people have brought me to this with hunger.

MARY: So you're taking my money? In spite of your new furniture? Where's Mother?

JOHN: Deserters are stood up against the wall.

MARY: Did you send her out on the streets?

JOHN: Be cynical, wallow in the gutter, drink grog. But I'm your father, you can't let me starve.

MARY: Where has she gone?

JOHN: You can go, too. I'm used to being left.

MARY: When did she leave here?

JOHN: At the end of my life I'm condemned to being poor and licking my children's spittle, but I won't have any truck with vice. I have no hesitation about throwing you out.

MARY: Give me back my money. It wasn't meant for you.

JOHN: Not a chance. You can sew me up in a shroud, I'll still beg for a pound of tobacco.

MARY: So long. *Goes out.*

JOHN: They've no more to say to a man than can be said in five minutes. Then they run out of lies. *Pause.* Actually everything there is to say could be covered in two minutes of silence.

GARGA *comes back:* Where's mother? Gone? Did she think I wasn't coming back up again? *He runs out and comes back.* She won't be back, she's taken her other dress. *He sits down at the table and writes a letter:* 'To *The Examiner.* I wish to call your attention to C. Shlink, the Malay lumber dealer. This man molested my wife, Jane Garga, and raped my sister, Mary Garga, who was in his employ. George Garga.' I won't say anything about my mother.

JOHN: That wipes out our family.

GARGA: I've written this letter. I'll put it in my pocket and forget the whole business. And in three years – that's how long they'll hold me – a week before I'm discharged, I'll send my letter to the newspaper. This man will be exterminated from this city, and when I come back he'll have vanished from my sight. But for him the day of my release will be marked by the howling of the lynch mobs.

8

C. Shlink's Private Office

20 October 1915, 1 p.m.
Shlink and a young clerk.

SHLINK *dictating:* Write to Miss Mary Garga, who has applied for a position as secretary, that I will never again have anything to do with either her or her family. To Standard Real Estate. Dear Sirs: As of today not a single share of our stock is in the hands of any outside firm and our business situation is secure. Consequently, there is nothing to prevent us from accepting your offer of a five-year contract.

AN EMPLOYEE *brings a man in:* This is Mr Shlink.

THE MAN: I've got three minutes to give you some information. You've got two minutes to understand your situation. Half an hour ago *The Examiner* received a letter from one of the state penitentiaries, signed by one Garga, showing you've committed a number of crimes. In five minutes the reporters will be here. You owe me a thousand dollars. *Shlink gives him the money. The man goes out.*

SHLINK *carefully packing his suitcase:* Carry on the business as long as you can. Mail these letters. I'll be back. *Goes out quickly.*

9

Bar Across the Street from the Prison

28 October 1915
Worm, Baboon, the Pugnosed Man, the Salvation Army Preacher,
Jane, Mary Garga. Noise from outside.

BABOON: Do you hear the howling of the lynch mob? These
are dangerous days for Chinatown. A week ago the crimes
of a Malayan lumber dealer came to light. Three years ago
he sent a man to prison, for three years the man kept quiet,
but a week before his release he wrote a letter to *The
Examiner*, telling the whole story.

THE PUGNOSED MAN: The human heart!

BABOON: The Malay himself, naturally, has skipped town.
But he's done for.

WORM: You can't say that about anybody. Consider the conditions on this planet. A man never gets finished off all at
once, but at least a hundred times. A man has too many
possibilities. For instance, let me tell you the story of
G. Wishu, the bulldog man. But I'll need the nickelodeon.
The nickelodeon is played. This is the story of the dog, George
Wishu. George Wishu was born on the Emerald Isle. When
he was eighteen months old a fat man took him to the great
city of London. His own country let him go like a stranger.
In London he soon fell into the hands of a cruel woman,
who subjected him to gruesome tortures. After much
suffering he ran away to the country, where he was hunted
down between green hedges. Men shot at him with big
dangerous guns, and strange dogs chased him. He lost a leg
and from then on he limped. After several of his under-
takings had failed, weary of life and half starved, he found
refuge with an old man who shared his bread with him.
Here, after a life full of disappointments and adventures, he

died at the age of seven and a half with great serenity and composure. He lies buried in Wales. – Now tell me, sir, how are you going to fit all that under one roof?

THE PUGNOSED MAN: Who is this man that's wanted?

WORM: It's the Malay they're looking for. He went bankrupt once before, but in three years he managed by all sorts of dodges to recover his lumber business, and that made him a lot of enemies in his neighbourhood. But no court could have touched him if a man in jail hadn't brought his sex crimes to light. *To Jane:* Exactly when is your husband getting out?

JANE: Yes, that's it: I knew it a while ago. Gentlemen, don't go thinking that I don't know. It's on the twenty-eighth, yesterday or today.

BABOON: Cut the comedy, Jane.

THE PUGNOSED MAN: And who's that woman in the indecent dress?

BABOON: That's the victim, the sister of the man in jail.

JANE: Yes, that's my sister-in-law. She pretends not to know me, but when I was married she never came home a single night.

BABOON: The Malay ruined her.

THE PUGNOSED MAN: What's she dropping into the sink behind the bar?

WORM: I can't see. She's saying something, too. Keep still, Jane.

MARY *lets a banknote flutter into the sink:* When I held the bills in my hand that day, I saw God's eye watching me. I said: I've done everything for him. God turned away, there was a sound like tobacco fields rustling in the wind. I kept them, though. One bill! Another! Pieces of myself! I'm giving my purity away. Now the money's gone! I don't feel any better . . .

GARGA *enters with C. Maynes and three other men:* I've asked you to come with me so you could see with your own eyes that I've been done an injustice. I've brought you with me, Mr Maynes, to witness the kind of place I find my wife in after three years of absence. *He leads the men to the table where Jane is sitting.* Hello, Jane. How are you?

JANE: George! Is this the twenty-eighth? I didn't know. I'd have been home. Did you notice how cold it is there? Did you guess I'd be sitting here just to get warm?

GARGA: This is Mr Maynes. You know him. I'm going back to work in his store. And these are neighbours who take an interest in my situation.

JANE: How do you do, gentlemen. Oh, George, it's awful for me that I missed your day. What will you gentlemen think of me? Ken Si, wait on the gentlemen.

BARMAN *to the Pugnosed Man:* That's the fellow from the pen who informed on him.

GARGA: Hello, Mary. Have you been waiting for me? My sister's here too, as you can see.

MARY: Hello, George. Are you all right?

GARGA: Let's go home, Jane.

JANE: Oh, George, you're just saying that. But if I go with you, you'll scold me when we get home. I'd better tell you right away that the housework hasn't been done.

GARGA: I know that.

JANE: That's mean of you.

GARGA: I'm not chiding you, Jane. We're going to make a fresh start. My fight is finished. I've driven my opponent from the city, and that's the end of it.

JANE: No, George. Things will keep getting worse and worse. People say things are going to get better, but they keep getting worse, they can do that. I hope you like it here, gentlemen. Of course we could go somewhere else . . .

GARGA: What's the matter, Jane? Aren't you glad I've come for you?

JANE: You know perfectly well, George. And if you don't, I can't tell you.

GARGA: What do you mean?

JANE: Don't you see, George, I'm different from what you think, even if I'm almost done for. Why did you bring these gentlemen? I've always known I'd end like this.

When they told me in Sunday school what happens to the weak, I said to myself: that's what will happen to me. You don't have to prove it to anybody.

GARGA: Then you won't come home?

JANE: Don't ask me, George.

GARGA: But I am asking you, my dear.

JANE: Then I'll have to put it a different way. I've been living with this man. *Points to Baboon.* I admit it, gentlemen. And what's the use? Nothing's going to get any better.

BABOON: She's out of her mind.

MAYNES: Dreadful!

GARGA: Listen to me, Jane. This is your last chance in this city. I'm ready to wipe the slate clean. These gentlemen are my witnesses. Come home with me.

JANE: It's nice of you, George. It certainly is my last chance. But I won't take it. Things aren't right between us, you know that. I'm going now, George. *To Baboon:* Come.

BABOON: That's that. *Both go out.*

ONE OF THE MEN: That fellow has nothing to laugh about.

GARGA: I'll leave the apartment open, Jane. You can ring at night.

WORM *steps up to the table:* You've probably noticed: there's a family here in our midst, or what's left of it. Moth-eaten as it is, this family would gladly give its last cent to find out where the mother, the mainstay of the household, is keeping herself. The fact is, I saw her one morning at about seven o'clock, a woman of forty, scrubbing a fruit cellar. She's started a new business. She'd aged but she was looking all right.

GARGA: But you, sir, didn't you work in the lumber business of the man they're combing every inch of Chicago for?

WORM: Me? No, I've never laid eyes on the man. *Goes out, on his way inserting a coin in the nickelodeon. It starts playing Gounod's 'Ave Maria'.*

THE PREACHER *at a corner table reads the liquor list aloud in a hard voice, savouring each word:* Cherry Flip, Cherry Brandy, Gin Fizz, Whisky Sour, Golden Slipper, Manhattan,

Curaçao extra dry, Orange, Maraschino Cusenier, and the specialty of the house, Egg-nog. This drink is made of egg – one raw egg – sugar, cognac, Jamaica rum, milk.

THE PUGNOSED MAN: Are you familiar with those drinks, sir?

PREACHER: No!

Laughter.

GARGA *to the men with him:* It has been necessary to show you my broken family, but you can see how humiliating it is for me. You will also have realized that that yellow weed must never again be allowed to take root in our city. My sister Mary, as you know, was in Shlink's employ for some time. In speaking to her now, of course, I shall have to proceed as carefully as possible, because even in her deepest misery my sister has preserved a certain trace of delicacy. *He sits down beside Mary.* Won't you let me see your face?

MARY: It's not a face any more. It's not me.

GARGA: No. But I remember once in church – when you were nine years old – you said: let him come to me beginning to-morrow. We thought you meant God.

MARY: Did I say that?

GARGA: I still love you, soiled and wasted as you are. But even if I knew that you knew you could do as you pleased with yourself if I told you I still loved you, I'd tell you all the same.

MARY: And you can look at me when you say that? At this face?

GARGA: That face. People remain what they are even if their faces fall apart.

MARY *stands up:* But I won't have it. I don't want you to love me that way. I like myself the way I was. Don't say I was never any different.

GARGA *in a loud voice:* Do you earn money? Do you live entirely on what you get from men?

MARY: And you've brought people to hear about it? Can I have some whisky? With plenty of ice. All right, I'll tell them. All right, I threw myself away, but as soon as I'd done it I asked for money, to make it plain what I am and that I can live on it. It's only a business arrangement. I've got a nice body, I never let a man smoke when he's with me, but I'm not a virgin any more, love is my job. I've got money here. But I'm going to earn more, I want to spend money, it's a craving I have; when I've made money, I don't want to save, here, I throw it down the sink. That's the way I am.

MAYNES: Horrible!

ANOTHER MAN: You wouldn't dare to laugh.

PREACHER: Man is too durable. That's his main fault. He can do too much to himself. He's too hard to destroy. *Goes out.*

MAYNES *standing up with the other three men:* We've seen, Garga, that you've suffered an injustice.

THE PUGNOSED MAN *approaches Mary:* Whores! *He guffaws.* Vice is a lady's perfume.

MARY: You call us whores. With this powder on our faces you can't see the eyes that were blue. The men who do business with crooks make love to us. We sell our sleep, we live on abuse.

A shot is heard.

BARMAN: The gentleman has shot himself in the neck. *The men bring in the Preacher and lay him down on the table among the glasses.*

FIRST MAN: Don't touch him. Hands off.

SECOND MAN: He's trying to say something.

FIRST MAN *bending over him, in a loud voice:* Do you want anything? Have you any relatives? Where should we take you?

PREACHER *mumbles:* 'La montagne est passée: nous irons mieux.' [11]

GARGA *standing over him, laughing:* He's missed, and in more ways than one. He thought those were his last words, but they're somebody else's, and anyway they're not his last words, because his aim was bad and it's only a small flesh wound.

FIRST MAN: So it is. Tough luck. He did it in the dark, he should have done it in the light.

MARY: His head is hanging down. Put something under it. How thin he is. I recognize him now. He spat in his face one time.

All except Mary and Garga go out with the wounded man.

GARGA: His skin is too thick. It bends anything you can stick into it. There aren't blades enough.

MARY: He's still on your mind?

GARGA: Yes, to you I can admit it.

MARY: Love and hate! How low they bring us!

GARGA: So they do. Do you still love him?

MARY: Yes ... yes.

GARGA: And no hope of better winds?

MARY: Yes, now and then.

GARGA: I wanted to help you. *Pause.* This fight has been such a debauch that today I need all Chicago to help me stop it. Of course it's possible that he himself wasn't planning to go on. He himself intimated that at his age three years can mean as much as thirty. In view of all these circumstances I've destroyed him with a very crude weapon. I didn't even have to be there in person. In addition, I've made it absolutely impossible for him to see me. This last blow will not be discussed between us, he won't be able to find me. You could call it a technical knockout, and on every street corner the taxi-drivers are watching to make sure that he won't show up in the ring again. Chicago has thrown in the towel for him. I don't know where he is, but he knows what's what.

BARMAN: The lumber yards in Mulberry Street are on fire.

MARY: If you've shaken him off, it's a good thing. But now I'm going.

GARGA: I'll stay here in the middle of the lynch mob. But I'll be home tonight. We'll live together. *Mary goes out.* Now I'll drink black coffee again in the morning, wash my face in cold water, and put on clean clothes, first of all a shirt. I'll comb a good many things out of my brain in the morning; there will be fresh noise and many things happening all around me in the city, now that I'm rid of that passion. It wanted to go down to the grave with me, but I've still got things to do. *Opens the door wide and listens laughing to the howling of the lynch mob that has grown louder.*

SHLINK *enters, wearing an American suit:* Are you alone? It was hard to get here. I knew you were getting out today, I've looked for you at your place. They're close at my heels. Quick, Garga, come with me.

GARGA: Are you out of your mind? I informed on you to get rid of you.

SHLINK: I'm not a brave man. I died three times on the way here.

GARGA: Yes. I hear they're hanging yellow men like linen on Milwaukee Bridge.

SHLINK: All the more reason for hurrying. You know you've got to come. We're not through yet.

GARGA *very slowly, aware of Shlink's haste:* Unfortunately your request comes at a bad time. I have company. My sister, Mary Garga, ruined in September three years ago, taken by surprise. My wife, Jane Garga, debauched at the same time. Last of all, a Salvation Army preacher, name unknown, spat on and destroyed, though it doesn't matter much. But most of all, my mother, Mae Garga, born in 1872 in the South, who disappeared three years ago this October and has vanished even from memory, now faceless. Her face fell off her like a yellow leaf. *Listens.* That howling!

SHLINK *also absorbed in listening:* Yes, but it's not the right kind of howling yet, the white kind. Then they'll be here. Then we'll still have a minute. Listen! Now! Now it's the right kind – white! Come! *Garga quickly leaves with Shlink.*

10

A Deserted Tent, formerly used by Railway Workers, in the Gravel Pits of Lake Michigan

19 November 1915, about 2 a.m.
Shlink, Garga.

SHLINK: The perpetual roar of Chicago has stopped. Seven times three days the skies have paled and the air turned grey-blue like grog. Now the silence has come, that conceals nothing.

GARGA *smoking:* Fighting comes as easy to you as digestion. I've been thinking about my childhood. The blue flax fields. The polecat in the gulches and the light-frothing rapids.

SHLINK: Right. All that was in your face. But now it's as hard as amber, which is transparent; here and there dead insects can be seen in it.

GARGA: You've always been alone?

SHLINK: Forty years.

GARGA: And now, towards the end, you've succumbed to the black plague of this planet, the lust for human contact.

SHLINK *smiling:* Through enmity?

GARGA: Through enmity.

SHLINK: Then you understand that we're comrades, comrades in a metaphysical conflict. Our acquaintance has been brief, for a time it overshadowed everything else, the time has passed quickly. The stations of life are not those of memory. The end is not the goal, the last episode is no more important than any other. Twice in my life I've owned a lumber business. For the last two weeks it has been registered in your name.

GARGA: Have you premonitions of death?

SHLINK: Here is the ledger of your lumber business; it begins where ink was once poured over the figures.

GARGA: You've been carrying it next to your skin? Open it yourself, it's sure to be filthy. *He reads.* A clean account. Nothing but withdrawals. On the seventeenth: the lumber deal. $25,000 to Garga. Just above: $10 for clothing. Below: $22 for Mary Garga, 'our' sister. At the very end: the whole business burned to the ground again. – I can't sleep any more. I'll be glad when you're covered with quicklime.

SHLINK: Don't deny the past, George! What's an account? Remember the question we raised. Brace yourself: I love you.

GARGA *looks at him:* That's disgusting! You're terrifyingly loathsome. An old man like you! [12]

SHLINK: Maybe I'll never get an answer. But if you get one, think of me when my mouth is full of dry rot. What are you listening for?

GARGA *lazily:* You show traces of feeling. You're old.

SHLINK: Is it so good to bare your teeth?

GARGA: If they're good teeth.

SHLINK: Man's infinite isolation makes enmity an unattainable goal. But even with the animals understanding is not possible.

GARGA: Speech isn't enough to create understanding.

SHLINK: I've observed the animals. Love, the warmth of bodies in contact, is the only mercy shown us in the darkness. But the only union is that of the organs, and it can't bridge over the cleavage made by speech. Yet they unite in order to produce beings to stand by them in their hopeless isolation. And the generations look coldly into each other's eyes. If you cram a ship full to bursting with human bodies, they'll all freeze with loneliness. Are you listening, Garga? Yes, so great is man's isolation that not even a fight is possible. The forest! That's where mankind comes from. Hairy, with apes' jaws, good animals who knew how to live. Everything was so easy. They simply tore each other apart. I see them clearly, with quivering flanks, staring into the whites of each other's eyes, sinking their teeth into each other's throats and rolling down. And the one who bled to death among the roots was the vanquished, and the one who had trampled down the most undergrowth was the victor. Are you listening for something, Garga?[13]

GARGA: Shlink, I've been listening to you now for three weeks. I've been waiting the whole time for a rage to take hold of me, under any pretext, however slight. But now, looking at you, I realize that your drivel irritates me and your voice sickens me.[14] Isn't this Thursday night? How far is it to New York? Why am I sitting here wasting my time? Haven't we been lying around here for three weeks now? We thought the planet would change its course on our account. But what happened? Three times it rained, and one night the wind blew. *Stands up.* Shlink, I think the time has come for you to take off your shoes. Take your shoes off, Shlink, and let me have them. Because I doubt if you've got much money left. Shlink, here in the woods of Lake Michigan I'm putting an end to our fight now going into its fourth year, because its substance is used up: it's ending right now. I can't finish it off with a knife, I see no need for high-sounding words. My shoes are full of holes and your speeches don't keep my toes warm. It's the old story, Shlink: the younger man wins.

SHLINK: Today we've heard the shovels of the railroad workers from time to time. I saw you pricking up your ears. You're standing up, Garga? You're going there, Garga? You're going to betray me?

GARGA *lying down lazily:* Yes, Shlink, that's exactly what I'm going to do.

SHLINK: And there will never be an outcome to this fight, George Garga? Never an understanding?

GARGA: No.

SHLINK: But you'll come out of it with nothing to show but your bare life.

GARGA: Bare life is better than any other kind of life.

SHLINK: Tahiti?

GARGA: New York. *Laughing ironically:* 'I will go and I will return with iron limbs and dark skin, with fury in my eyes. My face will make people think that I come of a strong race. I will have gold, I will be lazy and brutal. Women love to nurse wild, sick men, returned from the hot countries. I will swim, trample grass, hunt, and most of all smoke. And down drinks as hot as boiling metal. I will mingle with life and be saved.'[15] – What nonsense! Words on a planet that's not in the centre. Long after lime has covered you through the natural elimination of the obsolete, I shall be choosing the things that amuse me.

SHLINK: What kind of an attitude is that? Kindly take your pipe out of your filthy mouth. If you're trying to tell me you've gone impotent, take a different tone at least.

GARGA: Whatever you say.

SHLINK: That gesture shows me you're unworthy to be my opponent.

GARGA: I was only deploring the fact that you bored me.

SHLINK: What's that? You deploring? You! A hired pug! A drunken salesman! Whom I bought for ten dollars, an idealist who couldn't tell his two legs apart, a nobody!

GARGA *laughing:* A young man! Be frank.

SHLINK: A white man, hired to drag me down, to stuff my mouth with disgust or dry rot, to give me the taste of death on my tongue. Six hundred feet away in the woods I'll find all the men I need to lynch me.

GARGA: Yes, maybe I'm a leper, but what of it? You're a suicide. What more have you to offer me? You hired me, but you never paid up.

SHLINK: You got what a man like you needs. I bought you furniture.

GARGA: Yes, I got a piano out of you, a piano that had to be sold. I ate meat *once*. I bought one suit, and for your idiotic talk I gave up my sleep.

SHLINK: Your sleep, your mother, your sister and your wife. Three years off your stupid life. But how annoying! It's all ending in banality. You never understood what it was all about. You wanted me dead. But I wanted a fight. Not of the flesh but of the spirit.

GARGA: And the spirit, you see, is nothing. The important thing is not to be stronger, but to come off alive. I can't defeat you, I can only stamp you into the ground. I'll carry my raw flesh into the icy rains, Chicago is cold. I'm going there now. Possibly I'm doing the wrong thing. But I have plenty of time. *Goes out.*

Shlink falls down.

SHLINK *standing up:* Now that the last sword thrusts have been exchanged as well as the last words that occurred to us, I thank you for the interest you have shown in my person. A good deal has fallen away from us, we have hardly more than our naked bodies left. In four minutes the moon will rise, then your lynch mob will be here. *He notices that Garga has gone and follows him.* Don't go, George Garga! Don't quit because you're young. The forests have been cut down, the vultures are glutted, and the golden answer will be buried deep in the ground. *Turns. A milky light is seen in the brush.* November nineteenth. Three miles south of Chicago. West wind. Four minutes before the rising of the moon, drowned while fishing.

MARY *enters:* Please don't drive me away. I'm an unhappy woman.

The light grows stronger in the brush.

SHLINK: It's all piling up. Fish swimming into your mouth ... What's that crazy light? I'm very busy.

MARY *removing her hat:* I'm not pretty any more. Don't look at me. The rats have gnawed at me. I'm bringing you what's left.

SHLINK: That strange milky light! Ah, that's it! Phosphorescent rot, that's it!

MARY: Does my face look bloated to you?

SHLINK: Do you realize you'll be lynched if the mob catches you here?

MARY: It's all the same to me.

SHLINK: I beg you, leave me alone in my last moments.

N

MARY: Come. Hide in the underbrush. There's a hiding-place in the quarry.

SHLINK: Damn it! Are you out of your mind? Don't you see that I have to cast one last look over this jungle? That's what the moon is rising for. *Steps into the entrance of the tent.*

MARY: All I see is that you've lost the ground from under your feet. Have pity on yourself.

SHLINK: Can't you do me this one last kindness?

MARY: I only want to look at you. I've found out that this is where I belong.

SHLINK: Maybe so! Then stay. *A signal is heard in the distance.* Two o'clock. I've got to find safety.

MARY: Where's George?

SHLINK: George? He's run away. What a miscalculation! Safety. *He tears off his scarf.* The barrels are beginning to stink. Good fat fish, I caught them myself. Well-dried, packed up in crates. Salted. First set out in ponds, bought, overpaid, fattened! Fish eager for death, suicidal fish, that swallow hooks like holy wafers. Phoo! Quick now! *He goes to the table, sits down. Drinks from a flask.* I, Wang Yeng, known as Shlink, born in Yokohama in northern Peiho under the sign of the Tortoise. I operated a lumber business, ate rice, and dealt with all sorts of people. I, Wang Yeng, known as Shlink, aged fifty-four, ended three miles south of Chicago without heirs.

MARY: What's the matter?

SHLINK *seated:* You here? My legs are getting cold. Throw a cloth over my face. Have pity. *He collapses.*

Panting in the underbrush. Footsteps and hoarse curses from behind.

MARY: What are you listening for? Answer me. Are you asleep? Are you still cold? I'm here, close to you. What did you want with the cloth?

At this moment knives cut openings in the tent. The lynchers step silently through the openings.

MARY *going towards them:* Go away. He just died. He doesn't want anyone to look at him.

11

The Private Office of the late C. Shlink

A week later
The lumber yard has burned down. Signs here and there saying:
'Business for Sale'. Garga, John Garga, Mary Garga.

JOHN: It was stupid of you to let this place burn down. Now
all you've got is charred beams. Who's going to buy them?
GARGA *laughing:* They're cheap. But what are you two plan-
ning to do?
JOHN: I thought we'd stay together.
GARGA *laughing:* I'm leaving. Are you going to work?
MARY: I'm going to work. But not scrub stairs like my
mother.[16]
JOHN: I'm a soldier. We slept in watering troughs. The rats
on our faces never weighed less than seven pounds. When
they took away my rifle and it was over, I said: From now
on we'll all sleep with our caps on.
GARGA: You mean: we'll all sleep.
MARY: We'd better go now, Father. Night's coming on, and
I still have no room.
JOHN: Yes, let's go. *Looks around.* Let's go. A soldier at your
side. Forward march! Against the jungle of the city.
GARGA: I've got it behind me. Hello!
MANKY *comes in beaming, with his hands in his pockets:* It's me. I
read your ad in the paper. If your lumber business doesn't
cost too much, I'll buy it.
GARGA: What's your offer?
MANKY: Why are you selling?
GARGA: I'm going to New York.
MANKY: And I'm moving in here.
GARGA: How much can you pay?
MANKY: I'll need some cash for the business.

GARGA: Six thousand, if you'll take the woman too.

MANKY: All right.

MARY: I've got my father with me.

MANKY: And your mother?

MARY: She's not here any more.

MANKY *after a pause:* All right.

MARY: Draw up the contract.

The men sign.

MANKY: Let's all have a bite. Want to come along, George?

GARGA: No.

MANKY: Will you still be here when we get back?

GARGA: No.

JOHN: Good-bye, George. Take a look at New York. You can come back to Chicago if the going gets too rough.

The three go out.

GARGA *putting the money away:* It's a good thing to be alone. The chaos is spent. That was the best time.

The Life of Edward the Second of England
(after Marlowe)

a history

I wrote this play with Lion Feuchtwanger

BERTOLT BRECHT

Translator: JEAN BENEDETTI

Here is shown before the public the history of the troubled
reign of Edward the Second, King of England, and his
lamentable death / likewise the glory and end of his favourite,
Gaveston / further the disordered fate of Queen Anne / likewise the rise and fall of the great earl Roger Mortimer / all
which befell in England, and specially in London, more than
six hundred years ago

Characters

King Edward the Second · Queen Anne, his consort · Kent,
his brother · Young Edward, his son, afterwards King
Edward III · Gaveston · Archbishop of Winchester · Lord
Abbot of Coventry, afterwards Archbishop of Westminster ·
Mortimer · Lancaster · Rice ap Howell · Berkeley · Spencer ·
Baldock · The elder Gurney · The younger Gurney · Light-
born · James · Peers · Soldiers · A ballad-monger · A monk

14 DECEMBER 1307: RETURN OF THE FAVOURITE DANIEL GAVESTON ON THE OCCASION OF THE ACCESSION OF EDWARD THE SECOND

London

GAVESTON *reading a letter from King Edward:*
'My father is deceas'd. Come Gaveston
And share the kingdom with thy dearest friend
King Edward the Second.'
I come. These thy amorous lines
Whistled astern the brig from Ireland.
The sight of London to an exile's eyes
Is as Elysium to a new-come soul.
My father told me often: thou art
Already gross with drinking ale at eighteen years.
And my mother said: behind your corpse
Less men shall walk than a hen has teeth
In its beak. And now a king moves heaven and earth
For your son's friendship.
Holà. Reptiles!
What crawling things are these first cross my path?
Enter two poor men.

FIRST:
Such as desire your worship's service.

GAVESTON:
What canst thou do?

FIRST:
I can ride.

GAVESTON:
But I have no horses.
What art thou?

SECOND:
A soldier that has served against the Irish.

GAVESTON:

But I have no war. So God be wi' ye, gentlemen.

SECOND:

God be wi' us?

FIRST *to the second:*

England gives nothing
To old soldiers, sir.

GAVESTON:

England gave you Saint James' Hospital.

FIRST:

To rot to death in.

GAVESTON:

Death is a soldier's lot.

SECOND:

Is't so?
Then do thou die in thy England!
And perish by a soldier's hand!
Exeunt the two poor men.

GAVESTON:

He spoke just like my father.
Ah well!
This fellow's words move me as much
As if a goose should play the porcupine
And dart her plumes at me, imagining
To pierce me through the breast. But onward!
The day has come when many a man shall be paid
home.
For too much drinking ale and playing whist cannot
Fade the memory of that paper where they wrote
That I was Edward's whore and banished me.
Here comes my newly furbished king
With a herd of peers. I'll stand aside.
Enter Edward, Kent, Mortimer, the Archbishop of Winchester, Lancaster.

ARCHBISHOP:

Here, my lord, hasting to say mass
For the immortal relics of your father Edward

King of England, this I say:
On his death-bed Edward took his Peers —

LANCASTER:

He was already whiter than his sheets —

ARCHBISHOP:

To oath than he would never come again
To England.

GAVESTON *behind:*

Mort Dieu!

ARCHBISHOP:

If you love us, my lord, hate Gaveston.
Gaveston whistles between his teeth.

LANCASTER:

Comes he across the water there'll be naked swords
In England.

EDWARD:

I will have Gaveston.

GAVESTON:

Well done, Ned.

LANCASTER:

We mean we would not break our oath.

ARCHBISHOP:

My lord, why do you thus incense your Peers
Who naturally would love and honour you?

EDWARD:

I will have Gaveston.

LANCASTER:

There may be naked swords in England
My lords.

KENT:

If there be naked swords in England, Lancaster
Brother, methinks there will be heads
Set upon poles for trespass of their tongues.

ARCHBISHOP:

Our heads!

EDWARD:

Aye, yours. Now, I pray you, scuttle.

LANCASTER:

Our hands I think may fence our heads.
Exeunt Peers.

KENT:

Brother, leave Gaveston but bridle your peers.

EDWARD:

Brother, I live or die with Gaveston.

GAVESTON *coming forward:*

I can no longer keep me from my lord.

EDWARD:

What, Danny! Dearest friend!
Embrace me, Danny, as I do thee.
Since thou wert banished each day is parched.

GAVESTON:

And since I went from hence no soul in hell
Has felt more torment than poor Gaveston.

EDWARD:

I know it. Now rebellious Lancaster
Arch-heretic Winchester, conspire as you will
I here create thee Lord High Chamberlain
High Chancellor, Earl of Cornwall, Lord of Man.

KENT *darkly:*

Brother, enough!

EDWARD:

Brother, silence!

GAVESTON:

My lord, do not overwhelm me. What will men
Say? Perhaps: it is too much
For a simple butcher's son.

EDWARD:

Fear'st thou thy person? Thou shalt have a guard.
Wantest thou gold? Go to my treasury.
Woulds't thou be fear'd. Receive my ring and seal.
And in our name command, as thou wilt.

GAVESTON:

By your love am I made Caesar's equal.
Enter the Abbot of Coventry.

EDWARD:

Whither goes my lord of Coventry?

ABBOT:

To celebrate your father's exequies.

EDWARD *showing Gaveston:*

My ghostly father has a guest from Ireland.

ABBOT:

What, is that wicked Gaveston returned?

GAVESTON:

Yes, knave. In London there'll be tears and gnashing
teeth.

ABBOT:

I did no more than I was bound to do.
And, Gaveston, if thou art here unlawfully
I'll bring thy case once more before the Parliament
And thou shalt back again upon an Irish ship.

GAVESTON *grabbing him:*

Let's to it now. Here is the channel water
And since 'twas thou, sir priest, that wrote that paper
I will plunge thee, my Lord Abbot, in the gutter
As thou plungedst me into the Irish sea.

EDWARD:

Since thou dost it, 'tis good. What thou dost is good.
Aye, plunge him in, Gaveston. Wash his face
Barber thy enemy in the filthy stream.

KENT:

O brother! Touch him not with sacrilegious hand!
For he'll complain unto the See of Rome.

EDWARD:

Spare his life then! But seize upon his gold and rents!
Be thou Lord Abbot, be he exiled.

ABBOT:

King Edward, God will pay you home
For this misdeed.

EDWARD:

But in the meantime, Gaveston, away
And put his house and livings under seal.

GAVESTON:

What should a priest do with so fair a house?

MISGOVERNMENT UNDER THE REIGN OF KING
EDWARD IN THE YEARS 1307–12. A WAR IN SCOT-
LAND IS LOST BECAUSE OF THE KING'S INDIF-
FERENCE

London

Spencer, Baldock, the two poor men, soldiers.

BALDOCK:

The Archbishop of Winchester said in the pulpit the
wheat this year is worm-ridden. That means much.

SECOND POOR MAN:

But not to us. It's Winchester eats the corn.

FIRST POOR MAN:

The provisions for the Scottish troops have just been
seized by a Yorkshireman.

BALDOCK:

But in Neddy's house they're drinking beer at breakfast.

SPENCER:

Yesterday Ned fell into a swoon.

FIRST SOLDIER:

Why so?

SPENCER:

The Earl of Cornwall told him he was growing a beard.

BALDOCK:

Ned was sick the other day in Tanner's Lane.

SECOND SOLDIER:

Why so?

BALDOCK:

A woman made him liverish.

SECOND SOLDIER:

Have you heard the latest on the Earl of Cornwall? Now
he wears a false arse.

Laughter.

Enter a ballad monger.

BALLAD MONGER:

Neddy's woman has a beard on his chest.
Pray for us, pray for us, pray for us!
And so the Scot's war has been laid to rest.
Pray for us, pray for us, pray for us!
The Earl of Cornwall has silver at his rump
Pray for us, pray for us, pray for us!
But Pat has no arms and O'Nelly just a stump.
Pray for us, pray for us, pray for us.
Ned louses his Gavy and never has time.
Pray for us, pray for us, pray for us.
So Johnny fell in the bog at Bannockbride.
Pray for us, pray for us, pray for us.

SPENCER:

That song is worth a ha'penny, sir.

Enter Edward and Gaveston.

EDWARD:

My dearest Gaveston, thou hast me for thy friend.
Let them be! We'll to the pond at Tynemouth
Fishing, eating fish, riding, shooting
On the catapult walls, knee to knee.

SPENCER *grabbing the ballad monger:* This is high treason,
sir. And if you ripped to pieces my aunt's nephew yet
my mother's son could never once endure his dearest
Earl of Cornwall to be slandered.

GAVESTON:

What would'st thou, good friend?

SPENCER:

My lord, I am always well inclined to pretty couplets;
but high treason plainly goes against my stomach.

GAVESTON:

What is it?

SPENCER:

This worm-eaten peg-leg, my Lord.
The ballad monger runs out.

GAVESTON *to the King:*

Calumniare audacter, sempèr aliquid haeret.

SPENCER:

In your language: hang him the lower.

GAVESTON *to Spencer:*

Come follow me.
*He goes off with the King. Spencer signs to Baldock and they go
off together. Those left behind laugh.*
Enter the Archbishop and Lancaster.

ARCHBISHOP:

All London mocks us. Tax farmers ask how long the
   Parliament and Peers can let things be. In every alley
   'Civil war' is spoken.

LANCASTER:

One strumpet does not make a war.

London

MORTIMER *in his house, alone among his books:*
Plutarch tells of Gaius Julius Caesar
That he could at the same time read and write and dictate
   to
His clerk and beat the Gauls. It seems
That people of his stature owe their
Fame to a particular lack
Of insight into the vanity of man's
Concerns and deeds; coupled with an
Amazing lack of seriousness; in short, to their
Shallowness.
Enter archbishop and barons.

ARCHBISHOP:

You, Roger Mortimer, feed apart
On classic writings, meditations
Of times now dead
While like a seething ant-hill
London needs you.

MORTIMER:

London needs flour.

ARCHBISHOP:

If God should leave a hundred pigs to die
For lack of flour in Saint James's Hospital
We would not, certainly, for that
Mortimer, disturb you at your books.
But when this pig wallows in Westminster
Suckled with the milk of the land by him
Who is the guardian of the land, a king
Then it is truly time to leave the classics
To be classics.

MORTIMER:

The classics tell us: Great Alexander
Loved Hephaestion, Alcibiades was loved
Of grave Socrates and for
Patroclus Achilles drooped. Must I
For such freaks of nature drag my countenance
Into the market-place amid the sweaty rabble?

ARCHBISHOP:

Ned's long arms, the catapults
May bring to pass that you, head topped
May not enjoy this hard-defended leisure.
You step from the rain and drown in the flood.
You are cold in passion, at an age
For well-considered deeds, skilled and
Sharp in knowledge of man's frailty
Hardened by books and an active life
Great in name, goods, troops
Made to raise your voice in
Westminster.

MORTIMER:

Would you warm your soup on Etna?
You have mistook. He who sets himself
To pluck a cock, to eat it, or because
Its crowing jarred, to such a man the urge may come
At last, his hunger sated, out of love of skinning
To take the hide from the tiger. Have you
Thought of this?

ARCHBISHOP:

Let Westminster be rased to the ground
This peasant shall no longer plague us.

MORTIMER:

My lords, for your relief, this I propose:
We demand his exile, signed and sealed.

ARCHBISHOP *hastily:*

You speak to it in Parliament. In England's
Name we thank you, Earl Mortimer.
That you have sacrificed your learned studies
To England's weal.

Exeunt archbishop and peers.

MORTIMER *solus:*

Because some bonnets scrape the mud
Before a hound
These men will thrust our island
Underground.

London

Mortimer, Archbishop, Lancaster, the two lords.

LANCASTER:

The King of England shows the Earl of Cornwall
His catapults.

ARCHBISHOP:

It is to *us* he shows them.

LANCASTER:

Are you afraid, Archbishop?

MORTIMER:

Ah, this betrays our baseness, Lancaster.
Were the ancients present at this play
He'd long been out the bosom of the king
This butcher's son and hanged on a cur-gibbet
Swollen with venom, toothless.

LANCASTER *after a catapult shot:*

Well-aimed, Edward. That shot gives us
Pause for thought. The catapults
Are Edward's long arms. He'll reach
You in your Scottish castles, Winchester
With his catapults.
Enter Queen Anne.

MORTIMER:

Whither walks your majesty so fast?

ANNE:

Deep into the forest, gentle Mortimer
To live in grief and baleful discontent
For now my lord the king regards me not
But dotes on Gaveston.
He hangs about his neck and when I come
He frowns as who should say, 'Go whither thou wilt
Seeing I have Gaveston.'

MORTIMER:

My lady, you are widowed by
A butcher's son.

ARCHBISHOP:

How Mortimer consoles my lady!

LANCASTER:

She is devoted to this wicked Edward.
It is a piteous lot. God save her.

ANNE:

Oh Mortimer, can there be greater bitterness
Than this: the French king's sister is a widow
Yet no widow; since her husband lives
More wretched than a widow; it were better
For the earth to cover her, her steps are shadowed

By abuse, wife and yet no wife:
For her bed is cold.

MORTIMER:

Madame, too much weeping spoils the skin.
Widowed nights are ageing. Rank feelings
Tire the body. My lady, gratify yourself
Elsewhere. Raw meat
In general needs moistening.

ANNE *aside*:

O base Edward, how you shame me
That I dare not strike him in the face
But must stand silent, naked
When he falls on me in his lust.

Aloud:

You wrong me in my sorrow, Mortimer.

MORTIMER:

Lady Anne, return to court.
Leave these matters to the Peers; before the new
    moon
This butcher's son shall ship to Ireland.

ARCHBISHOP:

My lady, for us this Gaveston's
A thorn in the eye. We'll pluck him out.

ANNE:

But do not lift your sword against your king.
Edward is so far from us. Ah, my love
Betrays me. How could I take me to the forest, lords
If you should fall upon King Edward?
In distant lanes I'd hear him threatened
And straight return, to be beside him in
His danger.

LANCASTER:

Blood will be shed e'er Gaveston goes hence.

ANNE:

Then let him stay. Rather than my lord
Be threatened I will drag out my life
And let him have his Gaveston.

LANCASTER:

Patience, my lady.

MORTIMER:

My lords, escort we the queen back
To Westminster.

ANNE:

For my sake
Forebear to levy arms against the King.
Exeunt omnes.
Enter Gaveston.

GAVESTON:

The mighty Earl of Lancaster, the Archbishop
Of Winchester and with them the Queen
And some few carrion from old London
Are plotting something against
Certain people.

London

GAVESTON *alone in his house, writes his will:*
Through misunderstanding, on an ordinary Thursday
And from no desire for slaughter
Many a man's been wiped out, painfully.
And so I write, not knowing
What it was in me, or was not
Made this Edward, who is King now
Never leave my side. For my mother
Found nothing in me that was other than
Most commonplace, not goitre, not white skin –
And so I write, since I know nothing
Save, dull-witted as I am, this:
That nothing helps the life of one whom all wish dead
And so there's naught can save me in this London
Which I shall never leave again
Except feet first
My will.

I Daniel Gaveston, in my seven and twentieth year
A butcher's son, dispatch'd by favourable
Circumstance, blotted out by too much luck, leave
My clothes and boots to those are with me
At the end:
To the foolish wives of St James's street
The Abbey of Coventry, to the good
Ale-drinking folk of England my narrow grave
To good King Edward, my friend
God's mercy.
For it grieves me much I have not simply
Turned to dust.

9 MAY 1311: BECAUSE KING EDWARD REFUSES TO
SIGN THE BANISHMENT OF HIS FAVOURITE GAVE-
STON A WAR BREAKS OUT WHICH LASTS FOR
THIRTEEN YEARS.

Westminster

Mortimer, Lancaster, Archbishop, peers sign the document in turn.

MORTIMER:

This parchment seals his banishment.
Enter the Queen and Gaveston, who sits beside the King's throne, Kent, then Edward.

EDWARD:

What, are you moved that Gaveston sits there?
It is our pleasure: we will have it so.

LANCASTER:

Your grace does well to place him at your side
For nowhere else the new earl is so safe.

ARCHBISHOP:

Quam male conveniunt!

LANCASTER:

A kingly lion fawns on crawling ants.

FIRST LORD:

How this fellow sprawls upon his chair!

SECOND LORD:

A sight for London's citizens to feast their eyes:
King Edward with his two wives.
Parliament is opened to the people.

KENT:

Speak, Roger Mortimer.

MORTIMER:

After Paris had eaten bread and salt
In Menelaus' house, Menelaus' wife – so
Ancient chronicles relate –
Slept with him and he took her
In his hammock sailing home to Troy.
Troy laughed. To Troy it seemed laughable.
And to Greece it seemed but just this willing piece of
    flesh
Helen by name, should be returned
Since she was a whore, to her Greek husband.
Only Lord Paris, naturally, made trouble, said
It was her time of month. Meanwhile came ships.
Greek. Ships that multiplied
Like flies. One morning Greeks broke into
Paris' house to haul the Greek whore
Out. From his window
Paris roared this was his house
This his castle and the Trojans, judging
Him not wrong, applauded, sniggering.
The Greeks still lay fishing on their drooping
Sails until, in an ale-house
On the water-front, someone bloodied
Another's nose, pretending
It was for Helen's sake.

Before they knew it in the days that followed
Many hands grasped many throats.
From broken ships men speared other men
Like fishes as they drowned. By the moon's first quarter
Many were missing from their tents and in the houses
Many were found headless. The crabs
Were very fat those years in the river
Scamander, but went uneaten. Spying
The wind's direction early
Fretting only if the fish that night would nibble
By midnight, of confusion or design, they all
Were dead.
About ten o'clock still to be seen
With the faces of men
About eleven
Forgetting mother tongues, Trojan
Lost sight of Troy and Greek of Greece.
Many felt their men's mouths changing
Into tiger's jaws. At midday plunged their teeth
In their neighbour's tender flesh
Who roared pain.
Yet had there been on the embattled walls
One who knew
To call them by name, by kind
Many had stopped short. It had been better
Had they disappeared still fighting
On their quickly rotting ships
Sinking beneath their feet, before nightfall
Unnamed.
They killed each other with more horror.
And so this war went on ten years
And was called the Trojan and was
Ended by a horse.
Were understanding for the most part not
Unhuman, human ears not stopped –
What matter if this Helen was a whore
Or the grandmother of a sturdy line –

Troy would stand now, four times greater
Than our London, Hector had not
Died with bloody genitals, weak Priam's
Ancient head had not been spewed upon
By dogs, all this nation had not
Perished in the high noon of its manhood.
Quod erat demonstrandum. To be sure
We would not then have had the Iliad.
He sits. Pause.
Edward weeps.

ANNE:

What's the matter? Do you want water, husband?

KENT:

The king's unwell. End the sitting.
Parliament is closed.

EDWARD:

What do you see? Look not on me. God grant
Mortimer, thy lips have not lied.
Trouble not yourselves for me. If it appears
That I am out of sorts, then look away. 'Tis but
My cheek gone pale, blood frozen in my brain –
Not more.
Lay hands on that traitor Mortimer.

LANCASTER:

Take this Gaveston from out our sight, my lord.

MORTIMER:

Read here
What we in Parliament have written
For your intent.

ANNE *to Edward:*

My lord, come to your senses.
'Tis Thursday. 'Tis London.

MORTIMER:

Subscribe:
'The banishment of Daniel Gaveston, son
Of a meat peddler in the City of London
Banished a year or more ago by the English

Parliament, unlawfully returned and today
Banished for a second time by the English
Parliament.' My lord! Subscribe!

LANCASTER:

Will't please you to subscribe, my lord?

ARCHBISHOP:

My lord, will't please you to subscribe?

GAVESTON:

You did not think, my lord, matters would go so
fast.

KENT:

Brother Edward, throw off Gaveston.

MORTIMER:

'Tis Thursday. 'Tis London. Subscribe.
Lancaster, Archbishop, Lords place a table before the King.

EDWARD:

Never, never, never.
Ere Gaveston be taken from me
I'll leave this isle.
He tears up the paper.

ARCHBISHOP:

Now is England rent . . .

LANCASTER:

Much blood shall flow in England now
King Edward.

MORTIMER *sings:*

Maids of England in your widow's weeds mourn
For your lovers lost at Bannocksbourn
Cry aheave and aho.

The King of England bids the drums to roll
That no one may hear your mournful dole
With a rom rom below.

EDWARD:

Will you not sing on? Do you look
Upon your king as on some kine to slaughter?
Can a people live so?

Come, Gaveston. I am still here
And have a foot to crush these vipers' heads.
Exit with Gaveston.

MORTIMER:

This is war.

LANCASTER:

Not all the devils in the deep nor angels overhead
Shall halt the English army till this butcher's son is
dead.

THE BATTLE OF KILLINGWORTH (15 AND 16 AUGUST 1320). BATTLEFIELD AT KILLINGWORTH

About seven o'clock in the evening.

LANCASTER:

See! The tattered ensign of Saint George
Which swept from the Irish to the Dead Sea.
To arms!
Enter Kent.

KENT:

My lords, of love to this our native land
I come to join with you and leave the King.
My brother since, by his sinful passion
For this Gaveston, he destroys the realm.

ARCHBISHOP:

Thy hand, Kent!

LANCASTER:

March!
Drums.
None be so hardy as to touch the King.

ARCHBISHOP:

A hundred shillings for the head of Gaveston.
They march out.

About eight in the evening.
Marching troops, Edward, Gaveston.

FIRST SOLDIER:

Sire, come, the battle.

EDWARD:

Say on, Gaveston.

GAVESTON:

Many men on London say this war
Will never end.

EDWARD:

Our eye is greatly moved to see thee, Gaveston
At this hour, trusting in us, weaponless
Without defensive steel or leather, bare skinned
Standing before us in accustomed
Irish weeds.

SECOND SOLDIER:

Let's march, my lord! The battle.

EDWARD:

As this triangle flight of storks in the sky
Though moving yet seems still, still stays
In us thy image untouched by time.

GAVESTON:

My lord, this simple sum a fisherman performs
Before his rest, numbering nets and fish
Counting up the shillings
By his reckoning, will stay
With me for ever while I walk beneath the sun:
That many are more than one and that
This one lives many days but not all days.
Therefore do not stake your heart all on one.
That your heart should not be lost.

THIRD SOLDIER:

Sire, to battle.

EDWARD:

Thy beauteous hair.

Eight in the evening.

GAVESTON:

With these beating drums, bog gulping
Catapults and horses, my mother's-son's head
Whirls. Don't pant! Are all
Now drowned and done for and is there but noise
Hanging now between earth and heaven? Nor will I
Run any more. For there are only minutes left and
I'll not move a finger but just
Lay me down on the ground here, that I
Endure not until the end of time.
And when tomorrow morning King Edward
Rides by, calling, to torment me: 'Daniel
Where art thou?' I'll not be here. And now
Untie your shoes, Gav, and sit waiting
Here.
Enter Lancaster, Mortimer, Archbishop, lords, soldiers.

LANCASTER:

Upon him, soldiers.
The lords laugh.
Welcome, Lord Chamberlain!

FIRST LORD:

Welcome is the good Earl of Cornwall!

ARCHBISHOP:

Welcome, Lord Abbot!

LANCASTER:

Run you about to cool your villain's blood
Lord Abbot?

ARCHBISHOP:

Most noble Lords, his trial I think
Is short. His sentence: As Daniel Gaveston
Son of a meat-peddler in the City of London
Was King Edward's whore, suborning him
To luxury and other crimes
Since double banishment could not restrain him
He shall hang upon a tree. Hang him!

JAMES:

My lords, he will not budge. He's gone as stiff
As a frozen cod-fish. This is the tree.
Two hempen ropes. He's fleshy.

MORTIMER *aside:*

This man, alive, were worth half Scotland
And a man like me had given all
The army for this watery cod-fish. But
Tree, rope and neck are there and blood is cheap.
Now that the catapults, men clinging to them
Have pounded ceaselessly, herds of horses
With men up, startled by drums
Rushed each other, dustclouds and nightfall
Veiled all ways out of the battle
Now the catapults have laboured, drums drummed
Manned troops of horse
Devoured each other, a tottering
Red moon sucks all reason from the human brain, and from
The man steps forth the naked beast.
It is expedient now someone should hang.

JAMES:

Now the plank.

GAVESTON:

The rope's not running.

JAMES:

We'll soon soap it.

SOLDIERS *singing in the background:*

Neddy's woman has hair on his chest.
Pray for us, pray for us, pray for us.

A SOLDIER:

What do you feel, sir?

GAVESTON:

First take away the drum.

SOLDIER:

Will you scream, sir?

GAVESTON:

Pray you, remove the drum. I'll not
Scream.

JAMES:

Good sir, now shut your mouth.
Put the noose on him. His neck is short.

GAVESTON:

I pray you, have done quickly.
And I pray you read again my sentence.

JAMES *reads the sentence: then:*

Now, onward.

GAVESTON:

Edward! My friend Edward! Help me
If thou art still of this world. Edward!
Enter a soldier.

SOLDIER:

Stop! A message from the King!

GAVESTON:

He is still of this world.

ARCHBISHOP *reads:*

'I have heard that you have taken Gaveston
And I entreat you that I may
See him before he dies, since I know
That die he shall – and send my word
And seal: he shall come back.
And if you will so gratify me
I shall be mindful of the courtesy.
Edward.'

GAVESTON:

Edward!

ARCHBISHOP:

What now?

LANCASTER:

This paper, lords, is worth a battle won.

GAVESTON:

Edward. Thy name gives me life.

LANCASTER:
It need not. We might, for instance
Send the king thy heart.

GAVESTON:
Our good King Edward swears his bond and seal
He will but see me and then send me back.

LANCASTER:
When?
Laughter.
For his Danny, once he sees him
He'll break any seal, defying God.

ARCHBISHOP:
Ere a king of England breaks an oath
This isle shall break into the ocean.

LANCASTER:
So. Send him Gaveston and hang him
After.

MORTIMER:
Hang not Gaveston but send him not.

ARCHBISHOP:
You may deprive a king of his head
But not of his desire.

LANCASTER:
So, skin the hide from him but
Deny him not the slightest courtesy.
And now the fight against Edward Gloucester
Wife to a butcher's son.

ARCHBISHOP:
Cut him free.
And you, Lord Mortimer, see him delivered.

GAVESTON:
Another night-time's watch, there and back again.
I bear my death with me as it were my moon.

JAMES:
Much trouble for a low meat-peddler's son.
Exeunt all save Mortimer, James, and Gaveston.

MORTIMER:

This butcher's son's the alpha of the war
And its omega
A rope out of the bog, a shield against arrows; and I
Have him. Holà, James!
Take this man round about and should one ask
Whither, then say: To the knacker's yard. But handle
Him most gingerly. And bring him
In the morning at eleven to the wood
At Killingworth. Where I shall be.

JAMES:

And if some cause should hinder you?

MORTIMER:

Then what you will.

JAMES:

Come, sir.
Exit with Gaveston.

MORTIMER:

A gentle stench of carrion seems to rise
From my command. But since the moon began
To suck up blood, like mist, and these barons
To have death writ on their faces, I, who know
What's what and damn all moons, have been
A lump of cowardice.
One man's enough to kill
Another who might kill a thousand. So I wrap myself
Wily as a man once bitten, in another's
Skin, namely, the skin of this butcher's son.

About ten in the evening.

ANNE *alone:*

O most miserable Queen!
Ah had, before I left sweet France
And was embarked, the waters turned to stone!
Or that those arms that twined about my neck

Had strangled me on my wedding night.
Alas, now must I pursue King Edward
For, widowing me, he's gone to Killingworth
To battle for this devil Gaveston.
My skin crawls when I behold him.
But he soaks his heart in him as 'twere
A sponge.
And so I am for ever miserable.
O God, why hast thou brought me
Anne of France so low, that
This devil Gaveston might rise.
Enter Gaveston, James, Soldier.

JAMES:

Holà.

ANNE:

Are you soldiers of King Edward?

JAMES:

In no wise.

ANNE:

Who is that man in Irish weeds?

JAMES:

That is Daniel Gaveston, whore to the King
Of England.

ANNE:

Where are you taking him?

JAMES:

To the knacker's yard.

GAVESTON *upstage:*

If I had some water for my feet.

SOLDIER:

Here is water.

ANNE:

I pray you, do not deny him this.

GAVESTON:

Let me go to her, it is the queen.
Take me with you, my lady.

JAMES:

Stay there. Just wash your feet. I have my orders.

ANNE:

Why will you not let him speak with me?

JAMES:

Go you apart, your ladyship, that he may wash.
He pushes her away.

GAVESTON:

Stay, good lady, stay!
Unhappy Gaveston, whither goest thou now?

One in the morning.
Lancaster, lords, troops, on the march to Boroughbridge.

A SOLDIER:

Straight on to Boroughbridge.
The word is passed on.

SOLDIERS *singing:*

Maids of England in your widows weeds mourn.
(In the night)
For your lovers lost at Bannocksbourn.
(In the night)
With aheave and aho.
The King of England bids the drums to roll
(In the night)
That no one may hear their mournful dole
(In the night)
With a rom rom below.

LANCASTER:

All's well. We'll take Boroughbridge this very night.

Two in the morning.
Edward, Spencer, Baldock, Young Edward. The sleeping army.

EDWARD:

I long to hear the answer from the barons
Touching my friend, my dearest Gaveston.

Ah Spencer, not all England's gold
Can ransom him. He is marked
To die. I know the evil nature
Of Mortimer, I know the Archbishop is cruel
And Lancaster inexorable and never again
Shall I behold Daniel Gaveston.
And in the end they'll place their foot upon my neck.

SPENCER:

Were I King Edward, England's sovereign
Great Edward Longshanks' issue, I'd not bear
These rowdies' rage, and suffer that these
Ruffian lords should threaten me in my
Own land. Strike off their heads. Set them
Upon poles. This always works, for sure.

EDWARD:

Yea, gentle Spencer. We have been too mild
Too kind to them. Now that is ended.
Comes Gaveston not back their heads shall fly.

BALDOCK:

This high resolve becomes your majesty.

YOUNG EDWARD:

Why do they make such noise, father?

EDWARD:

They are hacking England's body, son.
Had I sent thee to them Edward
That they might do my will touching Gaveston
Hadst thou been afraid, boy, before those savage lords?

YOUNG EDWARD:

Yes, father.

EDWARD:

That's a good answer.
There are many evil birds in the field tonight.
Enter the Queen.

ANNE:

Are you the soldiers of King Edward?
Is this the quarry of Killingworth?
Where is King Edward, soldiers?

SPENCER:

What is it?

A SOLDIER:

A woman seeks King Edward.

ANNE:

Coming from London, for two days' ride
I have sought you, through bog and scrub and battle.

EDWARD:

Not welcome, madam.

SPENCER:

Two days the battle's laboured now, made worse
Since army looks like army and they both
Cry out for England and Saint George. By Saint
    George
Brother butchers brother and like two salamanders
Snarled in struggle army bites at army
And England's hamlets burn in England's name.
Toward evening, in the bog, amid the catapults and
    drowned
There, where Gaveston was taken, fell
So says certain news, Lord Arundel.
Soon after it rained hard. The night was unruly
With skirmishes. The king is somewhat cold but
In good spirits. Our positions are not
Bad, unless this night the barons
Have taken the town of Boroughbridge. Today
All will be settled. As to Gaveston
The lords have sworn to send him to us here.

ANNE *aside*:

But drag him to the knacker's yard.
Perhaps it is for the best. But it shall not
Be I who tells him at this hour the man's
No longer of this world.
Aloud:
Today the hunt's after thee, Edward.

EDWARD:

Aye

And my friend, Daniel Gaveston is taken.
And through the bog and undergrowth com'st thou.

ANNE:

My lord, if you will spit upon me
Here's my face.

EDWARD:

Your face is a tombstone. Whereon is writ:
'Here lies poor Gaveston.' Have you no
Small comfort even? 'Be comforted my lord
This Gaveston squinted in one eye.'
But I reply: 'All skins sicken me
And yours especially.'
I, Edward of England, tell you
Knowing, perchance mere hours divide me
From my wreck: you please me not.
In the eye of death: I love Gaveston.

ANNE:

Certain I shall not forget this cruel insult –
For the few things I hold in my poor head
Stay long therein and melt but very slow –
And so it is good that he is gone.

EDWARD:

Give him me again. All know
That Mortimer's all powerful. Go thou
To him, for this man is vain
His sort fall easy to a Queen.
Beseech him, use all arts and thine
Especial. The world will soon be wrecked.
What is an oath? I give thee absolution.

ANNE:

Jesu! I cannot.

EDWARD:

Then I banish thee from out my presence.

ANNE:

In these days, when war spreads that
They say, will never end, do you send
Me back through raw butchering army bands?

EDWARD:

Aye. And further give you this charge; to levy
Troops in Scotland for your son
Edward. For things go ill for his father.

ANNE:

Cruel Edward.

EDWARD:

He says this to you: it is your lot.
You are bound to this most cruel Edward, who
Knows you from your heart down to your thighs
Till, like a wild beast in a trap, you die.

ANNE:

Are you most certain of this?

EDWARD:

A thing, willed over to me. You are
Mine alone. Subscribed to me, unasked for
But never free except by my consent.

ANNE:

You send me forth but bind me to you?

EDWARD:

Aye.

ANNE:

Heaven is my witness that I love thee only.
My arms, I thought, could stretch to hold thee
Across this isle. The time to fear is
When they tire.
Do you bind me to you yet send me forth?

EDWARD:

Has no man any news of Gaveston?

ANNE:

He who bids me go but will not let me go
From him shall all men go and yet not let him go.
May his end elude him flayed and wandering.
If he should need a human hand
May the skin be hanging from it, leprous.
And if he would escape from them, to die
May they hold him and not let him go.

EDWARD:

Has no man any news of Gaveston?

ANNE:

If thou waitest for thy friend Gaveston
King Edward, then put an end to hope.
In the bog I saw a man in Irish weeds
And heard them say that he was for the knacker's
    yard.

SPENCER:

O bloody perjury!

EDWARD *kneeling:*

By earth the common mother of us all
By heaven and the movement of the stars
By this hard, sere hand
By all the steel that's in this isle
By the last oaths of a weary breast
By all England's glory – by my teeth:
I will have your misbegotten bodies
And change them so your mothers will
Not know you. I will have your white
Headless trunks.

ANNE:

Now I see he has become the slave
Body and soul, of this devil Gaveston.
Exit with Young Edward.
Enter a soldier.

SOLDIER:

The barons answer:
We have Boroughbridge, the battle's done.
If without bloodshed you would have
Relief and help England says to you:
Forget Gaveston, now not in dispute —

EDWARD:

Now not in this world.

SOLDIER:

And foreswear his memory and you'll
Have peace.

EDWARD:

Good. Tell the barons:
Since you have Boroughbridge and I, therefore
Can fight no further battles, and since
My friend Gaveston's no longer of this world
I take your offer; and let there be peace
Between you and me. Come about midday
To the quarry of Killingworth, where I
As you demand, will foreswear
His memory. And come you without arms.
For they would our kingly eye
Offend.
Exit soldier.

EDWARD *rousing his soldiers:*

Up, you sluggards! Lie in the quarry
Like the dead. Edward Softhand's
Expecting guests. And when they come
Leap at their throats.

Five in the morning.
Gaveston, James, the other soldier.

GAVESTON:

Where the devil are we going?
Here's the quarry once again.
We're going in a circle.
Why do you look at me so cold?
Fifty silver shillings!
Five hundred!
I will not die.
Throws himself on the ground.

JAMES:

Well, so you have shouted. Now we go on.
Enter two soldiers.

SHOUT: Saint George and England!
FIRST: What see'st thou yonder?

SECOND: Fire.

FIRST: That's Boroughbridge. What hearest thou?

SECOND: Clanging bells.

FIRST: Those are the bell-ropes of Bristol, they are tolling because the King of England and his barons are to conclude a peace.

SECOND: Why so sudden?

FIRST: So England won't be hacked to bits – they say.

JAMES: Now it seems that once again you are to get off cheap, sir. What time is it?

OTHER SOLDIER: About five o'clock.

Eleven in the morning.
Edward, Spencer, Baldock.

SPENCER:

The peers of England come unarmed
From the hills.

EDWARD:

The sentries are posted?

SPENCER:

Aye.

EDWARD:

Have they ropes?

SPENCER:

Aye.

EDWARD:

Are the troops drawn up, to fall upon
The headless army?

SPENCER:

Aye.

Enter Archbishop, Lancaster, peers.

BALDOCK:

My lord, your peers.

EDWARD:

Bind them with ropes.

PEERS *shouting:*

Treason! We are in an ambush! Your sworn oath!

EDWARD:

It is fine weather for breaking oaths.

ARCHBISHOP:

You had sworn.

EDWARD:

Drums!

The drums drown the shouting of the peers who are led away bound.

SPENCER:

Mortimer's missing.

EDWARD:

Then fetch him.
Have you crossbows, slings, catapults?
Bring me the maps!
Scour the land with steel. Comb it through!
Say, before you strangle him, to each man in the scrub:
England's king is changed into a tiger
In the wood at Killingworth.
Go!
Great battle.

Twelve noon.
Gaveston, James, the other soldier.

JAMES: Shovel, boy. The battle grows. Thy friend shall win.

GAVESTON: What's this hole for?

JAMES: The time has come to find shelter for our skins. And so we must carry out our orders. Shovel, good sir. Should you still want to relieve yourself you can do it here.

GAVESTON: Now it's moving more toward Bristol. When the wind blows you can hear the Welshman's horses. Have you ever read the Trojan war? Much blood will be shed for my mother's son too. Ned must often ask where his friend is.

JAMES: Hardly, sir. Everyone at Killingworth will tell him not to wait for you any longer. Shovel, good sir. The rumour goes that your worthy Irish corpse has been seen in the knacker's yard at Killingworth. If one dare believe a rumour you have lost your head, sir.

GAVESTON: Whose is this grave?

James is silent.

GAVESTON: Shall I not see the King again, James?

JAMES: The King of Heaven perhaps. The King of England, not.

SOLDIER: Today many a man shall perish by a soldier's hand.

JAMES: What time is it?

SOLDIER: About twelve o'clock.

Seven in the evening.
Edward, Spencer, Baldock, the captured barons, among them
Mortimer. Spencer counts the prisoners and notes down their
names.

EDWARD:

Now 'tis time. This is the hour
When the murder of my dearest friend
To whom, right well you knew, my soul was knit
The murder of Daniel Gaveston, shall be purged.

KENT:

Brother, all was done for you and England.

EDWARD *freeing him:*

So sir, you have spoken. Now be gone.
Exit Kent.

EDWARD:

Now lusty lords, not only chance of war
But sometimes the justice of the cause can conquer.

Methinks you hang your heads but
We'll advance them.
Recreants! Rebels! Accursed slaves!
Did you butcher him?
When we sent to ask by messenger
With seal and bond, also
By letter, that he come
And speak with us again.
Did you say yes? Say! Did you butcher him?
Behead him? Thou, Winchester, hast a great head.
Therefore thy head shall overlook the rest
As much as thou in rage outwent'st the rest.

ARCHBISHOP:

I look into your perjured face
And I have done, no words can penetrate.
For such as thee 'tis hard to trust the lips
Of one who speaks to save himself, spoke he the truth.
All proof hast thou blotted from the earth
And ours, thine, thy friend's strands
So tangled all eternity shall not unravel them.
Tis but temporal that thou canst inflict.

EDWARD:

What know'st thou, Lancaster?

LANCASTER:

The worst is death, and better die
Than live with thee in such a world.

MORTIMER *aside:*

But with me
Who more than Edward their butcher is
They'd go down to the worms
In harmony.

EDWARD:

Away with them! Their heads!

LANCASTER:

Farewell time.
Two nights since when the slender moon arose
God was with us. And now

A little larger moon's on high we're undone.
Farewell, good Mortimer.

ARCHBISHOP:

Good Mortimer, farewell.

MORTIMER:

Who loves his country as we do
Dies with light heart.
England shall weep for us. England forgets not.

Archbishop, Lancaster, lords – except Mortimer – are led off

EDWARD:

Have they found a certain Mortimer
Who, when I summoned them to Killingworth
Quarry, most cunningly came not?

SPENCER:

Indeed, my lord. Here he is.

EDWARD:

Take away the others. This one would not forget.
Our Majesty has special plans for him.
Release him so the memory of this day
Of Killingworth fade not in England.
You Mortimers reckon
Dim-eyed, are at home in books
Like worms. But Edward is not found
In books, he reads not, reckons not
Knows naught, but is nature's friend
And feeds himself on very different food.
You may go, Lord Mortimer. Go round and round
A wandering witness beneath the sun
How Edward Longshanks' son avenged
His friend.

MORTIMER:

As to your friend Daniel Gaveston
He walked at five o'clock
When the King of England turned a tiger
Alive still in the wood at Killingworth.
Had you, when my friends began to speak
Not drowned their cries with drumming

Had not too little trust
Too harsh a passion, too hot a rage
Clouded your eye, he'd be living now
Your favourite, Gaveston.
Exit.

EDWARD:

If Gaveston's corpse is found, take care
To give it honourable burial. Yet seek it not.
He was like a man who walks away into the wood:
Behind him bushes close again, grass
Springs up again and he is swallowed in the
Undergrowth.
But we will this day's sweat
Wash from our body, eat and rest
Till called to cleanse the realm of the last of fratricide
And war.
For I will not set foot again in London
Nor sleep save in a soldier's hammock
Until this generation like a raindrop
In the sea, is lost in me.
Come, Spencer.

Three in the morning.
Light wind.

ANNE:

Since Edward of England hears not prayers
Or urgent cries and throws me on Coldheart Mortimer
I will put on my widow's weeds.
Four times I let him spit upon my hair
But now, rather, do I stand bareheaded
Under heaven. For at the fifth time
The wind changes and heaven has another face
And changed is the breath upon my lips.
To London!
Mortimer has entered meanwhile.

MORTIMER:

Yet not so, my lady.
London warms but watery soup for our kind.

ANNE:

Where is your army, Earl Mortimer?

MORTIMER:

My army lies
Dead between meadows and a quarry.
And a pitiless bog has swallowed many
A mother's son. Where is your husband, lady?

ANNE:

With his dead Gaveston.

MORTIMER:

And France's sister?

ANNE:

At the crossroads between London and Scotland.
He charged me to levy troops in Scotland
On the day of Killingworth.

MORTIMER:

He charged me
To wander as a living witness
To the day of Killingworth.
Seven heads he struck from the hydra; may he
Find seven times seven when he wakes.
Enmeshed in marches and encampments
He will never free himself from war
Or from dead Gaveston.

ANNE:

He abused his wife for all to see.

MORTIMER:

He misused his kingdom like a pimp.

ANNE:

He bound me in chains and packed me off.

MORTIMER:

He gutted the land like a bleeding hunk of game.

ANNE:

Strike him, Mortimer!

MORTIMER:

Because he spurned you like a mangy bitch.

ANNE:

Because he spurned me like a worthless bitch.

MORTIMER:

You who were queen.

ANNE:

Who was a child in innocence
Not knowing the world or men.

MORTIMER:

Devour him!

ANNE:

I shall become a she-wolf
Ranging bare-toothed through the scrub
Not resting
Until the earth covers Edward long since dead –
Edward Gloucester, my husband sometime
Yesteryear – earth covers him.
She throws three lumps of earth behind her.
Rousing the poor from out the woods
Myself sullied by the wicked guile of the world and men
Ranging like a she-wolf, by wolves mounted
Drenched by the rain of exile
Hardened by foreign winds.

MORTIMER:

Earth upon Edward of England!

ANNE:

Earth upon Edward Gloucester!

MORTIMER:

To Scotland!

ANNE:

Ah Mortimer, war comes, whose end shall be
To drown this island in the deep wide sea.

AFTER FOUR YEARS OF WAR KING EDWARD IS
STILL LIVING IN CAMP. LANDING OF QUEEN ANNE.
THE DAY OF HARWICH (23 SEPTEMBER 1324)

Camp near Harwich

Edward, Spencer, Baldock.

EDWARD:

So, after many treacheries in four years' war
Triumpheth England's Edward with his friends.
Enter a courier with a message.

SPENCER:

What news, my lord?

EDWARD *tearing up the message:*

None. What news have you?

SPENCER:

None.

EDWARD:

Why man, they say there is a great slaughter.
And execution done through the realm.

BALDOCK:

That was, unless I do mistake, four
Years ago, my lord.

EDWARD:

Four good years. Living under canvas
And campaigning are a pleasure.
Horses are good. Wind cleanses the lungs.
And if skin shrivels and hair falls out
Rain washes the kidneys and all is better
Than London.

BALDOCK:

Would rather we could rail at London
In London.

EDWARD:

Have you still that list?

SPENCER:

Indeed, my lord.

EDWARD:

I pray you, let us hear it. Read it, Spencer.
Spencer reads the list of the executed peers.

EDWARD:

Methinks one name is lacking. Mortimer.
Have you proclaimed reward for such
As bring him in?

SPENCER:

We have, sire, and renew it every year.

EDWARD:

Shows he his face in England he'll soon be here.
Enter another messenger.

SECOND MESSENGER:

Rumours tell of ship on ship from the North.

EDWARD:

That means nothing. Those are herring fishers
Coming from the North.
Exit messenger.

EDWARD:

Touching the other names upon thy paper
They were still barking four years ago
Now they bark no more, nor bite.

BALDOCK *to Spencer:*

He credits nothing. Since his decline whatever's
Said to him he hastens to forget.

EDWARD:

Yet where are the Scottish troops?
Always you hear of troops. Falsely. Yet of
The Scottish troops for which we sent the Queen
Four years ago comes not a word.
Enter the army.

FIRST SOLDIER:

The king's army, proved in four years' strife
And having slain so many lords like rats
Lacking now uniforms, supplies, and footwear

Prays King Edward, son to Edward Longshanks
Father of the English army, that this year
They may eat Thames eels again.

SOLDIERS:

Long live King Edward!

SECOND SOLDIER:

Our women would be breeding. Only because
This war perchance may never end, now
The King has sworn he'll not sleep in a bed
Until the enemy are on their knees.

FIRST SOLDIER:

And now that many a man's gone home
Saying it was for a will, beer-licence, childbed
It were good to know if the king intends
To go to London or not.

THIRD SOLDIER:

Go you to London, sire?

FOURTH SOLDIER:

Or what shall you do?

EDWARD:

Wage war against the cranes of the air
The fish in the deep sea that faster spawn than die
Monday against the great Leviathan, Thursday in
    Wales
Against the vultures; now, to eat.

SPENCER:

The watery diet has given the king
A little fever. Go.
Spencer and Baldock push the soldiers out.

EDWARD:

Bring me to drink, Baldock.
Exit Baldock.

SPENCER:

They'll not come back again.
Will you really not to London, sire?
Enter third messenger.

MESSENGER:

My lord, armed men are moving through the wood at
 Harwich.

EDWARD:

Let them. They are the servants
Of Welsh traders.
He sits and eats.
Have ships been sighted?

THIRD MESSENGER:

Yes, sire.

EDWARD:

Villages burn in the North?

THIRD MESSENGER:

Yes, sire.

EDWARD:

It is the Queen with Scottish troops
For us.

SPENCER:

Hardly.

EDWARD:

I will not have you watch me whiles I eat.
Exeunt Spencer and Messenger.

EDWARD *alone:*

There is sorrow in my heart my son
Should be suborned to prop their wickedness.
Enter Spencer.

SPENCER:

Fly, sire! Tis not the time to eat!
Shall I call your army to the battle!

EDWARD:

No. Edward knows his army's far away and home.

SPENCER:

Will you not fight against Roger Mortimer?

EDWARD:

Help me God! He is like a fish
In home water.
Exit with Spencer and soldiers.
Off-stage marching, battle, retreat.

Enter Mortimer, Anne, Young Edward, troops.

ANNE:

Successful battles gives the God of Kings
To those that fight in the shadow of right. As we
Are proven by success and thus by right, thanks be
To Him that steered the planets for us. We are
Come in arms to this part of our isle
Lest a breed of men baser than all others
Knitting strength with strength lay England waste
Hacking its own body with its bloody
Weapons. As has been clearly shown
By the most dreadful fall of suborned Edward who —

MORTIMER:

If, my lady, you would be a soldier, you must
Not show passion in your speech.
Changed is
The face of this isle, today England's queen
Is landed with her son Edward.
Enter Rice ap Howell.

RICE AP HOWELL:

The fleeing Edward, by all foresaken
Is sailing with the wind to Ireland.

MORTIMER:

May it sink him or leave him in the lurch.
My lords, since now we hold the kingdom from
The Irish sea even to the Channel
Raise young Edward on our shields!
Let our party swear an oath to him!
Show the soldiers the Lord Warden of the realm!
*Young Edward is led out. Exeunt omnes except Mortimer and
the Queen.*

ANNE:

Now he has his Scottish troops
And his bitch comes and springs at him.
All that remains of him are half-eaten
Kitchen scraps and a tattered hammock
While my body, almost virgin-like, takes life.

MORTIMER:

We must send troops to the South.
Tomorrow morning you must be in London.
Still no news of the Irish fleet.
It will join with us, I hope. Are you weary?

ANNE:

Are you working?

MORTIMER:

I secure you England.

ANNE:

Ah, Mortimer, there is less pleasure than I thought
Tasting the fruit of this victory. It is stale
In the mouth, it's watery, it's not
Amusing.

MORTIMER:

Because of Edward?

ANNE:

Edward? I know him not. It is his smell
Here in the tent.
It was better in the Scottish hills
Than here in swampy lowlands. What do you think
To offer me now, Mortimer?

MORTIMER:

You are
Glutted. It is your bloated flesh.
Wait for London.
Enter Baldock with a drink.

MORTIMER:

Who art thou, fellow?

BALDOCK:

King Edward's Baldock, and I bring to drink.

MORTIMER *taking the drink from him:*

Hang him!

BALDOCK:

I cannot recommend that, noble sir.
Not that I am unwilling to depart;
It is our mortal lot and lasts not long.

But in Ireland my mother'd not rejoice to see it.
Leaving the tent to fetch him to drink –
Ah 'twixt fortune and misfortune there's not time
To drink a sip of water – I loved him much
And yet, returning to the tent
I must alas, so soon betray him. Indeed
Without me you'll not take him; for I alone
Have entry to his heart. And further
Madam, you'd not know him, nor his mother
Nor his innocent son
For time and life so have altered him.

MORTIMER:

Good, bring him to us!

BALDOCK:

The Bible teaches how it's done.
When your people come with manacles and
With thongs I will say to him: Beloved lord
Be of good cheer, here is a napkin. And the man
To whom I give the napkin, that is he.

Near Harwich

KENT alone:

With the wind's first breath he fled. He's sick.
Why have I thus all so unbrotherly
Borne arms against thee? Lying in thy tent
In their honeymoon this spotted pair
Aim against thy life, Edward. God rain vengeance
On my cursed head.
As running water cannot flow uphill
So wrong shall die and justice conquer still.

CAPTURE OF KING EDWARD IN THE GRANARY OF
NEATH ABBEY (19 OCTOBER 1324)

Neath Abbey

Edward, Spencer, Lord Abbot.

ABBOT:

Have you no doubt, my lord; have you no fear.
Forget that I was once abused by you
In times which have much altered. In these
Tempests you and we are merely pilgrims
To Our Lady of the Shipwrecks.

EDWARD:

Father, pierced by the sight of my flesh
All hearts must miss a beat, times have so changed.

ABBOT:

As you would hide from evil eyes
Here in this granary take this pillow.

EDWARD:

No pillow, Abbot. Let the soldier
Have his hammock.
Enter Baldock.

EDWARD:

Who comes?

BALDOCK:

King Edward's Baldock.

EDWARD:

And our only friend. 'Tis comfort to the hunted
When a brother seeks him in his lair.
Drink our water with us, eat our
Salt and bread.

BALDOCK:

Twice the moon has changed since I saw you
In the camp at Harwich.

SPENCER:

How stands it in London?

BALDOCK:

In London all is upside down, it seems.

EDWARD:

Come Spencer! Baldock come, sit by me
Make trial now of that philosophy
That in our famous nurseries of arts
Thou suckedst from Plato and from Aristotle.
Ah, Spencer
Since words are crude, dividing heart from heart
And understanding is not given us
In such deafness only bodies' touch is left
Between men. And this indeed's
But little, and all is vain.
Enter a monk.

MONK:

Father, a second ship is sailing into harbour.

ABBOT:

Since when?

MONK:

These few minutes.

EDWARD:

What does he say?

ABBOT:

Nothing, Sire.
To Spencer:
Did any see you come here?

SPENCER:

No one.

ABBOT:

Do you expect someone?

SPENCER:

No. No one.

MONK:

The ship puts to.

BALDOCK:

Tell me, King Edward, why, when you

Had Roger Mortimer in your grasp, did you
Spare him on the day of Killingworth?
Edward is silent.

BALDOCK:

Today you'd have a wind for Ireland.
Were you in Ireland you'd be saved.

SPENCER:

It left us in the lurch and all but sank us.

EDWARD:

Mortimer! Who talks of Mortimer?
A bloody man. Lord Abbot, on thy lap
Lay I this head, laden with care and violence.
O might I never ope these eyes again!

BALDOCK:

What is that noise?

SPENCER:

'Tis nothing. 'Tis a gust of snow.

BALDOCK:

I thought it was a cock-crow.
The noise deceived.

SPENCER:

Look up, my lord. Baldock, this drowsiness
Betides no good. We are betrayed already.
Enter Rice ap Howell and troops.

SOLDIER:

I'll wager Wales, these be the men.

BALDOCK *to himself:*

See him sitting there, hoping, unseen
As though flies covered him, to escape
From murdering hands.

RICE AP HOWELL:

In England's name which among you is the king?

SPENCER:

There is no king here.

BALDOCK *goes up to King Edward:*

Take this napkin, I pray you, good my lord.
You have sweat upon your brow.

RICE AP HOWELL:

Take him. This is he.

Edward as he goes between armed men, stares at Baldock.

BALDOCK *weeps:*

My mother in Ireland would eat some bread.
Sire, pardon me.

KING EDWARD, A PRISONER IN SHREWSBURY
CASTLE, REFUSES TO RENOUNCE THE CROWN.

Shrewsbury

*The Lord Abbot, now Archbishop of Winchester, Rice ap
Howell.*

ABBOT:

When he succeeded to his father Edward
He sported happy hours with a man
Named Gaveston
Who christened me with channel water
In a dark alley by Westminster Abbey.
Then through an error he embroiled himself
In a desperate oath and turned a tiger.
Some time after, the Queen, she who clung
To him so long, left him, with many others.
After many years it fell to me to see him
When he was a shipwreck, spattered
With much blood and vices, under my protection
At Neath Abbey.
Today am I Archbishop of Winchester
Successor to a man whose head he
Struck off, and I am charged
To ask him for his crown.

RICE AP HOWELL:

Now he is in chains he refuses
Food and drink. Go carefully, touch
Not his head but touch his heart.

ABBOT:

When you hear these words upon my lips:
'Allow me to begin with the set form'
Then draw nearer with some others
Witnesses that Edward the Second abdicated.
Unnoticed then and painlessly will I
This concession, like a bad tooth
Draw from him.
Enter Edward.

RICE AP HOWELL:

He still speaks. Hear him and say naught.
Better speak than think. See, he warms himself
With his words. Remember he is cold.
Will you not eat, my lord? Why do you refuse
To eat?
Edward is silent.
Exit Rice ap Howell.

EDWARD:

The forest deer, being struck
Runs to an herb that closeth up the wounds;
But when the tiger's flesh is gored, he rends
And tears it with his wrathful paw.
Often I think that all is ever change.
But when I call to mind I am a king
Methinks I should revenge me of the wrongs
That Mortimer and Anne have done to me.
And yet we kings when regiment is gone
Are perfect shadows in a sunshine day.
Truly I think most things are vain.
The nobles rule, I bear the name of king
And my unconstant queen
Once hateful to me for her bitch-like clinging
(And so debased that her love's not

Part of her like her own hair but a mere
Thing, changing with every change)
Now spots my nuptial bed
While sorrow at my elbow still attends
And grief still clasps me to his breast and I
Must bleed my heart out at this strange exchange.

ABBOT:

God paints with grief and pallor those he loves.
Would it please your majesty to ease
Your bosom in my ear?

EDWARD:

The starving fishermen of Yarmouth
I pressed for rent.

ABBOT:

What else weighs on thy heart?

EDWARD:

I kept my wife Anne in the city in fifteen.
In the August heat. A whim.

ABBOT:

What else weighs on thy heart?

EDWARD:

I spared Roger Mortimer for malicious pleasure.

ABBOT:

What else weighs upon thy heart?

EDWARD:

I whipped my dog Truly till he bled. Vanity.

ABBOT:

And what else weighs upon thy heart?

EDWARD:

Nothing.

ABBOT:

No bloodshed, no offences against nature?

EDWARD:

Nothing.
O wild despair of man's estate!
Say, father, must I now resign my crown
To make usurping Mortimer a king?

ABBOT:

Your grace mistakes, with all respect we crave
The crown for the child Edward's right.

EDWARD:

No it is for Mortimer, not Edward's head.
For he's a lamb encompassed by two wolves
That in a moment will rip out his throat.

ABBOT:

That child in London is in God's hands.
And many say your abdication
Were good both for your son and you.

EDWARD:

Why do they tell lies to one who
Scarce can ope his lids for weariness?
Say't, fear not my weariness: You do it
So that England's vine may perish
And Edward's name ne'er come within the Chronicles.

ABBOT:

My Lord, these last times must have been
Most cruel to make you hold such stark belief
In human wickedness. My son, since thou
Hast opened up thy heart to me, lay
Thy head once more upon my lap and hear me.

EDWARD *takes off his crown, then:*

Let me but wear it for today! Thou shouldst
Stay by me till evening and I
Will fast and cry: Continue ever, sun!
Let not the dark moon possess this clime!
Stand still you watches of the element
You moon and seasons, rest you at a stay
That Edward may be still fair England's king.
But day's bright beam doth quickly pass away.
He puts on his crown again.
Inhuman creatures nursed with tiger's milk
Lusting for your sovereign's overthrow.
See, you monsters, from Westminster Abbey, see!
I cannot take it off, my hair goes with it

It is quite grown with it. Oh it
Has at all times been an easy burden to me
No heavier than the maple's crown of twigs
So light and pleasing at all times to wear
And for all time now a little blood
A scrap of skin, black blood will stick to it
From Edward the Powerless, the Poor, the tiger's prey.

ABBOT:

Be patient. This is but the green discharge
Of a chastised body, a fantasy, a whistling wind
On a rainy night. Strip the linen from your breast.
I lay my hand straightway upon your heart
That it may lighter beat, for it is real.

EDWARD:

Were it reality and reality all this
The earth would open up and swallow us
Yet since it does not open and thus
'Tis as a dream, fantasy, and has naught to do
With the world's common reality nor with an
Ordinary day, I lay down this crown —

ABBOT:

Aye! Take it off! It is not thy flesh!

EDWARD:

Sure this is not real and I
Must wake in Westminster
After thirteen happily concluded years of war —
In London.
I, in the recorded births at Caernarvon
Edward, King of England, Edward Longshanks' son
Thus in the church register.

ABBOT:

You are in a sweat? You must eat!
I'll take it from your sight. Make haste!

EDWARD:

So quick? Here take it, seize it. But
If it please you with a cloth, 'tis wet.
Quick quick! 'Tis almost evening! Go! Tell them

At Shrewsbury Edward had no wish
To eat the icy wind with wolves
And gave it for a roof against the winter
That stands before the door.

ABBOT:

Permit me then
To begin with the set form: I, Thomas
Archbishop of Winchester, ask you
Edward of England, Second of that name
Son to Edward Longshanks: 'Art thou willing
To resign the crown and to renounce
Therewith all rights and claims.'
Rice ap Howell and his men have entered.

EDWARD:

No no no, you liars! Slaves! Measure you
The ocean with your little cups? Have I
Been tricked then? Have I babbled?
Have you come this time without a storm, man?
Have you another habit on, Lord Abbot?
Once before already, Winchester, I had
Your face struck off. Faces like yours
Do multiply ever in a most harmful way.
In such a case one named Mortimer
Was wont to say: like flies! Or did you
When I washed you in the gutter, lose
Your face there so I saw it not
When I laid my head upon your lap?
Aye, Lord Abbot, the things of this world are
Not constant.

ABBOT:

Make no mistake. Even if your hand's too good
To touch my face, be sure of this:
My face is real.

EDWARD:

Go quick! 'Tis evening. Tell the Peers: Edward
Dies soon. Less haste were courtesy.
Say too: he gave you leave not to

Mourn him greatly when you toll the knell
For him, but prayed you to go down
Upon your knees and say: Now
Is he the easier. Say: He bade us not to
Credit when, distractedly, he spoke
What seemed renunciation of the crown.
Thrice said he: No.

ABBOT:

My lord as you have said so be it done.
But as for us we are only moved by care
For Mother England. Two days
In London one was sought who
Was not your enemy and none was found
But me. And so we take our leave.
Exeunt Abbot and the others save Rice ap Howell.

EDWARD:

And now Rice ap Howell, give me to eat.
For Edward eats now.
He sits and eats.
Since I did not resign I know the next
News that they bring will be my death.
Enter Berkeley with a letter.

RICE AP HOWELL:

What bring you, Berkeley?

EDWARD:

What we know.
Pardon us, Berkeley, that we are at meat.
Come Berkeley
Tell thy message to my naked breast.

BERKELEY:

Think you, my lord, Berkeley
Would stain his hands?

RICE AP HOWELL:

An order from Westminster commands
That I resign my charge.

EDWARD:

And who must keep me now? You, Berkeley?

BERKELEY:
So 'tis decreed.

EDWARD *takes the letter:*
By Mortimer whose name is written here.
He tears the letter.
So may his limbs be torn as is this paper.

BERKELEY:
Your grace must straight to horse for Berkeley.

EDWARD:
Whither you will; all places are alike
And every earth is fit for burial.

BERKELEY:
And thinks your grace that Berkeley will be cruel?

EDWARD:
I know not.

IN THE YEARS 1324–6 THE PRISONER EDWARD
PASSES FROM HAND TO HAND.

Shrewsbury

RICE AP HOWELL *alone:*
His state moved me to pity. That is
The ground why Berkeley had
To take him hence.
Enter Kent.

KENT:
In London it is said the king's resigned.

RICE AP HOWELL:
Lies.

KENT:
Mortimer says so.

RICE AP HOWELL:
He lies. In my hearing thrice the king
Said no.

KENT:

Where is my brother?

RICE AP HOWELL:

These thirteen days Berkeley sent for him
To come.

KENT:

London believes he is with you.

RICE AP HOWELL:

Berkeley had an order signed by Mortimer.

KENT:

'Tis strange that no one's seen the king
Face to face and strange that no one's
Heard him and strange that now he speaks
In Mortimer's mouth.

RICE AP HOWELL:

'Tis strange indeed.

KENT:

Therefore to Berkeley swiftly will I hie
To learn from Edward's mouth what's truth, what lie.

THE QUEEN LAUGHS AT THE WORLD'S EMPTINESS.

Westminster

The Queen, Mortimer, the two brothers Gurney.

MORTIMER:

Did Berkeley give him to you willingly?

ELDER GURNEY:

No.

ANNE *aside:*

Here among the tapestries of Westminster it reeks
Of strangled chickens. You walked easier
In Scottish air.

MORTIMER *talking with the Gurneys:*
Look you, this Berkeley was a man
With milk in his bones, who wept too easy.
If he saw someone draw another's tooth
He'd faint on you. The earth lie easy on him.
You are not other such?

ELDER GURNEY:
Oh no, my lord, we are not of that sort.

ANNE:
Business! Business! The smell of too much
History between the walls of
Westminster. Will your hands not
Peel in London's lye? Your
Hands are scribbler's hands.

MORTIMER:
Where is your prisoner?

YOUNGER GURNEY:
North east south west from Berkeley, my lord.

MORTIMER:
See there are men whom cold air
Cannot harm. Know you aught
Of geography? Could you show England
To a man who knows it all too little?
In all directions?

ELDER GURNEY:
So we should lead him round about?

MORTIMER:
And specially where there's no sun nor men.

ELDER GURNEY:
Good, my lord, we are the men for that.

ANNE:
Ale! Ale! Jonah sat and waited
For the promised overthrow of Nineveh
But in those days God came that way
No more and Nineveh fell not. Now
I have richly eaten and am full of food
And I can eat more now than in the time

When I was growing. Are you learned still
In metaphysics, Earl Mortimer?

MORTIMER:

There are, to be sure, men who talk
From morn till night.

YOUNGER GURNEY:

We are other men than that.

MORTIMER:

Have you ever read a Chronicle?

ELDER GURNEY:

No. No.

MORTIMER:

'Tis good.
Exeunt the two Gurneys.

MORTIMER:

We hold an old wolf by the ear
That if he slip will seize upon us both.

ANNE:

Do you sleep badly? See something white at night?
Often? They are sheets, Mortimer, nothing else.
It comes from the stomach.

MORTIMER:

At his name the Commons turn to water.

ANNE:

He of whom it seems you speak, is silent.

MORTIMER:

Since he is obdurate and will not speak
Lies with lies must be o'erlain.

ANNE:

Business! Business! The days fly too slow
For me in Westminster and too many.

MORTIMER:

Husband's murder comes soon after father's murder
In the catechism.

ANNE:

You've an indulgence.

MORTIMER:

With knees wide and closed eyes
Catching at anything, you are insatiable, Anne.
You eat in your sleep and talk in sleep
Of things shall kill me.

ANNE:

I sleep, you say. How do you wake me?

MORTIMER:

With Westminster bells and grinding teeth
And in despite of these incredulous lords
You should crown your son in haste.

ANNE:

Not my son, I pray you!
Not this child, suckled by a she-wolf's milk
In weeks when she was wandering, dragged
Through bogs and hills in dark Scotland
Not this child
Too much night upon his lids to look up guiltless
Entangled in the filthy net with which you fish.

MORTIMER:

Dragging a little burden from
An age-old slimy pond, always
Though weary in the flesh, I see hanging from it
Human weed. More and more.
Hoisting myself up I feel ever a new
Weight.
And from the knees of the last another
Last. Human coils.
And at the moving wheel of this pulley block
Of human coils, breathless, lugging at them all
Myself.

ANNE:

Name the faces of those human weeds.
My husband Edward? My son Edward?

MORTIMER:

Yours.

ANNE:

Often I feared that these tired arms
With which I held a man upright perforce
Must yield, but now I know, when age
Has mingled weariness in my veins' flow
My outstretched arms are but a crude pretence
A vain machine that grabs – naught else
Remains. Roger Mortimer, I am
Tired and old.
Enter Young Edward.

MORTIMER:

Hook your dress up, Anne, so your son
See not tear-stained flesh.

YOUNG EDWARD:

Take this intruder, mother, from our sight.
We would have talk with you.

ANNE:

Earl Mortimer, child, is thy mother's prop.

YOUNG EDWARD:

I pray you for news of my father Edward.

ANNE:

If thy mother, child, hung on thy poor lips
This most fearful choice, say, wouldst thou
Go with her unto the Tower if by
Thy answer's colour the dice so fell?
Young Edward is silent.

MORTIMER:

You show wise caution, Edward.

YOUNG EDWARD:

You should drink less, mother.
Anne laughs.
Exit Young Edward.

MORTIMER:

Why do you laugh?
Anne is silent.

MORTIMER:

So prepare we in haste the boy's crowning.

For this our business wears another face
When a king's name is underwrit.

ANNE:

What has or ever will befall –
If Heaven will pardon it or no –
Your blood I've tasted and will not let you go
Till all this crack.
Meanwhile write, underwrite, decree
As you think fit. I will seal it for you sure.
She laughs.

MORTIMER:

Why do you laugh a second time?

ANNE:

I laugh for the world's emptiness.

Highway

KENT *alone:*

Berkeley is dead and Edward disappeared.
And Mortimer, in London, ever bolder, claims
In Berkeley's hearing Edward resigned the crown.
The light is murky now for us, Edward Longshanks'
Sons. Already there's a sign the sky will brighten.
The Commons were in uproar, clamoured
To be told the prisoner's whereabouts
And many called him poor Edward.
In Wales the people murmured against the butcher
      Mortimer.
Perchance now only crows and ravens
Know where lies Edward of England.
And I had hopes my rue came not too late!
Who is that poor man there mid pikes and lances?
Enter Edward, the two Gurneys, soldiers.

YOUNGER GURNEY:

Holà. Who comes there?

ELDER GURNEY:

Guard the King sure; it is his brother, Kent.

EDWARD:

O gentle brother, help to rescue me!

ELDER GURNEY:

Keep them asunder! Away with the prisoner!

KENT:

Soldiers, let me but talk to him one word.

YOUNGER GURNEY:

Stop up his mouth!

ELDER GURNEY:

Throw him in the ditch!
Edward is taken out.

KENT *alone:*

Edward, hast resigned? Edward! Edward!
Woe to us!
They drag England's king away like a calf.

3 DECEMBER 1325: THE MIGHTY EARL ROGER
MORTIMER IS TAKEN TO TASK FOR THE KING'S
DISAPPEARANCE

Westminster

Mortimer, Queen, Lord Abbot, Rice ap Howell.

ABBOT:

My Lord, like to a canker grows the rumour
Edward has not resigned.

MORTIMER:

At Berkeley, in Robert Berkeley's hearing
Edward the Second resigned, unforced.

ABBOT:

In my hearing, at Shrewsbury, clearly
Edward cried: No.

RICE AP HOWELL:

And thus often to me.

ABBOT:

It were good if this Berkeley
Could testify on oath before the Commons.
How and 'fore whom Edward put away the crown.

MORTIMER:

Today I have news from Lord Berkeley
That he is on his way to London.

RICE AP HOWELL:

And where is the king?

MORTIMER:

At Berkeley, where else? Too much knowledge, Rice
ap Howell
Dulls the appetite. Since I set aside
Books and learning I sleep better and digest.

RICE AP HOWELL:

Yes, but where is Edward?

MORTIMER:

I know nothing of your Edward, I love
Him not nor hate, he comes not
In my dreams. For things concerning him
Turn to Berkeley, not to me! Yourself, Winchester
Were against him.

ABBOT:

The Church was, with whom God was.

MORTIMER:

With whom was God?

ABBOT:

With him who conquered, Mortimer.
Enter Kent with Young Edward.

KENT:

We hear my brother
Is no more at Shrewsbury.

MORTIMER:

Your brother is at Berkeley, Edmund.

KENT:

We hear he is no more at Berkeley either.

MORTIMER:

Since Harwich rumours grow like
Mildew in the rain.

ANNE:

Come to thy mother, child.

MORTIMER:

How fares my honourable Lord of Kent?

KENT:

In health, sweet Mortimer. And you
My lady?

ANNE:

Well, Kent. Times are good for me and I
Am quite content. This past week I was
Fishing in Tynemouth.

MORTIMER:

To have gone fishing years ago at Tynemouth
Truly would have done a certain man
No harm.

ANNE:

Go fishing at Tynemouth next week with me, Kent.

MORTIMER *aside*:

You eat too much and do not chew, Anne.

ANNE *aside*:

I eat, I drink, I love with you.

ABBOT:

What were you saying, my Lord of Berkeley?

MORTIMER *to Kent*:

You were missed in London for three weeks.

KENT:

I rode across the mangled countryside
And meditated on my brother's tracks.

YOUNG EDWARD:

Mother, persuade me not to wear the crown

I'll not do it.

ANNE:

You should be pleased. The Barons wish it.

MORTIMER:

London wills it.

YOUNG EDWARD:

Let me speak with my father first
And then I will.

KENT:

That's a good answer, Ned.

ANNE:

Brother, you know it is impossible.

YOUNG EDWARD:

Is he dead?

KENT:

London says many things.
You must have knowledge, Roger Mortimer.

MORTIMER:

I? In Little Street at brightest noon
Five sharks were seen to go into a tavern
Take ale, and then, a little merry
To kneel in Westminster Abbey.
Laughter.

KENT:

They prayed, sure, for Berkeley's soul.

MORTIMER:

Inconstant Edmund, dost thou favour him
Who wast the cause of his imprisonment?

KENT:

The more cause now to make amends.

YOUNG EDWARD:

Aye aye!

KENT:

Ned, I counsel thee, be not wheedled
Take not the crown from thy father's head.

YOUNG EDWARD:

Indeed I will not.

RICE AP HOWELL:

He will not, Edward.

MORTIMER

takes Young Edward and drags him to his mother:

My Lady, signify to your son Edward
It is not England's wont to suffer
Contradiction.

YOUNG EDWARD:

Help, Uncle Kent. Mortimer will wrong me.

KENT:

Hands off England's royal blood!

ABBOT:

Would you really crown him in this bedlam?

MORTIMER:

So says the law.

RICE AP HOWELL:

So says your desire.

ABBOT:

Therefore I ask you by the law
In the presence of that man's brother, son, wife:
Has King Edward resigned?

MORTIMER:

Aye.

ABBOT:

Your witness?

MORTIMER:

Robert Berkeley.

KENT:

Who is dead.

RICE AP HOWELL:

Berkeley is dead?

KENT:

These seven days.

RICE AP HOWELL:

Said you not that you had news this very day
He was on his way to London?

ABBOT:

Since your witness, Lord Mortimer, is out this world

Be it these two or seven days
With your consent ride I to Berkeley
To bring a little light.

KENT:

At Berkeley you'll find blood upon the stones
But not the king.

RICE AP HOWELL:

Did you not say the king was at Berkeley?

MORTIMER:

And so I thought. Times pressed us hard.
In Wales the rebels gave us scarce a moment's
Breath. With greater leisure and
More opportune time much will be
Made clear.

ABBOT:

Thus is your first witness, Berkeley, dead
And your second, Edward, disappeared.

MORTIMER:

If I must fish through all the isle
With nets I shall
Uncover witnesses.

KENT:

First fish through your army, Mortimer.
I saw my brother among pikes and lances
Driven down the highway by a rout.

ABBOT:

Spoke your brother to you?

KENT:

His mouth
Was gagged. What think you, Archbishop
His lips had testified an they were able?

MORTIMER:

Wilt thou pretend that he has not resigned?
Strike off his head! He shall have martial law.

EDWARD:

My lord, he is my uncle and shall live.

MORTIMER:

My lord, he is your enemy and shall die.

KENT:

Wouldst have my head then, butcher Mortimer?
Where is the head of Edward Longshanks'
Firstborn son?

ABBOT:

The man is not at Berkeley nor at Shrewsbury.
Where is the man today, Roger Mortimer?

EDWARD:

Mother, permit him not to kill our Uncle
Kent!

ANNE:

Ask me not, child, I dare not speak a word.

KENT:

Plead you with the murderer for the murdered?
Seek in the Thames, seek in the Scottish pines
The resting place of him who found no refuge
Because his teeth held back that yes
You so desired.

RICE AP HOWELL:

Where is the man today, Roger Mortimer?

ABBOT:

Has he resigned?

MORTIMER:

Call the Commons for the eleventh of February.
Before them with his own lips Edward will
Affirm his abdication. And I
Reaping mistrust where I sowed thanks
Prepared to bring my heart and every hour
Lived out in Westminster before God's judgement
Relinquishing my office in your hands
O Queen, repairing to my books
Which I, my only true friends, bartered
Years ago for war's discomforts and the world's
Ill-will, I make charge before the Peers and you
Against this Kent, Edward Longshanks' son
Of high treason, and I claim his head.

ABBOT:

You dare greatly.

MORTIMER:

It is for you, my lady.

ANNE:

Thus say I:
Be Edmund Kent banished from London.

KENT *to Mortimer:*

You shall pay this to the very dregs.
Gladly Kent leaves Westminster
Where he was born and where now
A bull keeps house with his ruttish wife.

ANNE:

You, Earl Mortimer, are still the Lord Protector.

ABBOT:

And I summon the Commons for the eleventh of
    February.
That by what Edward himself shall say
The naked truth be made as clear as day.
Exeunt all save Mortimer.

MORTIMER *alone, brings in the two Gurneys:*

You'll make your man say aye
To every question. Engrave it on him.
But the eleventh of February be in London.
You have full power. He must say aye.

AFTER FOURTEEN YEARS ABSENCE KING EDWARD
SEES THE CITY OF LONDON ONCE AGAIN.

Before London

Edward. The two Gurneys.

ELDER GURNEY:

My lord, look not so pensive.

EDWARD:

Since you are come, each time that night falls
You lead me over land. Where must I go now?
Go not so fast. I have not eaten and
I am all weak, my hair falls out, my
Senses swoon from my body's stench.

YOUNGER GURNEY:

Are you in such good humour, sire?

EDWARD:

Aye.

ELDER GURNEY:

We come now to a great city.
Will it content you to see the Eel?

EDWARD:

Aye.

YOUNGER GURNEY:

Are those not willows there, sire?

EDWARD:

Aye.

ELDER GURNEY:

The Eel likes not men to visit him
Half washed. Here is channel water.
Sit down, I pray, that we may barber you.

EDWARD:

Not with puddle water!

YOUNGER GURNEY:

So you would have us barber you with
Puddle water?

They barber him with ditch water.

ELDER GURNEY:

The nights are beginning to draw in.

YOUNGER GURNEY:

Tomorrow is the eleventh of February.

ELDER GURNEY:

Was it not a certain Gaveston
That brought you to this pass?

EDWARD:

Aye. This Gaveston I do remember well.

YOUNGER GURNEY:

Hold still!

ELDER GURNEY:

Will you do everything we bid you?

EDWARD:

Aye. Is this London?

YOUNGER GURNEY:

This is the City of London, sire.

ELEVENTH OF FEBRUARY, 1326.

London

Soldiers and crowd before Westminster.

FIRST: The eleventh of February will count among the most important days in England's history.

SECOND: A man's toes freeze on such a night as this.

THIRD: And we have waited here for seven hours.

SECOND: Is Ned already in there?

FIRST: He must pass by to go to Parliament.

SECOND: There's a light again up there in Westminster.

THIRD: Will the Eel bring him round?

FIRST: I'll lay a silver shilling on the Eel.

SECOND: And I two shillings on Ned.

FIRST: What's your name?

SECOND: Smith. And yours?

FIRST: Baldock.

THIRD: It'll snow for sure about morning.

Westminster

Edward, blindfold, the two Gurneys.

ELDER GURNEY:
Are you content to be at last at the Eel's?
EDWARD:
Aye. Where is the Eel?
YOUNGER GURNEY:
That you'll soon see.
Exeunt the two Gurneys.
Enter Mortimer.

MORTIMER:
As London's sweaty market has so forced matters
That my head for these few minutes almost hangs
Upon a yea or nay from this man's humbled lips
So from him in his weakened state will I
Rip out this yea like a tooth.
Takes off Edward's blindfold.

EDWARD:
Is this Westminster and are you the Eel?
MORTIMER:
So men call me. It is a harmless beast.
You are weary; you shall eat
Drink, bathe perhaps. Would you like that?
EDWARD:
Aye.
MORTIMER:
You shall find yourself a friend.
Edward looks at him.
You shall be taken to England's Parliament.
There before the Peers you'll testify
You have resigned.
EDWARD:
Draw nearer, Mortimer.
We give you leave to sit. But for our

Broken health be brief
In your petition.
            MORTIMER *to himself:*
He is hard. Antaeus-like
He draws strength from Westminster's soil.
Aloud:
Brevity's the salt in watery soup. I
Have come for your reply if you'll
Resign in favour of your son Edward.
            EDWARD:
Thirteen years away from Westminster
After long campaigns, the thorny exercise
Of command, the flesh's needs have led me to
A commonplace concern with the welfare and
Decline of this my body.
            MORTIMER:
I understand you.
Nightly wanderings, human disenchantment
Give pause for thought. And do you
After all this weariness of which you speak
And which you've borne so patiently, with such
Broken health, still intend now
To continue office?
            EDWARD:
That is not in our plan.
            MORTIMER:
Will you consent?
            EDWARD:
That is not in our plan. The substance
Of these last days starts to clear. Edward, whose
Fall approaches, inexorable yet
Not fearful, knows himself. Not wishing much
To die he savours the usefulness of
Withering destruction. Edward, who no more
Poor Edward is, thinks death but little price
For such pleasure in his murderer. So then
When it is time, Mortimer, come yourself.

MORTIMER:

I see you grossly wrapped up in yourself
Whiles I, no longer sullied by a taste
For power, bear on my shoulders
This island that one workday word
Upon your lips can save from civil war.
Blunt perhaps in feelings, yet knowing much
No doubt not kingly, yet just perhaps
Not even that if you will, but yet
The rough stammering mouth of poor England
I ask you and I pray you:
Resign.

EDWARD:

Approach us not with such a mean request!
And yet at this hour when my body
Purifies I yearn to feel
Your hands about my throat.

MORTIMER:

You fight well. As one well versed in rhetoric
Whom men call the Eel, and valuing
Your taste, none the less I ask you
In this sober matter, at this night hour
For a brief answer.
Edward is silent.
Do not stop your ears! Lest the weight
Of human tongues, a moment's whim
And at the last misunderstanding, plunge
England in the ocean, speak now!
Edward is silent.
Will you resign before the Commons at noon
Today?
Edward is silent.

MORTIMER:

Will you not resign? You
Refuse?

EDWARD:

Though Edward must in swiftest time

Bring to a close more tangled matters
Than you, O busy Mortimer, can know
Yet while he's in this world he takes good care
For all that
Not to meddle arrogantly
In your affairs that from a growing
Distance seem to him most
Murky.
Therefore your question has no yea or nay.
Stitched up, his lips will nothing say.

Westminster

MORTIMER *alone:*

So long as he draws breath it can come to light.
Since not rough winds could snatch his foolish
Mantle from him, nor the warm sun draw it
Off, let it go rot
With him.
A scrap of paper cunningly prepared
Odourless, proving nothing, shall this
Chance resolve.
Since he gives my question neither yea or nay
I shall give an answer in like kind.
'Eduardum occidere nolite timere bonum est.'
I leave out the comma. Then can it read:
'Kill not the king, 'tis good to fear the worst'
Or depending on their state of innocence
Or whether they have dined or fasted:
'Fear not to kill the king, 'tis good he die.'
Unpointed as it is thus shall it go.
Now is England
Under us, above us God, who's very old.
My sole witness I take before the Peers.
Lightborn, come in.
Enter Lightborn.

If, when morning greys, the prisoner's
Learned nothing, he's not for saving.

Sewer in the Tower.
The two Gurneys.

ELDER GURNEY:

He speaks incessantly, tonight.

YOUNGER GURNEY:

It is
A wonder this king will not yield.
Worn out purposely, for when he would sleep
Our drum rolls, he stands
In a vault knee-deep in
Sewage, in which all the channels
Of the Tower run, yet he says not yea.

ELDER GURNEY:

That is most strange, brother. Just now I
Opened up the hatch to throw
Him meat and I was almost stifled
With the stench.

YOUNGER GURNEY:

He has a body more able to endure than we.
He sings. When you raise the hatch you hear
Him sing.

ELDER GURNEY:

I think he makes psalms
Against Spring's coming. Open up, we'll
Ask him again.

ELDER GURNEY:

Wilt thou say yes, Ned?

YOUNGER GURNEY:

No answer.
Lightborn has entered.

ELDER GURNEY:

Still he will not yield.
Lightborn gives a letter.

YOUNGER GURNEY:

What's this? I do not understand.

'Kill not the king, 'tis good to fear the worst.'

ELDER GURNEY:

'Fear not to kill the king' is there.

YOUNGER GURNEY:

Give the token.

Lightborn gives it.

ELDER GURNEY:

There is the key and there the vault.

Carry out the order. Need you anything besides?

LIGHTBORN:

A table and a feather bed.

YOUNGER GURNEY:

Here is a light for the cage.

Exeunt the two Gurneys.

Lightborn opens the door.

EDWARD:

This hole in which they hold me is the sink-hole

And upon me here, these seven hours, falls

London's filth. Yet its sewage hardens

My limbs. Now they are like cedar

Wood. The stench of rubbish makes my

Stature boundless. Great rolls on the drums

Keep him awake, though weak, so his death

Find him not in a swoon but rather

Waking.

Who's there? What light is that? Wherefore com'st

thou?

LIGHTBORN:

To comfort you.

EDWARD:

Thou would'st me kill.

LIGHTBORN:

What means your Highness to mistrust me thus?

Come out, brother.

EDWARD:

Thy look can harbour naught but death.

LIGHTBORN:

I am not without sin, yet not without
Heart. Come and lie down.

EDWARD:

Howell had pity, Berkeley was poorer
Yet he stained not his hand. The elder
Gurney's heart's a block
From Caucasus. The younger's harder. And
Mortimer, from whom thou comest, ice.

LIGHTBORN:

You are haggard, sire. Lie you
Upon this bed and rest awhile.

EDWARD:

Good was rain; hunger satisfied. But
The best was darkness. All
Were wavering, many hanging back but
The best were those betrayed me. Therefore
Whoever's dark let him dark remain, who's
Unclean, remain unclean. Praise
Want, praise cruelty, praise
The darkness.

LIGHTBORN:

Sleep, sire.

EDWARD:

Something buzzes in my ear and tells me
If I sleep now I never wake.
'Tis waiting makes me tremble thus.
Yet I cannot ope my eyes, they stick.
Therefore tell me wherefore thou art come.

LIGHTBORN:

For this.
Smothers him.

Westminster

MORTIMER *alone:*

Rise up eleventh of February
The others are shrubs beside me
They tremble at my name and dare not
Impeach me for his death.
Let come who will.
Enter the Queen.

ANNE:

Ah, Mortimer, my son hath news
His father's dead and now, new-hailed
As king, comes hither in the knowledge
We have murdered him.

MORTIMER:

What matter that he know since he's
A child so weak a drop of rain would
Kill him?

ANNE:

In to the Council Chamber he is gone
To crave the aid and succour of the peers, who
Like the people, wait since morning for this
Edward whom you promised. He tears
His hair and wrings his hands and vows
To be revenged upon us both.

MORTIMER:

Seem
I like one soon to be under earth?
*Enter Young Edward, Lord Abbot, Rice ap Howell,
peers.*

YOUNG EDWARD:

Murderers!

MORTIMER:

What sayest thou, boy?

YOUNG EDWARD:

Think not that I'm frighted with thy words.

ANNE:

Edward!

YOUNG EDWARD:

Stand off, mother! Had you loved him
As I did you'd not endure his death.

ABBOT:

Why speak you not, my lord, unto the king?

RICE AP HOWELL:

At this hour should Edward speak
Unto the Parliament.

A LORD:

At this hour
Is Edward's mouth dumb.

MORTIMER:

Who is the man who will
Impeach me for this death?

YOUNG EDWARD:

I am he.

MORTIMER:

Your witness?

YOUNG EDWARD:

My father's voice in me.

MORTIMER:

Have you no other witness, my lord?

YOUNG EDWARD:

Those not here are my witnesses.

ABBOT:

The Earl of Kent.

RICE AP HOWELL:

Berkeley.

A LORD:

The brothers Gurney.

ABBOT:

A man, Lightborn by name, seen
In the Tower.

ANNE:

No more!

ABBOT:

Who had a paper with him
In your writing.
The peers examine the paper.

RICE AP HOWELL:

Equivocal truly. The comma lacks.

ABBOT:

Purposely.

RICE AP HOWELL:

May be. Yet it stands not therein
That someone kill the king.

YOUNG EDWARD:

Ah Mortimer, thou knowest it was done
And so shall it be done to thee. Thou diest!
A witness to this world that thy
All too subtle wiles, by which
A kingly body in a grave now lies, too subtle were
For God.

MORTIMER:

If I see right you charge me with the murder
Of Edward the Second. Sometimes
The truth untruthful seems nor can we ever
Know which side the buffalo of state
Will roll. Good and moral
The side it rolls not on.
The buffalo has rolled and fallen on me.
Had I proof, how would proof serve me?
The man the state has called a murderer
Does well to play the murderer
Were his hand as white as Scotland's snow.
Therefore I am silent.

ABBOT:

Heed not the windings of the Eel.

MORTIMER:

Take away my seal! Squadron on squadron
France spits towards the isle. In Normandy
The armies rot. Banish me

To Normandy as your Governor
Or as a captain. As a recruiting officer
What you will, with naked arm to whip
The army for you 'gainst the foe. Send me as a
Soldier to be whipped on.
Yet do not thus
'Twixt meat and napkin, take my life
Because a young whelp yaps
For blood to see his father dead.
Ask yourself if now's the time
To clear the case of Edward's death,
Or whether this whole island, purged of one
Murder, should swim in blood.
You need me.
Your silence is heard as far as Ireland.
Have you a new tongue in your head
Since yesterday? If your hands are still
Unsullied, why, they are not sullied *yet*.
To be dispatched thus coldly smacks of morality.

ANNE:

For my sake, sweet son, pity Mortimer!
Young Edward is silent.
Be silent then, I never taught you speech.

MORTIMER:

Madam, stand off! I will rather die
Than sue for life unto a paltry boy.

YOUNG EDWARD:

Hang him!

MORTIMER:

See, boy, the strumpet fortune turns
A wheel. It bears thee upwards.
Upwards and upwards. Thou holdest fast. Upwards.
There comes a point, the highest. From whence thou
    see'st
It is no ladder, but now bears thee downwards
For it's round indeed. Who's seen that, boy

Does he fall or let himself go? The question
Is amusing. Savour it!

YOUNG EDWARD:

Take him away!
Mortimer is led out.

ANNE:

Bring not the blood of Roger Mortimer on you!

YOUNG EDWARD:

These words argue, mother, thou, perchance
Hast brought my father's blood on thee.
For thou, tied fast to Mortimer, I fear
Art suspect of his death and
We send you to the Tower for trial.

ANNE:

Not from thy mother's milk suckest thou
Such caustic wit, Edward the Third.
Dragged here and there, more than others
And not from love of change, I've ever seen
Evil nurturing its man and paying
Every triumph over conscience with success.
Now evil itself betrays me.
You say in these last hours died a man
Whose face yours dimly calls to mind
Who did me many wrongs, whom I forget
(Out of pity, you might say)
Even his face and voice I blotted out.
So much the better for him.
Now his son sends me to the Tower.
That is as good a place as anywhere.
You who have the excuse, that you
A child, have seen about you such hard
Lifeless things, what know you of the world
Where nothing's so inhuman as
Judgement and cold righteousness?
Exit Anne.

YOUNG EDWARD:

It yet remains for us to lay his body

Worthily to rest.

ABBOT:

And so it is of those who saw his crowning
In Westminster Abbey, not one shall see
His exequies. Of Edward the Second who
Not knowing, as it seems, which among his enemies
Remembered him, knowing not what
Breed lived in light above his head, knowing
Not the colour of the leaves, the season
Nor the pattern of the stars, oblivious
Of himself, in misery
Died.

YOUNG EDWARD *kneeling:*

God grant us mercy at this hour
That our house pay not these sins.
And God grant us too
Our house be not tainted
From its mother's womb.

A Respectable Wedding

Translator: JEAN BENEDETTI

Characters

The bride's father · The bridegroom's mother · The bride ·
Her sister · The bridegroom · His friend · The wife · Her
husband · The young man

A whitewashed room with a large rectangular table in the middle. A red paper lantern over it. Nine plain, wide wooden armchairs. Against the back wall, right, a sofa. Left, a cupboard. A curtained door between them. Upstage left, a low coffee table and two chairs. Left, a door; right, a window. Tables, chairs, and cupboard are in unpolished natural wood. It is evening. The red lamp is alight. The wedding guests are at the table, eating.

MOTHER *serving:* Here comes the cod.
   Murmurs of approval.
FATHER: That reminds me of a story.
BRIDE: Eat up, Dad. You always come off worst.
FATHER: Just you wait for it. Your poor old uncle – the one who was at my confirmation; but never mind, that's another story – anyway, there we all were, eating fish, when he suddenly choked – you have to look out for those damned bones, you know – anyway, he choked and started floundering about and flapping his feet and hands all over the place.
MOTHER: Take the tail, Jacob.
FATHER: Floundering about and going blue in the face like a carp; and then he knocked over a wineglass and scared the wits out of us; so we thumped him on the back and pummelled him this way and that way, and he spat the whole lot out all over the table. Nobody could eat any more after that – which was fine for us; we ate it up outside later; it was *my* confirmation after all – anyway, he spat the whole lot out over the table, and when we'd got him straightened up again he said in his splendid deep voice – he had a good bass voice, belonged to a choral society – anyway, he said . . .
MOTHER: Well, how's the fish? Can't somebody say something?
FATHER: Excellent. Anyway, he said . . .
MOTHER: You haven't had any yet.

T

FATHER: I'm eating it now. Anyway, he said . . .

MOTHER: Take some more, Jacob.

BRIDE: Mother, Father's telling a story.

FATHER: No, thanks. Anyway, to get back to the cod, well, he said: I nearly choked that time, kids. And it quite spoiled the meal.

Laughter.

GROOM: Damn good.

YOUNG MAN: He knows how to tell a story all right.

SISTER: Yes, and now I can't eat any more fish.

GROOM: Cows don't eat fish; they're vegetarian.

WIFE: I say, isn't the lamp ready yet?

BRIDE: You don't use a knife for fish, you know, Ina.

HUSBAND: Lamps are vulgar. I like it like this.

SISTER: It gives a more romantic light.

WIFE: Yes, but there isn't any.

FRIEND: It's a good light for cod.

YOUNG MAN *to sister:* Would you say so? Are you romantically inclined?

SISTER: Oh yes, very. I do so love Heine. He has such a sweet face.

FATHER: Died of consumption of the spine.

YOUNG MAN: That's a terrible illness to have.

FATHER: Old Weber's uncle's brother had it. It was frightening to hear him talk about it. Kept you awake at night. For instance, he told us . . .

BRIDE: Really, Father, it's too nasty.

FATHER: What?

BRIDE: Consumption of the spine.

MOTHER: Is that all right for you, Jacob?

WIFE: And on the one night you don't want to be kept awake!

FRIEND *to groom:* Cheers, old chap.

GROOM: Cheers, everyone.

They drink.

SISTER *to young man, sotto voce:* What a time to pick.

YOUNG MAN: Do you feel it's not fitting? *They talk quietly together.*

WIFE: Smells nice in here.

FRIEND: Out of this world.

MOTHER: The groom stood us half a bottle of eau-de-Cologne.

YOUNG MAN: Smashing smell. *Talks quietly to the girl.*

WIFE: Did you really make all the furniture yourself, the cupboard and all?

BRIDE: Every bit. My husband planned it, made the drawings, bought the wood, planed it all down, and glued it together, and it really looks quite nice.

FRIEND: It looks marvellous. I only wonder how you found the time.

GROOM: Evenings, quite often in the lunch hour, but mostly first thing in the morning.

BRIDE: He got up at five every day. And worked.

FATHER: It's a good bit of work. I always said I'd set them up with furniture. But he wouldn't have it. It was the same story with Johnny Segmüller. You know; he had . . .

BRIDE: He wanted to do the whole thing himself. Later on we'll show you the rest of the furniture.

WIFE: Let's hope it'll last.

BRIDE: Longer than you or any of us lot. When you think what went into it. He even made his own glue.

GROOM: You can't trust that rubbish you get in the shops.

HUSBAND: It's a very good idea. Things become part of you then. You take better care of them. *To his wife:* A pity you couldn't have made ours.

WIFE: Me, of course; not you. That's him all over.

HUSBAND: I didn't mean it that way. And you know it.

FATHER: That story about Johnny Segmüller is pretty funny.

BRIDE: I can never see anything funny in your stories.

SISTER: Don't be so rude, Maria.

GROOM: I think Father tells a wonderful story.

FRIEND: First-rate. Specially the way you make sure we don't miss the point.

BRIDE: They're too long.

GROOM: Rubbish.

FRIEND: Concise. Simple. Artistic.

WIFE: And anyway, there's plenty of time.

MOTHER *enters:* Here's the sweet.

FATHER: I could tell it you quite quickly, in just a few words, six or seven sentences perhaps, not more . . .

FRIEND: Smells like ambrosia.

MOTHER: It's pudding with whipped cream.

FRIEND: I've about got to my limit.

MOTHER: That's your one, Jacob. Don't take too much cream, though. There's not quite enough to go round. I hope you all like it.

SISTER: I'm mad about whipped cream.

YOUNG MAN: Really?

SISTER: Yes. What you have to do is cram your mouth full of it. Makes you feel as if you hadn't any teeth.

GROOM: More cream, Father?

FATHER: Go easy. You know, Johnny Segmüller always used to say . . .

BRIDE: Cream's good. Mother, you must let me have the recipe.

GROOM: She'll never cook as well as you, Mother.

MOTHER: It's got three eggs in it.

BRIDE: Oh well, if you're going to be extravagant.

SISTER: Of course you must. And beat them stiff. Or nothing'll come of it.

WIFE: Must be stiff.

FRIEND *giggles and chokes:* Stiff, ha ha ha, that's, ha ha ha, very good . . . Must be stiff, excellent . . . otherwise, ha ha ha, nothing'll come, ha ha ha, really excellent . . . ha ha ha. *As nobody else laughs he stops suddenly and quickly falls on his food.*

GROOM *thumping him on the back:* Hey, what's the matter with you?

SISTER: They *must* be stiff.

FRIEND *starts up again:* Very good! Excellent! I won't hear a word against being stiff.

FATHER: Eggs, yes. Your poor old mother once gave me one for a journey. I asked her if it was hard-boiled. 'As a rock,' she said. Well, I took her word for it and packed the egg. I wasn't even . . .

BRIDE: Cream please, Father.

FATHER: There you are. I wasn't even . . .

WIFE *archly:* Did you make the beds yourself too?

GROOM: Yes. I used walnut.

BRIDE: They look very nice.

SISTER: A bit on the wide side, I'd say.

WIFE: That comes of making them yourself.

HUSBAND: You haven't even seen them.

FATHER: I'd got some good beds I was going to let you have. Heirlooms, they are. Valuable antiques. Solidly made too.

FRIEND: Ah, people knew what they were up to in those days.

YOUNG MAN: Yes, but they weren't the same people.

FATHER: Other heads, other beds, as Fritz Forst used to say, and he was a funny chap if you like. For instance, he came into church once just as the parson was . . .

MOTHER *enters:* Now for the cake. Maria, you'll have to help me fetch the wine.

GROOM: And we'll sluice it all down.

FATHER: Wait a minute; there's a story about flush lavatories. I must just tell you that. When they were first brought in . . .

GROOM: Have a sup of wine first, Father. It oils the tongue. *The wine is poured.*

FRIEND: Fine colour; you only have to see it. And the bouquet!

MOTHER: You two seem to have a lot to say to each other.

SISTER *starting back:* What, us? Oh, nothing special. He was just saying . . .

HUSBAND *to young man:* Why do you keep treading on my foot? You've been doing it for the last three minutes. What do you take me for, a harmonium?

YOUNG MAN: I'm sorry. I thought . . .

HUSBAND: Oh yes, you thought. Thinking's all very well. But you don't think with your feet.

MOTHER: Where's your glass, Jacob?

WIFE: Better have a drink instead of uttering your pearls of wisdom. Wisdom, my God! You usually drink like a fish. *Silence.*

FRIEND: You were telling us about those heirlooms when you were interrupted.

FATHER: Oh yes, the beds. Thank you. Thank you very much. More than one member of the family has died in them, Maria.

GROOM: Just now, Father, we'd like to toast the living. Cheers.

ALL: Cheers.

HUSBAND *gets to his feet:* My dear friends.

WIFE: If you want them to stay your friends you'd better sit down.

The husband sits.

FRIEND: Go on. Your wife was only joking.

WIFE: He wouldn't know a joke if he saw one.

HUSBAND: I've forgotten what I was going to say.

The young man gets to his feet.

WIFE: Pssst!

MOTHER: Jacob, do up your waistcoat. Where are your manners? *At this moment the church bells outside start ringing.*

SISTER: The bells, Herr Mildner. It's the right moment for your speech.

FRIEND: Listen to that. A wonderful sound. Sort of awe-inspiring.

SISTER *to groom, who is eating:* Pssst!

BRIDE: Let him finish his meal.

YOUNG MAN *standing up very straight:* When two young people enter into matrimony – she a pure young bride, him a man matured in all the storms of life – then they say the angels sing in Heaven. When the bride – *he turns to her* – looks back at the happy times of her childhood she may perchance experience a few slight feelings of regret, for she is stepping out into the world, a hostile world – *the bride snivels* – with this well-tested man at her side, who has made a home, literally with his own hands in this case, and who will endure joy and sorrow with the bride his heart has chosen. And so let us drink to the happiness of these two, who today will belong to one another for the first time – *the wife laughs* – and thenceforward for all eternity. And also let us, in their honour, sing 'It must be a Wondrous Thing' by Liszt. *He starts singing, but as nobody joins in he stops. Silence.*

FRIEND *sotto voce:* None of us know it. That was a good speech, though.

SISTER: First class. Just like a book.

HUSBAND: Page 85. For weddings. He's got it word perfect.

WIFE: You ought to be ashamed.

HUSBAND: What, me?

WIFE: Yes, you.

FRIEND: Splendid wine.

The bells stop ringing.

All relax.

FATHER: Yes, well, I was telling you about the bed.

BRIDE: We've heard all about that.

FATHER: About how your great-uncle Augustus died?

BRIDE: Of course.

GROOM: How did great-uncle Augustus die exactly?

FATHER: No. You spoiled my story about the eggs, and then the one about the lavatory, which is a good one, and the Forst story on top of that – not to mention the one about Johnny Segmüller, because it really is a bit long, well not more than ten minutes, I suppose; perhaps I might later . . . Anyhow . . .

MOTHER: Fill their glasses, Jacob.

FATHER: Uncle Augustus died of dropsy.

HUSBAND: Cheers.

FATHER: Cheers. Dropsy. First it was just his feet, only the toes actually, then it was up to his knee in the time it takes to start a baby, and the whole thing had gone black. His belly was all swollen, and although they drained it off as best they could . . .

HUSBAND: Cheers.

FATHER: Cheers ... although they drained it off it was too late. Then there was the trouble with his heart, and that brought it all to a head. There he lay in the bed I was going to give you, groaning like an elephant, and looking like one too, the legs anyway. Then his sister, your grandmother, when it began to look like the end – it was around dawn, anyway there was grey light coming into the room; come to think of it I believe the same curtains are still up there – anyway, she said, 'Augustus, do you want a priest?' He didn't say a thing, just stared up at the ceiling – which he'd been doing for seven weeks, actually, ever since he'd been forced to give up lying on his side – and said, 'It's my foot mostly.' Then he groaned once more. But Mother, she wasn't going to give up, because she felt there was a soul at stake, so she let a good half hour go by and said, 'Do you want a priest, then, Augustus?' But Uncle didn't listen, and Father, who was standing there, said to her, 'Let him alone. He's in pain.' Father was always very soft-hearted. But she wasn't having any, because of his soul, and you know how obstinate women are, so she started up again: 'Augustus, it's for your immortal soul.' Then, Father told us later, Uncle looked away from the wall to the left where she was standing, so he had to look skew-eyed, and then he said something which I can't repeat here. It was something pretty crude, like Uncle Augustus always was. I don't think I can ... but then the story ... I'll have to say it, or the story won't make sense. He said, 'You can stuff ...' well, you know where. Well, as you can imagine, it was an effort to say that, and he died. I guarantee it's true. The bed's still there; I'll pack it up ready for you and you can take it away. *Drinks.*

Silence.

SISTER: I don't feel thirsty any more.

FRIEND: You shouldn't take it that way. Cheers. It's just a good story, that's all.

BRIDE *quietly to the groom:* Well, I do think he might have spared us that vulgar rubbish.

GROOM: Oh, if it makes him happy.

YOUNG MAN: I think that's a marvellous lighting arrangement.

MOTHER: Don't use a knife on your cake, Jacob.

FATHER: How about our having a peep at your furniture?

BRIDE: All right.

FRIEND: It's great, having those extra wide chairs. Room enough for two.

WIFE: The legs are a bit thin.

YOUNG MAN: Thin legs: that's very classy.

WIFE: Who told you that?

MOTHER: Jacob, can't you eat your cake with your fingers?

WIFE *gets up and walks round the room:* So that's the sofa. It's wide enough, but this kind of upholstery on top isn't very practical. Still, seeing that you made it yourself . . .

BRIDE *stands up:* Don't you think the cupboard's pretty? Specially the inlay work. I don't know; most people seem to have no feeling for that sort of thing. They just pay a bit of money for a bit of furniture, no soul or anything, merely in order to have a bit of furniture. But *we've* got our own things. Our own sweat's gone into them, we love them, because we made them ourselves.

HUSBAND: Come and sit down, woman.

WIFE: What's that supposed to mean? I want to see inside.

HUSBAND: You don't go looking into other people's cupboards.

WIFE: All I meant was – but then you always know better, don't you? All right, then. The cupboard's nothing special from the outside – people don't have that kind of inlay work now; they have glass doors with coloured curtains – but it might be quite good inside, and that's what I wanted to see.

HUSBAND: All right, all right; now just sit down.

WIFE: Oh, we've started talking like that, have we? You've had too much to drink again. I'm going to water it down, as your head's so weak.

GROOM: Go ahead if you want to look inside; I'm only too glad it interests you. Here's the key. Open it up, Maria.

BRIDE: I don't know . . . Sure this is the right key? It won't turn.

GROOM: Give it here; it's just a knack. I put the lock in myself too. *Tries it.* Shit! The bastard. *Angrily.* Bugger it!

BRIDE: There you are, you can't open it either.

GROOM: Perhaps somebody tried to force it. It beats me.

WIFE: Perhaps it's not all that special inside. So why bother? It's certainly a business getting the lock on this cupboard open. That's something to be said against it.

HUSBAND *threateningly:* You come and sit down. That's enough of that.

SISTER: Oh no, now we're on our feet, why don't we dance?

YOUNG MAN: Yes, let's. We can push the table back.

GROOM: Dance, that's a good idea. But where's the music to come from?

FRIEND: I can play the guitar. It's in the hall. *Goes and fetches it.*

All stand. The father and the husband go left and sit. They smoke. The groom and the young man lift the table and carry it to the right.

YOUNG MAN: Careful how you put it down.

GROOM: Don't bother. It's got to take some knocks. *Puts it down heavily. One leg goes askew.* Now let's dance.

YOUNG MAN: Look, one of the legs has gone. You shouldn't have put it down so hard.

BRIDE: What has gone?

GROOM: Nothing that matters. Let's start dancing.

BRIDE: Why can't you look out what you're doing?

WIFE: Think of all that sweat that went into it. Proper glue might have been better.

GROOM: Sharp tongue you've got. May I?

WIFE: Don't you want the first dance with your wife?

GROOM: Of course. Come on, Maria.

BRIDE: No, I want to dance with Hans.

SISTER: Who am *I* to dance with, then?

BRIDE *to husband:* Aren't you dancing?

HUSBAND: No. My wife'll never let me hear the last of it if I do.

SISTER: You ought to dance. Otherwise I've got to sit and watch.

HUSBAND: It's not fair if I don't want to. *Gets up and gives her his arm.*

FRIEND *sits on the sofa with his guitar:* I can play a waltz. *Begins to play.*
They dance: the groom with the wife, the bride with the young man, the sister with the husband.

WIFE: Faster! Faster! It's like a roundabout.
They dance quite fast, then stop.

WIFE: That's what I call classy. Not bad dancing. *She sits heavily on the sofa. It cracks. The wife and the friend jump up.*

FRIEND: It went crack.

WIFE: Something's broken. It's my fault.

GROOM: Doesn't matter. I'll mend it.

WIFE: Yes, you know all about furniture. That's the main thing.

BRIDE: It must have been *too* fast for you to make you come down like that.

WIFE: Yes, that husband of yours does swing one round.

SISTER: Didn't you enjoy it?

HUSBAND: Today I did. Oh yes.

WIFE: You should watch that heart of yours.

HUSBAND: You worried?

WIFE: I have to carry the can always.

GROOM: Shall we sit down again?

BRIDE *to the friend:* You play wonderfully.

FRIEND: It's easy when I see you dancing.

GROOM: Cut the chatter. Let's sit down. How did *you* like that dance?

YOUNG MAN: Very much. Aren't we going to go on?

GROOM: No.

FATHER: Can't we have some wine? Helps the conversation.

GROOM: Let's just put the table back in the middle. *Does so, helped by the young man.* But carefully this time. *The mother brings wine. The chairs are pushed back, and all sit.*

WIFE: Sing something. I love it when people sing.

FRIEND: I'm not much of a singer.

GROOM: Doesn't matter. Just sing so there's some sort of entertainment.

WIFE: My husband sings now and again. He can play the guitar too.

YOUNG MAN: Oh yes, do play.

WIFE: Here's the guitar.

HUSBAND: I'm too out of practice.

SISTER: Go on, do.

HUSBAND: Suppose I get stuck . . .

WIFE: You always do.

SISTER: Just once.

HUSBAND: I might be able to, just once.

WIFE: He used to play a lot, but since we've been together he's stopped. He just concentrates on being a bore. He used to know a whole heap of songs, then he forgot most of them; there were less and less of them he could get through, he got stuck more and more often, you'd think he was going senile, till in the end he could only manage one single song. You'd better sing it now.

HUSBAND: All right, I'll sing it. *Tunes guitar, and begins, lively:*
The ghost of Liebenau, o hear!
Who many a . . .
Stops.
Who many a . . . I don't know . . . Now I've forgotten that one too . . . It was the only one I had left . . .

WIFE: Senile.

GROOM: Doesn't matter. I can't sing at all.

YOUNG MAN: How about dancing a bit more?

FRIEND: Yes, a good idea. Me too this time. You can play a waltz, can't you? A major with the seventh. Please, Frau Maria, it's my turn now.

WIFE: I've had enough.

GROOM: We'll watch, then.

FATHER: Maria dances nicely.
The bride and the friend dance.

HUSBAND *strums guitar:* A major: there we are.

FRIEND: You're a wonderful dancer. Faster.

GROOM: Don't fall over, that's all.

WIFE *to the groom:* Catch me dancing like that.

SISTER: Could you?

WIFE: Depends on the man.

FRIEND *breaking off:* It gets into your veins. Here's your wife. She's a classy dancer. May I have a drink, though?

FATHER: Why don't we sit at the table again? Nobody can talk like this.

GROOM: Yes, do sit down. *To the bride, quietly:* Unless you'd rather go on dancing?

BRIDE: Let's sit a different way this time. *To the friend:* You sit here. And do you mind sitting – *to the wife* – there? *The wife sits next to the groom.* Dad, you sit at the head.

GROOM *opening bottles:* Now, let's drink. To comfort and cosiness.

YOUNG MAN: In your own home.

FRIEND: That you made yourself.

FATHER: Cheers. When you were in short skirts, Maria, you had a drop of wine once. Your grandfather was delighted. He wanted you to dance, but you went to sleep instead.

WIFE: So you'd better not drink today, eh?

HUSBAND: I've never seen anyone dance better.

FRIEND: I'm in smashing form now. It was a bit sticky here earlier. Apart from that, wonderful. *Gets up:* What the . . .? *Looks at the chair.* There's something caught here.

BRIDE: Have you hurt yourself?

FRIEND: A splinter.

GROOM: Doesn't matter.

FRIEND: The chair doesn't. But those are my best trousers.

GROOM: Do you mean to say you put them on in my honour?

FRIEND: Yes; but now I'm going to sing.

GROOM: Don't if you don't really want to.

FRIEND *taking the guitar:* But I do want to.

GROOM: I mean, if you feel put out . . .

FRIEND: I'm not put out.

GROOM: On account of your trousers.

FRIEND: Set that off against the dance.

FATHER: There's a providence rough-hews our ends. That was another of Forst's sayings.

FRIEND *sings the 'Ballad of Chastity in a Major Key'*:

See them melting with desire!
Mine! he thought. If she is free.
And the darkness fanned their fire.
And she thought: just him and me.
And he said: 'I'll never hurt you.'
Not a girl of easy virtue
And she didn't want to be.

Oh, their fingers' sweet sensations
As with beating heart she lay!
What about his hesitations?
Each of them could only pray.
And he said: 'I mustn't hurt you.'
Not a girl of easy virtue
(Not yet having learnt the way . . .)

Sooner than profane that moment
Off he went to find a tart
Who could teach him what to come meant
Helping nature out with art.
But he found the pace was killing:
Once he had been very willing
Now he swore to stay apart.

Still red-hot, but still unsullied
Quick release was now *her* prayer
So she found herself a solid
Chap who simply didn't care.
(And who beat her something horrid
Laying her across the stair.)
Being manhandled rejoiced her –

Not for her the holy cloister –
And at last the urge was there.

So he sees his hesitation
To have been entirely right:
Thinks it was by inspiration
That he spared her that May night.
She's all vice now, he's all virtue:
Each is anxious to alert you
Not to play with dynamite.

The wife laughs.

GROOM: I know that one. One of your best songs. *To the wife:* Did you like it? I'll go and get some wine.

FRIEND: Yes, it is good. Specially the moral. *To the bride:* Did you like it?

BRIDE: I'm not sure I understood it.

WIFE: Anyway, it wasn't meant for you.

FATHER *anxiously:* Where's Ina?

BRIDE: Don't ask me.

GROOM: Herr Mildner's missing too. Why was he asked, anyway?

BRIDE: He's the porter's son.

GROOM: Oh, a menial.

BRIDE: They must have gone out.

FATHER: Then they didn't hear the song. That's just as well. Go and look, Maria.

WIFE: Perhaps they *did* understand it.

HUSBAND: And your mother's in the kitchen.

GROOM: Making blancmange.

BRIDE *in a low voice to him:* I thought that was smutty.

GROOM: After you'd danced with him like that.

BRIDE: I'm ashamed.

GROOM: Of the way you danced?

BRIDE: No: of the sort of friends you have.

FRIEND: I don't know when I've felt in better form. When I've had a drink or two I feel like God.

GROOM: You mean when God has had a drink or two he feels like an office clerk.

FRIEND *laughs, a little piqued:* That's very good. What's made you so witty all of a sudden?

HUSBAND: That reminds me of a story. One day God tried to go for a walk incognito. He forgot to put his tie on, so they recognized him at once and put him in a mental home.

FRIEND: You've told it all wrong. It ruins the whole point of the story.

FATHER: That was a good one. But Joe Schmidt really was sent to a mental home. It was like this . . .

The sister, the bride, and the young man come in.

SISTER: We've been helping Mother with the blancmange.

GROOM: Doesn't matter. We're all in excellent form here. We've been swapping stories.

YOUNG MAN: It's going to be a smashing blancmange.

WIFE: Made it on the cooker, did you?

SISTER: No. Blancmange is never made on the cooker in *this* house.

WIFE: I only thought you'd say you made it on the cooker because the two of you have got such red faces. *Laughs and drops into a chair.* Oh! *Gets up.*

FRIEND: Was that something going?

WIFE: Oh dear, the chair . . .

GROOM: It can't have. You can bounce about on that as much as you like. Two-inch pegs, I used.

WIFE: I'm not going to risk sitting on it any more. I'll sit on the sofa.

SISTER: You've already sat there. A leg's come off.

FRIEND *feeling under her chair:* There really is something wrong here. It isn't a splinter this time. But better watch out for your clothes.

GROOM *coming across:* Oh yes, that chair was a bit of a teaser. I ran out of pegs. I didn't realize it was that one, or I'd have asked you to sit somewhere else.

BRIDE: Then it would have been that one.

HUSBAND: Here's one going begging.

Silence.

MOTHER: Here's the blancmange. And the mulled claret.

FRIEND: Splendid. Mulled claret. *He sprawls in his chair.* That was just one of the arms. And I haven't torn anything. Let's have a drink. *The arm of the chair is broken.*

GROOM: That's more like it. Cheers.

ALL: Cheers.

GROOM: And here's to *you*, Mother.

MOTHER: Don't splash your nice waistcoat with the wine. There's a spot on it already.

FATHER: Talking of chairs . . . Rosenberg and Co. used to have chairs for the customers in their office with the seats so low your knees came up to your chin. You felt so much at home that Rosenberg and Co. got rich on it. He got a better place and better fittings, but he kept the chairs. He used to say in a very emotional way, 'That's the kind of simple furniture I started out with. May God punish me for my pride if I ever forget it.'

WIFE: I didn't ask your chairs to break. It's not my fault.

HUSBAND: No one said it was.

WIFE: That's just it. You want to put me in the wrong.

FRIEND: I detect a discordant note. Shall I get my guitar and sing something?

GROOM: Aren't you tired?

FRIEND: What from?

GROOM: Dancing, drinking. With your stomach trouble.

FRIEND: I have not got stomach trouble.

GROOM: You're always taking bicarbonate of soda.

FRIEND: That doesn't make me ill by a long chalk.

GROOM: It was only in your own interest.

FRIEND: Thanks, but I'm not tired.

Pause.

YOUNG MAN: Have you been to see that play *Baal*?

HUSBAND: Yes; it's a load of filth.

YOUNG MAN: A lot of punch in it, though.

HUSBAND: All right: so it's a load of filth with punch in it.

That's worse than having none. It's no excuse for a man to say that he's got a gift for writing filth. Filth should be kept off the stage.

Pause.

FATHER: Those modern writers are always dragging family life in the mud. When it's the best thing we Germans have.

FRIEND: True enough.

Pause.

GROOM: Well. Now cheer up, everyone. I don't get married every day. Drink up, and don't sit there like a lot of stiffs. Look, I'm going to take my coat off. *He does so.*

Pause.

FRIEND: Got any cards? We might play pontoon.

GROOM: They're in the cupboard.

WIFE: Which won't open.

FRIEND: You might do it with a crowbar.

BRIDE: Be serious.

FRIEND: Well, you'll have to get it open some time.

BRIDE: But not today.

GROOM: Just to get a few cards out.

FRIEND *rudely:* All right, then you tell us just what else one can do in this place.

WIFE: It might be the moment to look at the rest of the furniture.

GROOM: That's an idea. I'll lead the way.

All get up.

SISTER: I think I'll go on sitting here.

BRIDE: All by yourself? You can't.

SISTER: Why not?

BRIDE: Because there are limits.

SISTER: Then let me tell you I didn't want to get up because the chair's bust.

BRIDE: How did you bust it?

SISTER: It just went.

FRIEND *feeling the chair:* As long as you take care and sit down gently it won't matter.

FATHER: Perhaps we could go and look at the rest of the furniture now.

FRIEND *quietly to the wife:* The table's still intact.

GROOM: They're nothing special really . . .

WIFE: So long as they hold up.

GROOM: Come on, Maria.

BRIDE *stays seated:* I'll be along in a minute. You go on.

All leave through the centre door. As they go:

WIFE *to the friend:* The bridegroom's taken his jacket off.

FRIEND: That's rash of him. No holds barred now.

The bride sits at the table and snivels.

GROOM: I must go and look for the torch; something's wrong with the wiring.

BRIDE: Why didn't you get a proper electrician to do it?

GROOM: What's the matter with you? I didn't care for the way your sister behaved, either.

BRIDE: How about your friend?

GROOM: That's no way to dance if you want to keep people's respect.

BRIDE: And Mildner too. All that stuff about the pure young bride was deliberate. I went all red, and everybody noticed. He kept staring at me, too. And then that awful song. He's been getting his own back for something.

GROOM: Those dirty jokes. All because he thought you're the sort of person it doesn't matter with.

BRIDE: Don't forget he's *your* friend. And I'm not that sort of person.

GROOM: How can we get rid of them? There they are, stuffing themselves, smoking, chattering away; they just don't want to go. After all it's *our* party.

BRIDE: A nice party!

GROOM: Don't act that way. Once they've gone . . .

BRIDE: They've spoilt everything now.

GROOM: I wish we were alone. Here they are.

BRIDE: I don't want them to go. That'll be even worse.

GROOM *puts his coat on again quickly:* It's chillier than I thought.

The others appear in the door.

FATHER: We had to wait in the kitchen as the bedroom light wasn't working.

FRIEND: Are we intruding?

The wife has a fit of laughter.

HUSBAND: What is it now?

WIFE: It's so funny.

HUSBAND: What's funny?

WIFE: Everything. Everything. The broken chairs, the home-made furniture. The entertainment. *Laughs horribly.*

BRIDE: Emmy, really!

WIFE: All broken. *Laughing, she drops into a chair which breaks.* There goes another. There goes another. Now I'll have to sit on the floor.

FRIEND *joins in the laughter:* That's a fact. We ought to have brought camp stools.

HUSBAND *grabs his wife:* You must be ill. If you go around behaving like that and the furniture breaks it won't be the furniture's fault. *To the groom:* I'm sorry.

FRIEND: Let's sit down as best we can. So long as we keep cheerful that's all that counts.

They sit.

SISTER: A pity we couldn't see. The beds are really very nice.

WIFE: No, the light didn't work either.

BRIDE: Won't you fetch some more wine, Jacob?

GROOM: It's in the cellar. Let's have the key.

BRIDE: Just a moment.

They go out.

WIFE: There's a peculiar smell here too.

FRIEND: It didn't seem to be there before.

SISTER: I don't smell anything.

WIFE: I know what it is. It's the glue.

FRIEND: That's why they wanted that eau-de-Cologne I gave them. An entire half bottle.

WIFE: But the smell of the glue's coming through; there's no hiding it now.

The bride returns.

FATHER: You're a pretty sight, standing in the door like that.

You always were pretty to look at, even as a child. But now you're blooming.

WIFE: That's a well-cut frock.

BRIDE: No camouflage needed, thank God.

WIFE: Was that aimed at anybody?

BRIDE: If the cap fits.

WIFE: People who live in glass houses shouldn't throw stones.

BRIDE: And who's in a glass house?

WIFE: That frock's a very good piece of work, because no one would imagine you were . . .

FRIEND: Cheers. Fine wine, that.

BRIDE *crying:* That's, that's . . .

HUSBAND: What's all this about?

GROOM *returns:* Here's the wine. What's the matter with you?

SISTER: A remark in bad taste.

WIFE: Where was the bad taste?

FATHER: Calm down now. Cheers.

GROOM *to the sister:* You're not to insult our guests.

SISTER: But the guests can insult your wife.

WIFE: I never said a thing.

HUSBAND: Oh yes you did. You were offensive.

WIFE *annoyed:* I only spoke the truth.

GROOM: And what truth was that?

WIFE: Be your age.

HUSBAND *leaning towards her:* Just you control yourself.

WIFE: When a woman's pregnant she's pregnant.

The husband rips a leg from the table and throws it at his wife, but it hits a vase on top of the cupboard. The wife cries.

GROOM *angrily, to the sister:* That was the vase *you* gave us.

SISTER: You can't have thought much of it, or you wouldn't have put it up there.

GROOM: I've no time to argue with you now, because it was my table as well. *He feels it to see if it will hold up.*

HUSBAND *walks agitatedly up and down:* There: I've lifted a hand to her. So now *I'm* the brute. It's always the same story: she's the martyr, I'm the brute. Seven years I've put

up with it, and you may well ask who made a brute of me.
My hands were always too tired from working for her to be
able to hit her. If I'm on top of the world she's got a pain; if
I have a drink she counts the pennies; but if I count the
pennies she bursts into tears. Once I had to throw out a
picture I was very fond of, because she disliked it. She disliked it because I was fond of it. When I had thrown it out
she picked it up and hung it in her room. As soon as I saw
it there she was happy and said, 'It's good enough for me.'
Then she was sorry for herself for being reduced to picking
up my throw-outs. I got angry and took it off her, and then
she cried because she couldn't even have that. 'Not even
that' was her phrase, even when it was something we
couldn't possibly afford. But that's the way she is, and that's
the way they all are. As soon as the wedding's over you're
no longer a beast working for its mistress, you're a man
working for a beast; and it drags you down till there's
nothing you don't deserve.

Pause.

GROOM *with an effort:* Have something more to drink? It's
only nine.

FRIEND: We've run out of chairs.

YOUNG MAN: We could still dance.

FRIEND: I've had enough of that.

GROOM: You liked it earlier on all right.

FRIEND: I hadn't got the splinter.

GROOM: Oh, I see. *Laughs.* Is that why you've been standing
in that subdued way?

FRIEND: It wasn't *my* chair, was it?

GROOM: No, it was mine. Was. Now it isn't any more.

FRIEND: Then we may as well go. *Goes out.*

YOUNG MAN: Thank you. That was very nice. But it's time
for me to put my coat on.

WIFE: Take me home.

HUSBAND *goes out and comes back with his wife's things:* And I
must apologize again for this wife of mine.

GROOM: You don't have to.

WIFE: I daren't go home.

HUSBAND: That's *your* revenge. But the play-acting's all over now, and we're coming to the serious bit. *Takes her arm:* Off we go. *He leaves with his wife, who is silent and dejected.*

GROOM: Now they've gorged they're anxious to get away. After that we'll be on our own, with half the evening to fill.

BRIDE: A moment ago you were longing for them to get out. One never knows where one is with you, does one? And of course you don't love me, either.

FRIEND *comes back with his hat on. Spitefully:* The stink has become almost unbearable.

GROOM: What stink?

FRIEND: That glue that wouldn't stick. I call it cheek asking people to such a rubbish dump.

GROOM: Then you'd better forgive me for not appreciating your dirty song and having let you break my chair.

FRIEND: Why don't you wait for your nuptial dropsy bed? I wish you a very good night. *Goes.*

GROOM: Go to hell.

FATHER: I think we'd better go too. We can talk about the furniture another time, and the beds are there if you want them. I thought it'd be a help if I told stories that had no connection with the company. It's always a mistake to leave people to their own devices. Come along, Ina.

SISTER: It's a pity such a nice evening should end like this. After all, you only have it once. Life begins tomorrow, as Hans says.

BRIDE: You did your best to contribute. And just how long have you been calling Herr Mildner Hans?

YOUNG MAN: Thanks again. I thought it was a very nice evening.

All three go.

GROOM: Thank God they've gone at last.

BRIDE: Yes: to spread our disgrace all over the town. I don't know how I can face it. Tomorrow they'll all know what happened. And how they'll laugh. They'll sit sniggering behind their windows. They'll stare at us in church as they think of the furniture and the lights that wouldn't work and the blancmange that went wrong, and, to cap it all, that the bride was pregnant. And there was I going to say the baby was premature.

GROOM: What about the furniture too? Five months' work! Have you thought of that? They only pissed themselves laughing over that dirty song because you'd danced with them as if you were in a whorehouse, till all the best chairs were bust. A friend of yours, she was.

BRIDE: And it was a friend of yours who sang that song. To hell with your furniture. It isn't even stained, because you said the look didn't matter so long as it was solid and comfortable. Five months wasted while you got it finished, and by then I was showing. This rubbish, this trash, this shoddy workmanship. What on earth did we get married for?

GROOM: Well, they've gone now, and this is the start of our wedding night. This is it.

Pause. He walks up and down. She stands at the window, right.

BRIDE: Why did you have the first dance with that awful creature? It's not done. I never knew her till today. I thought she was my friend. It's all so shameful.

GROOM: Because she'd been nasty about the furniture.

BRIDE: And you wanted her to think well of you at any price. A lot of help that was.

Pause.

GROOM: The trouble is that when you do anything different from other people they turn nasty. Specially when they know it's something they've missed out on. Then they take it out on you. They couldn't for a moment make even one of these bits of furniture, not even design it and get the wood cut. But one little slip-up, like bad glue, and they think they're justified. I shall put the whole thing out of my mind. *Goes to cupboard and tries to open it.*

BRIDE: They'll remind you. And I won't forget ever. *Sobs.*

GROOM: The bad glue, do you mean?

BRIDE: God will punish you for jeering at me.

GROOM: He's started already. To hell with this damned lock. What does anything matter now? *He breaks in the door.*

BRIDE: Just because the lock was bust you've gone and bust the cupboard.

GROOM: I've got my house-jacket out now, and you can clear away. How long am I supposed to wallow in this pigsty? *The bride gets up and begins to clear.*

GROOM *standing by the cupboard in his house-jacket and counting money:* It wasn't cheap either. And we didn't really need to get that wine up from the cellar.

BRIDE: The table's wonky. There are two legs missing.

GROOM: The mulled wine. The food. On top of that the repairs.

BRIDE: The chairs, the cupboard, the sofa.

GROOM: Bloody bastards.

BRIDE: And *your* furniture.

GROOM: The home we'd made.

BRIDE: You know just what's there.

GROOM: And take better care of it.

BRIDE *sits and buries her face in her hands:* It's all such a disgrace.

GROOM: Was it necessary to clear away in your wedding frock? It'll be spoiled. There's a wine-stain already.

BRIDE: You look so insignificant in that jacket. Your face seems quite changed. And not for the better.

GROOM: And you're an old bag. Crying brings it out.

BRIDE: Nothing's sacred any longer.

GROOM: It's our wedding night.

Pause, then the groom goes to the table.

GROOM: Drunk every drop. The tablecloth got more than I did. Bottles empty, but there's some left in the glasses. Mustn't be wasteful.

BRIDE: What are you doing?

GROOM: Finishing off what's left in the glasses. Look, here's a full one.

BRIDE: I'm not in the mood.

GROOM: But it's our wedding night!

The bride takes the glass, looks away, drinks.

GROOM: Not that anybody can say I'm drinking to your innocence, what with you being pregnant . . .

BRIDE: That's the worst thing you've said today. You've really outdone yourself. Whose fault was it? You were like a ram.

GROOM *not to be put off:* Now comes the night when, within our four walls and under the eyes of the family . . .
The bride laughs bitterly.

GROOM: . . . we must be fruitful and multiply. A holy occasion, so to speak.

BRIDE: You can talk.

GROOM: I drink to your good health, my dear wife, and may it all turn out right for us.
They drink.

BRIDE: Well, you said one true thing tonight: this is a party, and one can't be too fussy.

GROOM: It could have gone worse.

BRIDE: What with your friend . . .

GROOM: And your relatives.

BRIDE: Must we quarrel all the time?

GROOM: No. On our wedding night.
They keep on drinking.

BRIDE: Our wedding night. *Chokes. Laughs heartily.* What a scream. Some wedding night.

GROOM: Well, why not? Cheers.

BRIDE: That song was dirty. *Sniggers.* 'And who beat her . . .' That's you men all over. 'Laying her across the stair.'

GROOM *jumping up:* And those stories of your father's!

BRIDE: And my sister out in the passage! It's enough to kill a cat.

GROOM: And the way that silly bitch nearly fell on the floor!

BRIDE: And the way their eyes popped when the cupboard wouldn't open!

GROOM: Well, at least they couldn't see inside.

BRIDE: I'm glad they've gone.

GROOM: They just create noise and dirt.

BRIDE: Two's company.

GROOM: Alone at last.

BRIDE: I don't think much of your jacket.

GROOM: I don't care for that frock. *He rips it down the front.*

BRIDE: You've ruined it.

GROOM: Who cares? *Kisses her.*

BRIDE: You're so wild.

GROOM: You're pretty. Your breasts are so white.

BRIDE: Oh, you're hurting me, darling.

GROOM *pulls her to the door, opens it. The knob comes off in his hand.* There goes the knob. Ha ha ha. What next? *Throws it at the lamp, which goes out and falls down.* Come along.

BRIDE: But the bed! Ha ha ha.

GROOM: Well, what about the bed?

BRIDE: That'll break too.

GROOM: Doesn't matter. *Drags her out. Darkness. Noise of bed collapsing.*

The Beggar or The Dead Dog

Translator: MICHAEL HAMBURGER

Characters

The Emperor · The beggar · Soldiers

A gate. To the right of it crouches a beggar, a great ragged fellow with a white forehead. He has a small hurdy-gurdy which he keeps concealed under his rags. It is early morning. A cannon shot is heard. The Emperor arrives, escorted by soldiers; he has long reddish hair, uncovered. He wears a purple woollen garment. Bells are ringing.

EMPEROR: At the very moment that I go to celebrate my victory over my worst enemy and the country blends my name with black incense a beggar sits in front of my gate, stinking of misery. But between these great events it seems fitting for me to converse with nothingness. *The soldiers step back.* Do you know why the bells are ringing, man?

BEGGAR: Yes. My dog has died.

EMPEROR: Was that a piece of insolence?

BEGGAR: No. It was old age. He struggled on to the end. I wondered, why do his legs tremble so? He had laid his front legs over my chest. Like that we lay all night, even when it turned cold. But by the morning he had been dead a long time, and I pushed him off me. Now I can't go home because he's beginning to putrify, and stinks.

EMPEROR: Why don't you throw him out?

BEGGAR: That's none of your business. Now you have a hollow in your chest, like a hole in a drain; because you've asked a stupid question. Everyone asks stupid questions. Just to ask questions is stupid.

EMPEROR: And yet I shall ask another: who looks after you? Because if no one looks after you, you'll have to remove yourself. This is a place where no carrion may rot and no outcry may rend the air.

BEGGAR: Am I crying out?

EMPEROR: Now it's you that are asking, though there is mockery in your question, and I do not understand the mockery.

BEGGAR: Well, I don't know about that, though I'm the person involved.

EMPEROR: I take no account of what you say. But who looks after you?

BEGGAR: Sometimes it's a boy whom his mother got from an angel while she was digging potatoes.

EMPEROR: Do you have no sons?

BEGGAR: They've gone.

EMPEROR: Like the Emperor Ta Li's army, buried by the desert sand?

BEGGAR: He marched through the desert, and his people said: It's too far. Turn back, Ta Li. To that he replied every time: This territory must be conquered. They marched on each day, till their shoe leather was worn away, then their skin began to tear, and they used their knees to move on. Once the whirlwind caught a camel on the flank. That camel died in front of their eyes. Once they came to an oasis and said: That's what our homes are like. Then the Emperor's little son fell into a cistern and drowned. They mourned for seven days, feeling an infinite grief. Once they saw their horses die. Once their women could go no farther. Once came the wind and the sand that buried them, and then it was all over and quiet again, and the territory belonged to them, and I forgot its name.

EMPEROR: How do you know all that? Not a word of it is true. It was quite different.

BEGGAR: When he got so strong that I was like his child, I crawled away, for I allow no one to dominate me.

EMPEROR: What are you talking about?

BEGGAR: Clouds drifted. Towards midnight stars broke through. Then there was silence.

EMPEROR: Do clouds make a noise?

BEGGAR: Many, it's true, died in those filthy hovels by the river that flooded its banks last week, but they didn't get through.

EMPEROR: Since you know that much – do you never sleep?

BEGGAR: When I lie back on the stones the child that was born cries. And then a new wind rises.

EMPEROR: Last night the stars were out, nobody died by the river, no child was born, there was no wind here.

BEGGAR: In that case you must be blind, deaf, and ignorant. Or else it's malice on your part.

Pause.

EMPEROR: What do you do all the time? I've never seen you before. Out of what egg did you creep?

BEGGAR: Today I noticed that the maize is poor this year, because the rain hasn't come. There's such a dark warm wind blowing in from the fields.

EMPEROR: That's correct. The maize is poor.

BEGGAR: That's what it was like thirty-eight years ago. The maize perished in the sun, and before it was done for the rain came down so thick that rats sprang up and devastated all the other fields. Then they came into the villages and took bites out of people. That food was the death of them.

EMPEROR: I know nothing of that. It must be a fabrication like the rest. There's nothing about it in history.

BEGGAR: There's no such thing as history.

EMPEROR: And what about Alexander? And Caesar? And Napoleon?

BEGGAR: Stories! Fairy tales! What Napoleon are you talking about?

EMPEROR: The one who conquered half the world and was undone because he overreached himself.

BEGGAR: Only two can believe that. He and the world. It is wrong. In reality Napoleon was a man who rowed in a galley and had such a fat head that everybody said: We can't row, because we haven't enough elbow-room. When the ship went down, because they didn't row, he pumped his head full of air and kept alive, he alone, and because he was fettered he had to row on – he couldn't see where to from down there, and all had drowned. So he shook his head over the world, and since it was too heavy, it fell off.

EMPEROR: That's the silliest thing I have ever heard. You have greatly disappointed me by telling me that yarn. The others were at least well told. But what do you think of the Emperor?

BEGGAR: There is no such person as the Emperor. Only the nation thinks there is such a person, and one individual thinks that he is the one. Later, when too many military vehicles are being made and the drummers are well rehearsed, there is war and an adversary is looked for.

EMPEROR: But now the Emperor has defeated his adversary.

BEGGAR: He has killed him, not defeated him. One idiot has killed another.

EMPEROR *with an effort:* He was a strong adversary, believe me.

BEGGAR: There is a man who puts stones into my rice. That man is *my* enemy. He bragged, because he has a strong hand. But he died of cancer, and when they closed the coffin they caught his hand under the lid and didn't notice it when they carried the coffin away, so that the hand hung out of it, limp, helpless, and empty.

EMPEROR: Don't you ever get bored, then, with lying about like this?

BEGGAR: In the past clouds used to drift down, along the sky, endlessly. I look at those. There is no end to them.

EMPEROR: Now there are no clouds moving in the sky. So your talk makes no sense. That's as clear as the sun.

BEGGAR: There is no such thing as the sun.

EMPEROR: Perhaps you are even dangerous, a paranoiac, a raving madman.

BEGGAR: He was a good dog, not just an ordinary one. He deserves a good deal of praise. He even brought me meat, and at night he slept in my rags. Once there was a great uproar in town, they all had something against me because I don't give anyone anything worth talking about, and even soldiers were brought in. But the dog drove them off.

EMPEROR: Why do you tell me that?

BEGGAR: Because I consider you stupid.

EMPEROR: What else do you think of me?

BEGGAR: You have a feeble voice, therefore you are timid;

you ask too many questions, therefore you're a flunkey; you try to set traps for me, therefore you're not sure of anything, even the surest thing; you don't believe me but listen to me all the same, therefore you're a weak man, and finally you believe that the whole world revolves around you, when there are people far more important, myself for instance. Besides, you are blind, deaf, and ignorant. As for your other vices, I don't know them yet.

EMPEROR: That doesn't look good. Don't you see any virtues in me?

BEGGAR: You speak softly, therefore you are humble; you ask many questions, therefore you seek knowledge; you weigh up everything, therefore you are sceptical; you listen to what you believe to be lies, therefore you are tolerant; you believe that everything revolves around yourself, therefore you are no worse than other men and believe nothing more stupid than they do. Besides, you are not confused by too much seeing, don't bother with things that don't concern you, are not made inactive by knowledge. As for your other virtues, you know them better than I do, or anyone else.

EMPEROR: You are witty.

BEGGAR: Every bit of flattery is worthy of its reward. But I am not going to pay you now for paying me.

EMPEROR: I reward all services done me.

BEGGAR: That goes without saying. That you expect approval reveals your vulgar soul.

EMPEROR: I hold nothing against you. Is that vulgar too?

BEGGAR: Yes. For there is nothing you can do to me.

EMPEROR: I can have you thrown into a dungeon.

BEGGAR: Is it cool?

EMPEROR: The sun doesn't penetrate there.

BEGGAR: The sun? There's no such thing. You must have a bad memory.

EMPEROR: And I could have you killed.

BEGGAR: Then the rain will no longer fall on my head, the vermin will disperse, my stomach will no longer grumble, and there will be the greatest quiet that I've ever enjoyed.

A messenger comes and speaks softly to the Emperor.

EMPEROR: Tell them I shan't be long. *Exit messenger.* I shall do none of those things to you. I am considering what I shall do.

BEGGAR: You shouldn't tell anyone that. Or he will draw conclusions when he sees what your actions are.

EMPEROR: I do not find that I am despised.

BEGGAR: Everyone bows to me. But it means nothing to me. Only importunate people trouble me with their chatter and questions.

EMPEROR: Am I troubling you?

BEGGAR: That's the stupidest question you have asked to-day. You're an impudent man! You do not respect a human being's essential privacy. You do not know solitude, therefore you want the approval of a stranger like myself. You are dependent on every man's respect.

EMPEROR: I rule men. Hence the respect.

BEGGAR: The bridle too thinks that it rules the horse, the swallow's beak thinks that it steers the swallow, and the palm tree's topmost spike thinks that it pulls the tree after it up to heaven!

EMPEROR: You are a malicious man. I should have you destroyed if I wouldn't then have to believe that it was out of injured vanity.

The beggar takes out the hurdy-gurdy and plays.

A man passes quickly and bows.

BEGGAR *puts away the hurdy-gurdy:* This man has a wife who steals from him. At night she bends over him to take money from him. At times he wakes up and sees her above him. Then he thinks that she loves him so much that she can no longer resist the impulse to gaze at him at night. For that reason he forgives her the little deceptions which he detects.

EMPEROR: Are you at it again? Not a word of it is true.

BEGGAR: You can go now. You're becoming coarse.

EMPEROR: That's incredible!

The beggar plays on the hurdy-gurdy.

EMPEROR: Is the audience over now?

BEGGAR: Once again now they all see the sky beautified and the earth more fruitful because of this bit of music, and prolong their lives and forgive themselves and their neighbours, because of this bit of sound.

EMPEROR: Well, at least tell me why you simply cannot bear me and have yet told me so much?

BEGGAR *nonchalantly:* Because you were not too proud to listen to my chitchat, which I only used to forget my dead dog.

EMPEROR: Now I am going. You have spoilt the best day of my life. I should never have stopped here. Pity is no good. The only thing in your favour is the courage to speak to me as you have done. And for that I've kept everyone waiting for me! *He leaves, escorted by the soldiers. The bells ring again.*

BEGGAR *one sees that he is blind:* Now he's gone. It must be before noon, the air is so warm. The boy won't be coming today. There's a celebration in town. That idiot just now is going there too. Now I have to think again of my dog.

Driving out a Devil

Translator: RICHARD GRUNBERGER

Characters

The girl · The lad · The mother · The father · The night-
watchman · The schoolmaster · The mayor · Farmers

A single-storey farmhouse with a very large red-tiled roof. There is a bench in front of the house. An evening in August.

I

The lad and the girl are sitting on the bench.

LAD: Lovely evening.
GIRL: There's a dance on at the Red Cow tonight. Heard the band?
LAD: A couple of trumpets.
GIRL: Mother won't let me go.
LAD: Why not?
GIRL: Says it's dangerous.
LAD: Ah, you got to watch out.
GIRL: You can hear it all the way from here now. That'll be the wind.
LAD: Might have a storm. Today was a scorcher.
GIRL: Stars should be out soon. Then I'll have to see to the cows.
LAD: Lucky them.
GIRL: Why?
LAD: Because you have to see to them.
GIRL: A lot of good that does them.
LAD: Don't see to me, do you?
GIRL: Don't have to.
LAD: Don't want to, you mean.
GIRL: There won't be any storm if you ask me.
LAD: Have to get out of your bed if there is.
GIRL: Down to the parlour. So Mum can pray.
LAD: Sooner than pray in bed.
GIRL: Nearly time for those cows.
LAD: There aren't any stars I can see.

GIRL: You bet not.
Pause.
LAD: What's that mean?
GIRL: Something.
LAD: Better say.
GIRL: Better hell.
LAD: You going to?
GIRL: Not to you, silly.
LAD: I'll make you pay for that.
GIRL: You make me laugh.
LAD *tries to kiss her:* Go ahead, laugh then.
GIRL: That was nowhere near my mouth.
LAD: That's what you think.
GIRL: So you think it was, eh?
LAD: You know it was.
GIRL: Bit too dark for you, is it?
LAD: Ah, I'm scared.
GIRL: Get that arm away. I don't like it.
LAD: That's your arm, that is.
GIRL: *That's* the arm I mean.
LAD: It's all yours.
GIRL: I'm off to the cows.
LAD: Got legs too, have you?
GIRL: Then into bed.
LAD: Legs and all?
GIRL: What's that supposed to mean?
LAD: What?
GIRL: All that nonsense of yours.
LAD: I don't give it a thought. Look, there are the stars.
GIRL: Do you usually see to the cows too?
LAD: You pulling my leg?
GIRL: I suppose it rings when it's pulled.
LAD: I don't get you today.
GIRL: You're not with us any more, are you?
LAD: Was I?
GIRL: You've mucked it all up.
LAD: What have I said?

GIRL: Nothing. That's the trouble.

LAD: You'll hear something different now, though.

GIRL: I should think so when you see who's coming.

2

The mother enters.

MOTHER: Good evening, Richard.

LAD: Evening.

MOTHER: Have you done the cows yet?

GIRL: Plenty of time for that.

MOTHER: But not for *you* to do them, eh?

GIRL: Oh? Why not? *Gets up.*

LAD: We've been having a long talk about the cows.

MOTHER: Is she as fond of them as all that?

LAD: She says she's got to see to them.

MOTHER: And doesn't.

LAD: You know how girls are.

GIRL: A lot of experience you've had!

LAD: Not hard to tell that.

MOTHER: It's much too late to be out.

GIRL: I've been at it all day.

LAD: That's a fact.

MOTHER: Thick as thieves, aren't you?

LAD: It's a fact, though.

MOTHER: The bell will be going for prayers.

GIRL: I can stay out till then, can't I?

MOTHER: You'll have to be in for that.

LAD: Go on, why?

MOTHER: Because it's the proper thing.

LAD: And supposing it's nicer out here?

MOTHER: That's just why.

GIRL: Ah, it's dangerous out here.

MOTHER: What do you know about it? I won't have that way of talking. You don't know anything.

LAD: But it's a fact.

MOTHER: What, another one?

LAD: It does happen.

MOTHER: Nothing happens. Go and do the cows.

GIRL: It's much too early.

MOTHER: What do you mean, too early? It's pitch-dark.

LAD: Light enough to be seen.

MOTHER: But not to see the cows.

GIRL: I can see a donkey all right.

MOTHER: Don't take it amiss, Richard. She's very young.

LAD: They always are at that age.

GIRL: Clever.

FATHER'S VOICE: Missus!

MOTHER: He's calling. We'll have to go in. Good night, Richard.

LAD: Good night. Can't she stay out a bit longer?

GIRL: No. I'm off.

LAD: Till the stars are out?

MOTHER: You get down to those cows. *Goes inside.*

LAD: Why don't you want to stay?

GIRL: Because I don't feel like it.

LAD: She'd have let you.

GIRL: Only because I didn't feel like it.

LAD: Is that why you didn't feel like it?

GIRL: Think what you please.

LAD: I'm not thinking at all.

GIRL: I'm off.

LAD: Better, or they'll beat you.

GIRL: You been listening?

LAD: Yes: smack smack.

GIRL: You ought to be ashamed of yourself.

LAD: I quite like it.

GIRL: Don't you take anything seriously?

LAD: You wouldn't want me to.

GIRL: What ideas you get.

LAD: What have they got against it, I'd like to know?

GIRL: Against what?

LAD: People getting together.

GIRL: You having me on?

LAD: Do you think they could be right?

GIRL: Me? Go on.

LAD: There you are.

GIRL: Father and Mother do, though.

LAD: Why?

GIRL: They don't know me.

LAD: You know yourself, though.

GIRL: *And* I know you.

LAD: Smart friends you've got.

GIRL: Well, I'm going in.

LAD: Tired?

GIRL: And if I am?

LAD: Then I'll carry you in.

GIRL: Fall flat on your face, you will.

LAD *picks her up:* Think so?

GIRL: No. Let me go. Suppose they see us.

LAD: They'll see us all right.

GIRL: Let go of me.

LAD: Give us a kiss.

GIRL: My mother . . .

LAD: Doesn't like the idea. *Puts her down.*

GIRL: That wasn't nice.

LAD: Yes, it was. You kiss pretty well.

GIRL: That's why I'm going in now.

LAD: All right, better go.

GIRL: Now you've satisfied the animal in you.

LAD: Want me to stay, then?

GIRL: I didn't say that.

LAD: Stars are out now.

GIRL: I'll see to the cows, then.

LAD: Been no thunder today.

GIRL: Any objection?

LAD: Yes. There's a crack in your wall.

GIRL: Anything wrong with that?

LAD: Nothing wrong. On the contrary.

GIRL: Oh, you and your nonsense.

LAD: When it's thundery.

GIRL: Well, what?

LAD: A fellow can see you.

GIRL: Can't he see me now?

LAD: Not in your slip.

GIRL: Is that what they see when it's thundery?

LAD: Ah, when you're saying your prayers.

GIRL: And you've seen it?

LAD: Like to know, wouldn't you?

GIRL: You've seen nothing.

LAD: That's right: nothing to see. Only that your slip's darned on the right shoulder.

GIRL: It's not true.

LAD: Want me to show you?

GIRL: What else do you know about?

LAD: Sleep over the byre, don't you?

GIRL: Is that something else you saw through the crack?

LAD: You haven't been sleeping there all that long.

GIRL: Who told you that?

LAD: I've seen worse lookers.

GIRL: Oh, get on.

LAD: Much worse lookers.

GIRL: Seen them, eh?

LAD: You're not the worst of them.

GIRL: Swank.

LAD: Maybe. But you're all right up front.

GIRL: Pooh, you dirty old man.

LAD: What's dirty about being all right up front and not flat as a pancake?

FATHER *calls from the house:* Anna!

The girl is scared.

The lad puts his arm round her waist; they listen.

GIRL: Let go of me. I was scared.

LAD: You might be scared again.

GIRL: I'll have to go in. I haven't any excuse now.

LAD: Because the stars are out?

GIRL: Yes. And because he's calling.

LAD: Put your head here and you won't see the stars.

GIRL: I'm not putting my face there, though.

LAD: Why? It won't bite, will it?

GIRL: I'll take it away at once, though.

LAD: You do that.

GIRL: I'm sure they can see us.

LAD: It's pitch-dark.

GIRL: But you're to take that hand away.

LAD: Which hand?

GIRL: That one and that one. No, you can't.

LAD: But I can, you see.

GIRL: No, I'll have to go in.

LAD: You've got such a soft body.

GIRL: You're hurting.

LAD: Can you see me?

GIRL: If I look up.

LAD: That means you've got your eyes shut.

GIRL: Leave me alone.

LAD: Does that hurt?

GIRL: Let me go in. Don't!

LAD: You're so warm.

GIRL: And you've got cold hands.

LAD: They'll warm up in no time.

GIRL: Look out! *They separate.*

LAD: Bloody hell. *Slips behind the house.*

3

The father arrives.

FATHER: What's going on, Anna?

GIRL: Is that you, Father?

FATHER: What are you up to?

GIRL: Nothing. Just sitting.

FATHER: Sitting, eh?

GIRL: Yes, I was feeling tired.

FATHER: All by yourself too?

GIRL: Yes. Nobody ever comes to visit us.

FATHER: Nobody comes, eh?

GIRL: Should I see to the cows now?

FATHER: I should think you bloody well will see to the cows. *Hits her.* I'll teach you to gallivant about at night with boys and get yourself a bad name!

The girl goes off crying.

The father exit in pursuit.

LAD: Ah, now she's copped it. Now she's ripe. Now for the other thing. *Exit.*

The bell rings for prayers.

4

Candlelight in the parlour.

MOTHER *puts her head out of the window:* Such a beautiful evening. You can smell Bellinger's wheat all the way up here. Nice wind. *Pulling her head in:* Days like this aren't easy. I'm glad the night's come. *Her head disappears. The light goes out. Cassiopeia is visible above the roof.*

5

Enter the lad with a ladder. He moves quietly.

LAD: No light. So let's go. I'll comfort her. It's always good when they're crying. It goes with a swing then. The old folk are quite right. *He leans the ladder left against the unseen front of the house.* People can see you out here. This way they won't have anything to worry about. *Climbs the ladder. At the top:* Hey! What's happening?

GIRL'S VOICE: For God's sake. Suppose they saw you.

LAD'S VOICE: All the more reason to open the window wid.
GIRL'S VOICE: But you can't come in here.
LAD'S VOICE: Is that what your old man said?
GIRL'S VOICE: You've got some cheek.
LAD'S VOICE: There we are. Nobody's going to see me now.
Silence. Wind. And a bed creaks.

6

The father approaches down below from the right. Listens.

FATHER: A fine bloody business. In the middle of the night
too. *Sees the ladder.* Hullo there. *Takes the ladder away.* That's
for a start. *Fetches a cudgel, reappears and goes off right. Then a
sound of stamping on the stairs and a shrill scream, followed by
thumps.*
FATHER'S VOICE: Open up! Christ and damnation! Bloody
cow!

7

*The lad and the girl climb through an attic window on to the roof,
shutting the window behind them.*

LAD: Sh!
GIRL: He'll kill me.
LAD: Shut up.
Pause.
GIRL: He'll find us.
LAD: He will if you don't keep quiet.
Noise of the door being broken open.
GIRL: He's busting open the door.
LAD: And he can hear us, damn it.
GIRL: He's looking for us. Now he's going downstairs. What
will he think?

AD: He's going back to bed.

GIRL: He's taken away the ladder. He's not going to bed.

LAD: I suppose he's looking for you.

GIRL: What did I come for?

LAD: You could perfectly well have stayed.

GIRL: Then there wouldn't have been any trouble.

LAD: This way it's touch and go.

GIRL: Shall I go down?

LAD: It's dull on one's own.

GIRL: But suppose he asks where I've been?

LAD: On the toilet.

GIRL: Whatever did I let you in for?

LAD: Oh, drop it. Things went wrong, that's all. It was good earlier.

GIRL: He'll chuck me out.

LAD: He won't do that. Think what the neighbours would say. But I'll never hear the end of it.

GIRL: Always thinking of yourself.

LAD: What did you have to hang your washing up in the yard for?

GIRL: Do you mean you didn't look through the crack?

LAD: How about going down now?

GIRL: Are you trying to get rid of me? I'm so frightened.

LAD: Ah. And up here you can look at the stars. Quiet!

8

The father arrives muttering. Stands left front and looks up.

FATHER: Anna! If I wake the missus up the whole village will hear about it. She can't have gone. He wouldn't have climbed in otherwise, sod it. And I was on the stairs. *Mutters his way off right.*

LAD: Quick now.

GIRL: My body's not so soft now, is it?

LAD: You'd better think about how to get down. Or he'll
have the hide off you.

GIRL: I wish I hadn't come up here.

LAD: Just what I'm feeling.

Girl sets out to crawl to the attic window.

LAD: Whoa, somebody coming. Keep quiet or I'll bash your
teeth in.

GIRL: The vicar!

9

The parson and the nightwatchman.

PARSON: Who did you see today?

WATCHMAN: Nobody so far. You can't look inside the
houses.

PARSON: True, true. That is why they are such hotbeds of
immorality.

WATCHMAN: Ah. More babies made there than any other
place.

PARSON: It is a beautiful night. I've been for a last stroll. It is
much pleasanter out of doors. Inside it is stuffy.

WATCHMAN: I thought we were going to have thunder at
first. But it's turned out beautiful.

PARSON: The wind has driven the clouds away. And it's
light.

WATCHMAN: It's getting lighter pretty well every minute.
That's the stars.

PARSON: There's Cassiopeia. Like a big W. See her?

WATCHMAN: Ah. It's marvellous.

PARSON: What are you looking that way for? It's over there.

WATCHMAN: Your Reverence.

PARSON: Yes; what?

WATCHMAN: Somebody's sitting up there.

PARSON: Where?

WATCHMAN: On Fisher's roof.

PARSON: Indeed yes. Two of them.

WATCHMAN: Let's get closer.

They do so.

PARSON: Of diverse sex. A scandal.

WATCHMAN: Well I never!

PARSON: They've started doing it on the roofs now.

WATCHMAN: Maybe it's too stuffy for them downstairs.

PARSON: That's Anna.

WATCHMAN: Or they might want to look at Cassiopeia too.

PARSON: Don't joke about it. It's a terrible thing. Hullo, who's that sitting up there?

Silence.

WATCHMAN: They think they can't be seen if they don't say anything. And perhaps they can't think of anything to say.

PARSON: But it *is* Anna. Can't you hear me, you there up on the roof?

SCHOOLMASTER'S VOICE: What's happening?

PARSON: Do come here. Something absolutely disgraceful.

SCHOOLMASTER *enters with the mayor:* What's the trouble? How about a hand of whist?

PARSON: Look: up on the roof.

SCHOOLMASTER: Holy smoke! That's a fine view they've got.

MAYOR: Well, what a business. What are they doing up there?

WATCHMAN: Been waiting for us, I expect. They're deaf.

PARSON: Go and wake up Mr Fisher.

SCHOOLMASTER: Tell him there's something worth seeing.

MAYOR: Our new weathercock.

WATCHMAN: Stork's nest, you mean. *Knocks.*

FARMERS *entering:* Good evening, your Reverence. Ho, on old Fisher's roof! That beats the band. They can't hear a thing. All that way up!

Laughter.

FATHER *comes out:* What is it? A fire?

Farmers laugh uproariously.

SCHOOLMASTER: No. No fire.

FATHER: What's it about then?

Laughter.

MAYOR: Nothing. We're just having a good time.

FATHER: What the hell! Tell me.

Laughter.

PARSON: The way you run your house is an abomination to the Lord.

FATHER: I don't know what you're talking about.

Laughter.

WATCHMAN: The devil has come for your daughter.

FATHER: Well, where the devil is she?

WATCHMAN: He's settled down with her on your roof!

Gigantic laughter.

Lux in Tenebris

Translators: EVA GEISEL and ERNEST BORNEMAN

Characters

Paduk · Frau Hogge · The reporter · The chaplain · The assistant · People · Frau Hogge's girls

Brothel alley. To the right and at the back brothels, their red glass doors open, red lanterns above them. The alley leads to the back and turns sharply left. Left front, a large canvas tent, its entrance closed by a flap. Right of the entrance, a table and a chair. A picket fence surrounds the tent. On the top of the tent a large sign, 'Let there be Light! Mass education!' From the top of the tent a floodlight pours chalky white light over the alley.

I

Night. At the table outside, Paduk, a red-haired man, a cash box before him. People are buying tickets.

PADUK: Soft chancre one mark! Clap one sixty! Syphilis two fifty! Don't push!

A MAN: Is there a lecture on now?

PADUK: In three minutes.

A WOMAN: Is it made of wax?

PADUK: Here, forty pfennigs change. You don't want syphilis?

THE WOMAN: Is it wax or . . .

PADUK: Wax and things in alcohol.

THE WOMAN: All right, then syphilis too.

PADUK: That'll be two marks fifty.

A MAN: The clap.

PADUK: There you are! Correct.

A WOMAN: Syphilis. No, only syphilis. That's the most gruesome of the lot, isn't it?

PADUK: You can't have syphilis by itself. The lecture starts with clap. The clap it is, then.

A WOMAN *among those queuing up:* My sister couldn't sleep a wink all night, she was that excited.

ANOTHER WOMAN: Why not come here for a change, I said to myself. Normally I go to the cinema Thursdays.

FIRST WOMAN: That alley alone's worth *my* money.

PADUK: Move along, please! Keep your money ready! Clap one mark. Soft chancre one sixty. Syphilis two fifty.

MAN: Clap.

PADUK: One mark. That's only fifty pfennigs.

MAN: That's all I intend to pay.

PADUK: Then you can't get in. Next one!

MAN: Let's see about that. D'you mean I must catch these hideous diseases just because I haven't got more than fifty pfennigs on me?

PADUK *addressing the man behind:* Syphilis two marks fifty. Right.

MAN: I won't get a ticket then?

PADUK: No.

MAN: And what about my health? My wife! The kids!

PADUK: What about me? My equipment? Expenses? Taxes? The whole lecture? Run along, or I'll call the police! *The man leaves, cursing, right.*

WOMAN: He's in the mood, that one.

SECOND WOMAN: Wonder where he'll go now?

THIRD WOMAN: He looked as if he was going to pay him back!

FIRST WOMAN: Well I never! He's going *that* way!

MAN *disappears right into the brothel:* Bloody swine!

PADUK: On fifty pfennigs! That's a laugh! The clap one mark. Ladies and gentlemen, lecture's starting right now. If you can't get in now, come back in half an hour. We're open all night. *He gets up, pulls the tent flap shut. Some people are left standing left. They are joined by fresh arrivals. From inside the tent a monotonous, unintelligible voice.*

2

THE REPORTER *to Paduk:* My name is Schmidt. I represent the *Evening Chronicle*. Have you got a moment?

PADUK: The gentleman is from the Press? Certainly.

REPORTER: Quite a show you're having here.

PADUK: Sold out!

REPORTER: That must be gratifying! *Very* gratifying!

PADUK: You're right.

REPORTER: In view of the good cause, I mean.

PADUK: That's what I meant.

REPORTER: Tell me, what is it you're actually showing?

PADUK: In my hestablishment you can view the dread harvest of venereal disease. A warning against that whoredom which undermines our society. A fiery call to the victims to have themselves treated before the poison destroys body and mind.

REPORTER: Are you drumming up trade for any particular physician?

PADUK: What do you mean by that? Sir, I'm doing this out of pure concern for my fellow-beings! Think of those thousands of sufferers!

The reporter makes notes.

PADUK: Thousands of victims, led astray in a moment of weakness, driven by the demon alcohol into the arms of diseased harlots.

REPORTER: I see you're an idealist. What made you decide to devote your life to the service of your fellows?

PADUK: For years I have observed the wanton ways of our cities. How they destroy the soul and wear away the body. How drink and alcohol only prepare the way for prostitution and crime.

REPORTER: And crime. You speak excellent prose, did you know that? As if you had worked for years in a newspaper office. Did you have the advantage of a higher education?

PADUK: Only elementary school, I'm afraid. My parents were too poor to make a good breadwinner of me.

REPORTER: Make a good breadwinner of me. Beautiful. May I ask you a few questions about your life and career? In view of the public interest your enterprise has aroused.

PADUK: My life is an open book. I am a man who likes things tidy. A self-made man. My father was a small shopkeeper ruined by drink. My mother was always ailing. My early years were marked by poverty, deprivation, and humiliation.

REPORTER: So you acquired your profound understanding of social injustice quite young?

PADUK: Precisely.

REPORTER: And realized that prostitution lay at the root of it all?

PADUK: That's right!

REPORTER: And accordingly selected this alley for your mission?

PADUK: Of course. The enemy has to be fought on the spot. The frequenters of these dens of vice must be confronted right here with the consequences of their iniquity. I shall not rest until the last of these unfortunates turns his back on those breeding places of misery.

REPORTER: It's a pleasure to listen to you. Are you open only at night?

PADUK: Yes, sir. For just that reason.

REPORTER: But it means sacrificing your nights?

PADUK: I'm used to that.

REPORTER: May I ask what has led you to choose such a highly ingenious form of attack upon this social evil? It strikes me that only fanatical hatred could hit upon a scheme of such ingenuity.

PADUK: What do you mean?

REPORTER: Was it something you'd read somewhere; did you have a model and if so, what? Or was it a personal experience, some kind of revelation?

PADUK: Let's say it was a revelation.

REPORTER: Like what?

PADUK: I saw people deprived of their money so that they could be deprived of their health as well. How much better, I thought, if in exchange for that money they at least got a chance to keep their health.

REPORTER: So it was primarily for financial reasons . . .

PADUK *taken aback*: Good God, no. What gave you that idea?

It was for purely moral reasons. I thought ignorance of danger drives these souls to their destruction. One must show them what these dens of vice do to them. Then the stews will go bankrupt, and the customers be saved.

REPORTER: But you charge admission. For educational reasons?

PADUK: Yes. What people don't have to pay for they don't appreciate. I charge them two marks fifty for syphilis. Over there they have to pay at least five marks, wine not included.

REPORTER *titters:* But at least they get the real thing.

PADUK: This is no laughing matter, sir.

REPORTER: I'm sorry. And what has been the effect of your lectures?

PADUK: Sold out every night.

REPORTER: I mean on your audience.

PADUK: The best that could be imagined. Fainting and vomiting.

REPORTER: That's splendid.

PADUK: And what's more: those brothels over there are empty now. To let.

REPORTER: How do you know?

PADUK: Under my floodlight here no visitor remains unnoticed. Do you notice any now? And you can tell by the piano if there's anyone inside to be led astray.

REPORTER: Excellent way to check on your success! Positively ingenious. It can't have been easy to organize all this.

PADUK: It's always hard to break new ground. The municipal authorities were against it, naturally. Particularly because of the late hour.

REPORTER: But in the end they put the site at your disposal?

PADUK: They did.

REPORTER: And the whole thing was financed by anonymous private benefactors?

PADUK: It was. But the lecture's just finished now.

REPORTER: I have enough for my editor. Thank you very

much. It will all appear in the newspapers. I love the newspapers!

PADUK: A pleasure. Would you like to attend the next lecture?

REPORTER: No, thanks. I don't care for that sort of thing.

PADUK: But perhaps you'll wait a few moments before the next performance starts? I'm giving a brief address.

REPORTER: Thank you very much. That I'll do. You're such a good speaker.

3

People come out and disperse.

PEOPLE: I feel quite sick. – I've thrown up. Thank God they've provided buckets. – That feeling of disgust afterwards, it's just like coming out of a brothel oneself.

A MAN *waiting to go in*: Is it worth it?

A MAN WHO HAS JUST COME OUT: Absolutely. Specially the syphilis section. Some beautiful things there.

A CHAPLAIN *to Paduk:* Allow me. My name's Benkler. Chaplain. President of the Christian Catholic Young Workers' Association. We were thinking of visiting your exhibition.

PADUK: It's open to everyone.

CHAPLAIN *with Young Workers lining up behind him:* May I ask if there are any reductions?

PADUK: No. Not as a rule. But you're from the official Young Workers' Association?

CHAPLAIN: We are.

PADUK: Catholic?

CHAPLAIN: Christian Catholic.

PADUK: Then we'll make an exception. How many gentlemen are there?

CHAPLAIN: Unfortunately only half of them. Seventy-three.

PADUK: Then you can book the whole lecture. That will be one hundred marks the lot.

CHAPLAIN: And would that cover all sections?

PADUK: Yes. Gonorrhoea, chancre, *and* syphilis.

CHAPLAIN: Here you are. One hundred marks.

PADUK: But mind you, no singing.

CHAPLAIN: Of course not.

PADUK *waggish:* Can't disturb people's sleep.

CHAPLAIN: Sleep? Nobody's living here.

PADUK: How about there, across the street? *They* sleep all night now I'm here.

CHAPLAIN: Oh yes, I see, that's splendid. No, we won't sing.

PADUK: Please recommend me to your friends. *Leads the Young Workers' Association into the tent. Re-emerges.* Ladies and gentlemen, kindly be patient for another quarter of an hour. I can assure you it won't take longer this time. *To the reporter:* Perhaps you'll look in tomorrow night?

REPORTER: I will. Thank you. *Exit.*

PADUK *alone:* How quiet it is now. After midnight there'll be no customers. It's hell having to stay up after that. But it's the light ... *Looks up.* The light is beautiful. *Goes to the picket fence.* Silence. Bankruptcy. A dry river bed. The water's gone. How quiet they are! I wonder when they will be able to get that piano going again.

4

Frau Hogge appears on the right, in the red doorway.

FRAU HOGGE: Paduk!

PADUK: Eh?

FRAU HOGGE *emerges into the alley:* Have you a moment?

PADUK: By all means. The lecture's on.

FRAU HOGGE: Business booming?

PADUK: Sold out.

FRAU HOGGE: Paduk ...

PADUK: Mister Paduk to you.

FRAU HOGGE: Beg your pardon. Mr Paduk. I merely thought you're an old friend.

PADUK *mumbles:* Not to my knowledge.

FRAU HOGGE: Old customer, then.

PADUK *glances around:* What do you want now? Haven't you got anything to do?

FRAU HOGGE: We're spring-cleaning. I want to apologize because of that misunderstanding the other day.

PADUK *aloof:* Oh, don't bother.

FRAU HOGGE: Because of the way you were treated!

PADUK: I'm overwhelmed.

FRAU HOGGE: We were so busy, and you know how it is . . .

PADUK: You're still busy?

FRAU HOGGE: Now you're being sarcastic again!

PADUK: I thought I was doing you a favour, reducing your business a little so that you can treat your customers better.

FRAU HOGGE: But you didn't have any cash on you.

PADUK: That's right. And that's why I thought I'd better earn some.

FRAU HOGGE: But it's *our* money you're earning!

PADUK: But *decently*, mind you.

FRAU HOGGE: What d'you mean, decently? You're taking the bread out of our mouths.

PADUK: You've got wine, and you've got it all to yourself now.

FRAU HOGGE: And my poor girls, what of them?

PADUK: They're only poor because they're your girls.

FRAU HOGGE: You're making things very difficult for an old woman like me. Listen: I'm sorry you were thrown out of our house like that.

PADUK: I was sorry too. But unlike you, I did something about it.

FRAU HOGGE: You were one of our best customers.

PADUK: And yet you threw me out because I was temporarily embarrassed.

FRAU HOGGE: Now tell me frankly, what's all this nonsense?
Why are you exhibiting these disgusting things to people?
As if you could change the world.

PADUK: You know very well that *that's* not the point. I
simply figured on a way to bring some *light* into this alley.
To illuminate your disgusting trade!

FRAU HOGGE: So it was out of spite? All you wanted was to
fix an electric floodlight – *looks up* – somewhere? And that's
why you staged this farce? All those petitions? The benefactors? Your hestablishment? Just for the floodlight?

PADUK: I couldn't very well stand here all by myself and hold
it in my hand like a lamp-post. I couldn't afford that. You
yourself said one can't do anything without money.

FRAU HOGGE: What a miserable specimen you are!

PADUK: You overestimate me. It just happened to be a good
idea that turned into a blessing for thousands.

FRAU HOGGE: Yes. We all know *you*.

PADUK: Right. I did draw attention to myself.

FRAU HOGGE: Maltreating my girls so that they come running to me. Howling, half naked. Refusing to pay, kicking
up a row, yourself the worst of the lot, a miserable scoundrel we had to throw out – *we* had to throw out!

PADUK: And risen from the dead. On the third day resur-
rected and ascended to Heaven! Creator of a welfare institu-
tion! Champion of public morality! Capitalist!

FRAU HOGGE: Bastard! Pig! Degenerate! *Exit into brothel.*

5

PADUK *returning to the table:* Baggage. Common, uneducated
lot! And all of it just because the Young Workers' Association is honouring *me* with a visit! Envy, that's the trouble.

A MAN *on the left, one of those waiting in the queue:* What's all the
fuss with that woman?

PADUK: May I ask what business of yours that is?

THE MAN: I'm a public servant. That's why it's my business.

PADUK: Common slander, that's all it is. Slander to which we pioneers of decency have always been exposed.

THE MAN: I'll get someone to look into it tomorrow. This thing's been built with outside money! *Exit unceremoniously.*

PADUK *stares after him:* Damn. Those fellows have long ears! This could be awkward . . . But I've got the gift of the gab, as that idiot said, and tomorrow my life story will be in the papers. Full of touching details. Hm. Still, it might do no harm to dispel lingering doubts about my high moral purpose!

6

Another performance has ended. The Young Workers' Association comes trooping out.

PADUK *to the chaplain:* How did you like it?

CHAPLAIN: Very much. *Pause.* But it's really hell on earth, isn't it?

PADUK: Isn't it? Absolute hell. And all because of prostitution! Padre, if you will permit I'd like to talk to you for a moment. Get it off my chest. For out of the abundance of the heart the mouth speaketh, you know . . . *He goes into the tent and reappears with the assistant who is carrying specimen jars which he deposits on the table. Young Workers hover uncertainly. They are joined by members of the queue. During the first sentences of Paduk's address the alley comes to life. From the brothels issue the girls, singly or in groups of two or three, dressed in sombre street clothes. Some tiptoe towards the fence, others saunter across the alley, giggling noisily. But in the end they all stand gazing silently over the fence.*

PADUK: My dear young friends! You have been shown the dread effects of vice, the horrible diseases that result from prostitution. It is no accident that this hestablishment destined to serve a high moral purpose is situated at this particular spot. It is an act of protest. *He notices the girls*

beyond the fence, climbs on the table, a specimen jar in each hand.
My dear young friends! I'm not attacking the poor unfortunates who dwell in these places, I'm attacking the
places themselves, I'm attacking their very spirit! I don't
condemn the unfortunate young women compelled like
slaves to sell their bodies that were once the work of God –
without even being allowed to keep the money. *He turns to
the girls.* Only a brute would turn against them. They are
the victims. Their lot is more pitiful than that of cart-
horses, more harrowing than that of convicts, more terrible
than that of the mortally sick. They feel their immortal soul
decaying, their body rotting away, they have to comply
with the wishes of dirty rotters and degenerate scoundrels,
must serve men's bestial lusts and let themselves be in-
fected with incurable diseases. *Holding specimen jar aloft in his
left hand.* Look at these lips, these rotting gums – once they
sang the Lord's praises in church as loudly as yours did.
This ravaged head, like yours it was once caressed by a
loving mother's hand. Above this breast – *he stoops to pick up
a wax model* – now pitted by pus, hung a little golden
crucifix, just as above yours. These eyes, or what's left of
them – *he stoops and picks up another wax model* – bleary,
rotting in their sockets; they gladdened a parent's heart
when they first opened, just like yours! Don't ever forget
that! Don't forget it when temptations whisper and the
devil beckons. Perhaps there is still time, perhaps you will
be spared, perhaps it is not too late. Be grateful for your
chance of salvation. Don't pile new wrongs on to the old!
He steps off the table.

CHAPLAIN: Very well spoken. Only someone chosen by the
Lord could speak like that. We thank you.

PADUK *with specimen jars:* Padre, I was only doing my duty.
*Chaplain extends his hand. Paduk shakes it after putting down the
jars. The chaplain and Young Workers file out silently.*

PADUK: No more performances tonight. It's cleaning time.
Goes upstage.

7

People disperse. The girls, too, disappear again into the houses.

PADUK *returns, followed by the assistant:* Any tips?

ASSISTANT: A few marks.

PADUK: Let's have 'em!

ASSISTANT: But they're mine!

PADUK: They're not. Don't be insolent. You're being paid by me.

ASSISTANT: Then you can rattle off that junk yourself from now on. Anyway, who wants to work in that smell?

PADUK: You're fired.

ASSISTANT: Suits me. And this time I'll really go. This time you've made a mistake. I'm through. Can't pay for any fun on *those* wages. And besides, it turns one's stomach. I'm through, I tell you!

PADUK: Are you serious?

ASSISTANT: Changed your mind again? Naah! This time it won't work. I'm going inside to pack up. You can keep an eye on your own dirty stuff from now on. *He throws the money on the table.*

PADUK: Keep it. You've misunderstood me. You're too touchy, boy.

ASSISTANT: Naah, this time I've had it. For good. And don't call me 'boy'. *Goes inside.*

PADUK: Damn! What a day! And just when I've never spoken better. Now I know what Whitsun means – I was filled with the Holy Ghost. But fortune's a woman: she protects fools. *Sits down.* All this hanging around now! On an empty stomach, too! Who can eat in a place like this? I even dream about it. When I think of the time it's going to take to coach the next one and teach him all those Latin words! Damn drudgery! And on top of it that bloody official! Jackass! Stool pigeon! *Turns round suddenly as if struck by apoplexy. Some men have appeared at the brothel door on the right. They ring the bell.*

FIRST CUSTOMER: What the hell's the matter? Are they closed?

SECOND CUSTOMER: As if that damn floodlight wasn't enough!

THIRD CUSTOMER: Open up! Or are you all on holiday? *The door is opened. They go inside.*

PADUK: Wonder what they want. *Goes up to the fence.* First lot in a fortnight!

8

Paduk returns to his table, shakes his head, takes out the cash box and starts counting money.

FRAU HOGGE *right, opens the door, silently crosses the street, listens. Tiptoes through the gate and stands behind Paduk:* Enough in the kitty, Mr Paduk?

PADUK *startled, furious:* What's that? Clear off, will you?

FRAU HOGGE: Don't lose your temper, Mr Paduk – we've got our old customers back again.

PADUK: Where's the music, then?

FRAU HOGGE: Music isn't just for everyone. Tonight it's only five-mark customers. But things will improve.

PADUK: You should know.

FRAU HOGGE: Listen, Mr Paduk, could you let me have a chair?

PADUK: That all?

FRAU HOGGE: Yes. And I don't want it for nothing, either.

PADUK *locks up the cash box:* After all those insults you were hurling at me only ten minutes ago . . .

FRAU HOGGE: Since then quite a lot has happened. Quite a lot, I said.

PADUK: I haven't noticed anything.

FRAU HOGGE: In the first place, our old customers have

started coming back. One up to me. In the second place,
you made a speech.

PADUK: Right. One up to me. Your powers of observation do
you credit.

FRAU HOGGE: Yours don't. That speech was rubbish.

PADUK: Rubbish, was it?

FRAU HOGGE: Yes. From your point of view. Not from the
chaplain's. But from yours and mine.

PADUK: Haha. Very funny. *Fetches the chair*. Here's your chair.
Now will you explain?

FRAU HOGGE: I will. *Sits down*. Because I am grateful to you,
that's why. And I wanted to apologize for our little misunderstanding a short while ago.

PADUK: Let's get back to my speech.

FRAU HOGGE: The point of your speech was, if I understand
it correctly, that the girls were being exploited. You put
that very well. But it isn't quite correct. Instead of going on
and on about those lips that once sang the Lord's praises,
you might as well have mentioned the schnaps they once
guzzled – less effective, perhaps, but nearer the truth.
Instead of saying how those heads were caressed by
mothers' hands, you might have mentioned the less familiar
fact that they were bashed by pimps' fists. But I don't want
to dwell on that. You know it, anyway; you studied long
enough with us. That my business has got to show a profit
was correct. Normally my takings are considerably higher
than yours.

PADUK: You're an excellent speaker. It is a pleasure to listen
to you. But why was my speech rubbish? Is that the way to
thank me for my chair?

FRAU HOGGE: Don't rush me. I'll break it to you gently.
Let's look at your business prospects first. You're doing
quite well because no one has seen your exhibits before unless he's been one himself, which is a high price to pay.
But no one will visit your show twice – you can take my word for
it – and that means there'll be an end to it some day. You'll
go bankrupt, and *my* business will restart two weeks after.

My clientele numbers about six thousand. Thanks to the educational measures which we immediately put into effect a high proportion have been discouraged from visiting your disgusting, vulgar establishment, with its appeal only to the basest instincts in men, cowardice, and cant. The rest can't be prevented from letting you spoil the delights of love for them, the greatest delight life has to offer in and out of wedlock; they will avoid us for a couple of weeks, I admit that the loss of revenue is considerable, but nevertheless it is non-recurring. *And visitors to our institute always come back.*

Silence.

PADUK *sits across from her at his table, his forehead bathed in sweat:* That's got nothing to do with my speech.

FRAU HOGGE: Yes, it has. As far as I gather, the idea of your business is to exploit the venereal infection spread by prostitution. That'll hurt prostitution only as long as you can tell people about it. Then it'll be over and we'll flourish as before. The point of your speech, however, was that you wanted to destroy the origin of the infection, prostitution itself. But that means doing away with the source of your own business which flows from it like water from a tap. In short, if you choose to educate the customers about infection, that's your business. *But if you educate my girls*, then prostitution will perish and with it the source of infection and you yourself too! *Triumphantly yet still anxious:* And that's what you were doing when you sent my girls back to me *again*, weeping, as you did today. Now wasn't I right to call your speech rubbish?

Silence. Paduk is breathing hard. Frau Hogge passes a handkerchief across her forehead.

PADUK *pretends to be unmoved:* All right then. Very well. What next? *Silence.* You talk like a book.

FRAU HOGGE: I *did* have a higher education.

PADUK: All right. So I allowed myself to be carried away, the same as you did. Now what?

FRAU HOGGE *breathes a sigh of relief:* At last! That's better!

And now I'll thank you for your chair by giving you a piece of advice: close down and invest your earnings in our business!

PADUK *rises:* What's that?

FRAU HOGGE: What I said.

PADUK: And what about my reputation? What about the municipal authorities who let me have the site? What about the interview I gave the paper?

FRAU HOGGE: Small inconveniences. But think of the results!

PADUK: I can't. Because of my reputation. What you're proposing I had already figured out myself. But it won't do.

FRAU HOGGE: What do you mean, your reputation? If you want to go on ruining me – and yourself – I must protect myself as best I can. I'll have to show up your real motives! With the reputation you'll have after that, they'll make you Minister of Finance.

PADUK: Haha. Very amusing. But what of my marvellous idea? And what about the way you treated me when . . .

FRAU HOGGE: I didn't. Carmen did. And that was when you were still a nobody without cash. Now that you're my partner, you can do what you want with her. Have you seen the new photos?

PADUK: No, I've been out of touch.

FRAU HOGGE *pulls some photos out of her blouse and shows them to him:* That's Carmen from the back and here she is in profile. And here, very sexy, Ludmilla *en face.* Full length. Look at those eyes! Those breasts! That mouth! That charming little head!

PADUK *with a jerk:* All right. I shall inspect your hestablishment! *Takes the cash box under his arm.* No more customers now, I'm sure. And anyway, my assistant is still here. *Calls into the tent:* Just stick around another few minutes, will you? I'm going out on business.

ASSISTANT *from inside the tent:* Not another minute!

PADUK *to himself:* This place is going to pot anyway. *Follows*

*Frau Hogge to the right. Both disappear through the red door. The
piano starts up at once. A girl screams. Noise of dancing.
The stage darkens. The music fades.*

9

PADUK *enters from the right, his hair somewhat dishevelled, his
clothes in disorder but the cash box still under his arm:* Let that
stupid jackass make his inquiries. I'll tell him myself. *Halts
near the table.* Hey, you! Where are you?

ASSISTANT *crawls out:* You were calling me, Mr Paduk?

PADUK: Have you changed your mind again?

ASSISTANT: Only on condition that . . .

PADUK: On no condition. You're fired! *Choking with triumph:*
Get out! Or I'll toss you out bodily! You exploiter!
Rotter! Degenerate scoundrel!

ASSISTANT: I'll make you pay for this. I'll tell the world
about you and your past!

PADUK: You do that, my friend! Tell 'em I'm a brothel-
keeper. Tell them I make a hundred marks a day. Run along
and tell every man who's still got something between his
legs. Off with you!

ASSISTANT *exits:* Bastard!

PADUK *hums the piano melody:* Well now, to give the whole
thing a bit of tone – *climbs up on his table and removes the sign –*
we might install a projector and show sex education films,
we'd certainly get police permission for that. And then,
with our contacts, we might get a law passed punishing
private fornication with penal servitude and abortion with
death! That'd make business boom unbelievably! That's
that, then. Finished. All you need is ideas. *Takes the sign
off the entrance. Looks around. Grins.* Two weeks at most, and
business will start up once more. Some of our old customers
came back today. *Presses the switch that extinguishes the floodlight. Picks up the cash box, saunters slowly, humming, across the
stage and disappears right behind the red door. Piano and noise of
dancing feet.*

The Catch

Translator: JOHN WILLETT

Characters

The fisherman · His wife · First man · Second man · The six
fishermen · The beggar · The beggarwoman

*A fisherman's hut. Background: left, a window with muslin curtains.
To the right of that, more or less in the middle, a curtained bed.
To the right of that a fairly heavy square wooden door. A large
wooden table in the centre of the room. Against the left-side wall a
leather sofa with a net above it. Right, a door.*

It is night-time. The fisherman's wife is in bed.

WIFE *sleeping uneasily, rolls over and talks in her sleep:* Tom!
Tom! Leave me alone! . . . *Wakes, and sits up in bed.* It must
be long past midnight. Not back yet . . . Didn't catch a
thing today and now he's on the drink . . . Oh . . . *Lies
down.* Oah . . . *Falls asleep. Silence. Then thumps on the door.*

FISHERMAN *outside:* Hey! Open up!

WIFE *with a start:* Tom! *Gets out, goes to the door with a candle,
opens it and jumps back.*

The fisherman staggers in, supported by two men.

FISHERMAN *angrily:* What's door . . . locked for? When I get
home?

WIFE *wrapping herself:* I was asleep.

FISHERMAN: You see that door's kept unlocked, damn you.
How are people to get in?

WIFE: What, with me lying asleep?

FISHERMAN: It'll be unlocked from now on, I tell you.
Staggers to the table.

FIRST MAN: He's had a bit too much, Missus. But the three of
us made it.

WIFE: Oh, it's you, Mac? Well, well, there he is, full as a
herring barrel. Not much in *his* barrels, though.

FISHERMAN: That's not right. All my best ideas come to me
when I go on the booze.

WIFE: And how's that going to feed us?

FISHERMAN: You don't need food when you've been boozing.

SECOND MAN: The right place for you is bed.

FISHERMAN: He's worse than I am. He'll pass out as soon as he sits down. Can't take it. Tacking about like a yawl in a squall. Give him a coffee.

WIFE: Expect me to cook in the middle of the night?

FIRST MAN: Not for my sake, Missus.

FISHERMAN: Would you rather I came home in the morning? Get along into that kitchen! And make it hot.

WOMAN *exits right:* Wish the drink would kill you.

FIRST MAN: Not much fun for her.

FISHERMAN: It isn't for anybody. God, I'm sleepy. Missus!

WIFE *returning:* What are you yelling about now?

FISHERMAN: Give us a wash.

WIFE: At this time of night?

FISHERMAN: Wash, wash, wash. I shut my eyes and there's the sky as pink as a bloody rosebush. Like the Kingdom of Heaven, except it makes me belch.

The wife washes his head. He almost drops off to sleep.

SECOND MAN *grinning:* Just out of bed.

FIRST MAN: That's not hard to see.

SECOND MAN: Makes them look like ruffled cats.

FIRST MAN: She's got some meat on her.

SECOND MAN: He's a bloody fool.

FISHERMAN: Sod it. I left my pipe across the road. Get it, woman.

WIFE: In my nightdress?

FIRST MAN: One of us could go.

SECOND MAN: Yes, one of us could go.

FIRST MAN: Shall I?

SECOND MAN *to the wife:* Tisn't a night for you to be going over there.

FIRST MAN: Their eyes would pop out of their head.

SECOND MAN: I'll go.

FIRST MAN: I don't mind going.

Nobody moves.

WIFE: They'll laugh at me over there.

SECOND MAN: All right, one of us'll go.

FIRST MAN: It wouldn't take a moment for one of us, really.

SECOND MAN: Isn't as if it were all that far.

FIRST MAN: No reason why you should go out in your nightdress for him.

SECOND MAN: Can't have that.

FIRST MAN: So he'll just pop across. We can't have that.

FISHERMAN: But mind you're back for your coffee, Fred.

SECOND MAN: Watch my smoke. *Goes reluctantly off.*

WIFE: Coffee won't be long. It's nearly boiling.

FIRST MAN: That's all right: I'm not cold.

WIFE: Won't hurt you to have a cup.

FIRST MAN: I can still see pretty well, thanks.

WIFE: Then shut your eyes, Mac.

FIRST MAN: Light's not good enough.

WIFE: He's nearly asleep.

FIRST MAN: He's too drunk.

WIFE: He's a pig.

FIRST MAN: Coming home like that.

WIFE: As usual.

FIRST MAN: You look all right, though . . .

WIFE: I'm just in my nightdress.

FIRST MAN: What's wrong with that?

FISHERMAN *starting up:* Shut the door, damn it. Water's too bloody cold. Get the coffee. Wrong with what?

WIFE: The water being cold.

FISHERMAN: Get moving, you cow.

WIFE: Fred's gone over the way for me, though.

FIRST MAN: I felt like staying.

The wife laughs and exit.

FISHERMAN: Nag nag nag, because I got her up. Treating me like a bloody animal. Laziness, that's all. A lot of sluts, they are.

FIRST MAN: Well, I'm off.

FISHERMAN: Not had enough yet?

FIRST MAN: The room's going round.

FISHERMAN: Sit down.

FIRST MAN: I'll pass out.

FISHERMAN: What, can't you take it? You two lead immoral lives; saps your energies. I can take anything.

FIRST MAN *in the doorway, speaks to the right:* Must have been nice and warm in bed.

WIFE: Trying to make me go out.

FIRST MAN: Half naked.

WIFE: All on account of that old soak.

FIRST MAN: Bet those tiles on the kitchen floor are cold.

WIFE: Hell.

FIRST MAN: With those warm feet of yours.

WIFE: What do you men have to get so drunk for always?

FIRST MAN: With me it's because I haven't got a wife.

WIFE: And if you had?

FIRST MAN: Everything would be different.

WIFE: That's what they all say.

FIRST MAN: I'm not like that. I'm not drunk, either.

WIFE: Hold the pot for me a minute.

FIRST MAN: I'm not that drunk.

Goes into the kitchen.

FISHERMAN *raises his head from the table:* My head's buzzing. Like a roundabout. And that damned curtain. Mac! Rotten drunken bastard. Drinks like a fish. As if it was free . . . Where's the bugger got to? Aha! Pull yourself together, Hansen, and get sober. On your feet! Attention! Right wheel, quick march. *Goes upstage left to a bucket of water.* Knees bend! Now the high dive! *Dips his head.* Brr! *A pan falls in the kitchen.* Hullo, what's going on? *Steps over to the right, stooping with his head down dripping water, and listens. Then unsteadily back to the left.* Missus!

WIFE *comes a shade too hastily:* Well? What is it this time?

FISHERMAN: Give me your apron. Quick. *Stamps his foot.*

WIFE: What have you been sticking your head in? That's the washing-up water.

FISHERMAN: It's clean enough. Apron!

WIFE *takes an apron from the peg and wipes him with it. To the right:* Mind it doesn't boil over, Mac!

FISHERMAN: Now get a move on. Coffee! Do you want us to

stay up all night? Won't it boil without a kick up the arse?
Ties his wife's apron on her. And you wear that. Want me to
fetch the parson? Quick march! *Gives her a kick, and she goes
off right. He sits at the table, thinking* 'Isn't boiling over.
He's pissed as arseholes. She's half naked, the little tart.
Anyhow, I'm going to sleep. Sleep! Don't care if he does
her or not. Sleep. Birds of a feather flock together. Under
my own roof, too. Suppose I chuck him out and bolt the
door, then they'll slip the bolt and laugh like drains. And if
I stop them getting down to it here, then she'll nip off and
I won't see what happens. Shit. The bleeders. Sleep, that's
the answer.

WIFE *bringing coffee:* Drink that.

FIRST MAN *behind her:* It's a life-saver. *They drink coffee.*

FISHERMAN: Sit down. There. Get my net.

WIFE: What do you want your net for?

FISHERMAN *bangs the table:* I said get it.

FIRST MAN: What, at this time of night?

WIFE *gets it:* Thinking of going out fishing?

FISHERMAN: Fishing, ha ha ha!

WOMAN: Caught nothing all day. Just boozed, you did.

FISHERMAN: All my best ideas come to me when I go on the
booze. When I go on the booze I go fishing. Mend the net.

WOMAN: What, at this time of night? *Starts mending it.*

FISHERMAN *bangs the table:* At this time of night!

FIRST MAN: That's not right. Nobody ought to do anything
now but sleep. Don't *you* feel sleepy?

FISHERMAN: Like after a booze-up. You finished?

FIRST MAN: They're still boozing over the way.

FISHERMAN: It's Midsummer Day.

FIRST MAN: They ought to go to bed.

WIFE: Like Christians . . .

FISHERMAN: Like us. You know, when you get in and let
go – there's another hole there, Missus – and feel heavy as
an anchor and down you sink – lazy cow – and forget
everything, so utterly pissed, and don't give a bugger . . .
Finished?

FIRST MAN: I seem to have got heavier too. Thanks for the coffee. Sleep well. *Leaves.*

WIFE: Good night, Mac. And thanks for bringing that drunken layabout home.

FISHERMAN *bangs the table:* Clear it away.

WIFE: It can wait.

FISHERMAN: Lazy bitch. Get into that kitchen. Clear up. Wash up.

WIFE *taking the candle:* Oahh, I can't keep awake.

FISHERMAN: Leave the candle there. Get on. *Exit wife.* Footy-footy under the table. Right. I'll make that bastard pay for his coffee. He'll have worked out that those feet lead up to thighs and so on, on and on, keen eye and steady hand will bring you to the promised land. Smashing. *Gets up, picks up the net and performs the following actions as he mutters to himself. He fixes the net above the bed, gets a heavy rock anchor and rolls it on to the edge of the bed below. None of this is very clearly seen, though in the process he has to stand on the bed.* There we are, that goes there, and there; right, smashing, and . . . enjoy your little arrangement, my . . . darlings. Immorality! Boozing! Think you're so bloody clever! Like cats. *Climbs down.* Now let me dip my head in the trough and just watch me sleep . . . *Lurches out. The two men reappear.*

FIRST MAN: Might as well see each other home. Two are tougher than one.

SECOND MAN: So I fetched his pipe and you got your way.

FIRST MAN: Afraid the coffee's finished.

SECOND MAN: What a pal, drinking my coffee while I was wandering around in the dark so you could have a chance to stay.

FIRST MAN: Weren't keen, were you?

SECOND MAN: I fell over twice.

FIRST MAN: Shouldn't have drunk so much.

SECOND MAN: Or gone across there.

FIRST MAN: You're too young.

SECOND MAN: Just why I went. I thought an old man wouldn't be up to it physically.

FIRST MAN: Let's go. There's nobody here.

SECOND MAN: I must say good night.

FIRST MAN: Why not just leave the pipe?

SECOND MAN: What, and not say good night?

FIRST MAN: They won't want to be interrupted. They're on their own.

SECOND MAN: They aren't in bed yet.

FIRST MAN: A man and his wife.

SECOND MAN: Oh, you make me sick, you and your poaching.

FIRST MAN: What do you mean?

SECOND MAN: I'll spell it out for you. I'm attracted too.

FIRST MAN: Who by?

SECOND MAN: You watch it, Mac.

FIRST MAN: Ought to be ashamed of yourself. Young whipper-snapper like you.

SECOND MAN: As for a fellow of your age . . .

FIRST MAN: She's faithful.

SECOND MAN: Which bit of her?

FIRST MAN: Her heart.

SECOND MAN: It's her legs we're interested in.

FIRST MAN: If you want to talk dirty you can count me out.

SECOND MAN: Just that I want a go too.

FIRST MAN: I'll tell Tom.

SECOND MAN: I'll sodding do you.

FIRST MAN: Go on, then.

SECOND MAN: Cowardy.

FIRST MAN: All piss and wind.

SECOND MAN: Rotten bastard.

FIRST MAN: Get some hair on your chest.

They wrestle.

FISHERMAN *enters with his head bent forward, dripping water:* What's the matter with you? You're disgustingly drunk. In my cottage too. I'd kick your arsehole up through your neck if I wasn't too tired.

They break off.

FIRST MAN: He started it!

SECOND MAN: Liar!

The fisherman lies down on the leather sofa.

FIRST MAN: Come on out.

SECOND MAN: Suits me.

FIRST MAN: Night, Tom.

SECOND MAN: Already asleep? Well, we'll see who wins.

Exeunt both. Silence. Distant sound of the sea.

WIFE *appears in the doorway:* Tom! Tom! Asleep. *Stretches.*

FISHERMAN *half asleep:* Shut the window! Bleeding music.

WIFE *shuts the window:* What are you lying on the sofa for?

FISHERMAN: Shut up.

WIFE: Can't even be fagged to take his trousers off. What a beast. Sprawled out. Asleep already. He'll never wake up either. And the bed's all ours. He's daft. Well, he's only got himself to blame. I'm flesh and blood too. *Sits on the bed.* It's two o'clock. It'll be light at four. He'll sleep till eleven, though. But everybody can see our door then. And the others'll be off fishing, not like him. Why shouldn't I have some fun? He's asleep all right. *Takes the candle and puts it in the window.* Where's he got to? Think he's passed out? He wasn't all that sober. Here he comes. What in God's name is he making all that row for? *Sounds of panting and wrestling. Wife looks out. Exclaims:* Christ . . . Fred! And they're fighting. O my God, save us. Our Father, which art . . . That's fixed him, thank heaven.

FIRST MAN *rushing to the window:* Hey, love.

WIFE: What are *you* after?

FIRST MAN: Don't ask silly questions.

WIFE: I've every right to ask what you're doing at my window.

FIRST MAN: What did you put the light there for?

WIFE: So you could tell he was asleep.

FIRST MAN: You said you'd put the light there once he'd gone to sleep.

WIFE: And that's what he's done.

FIRST MAN: And that's why I'm here.

WIFE: I never said so.

FIRST MAN: What's the point of telling me, then?

WIFE: You said you were frightened he might strike me.

FIRST MAN: Didn't he?

WIFE: What for?

FIRST MAN: For acting like that in the kitchen.

WIFE: Oh, he was drunk.

FIRST MAN: So why did you put the light in the window?

WIFE: Oh, come on, or they'll see you.

FIRST MAN *climbs right in:* There we are. A proper puzzle, you women. *Picks up the light.*

WIFE: What's happened to your friend?

FIRST MAN: He got a belt in the earhole.

WIFE: Where is he?

FIRST MAN: Happy as a sandboy.

WIFE: So long as you didn't hurt him.

FIRST MAN: Um.

WIFE: Won't you come over here? There's room enough.

FIRST MAN *carrying the light around:* In a minute.

WIFE: He's sleeping on the sofa.

FIRST MAN: Hadn't we better go outside?

WIFE: What, now? They'd see us. What are you up to?

FIRST MAN *shining the light on the fisherman's face:* See if he's asleep.

WIFE: Of course he is. You'll wake him up like that.

FIRST MAN: Suppose we go outside . . .

WIFE: Don't you like it here?

FIRST MAN: I like you.

WIFE: Can you feel your way over this way?

FIRST MAN: Why not?

WIFE: Then we'd save the candle. *Trembling.* It's got to do for tomorrow.

FIRST MAN *puts out the light, feels his way:* He's pissed to the eyebrows.

WIFE: On the sofa.

FIRST MAN: Not in the bed. Those your knees?

WIFE: Yes. Look out. Sit down there.

FIRST MAN: He's completely pissed.

WIFE: He's like an animal.

FIRST MAN: Is that your hand?

WIFE: What's he want to get so boozed for?

FIRST MAN: So I can carry him home.

WIFE: And to get me out of bed.

FIRST MAN: Warm, was it?

WIFE: I was waiting.

FIRST MAN: In your nightdress . . .

WIFE: He caught nothing all day.

FIRST MAN: What about putting out his nightlines?

WIFE: He's a pig, I tell you.

FIRST MAN *more laboriously, like her:* That your breast?

WIFE: Leave me alone.

FIRST MAN: Does it hurt?

WIFE: Leave me alone, Mac.

FIRST MAN: You put the light there.

WIFE: But you – you mustn't do that.

FIRST MAN: So the Sixth Commandment says.

WIFE: Your breath doesn't stink of brandy; that's something.

FIRST MAN: I'm respectable.

WIFE: Leave my knee alone.

FIRST MAN: It'll be more comfortable for you.

WIFE: Ow!

FIRST MAN: Let's get rid of that.

WIFE: You get rid of it.

FIRST MAN: That's better.

WIFE: No, no.

FIRST MAN: Can't you keep still for a minute?

> *The stone falls to the floor with an immense crash. The wife gives a subdued scream, the man curses, then the two of them lie quite motionless.*

FISHERMAN *lifts his head:* The sky's fallen in. Hullo. That's going to cost her a packet. Waking me up. *Gets up and lights the candle.* Must have blown it out almost at once. Bastards. *Addressing the bed:* Cheers, Mac. Back here again? Are you all that pissed? That's fine. Right over the top? Ha ha ha!

Bastards! – How's that for a draught of fishes? Glory be to God. The Lord rewardeth the just even as they sleep, Mac. *Goes to the window.*

FIRST MAN *rolling about and cursing:* Bloody buggery, a net.

FISHERMAN: Right first time. Don't bust yourselves. It'll hold. *She* mended it. And to think I caught nothing all day. I felt so sleepy. *Drumming on the window-sill.* Hey, fish! fish! Something worth looking at here, boys. Come along over. Got something here. Dearly beloved brethren, I've made a catch.

VOICES: You all right in the head? – What's it about?

FISHERMAN: Fish! Fish!

VOICES: You're bloody drunk.

FISHERMAN: Across here! Fish!

FIRST MAN: For Christ's sake. It's *your* reputation that'll suffer.

FISHERMAN: It did suffer, Mac. Fish! Fish! *Goes to the door.*

FISHERMEN *come crowding in:* What's up? – What's all the row about? – Had a baby?

FISHERMAN: Something's happened. I've caught some fish.

THE OTHERS *craning their heads:* Here? – A minute ago you were pissed as arseholes.

FISHERMAN: Too pissed, I was. That's why I couldn't go out. I did my fishing here.

THE OTHERS: O he's too far gone. – Where's his wife? You can get some sense out of her.

FISHERMAN: My wife's gone. I'm so stinking pissed I think she must have turned into a fish. Hear that wind? That's God Almighty coming in the storm-cloud. Go forth, says he, and thou shalt make a great catch.

THE OTHERS: Better slop some water over his head. – He's wandering.

FISHERMAN *moves away shouting, having blocked the view up to now:* Fish! Fish!

THE OTHERS *pressing forward:* She dead? Is that a body? – Look, there's another. There are two of them. – Is that a body? *All laugh.* It's his wife with Mac!

FIRST MAN *on the bed, under the net:* For Christ's sake get that thing off us. For ... Christ's sake ... put some kind of sheet over us, will you?

THE OTHERS *roaring with laughter:* It's all a matter of habit, as the woman said to the eel when she skinned him. – What's sauce for the goose is sauce for the gander, as the wife said on her wedding night. – That was a bright idea, getting in there, mate. – You're in clover. Must have had a struggle to make it, eh?

FISHERMAN: I bet he'd stand the company a bucket of rum to be allowed out.

FIRST MAN: A bucket of rum, you old devil, but let's have a sheet first.

FISHERMAN *to one of the spectators:* Go and get the rum, mate, before he thinks better of it. Now then, boys, let's take these fish and drop them in the bay to cool off. Take that pole and carry them carefully, like in a procession, with some nice singing. This isn't something you'll see every day.

THE OTHERS *loop the net over a pole. Two of them carry the couple out, amid great laughter:* Take it easy, kids! Don't burst yourselves laughing. – Better knock off a moment. – If you come back you'll have done better than a fart; they only go one way.

FISHERMAN: Fine fish! Glistening fish! Fresh fat frisking fish! They can swim away; I don't want them. Let them go, I give up. But it was a splendid catch. And all of you must stay here, because you're invited to the wake. My wife's died; she was a good soul. So have some of the rum her lover's bought us and let's celebrate my being in the shit. Sit down with me; you can help me drown my sorrows.
The fishermen sit down. A jar of rum is brought in. Some of them sing. A game of cards starts.

FISHERMAN *lights candles:* Those are the lights of the dead, those candles in the mugs. Careful not to blow them out when you laugh. This table's in a house of mourning. Kindly turn your heads away when you throw up. I'm giving you glasses from the pub, because my wife's dead and I don't know where our own are kept.

Wind blows. Fishermen sing.

A FISHERMAN: Wind's getting up. It's chilly outside. Drink up and keep warm.

A SECOND: God, how I laughed. I liked it when they wriggled, but it was still better when they lay doggo and pretended they weren't there and hid their faces in the sheets. Ha ha ha!

FISHERMAN: This is a house of mourning, and I must ask you not to laugh. Can't you get drunk without making all that noise? Don't you see I want to pass out?

A THIRD: Ah, she was a good wife, she was: she kept you going. Washed your face and brushed your hair and let you kick her about.

THE FIRST: What a wind! Just you listen to that wind.

A FOURTH: Better drink up. That wind's no business of *yours*.

THIRD: She didn't half look good in that nightdress, let me tell you.

SECOND: That wasn't a nightdress. That was a shroud.

FIRST: When she clasped the top of it and pressed up to Mac so as to stop us seeing, that was your fault, Tom.

FOURTH: It started with a bang, and the rum's good, but there's no real atmosphere.

The two fishermen (fifth and sixth) come back.

FIFTH: There was a bloody great splash.

SIXTH: They asked for it.

FIFTH: Your own bed; I ask you.

SIXTH: Didn't half yell, they did.

FIFTH: Go on, can't you lot say anything? It's like a funeral here.

SIXTH: Rum, no wife: what else do you want?

FISHERMAN: Sit down and shut up. My wife's dead. The wind's up now, and when it drops she won't be there. She was a good wife, and God has come and taken away his own. The wind's got up, listen, drink, and let's say my wife drowned in the wind.

SECOND: Don't take it too hard. She lost her head.

FOURTH: She oughtn't to have done it, not in your bed.

FISHERMAN: God has punished me. I've drunk too much. She was the best wife I've got. The wind came, and the boat went down with her. Drink up and say a rosary for her and her soul. Hail, Mary, full of grace, the Lord is with thee. Lord grant her eternal rest. *He prays on his own.*

FIFTH: That's a lot of nonsense. Blasphemous too.

SIXTH: He's plastered.

THIRD: You have to draw the line somewhere, as the man said when he beat his wife to death.

SECOND: Why weren't you in that bed yourself? There's only room for one man.

FOURTH: Or you could have given her a good hiding. As it is, you ought to be ashamed.

THIRD: It's immoral.

FISHERMAN: Immoral, is it? You're immoral. God has smitten me and you think it funny. Which of us lost his wife? I'm a miserable sinner, a drunkard, a poor good-for-nothing, but now the Lord has punished me and no one's got a right to laugh.

THE OTHERS *getting up:* He's gone crazy. – Come on. Let's take the rum. – Poor woman, serve the old soak right. – She can get another one like him any time.

FISHERMAN: You blaspheme. Show me the man who has suffered as much as me. Where's your sense of shame, ye of little faith? I am exceeding sorrowful. *Drinks.*

THE OTHERS: Get the jar off him and let's go to the pub. – He's going gaga.

FISHERMAN *gets up and hugs the jar:* This is a wake and you're the mourners. And now you're drunk and saying wicked things. You should be ashamed for the sake of your miserable souls.

THE OTHERS *trying to get the jar away from him:* Leave go, you old villain. Give us that jar! – We'll do you!

FISHERMAN: Lust was written on your countenances as you watched them, and you slavered with envy as you carted them off. *You* are the villains. You degenerates. Degenerates!

THE OTHERS *thronging to the door:* Good God, he's gone mad. – He's delirious, he dreamt it all up. – Gives me the creeps, no more rum for me. – Leave him lying among his candles. Perhaps God'll work a miracle and drown him in the jar. *Exeunt. The fisherman blows out all but three candles. Kicks away the chairs. Stares in front of him.*

SECOND MAN *at the window, left:* Hey!

FISHERMAN *turning round:* Who is it? Oh, you. Come in. My wife's died.

SECOND MAN *climbs in. His face is bleeding:* Are you drunk?

FISHERMAN: Hear that wind? She's been drowned.

SECOND MAN: When?

FISHERMAN: Just now.

SECOND MAN: How do you know?

FISHERMAN: God woke me up. There was my wife lying dead in bed. She looked like a fish, see? Have a drink with me. I'm so terribly lonely.

SECOND MAN: I don't get you. There's a creepy feeling round here. That your rum?

FISHERMAN: Yes. Have some. A present from her bloke.

SECOND MAN: Had she got a bloke, then?

FISHERMAN: Dozens. But this was the only one I got rum from.

SECOND MAN: How long have you been sitting here by yourself?

FISHERMAN: Not long. There were some people here. They laughed, then they went off. They saw my disgrace and they're going to tell everyone about it.

SECOND MAN: I don't like it. I'm off.

FISHERMAN: Why's your face got blood on it? You been attacked too?

SECOND MAN: Had a bit of a fall. I'd been drinking.

FISHERMAN: You're the only friend I've got, because you've had bad luck too. I've been smitten by God in person. I'd have handed my heart over to him and said,

'It's yours.' But he took my wife, who was dearer to me still. And now I'm drinking and going to the bad. It's all his fault.

SECOND MAN: When did that happen?

FISHERMAN: Just now. When my turn comes and the Lord says, 'Where am I to put a good-for-nothing like you?', then I'll say, 'In hell, so I can meet up with my wife.'

BEGGAR *in the doorway, with a beggarwoman behind him:* Come along! – This where the rum is? They said there was some rum going here.

FISHERMAN: Come in and sit down. We're having a wake. My wife's died. Thank you for the honour of your company.

BEGGAR *and the beggarwoman sit down:* A good wife, was she, eh?

FISHERMAN: Mustn't speak ill of the dead. Drink up.

BEGGARWOMAN: That wind outside. It's warm in here.

BEGGAR: Good rum that. It's very sad when one loses a wife.

FISHERMAN: One's left all on one's own. But they're a lot of animals. *Bangs on the table:* Animals! That idea about the net came to me as I was wetting my head. I looked up at the stars and thought 'that'll be useful'.

BEGGAR: It's like as if the spirit was speaking through you. Very moving. *Drinks a lot.*
The two of them retire to the sofa, rear left, during what follows. Occasional murmurs and giggles.

FIRST MAN *in the doorway, right, dripping water:* Hey, Tom, is it all right if I have a tot of my rum?

FISHERMAN *ecstatically:* I stood in the doorway just like that after wetting my head.

FIRST MAN: Right. You shouldn't have got pissed, though.

FISHERMAN: Join us if you like, but mind you keep quiet. I'm not angry any longer. Were you dried off by the same wind drowned my wife? Sit down and have a drink. All is vanity. *He speaks drunkenly and laboriously.*
The first man approaches the table.

SECOND MAN *stands up. They confront each other:* I wouldn't advise you to sit down here.

FIRST MAN *unsure:* I must talk to him.

SECOND MAN *steps forward, but starts to sway:* Want me to knock you down? You swine.

FIRST MAN *drinking:* I'm sober as a judge now.

SECOND MAN *as he sits down:* And I'm going to knock you down. Tomorrow.

FIRST MAN: There's something I must say to him. *Drinks.*

SECOND MAN: He will keep on about God. What happened?

FIRST MAN: Something. *Drinks.*

SECOND MAN: Not exactly cosy, is it?

FIRST MAN: What's going on over there?

SECOND MAN: Two of the mourners.

FISHERMAN *thickly:* God punished me. God fished me out of the booze. Hear that wind? That's where I was, in *that* wind.

FIRST MAN: Not shy, are they?

SECOND MAN: It's the fault of your rum.

FIRST MAN: His wife's going around outside, she's scared to come home. In that wind. He must be terribly angry.

SECOND MAN: He's terribly pissed.

FIRST MAN *to the fisherman:* We're all sinners together, mate.

FISHERMAN *embracing him:* Now she's drowned and I'm alone, and there's no one around here.

FIRST MAN *drinks:* You'll have to take her back. *Goes on drinking. The fisherman lays his head on the table.* I've got five kids. You'll have to take her back. *To the second man, who has slid under the table:* You tell him. He's absolutely dead drunk. Oh, I feel so miserable. *Weeps.* You'll have to take her back. They all saw us. I feel dreadful.

FISHERMAN: We are alone. Completely alone. Listen! The wind.

Silence. Wind.

WIFE *stands in the doorway, likewise dripping, with the net over one shoulder:* Still angry, is he?

FIRST MAN: He's asleep. *Staggers towards her and tries to embrace her. She pushes him away.*

FIRST MAN: I put in a word for you.

WIFE: You get out of here. *Drops the net to the ground.*

FIRST MAN: You've had a pretty rough time . . .

WIFE: Go on home. *Shoves him as far as the door, turns round, tugs the second man out and drags him after.* Pig. Bastards! Come on out, both of you.

FISHERMAN *gets up laboriously*: All a lot of beasts. Pray, will you? A mass for her soul. Beasts. Wind. Soul. *Sits down, falls asleep.*

Both men, drunk, leave together as before.

WIFE *shuts the window. Shakes out the jar, mops the floor with the remains of the rum. Comes on the beggar and beggarwoman*: What's this trash?

BEGGAR: Two poor people.

WIFE: Get out. Have you got no sense of shame?

BEGGARWOMAN: It's cold outside. And what a wind!

WIFE *drives them out with her broom*: Out with you, get on. *Half turning to the fisherman as she mops*: What did you want to get so drunk for? Shall I make some coffee? *No answer.* They must have dropped the net into the well, those bastards. *Looks at him.* Asleep. *She dowses the light, puts him on her back, and carries him to bed.*

Notes and Variants

BAAL

The subject of this play is the very ordinary story of a man who sings a hymn to summer in a grog-shop without selecting his audience – together with the consequences of summer, grog and song. The man is not a particularly modern poet. Baal has not been handicapped by Nature. He belongs to the period of the play's performance. Remember Socrates and Verlaine, with their lamentable skulls. For actors (who love extremes, except when they can get away with mediocrities), Baal is neither a specially comic character nor a specially tragic one. Like all wild animals he is serious. As for the play, the author has managed to find a message in it: it sets out to prove that you can have your cake if you are prepared to pay for it. And even if you aren't. So long as you pay . . . The play is the story neither of a single incident nor of many, but of a life. Originally it was called *Baal eats! Baal dances!! Baal is transfigured!!!*

[GW *Schriften zum Theater*, p. 954.]

PROLOGUE TO THE 1926 VERSION

This dramatic biography shows the life story of the man Baal as it took place in the first part of this century. You see before you Baal the abnormality trying to come to terms with the twentieth-century world. Baal the relative man, Baal the passive genius, the whole phenomenon of Baal from his first appearance among civilized beings up to his horrific end, with his unprecedented consumption of ladies of high degree, in his dealings with his fellow-humans. This creature's life was one of sensational immorality. In the stage version it has been considerably toned down. The performance begins

with Baal's first appearance as a poet among civilized beings
in the year 1904. As a preliminary you will see Baal in the
round from several aspects and hear his version of how he
used to perform his famous Hymn of Baal the Great, ac-
companied on his own unique invention, the tin-stringed
banjo.

[Ibid., pp. 954–5.]

THE MODEL FOR BAAL

The dramatic biography called *Baal* treats of the life of a man
who really existed. This was a certain Josef K., whom I heard
about from people who retained clear memories of the man's
person and the commotion created by his activities. K. was
the illegitimate son of a washerwoman. He soon made a bad
name for himself. Though without formal education of any
sort he is said to have been able to impress the most highly
educated people by his extraordinarily well-informed talk.
A friend told me that the idiosyncrasy of his movements
(when taking a cigarette, when seating himself on a chair, and
so on) made such a mark on a number of (mainly) young
people that they wanted to imitate him. His carefree way of
life, however, led him to sink ever deeper, particularly since
he never started anything himself but shamelessly took
advantage of every opportunity offered him. A number of
shady episodes were laid at his door, including a girl's suicide.
He was a trained mechanic, though so far as we know he
never worked. When A. became too hot for him he went off
on protracted wanderings with a broken-down medical
student, returning to A. in about 1911. There his friend was
killed in an affray with knives in a grog-shop on the Lauter-
lech, almost certainly by K. himself. At all events he then
disappeared with remarkable suddenness from A., and is
supposed to have died miserably in the Black Forest.

['Das Urbild Baals', from *Die Szene*, Berlin, January 1926,
reprinted in GW *Schriften zum Theater*, p. 955. Elisabeth Haupt-

mann's 'Notizen über Brechts Arbeit 1926' on p. 241 of the *Sinn und Form* special Brecht issue of 1957 cites her diary for 18 January: 'Wrote the "Model" for Baal for *Die Szene* in the form of a newspaper report. The model for Baal, the "anti-social" man, is an Augsburg mechanic.' This has not prevented commentators from taking at their face value both the report and Brecht's claim to have written it.]

BAD BAAL THE ANTI-SOCIAL MAN

but that is what makes bad baal the antisocial man great
that the report of his enemy
describing him with my voice is
permeated by his
accusing me that i
a delighted onlooker
while he was exploiting the exploiters
and making use of the users
started treating him more harshly
as soon as he derided my own rules
but that is his offence
and why he is called antisocial
because in making trivial demands of him
the perfect state would appear like an exploiter.

['Baal', from Dieter Schmidt (ed.): *Baal. Der böse Baal der asoziale*, Suhrkamp, 1968, p. 90. This poem, which is not included in GW, is part of the material relating to the Baal *Lehrstücke* project discussed on pp. 372-3 below.]

ON LOOKING THROUGH MY FIRST PLAYS (ii)

Baal is a play which could present all kinds of difficulties to those who have not learnt to think dialectically. No doubt they will see it as a glorification of unrelieved egotism and nothing more. Yet here is an individual standing out against the demands and discouragements of a world whose form of production is designed for exploitation rather than usefulness. We cannot tell how Baal would react to having his talents employed; what he is resisting is their misuse. Baal's art of life is subject to the same fate as any other art under capitalism: it is attacked. He is anti-social, but in an anti-social society.

Twenty years after completing *Baal* I was preoccupied with an idea (for an opera) related to the same basic theme. There is a carved wooden Chinese figure, two or three inches high and sold in thousands, representing the fat little god of happiness, contentedly stretching himself. This god was to arrive from the East after a great war and enter the devastated cities, trying to persuade people to fight for their personal happiness and well-being. He acquires followers of various sorts, and becomes subject to persecution by the authorities when some of them start proclaiming that the peasants ought to be given land, the workers to take over the factories, and the workers' and peasants' children to seize the schools. He is arrested and condemned to death. And now the executioners practise their arts on the little god of happiness. But when they hand him poison he just smacks his lips; when they cut his head off he at once grows a new one; when they hang him from the gallows he starts an irresistibly lively dance, etc., etc. *Humanity's urge for happiness can never be entirely killed.*

For the present edition of *Baal* the original version of the first and last scenes has been restored. Otherwise I have left the play as it was, not having the strength to alter it. I admit (and advise you): this play is lacking in wisdom.

['Bei Durchsicht meiner ersten Stücke.' Foreword to *Stücke I*, all editions but the first. GW *Schriften zum Theater*, pp. 947–8. For a more accurate view of the revisions to the first and last scenes, see p. 372 below.]

Editorial Note on the Text

For the following note and for the writings by Brecht quoted in it the editors have drawn gratefully and extensively on the two volumes of 'materials' edited by Dieter Schmidt, *Baal. Drei Fassungen* and *Baal. Der böse Baal der asoziale. Texten, Varianten und Materialien*, published by Suhrkamp-Verlag in 1966 and 1968 respectively ('edition suhrkamp' numbers 170 and 248).

Brecht's first play was not written in four days and for a bet, as has been alleged, but developed from a paper which he read in the spring of 1918 to Professor Artur Kutscher's theatre seminar at Munich University. His subject was Hanns Johst, the Expressionist novelist and playwright who later wrote the Nazi play *Schlageter* and at the end of 1933 became president of the (purged) Prussian Academy. Brecht undertook to write a 'counter-play' to Johst's *Der Einsame* (The Lonely One), an emotionalized account of the life of the nineteenth-century dramatist Christoph Dietrich Grabbe, which the Munich Kammerspiele were presenting. A first draft was complete by mid-May, and a month later he could write to his lifelong friend Caspar Neher:

> My play:
> > Baal eats! Baal dances!! Baal is transfigured!!!
> > > What's Baal up to?
>
> > > > > > 24 scenes
>
> is ready and typed – a substantial tome. I hope to get somewhere with it.

He revised the play in the spring of 1919, after his military service and the writing of the earliest draft of *Drums in the Night*. That was the version first submitted to publishers and theatre managements, but Brecht appears to have decided that it was too long – there were 29 scenes – and too wild, and before its publication he overhauled it yet a third time, jettisoning about one-third of the 1919 text. Publication should have taken place some time in the second half of 1920, but the original publishers were by then already in trouble with the censorship over other books, and only a few copies for Brecht's own use were ever printed. The rights were transferred to another firm (Kiepenheuer of Potsdam) who brought the book out two years later at the time of the première of *Drums in the Night*, virtually unchanged apart from the addition of the first woodcutters' scene.

This first published version was the play as we now have it, apart from the first and last scenes. It was republished in 1953 as the first volume of Brecht's collected *Stücke*; then in 1955 scene 1 was given its present form (including the two poems quoted from the Munich Expressionist periodical *Revolution*, which are in fact Georg Heym's 'Der Baum' and 'Vorbereitung' by the then East German Minister of Culture, Johannes R. Becher), while Brecht restored the final scene which he deleted from the proofs in 1920. What Brecht says in his own note of 1954 is not precisely right, since neither of these scenes is in its original form. But clearly he was content to leave it as an early work.

In the later 1920s he felt otherwise. The version which he himself staged at the Deutsches Theater in February 1926 (a single afternoon performance by the 'Junge Bühne' – and *Baal's* only performance in Berlin to this day) was a largely new, much shorter play called *Life Story of the Man Baal*. As will be seen below, it retained only eleven of the published scenes, which were altered so as to set Baal in the emergent technological society of the first decade of the century. They were stripped of much of their original lyricism and given an 'epic' framework by means of titles to each scene. Brecht wanted this version to appear as an appendix to the *Stücke* edition of the 1950s, but it remained unpublished till 1966. Its only other known performances were in Vienna in 1926 (with a prologue by Hofmannsthal) and in Kassel the year after.

Around 1930 – the dates and also the intended arrangement of the fragmentary typescript are uncertain – he planned a number of linked *Lehrstücke* (or didactic playlets) about the character he now called *Bad Baal the Antisocial Man*. Here he thought of making Baal appear in various guises –

guest/whore/judge/dealer (bulls)/engineer (only concerned with experiment)/suppliant – in need of help (exploiting other people's wish to be exploited)/nature-lover/demagogue/worker (strikebreaker)/mother/historian/soldier/lover (baker's apprentice scene from 'breadshop')/as parson/as civil servant/the 2 coats

– but apart from a reception where Baal is guest and the Baal Hymn is sung this plan has very little to do with the play. The writing is deadpan, with strange word order and virtually no punctuation apart from full stops. Brecht's aphoristic *alter ego* Herr Keuner appears, and the only *Baal* character apart from Baal himself is Lupu. Some idea of the style can be got from the beginning of 'Bad Baal the Antisocial Man and the Two Coats', which is one of the few complete episodes:

BAAL: all night i have been going in increasing cold through the forests towards where they get darker. the evening was icy. the night was icier and a crowd of stars crept into a whiteish fog towards morning. today the bushes occupy the least space of the entire year. whatever is soft freezes. whatever is hard breaks.

THE LEFT-HAND CHORUS the best thing is
the cold comes before the warmth
everything makes itself as small
as it can. everything is
so sparingly silent only
thinking becomes im-
practicable and then
comes the warmth

THE POOR MAN it is cold. i have no coat. i'm freezing. perhaps that grand gentleman can tell me what i can do against the cold. good day sir . . .

In 1938 Brecht again looked at the play with a view to the Malik-Verlag collected edition of his work (which was never completed). 'A pity,' he then noted: 'it was always a torso, and on top of that it underwent a number of operations . . . Its meaning almost disappeared. Baal the provocateur, the admirer of things as they are, who believes in living life to the full, other people's lives as well as his own. His "do what amuses you" could be very rewarding if properly handled. Wonder if I could find the time'. That is, aside from the *Lehrstücke* plan, which was still on the agenda. A few months later he seems to have written that off, to judge from a diary note of 4 March 1939:

Today I finally realized why I never managed to turn out those little *Lehrstücke* about the adventures of 'Bad Baal the Antisocial Man'. Antisocial people aren't important. The really antisocial people are the owners of the means of production and other sources of life, and they are only antisocial as such. There are also their helpers and their helpers' helpers, of course, but again only as such. It is *the* gospel of humanity's enemies that there are such things as antisocial instincts, antisocial personalities and so on.

He also came to feel that he had made a mistake in seeing socialism as a matter of social order rather than of productivity, which may have been another reason underlying his more sympathetic judgement of Baal at the end of his life.

THE VERSIONS OF 1918, 1919 AND 1920–2 (*first published version*)

Numbers in square brackets refer to the scene order of the final text. Other numbers to that of the particular script under discussion

Though *Baal* at first appears to have little structure, so that Brecht could change scenes around, or add or delete them, without greatly affecting the play's character, there are nine basic scenes which recur in the same order in every version, together with four others* which are in all except the 1926 text. They are: [1] (the opening party scene), [2] (Baal and Johannes), [3] (the first tavern scene), [4 i] (Baal and Johanna, after the seduction), [4 iii] (first scene with Sophie), [6]* (second ditto), [7] (cabaret scene), [8]* (Baal and Ekart), [15] (Baal reading a poem to Ekart, who speaks of his girl), [17]* (Baal reads 'Death in the Forest'). [18] (last tavern scene, with the murder of Ekart), [20]* (the two gendarmes), and [21] (the death scene in the forest hut). Accordingly, we shall start by describing the more significant changes in these scenes, from one version to another up to 1922.

[1] In the first two versions it is a grand party: full evening dress. The host and other guests are not named; the host's wife is not mentioned. Unspecified poems by Stramm and Novotny (whoever *he* was) are read; Baal, who is a clerk in the host's office, calls them drivel. The servants try to throw him out, but he fights them off, saying, 'I'll show you who's master.'

The 1922 version is virtually the same as the final text, less the character of Pschierer and all between the first remark of the Young Man and the last remark of the Young Woman. The scene ends, after Piller's last jibe, with Johannes asking Baal if he may visit him and Emilie saying, 'I'm sorry for him.'

[2] Baal's speeches are longer than in the final version, but the scene is not essentially changed.

[3] In 1918 it is a bourgeois bar. Baal reads the 'Ballad of Evelyn Roe' (now in Brecht's collected poems), is applauded and introduces Johannes and 'Mr Ekart, a brilliant composer who is passing through'. He insults the bourgeois, who fail to pay for his drinks; he refuses to join Ekart on his wanderings because Marie the waitress, who is in love with him, cannot come too. Johannes leads him away.

In 1919 this becomes the Inn with an audience of drivers to whom he sings 'Orge's song'. Johannes brings Johanna; Emmi arrives, identified by Baal as 'wife of my office boss' and described as *well-dressed, nervous, rather domineering*. It is virtually the final version.

[4 i] Essentially the final version, though in 1918 Johanna is called Anna. Instead of asking Baal if he still loves her, she asks, 'Do you love me?' *in a small voice, breathlessly*.

[4 iii] Sophie Dechant in 1918 appears dressed in white. She is an actress, on her way to play (presumably Hebbel's) Judith. Much of the final version is there – Baal calling her a white cloud, her reference to Baal's ugliness, her virginity, her declaration that she loves him – till Baal's mother comes in, accusing him of having whores in his room. He says Sophie is to be his wife, and asks her if she will. A piano is playing all the time, off.

In 1919 the scene has been largely rewritten. Sophie ceases to be an actress and takes her eventual form. Baal still says she is to be his wife, but no longer asks her.

By 1922 the mother is cut out of the play. Baal's long opening speech, which originally introduced another scene with his mother (see below) is added to this one. Johannes makes his brief appearance. Sophie's name is changed to Barger, and there is no mention of her becoming Baal's wife. Instead of the piano there is intermittently the beggar's hurdy-gurdy playing *Tristan*.

[6] In 1918 it is 'Night', with no place given. Sophie says they are penniless, and wants to go back to the stage. Baal says he will go on the stage: in a cabaret. He sings the verse which later introduces 4 (ii).

In 1919 the scene is rewritten. It is a bedroom in the summer, and several phrases of the dialogue survive into the final version. It is now Baal who says, 'Do you realize we've got no money?' The cabaret is not mentioned.

In 1922 there is no song, and the scene is set out of doors in May, as we have it.

[7] In 1918 there is an unnamed compère instead of Mjurk. There is no Lupu and no mention of the agreement about schnaps. The dialogue is differently phrased, but the only major differences from the ultimate version are: (1) the irruption of a group of Young Artists, who tell Baal: 'Your latest poem in the *Phoebus* is good, but too affectedly simple – Princess Ebing's taking an interest in you. She's hot stuff. Lucky fellow!'; (2) the song which Baal sings, dressed in tails and a child's sailor hat, which goes roughly:

> If a woman's hips are ample
> Then I want her in the hay
> Skirt and stockings all a-rumple
> (cheerfully) – for that's my way.
>
> If the woman bites in pleasure
> Then I wipe it clean with hay
> My mouth and her lap together
> (thoroughly) – for that's my way.
>
> If the woman goes on loving
> When I feel too tired to play
> I just smile and go off waving
> (amiably) – for that's my way.

The 1919 version is textually the same, except for the replacement of 'Compère' by 'Nigger John' throughout. For Nigger John, see below.

In 1922 Mjurk, Lupu, and the final song make their appearance. There is a typescript of the song dated 21 January 1920.

[8] Basically the same in all versions.

[15] 1918 and 1919 (slightly lengthened) versions show Ekart talking about his pale-faced girl as an experience of the past; Baal goes to sleep while he is talking about her. The poem which Baal recites to him is not the 'Drowned Girl' (as in the 1922 text) but 'The Song of the Cloud in the Night' (in the collected poems).

[17] In 1918 the scene is set outside a country tavern. The text is almost word for word the same as in the final version, apart from some slight variations in the poem 'Death in the Forest', until what is now the end of the scene. Thereupon Baal says 'I'll go and get one' (i.e., a woman), and breaks into the dance which has started inside the tavern. There is almost a fight with the man whose

partner Baal pulls away from him, then Baal suddenly crumples and leaves.

In 1919 the setting becomes 'Maple Trees in the Wind', and the dance episode is detached to make a separate short scene, which Brecht dropped in the third version.

[18] The 1918 and 1919 versions are almost identical apart from the absence of Johannes from the former and certain differences in the arrangement of the verses. Baal here arrives, on the top of his form, having sold a book of his poems to a publisher. 'I want meat! What's your name, kids, and what's your price? I'm as choosy as a vicar. But watch what I can do. I'll pay for everything!' He orders champagne (in the final version there is an allusion to this left after the third verse of the Ballad) and, with Luise on his knee (who does not yet look like Sophie) sings an obscene, blasphemous, and largely untranslatable song about the Virgin. Watzmann, whose character was even then unexplained, sings in lieu of 'The trees come in avalanches':

When the hatred and venom he's swallowed
Are more than his gullet can take
He may well draw a knife from his pocket
And languidly sever his neck.

At the end of the scene, before Baal attacks Ekart, Ekart tries to get Luise off his lap, saying, 'Oh, rubbish! Gentlemen! Let's drink to fair shares between brothers!'

There is a draft of January 1920 showing the waitress with Sophie's features and Baal a wreck, as in the 1922 text, which also substitutes the new dialogue between Baal and Ekart at the end.

[20] The dialogue between the two policemen is little changed. In 1918 and 1919 three other professions are attributed to Baal: gardener, city clerk, and journalist. Those of roundabout proprietor, woodcutter, and millionairess's lover only appear in the 1922 version.

[22] This scene has remained essentially unchanged from the 1918 version, apart from Baal's last speech, which both there and in 1919 runs:

Dear God. Gone. *Groans*. It's not so simple. My God, it's not so simple. If only I. One. Two. Three. Four. Five. Six. Not much help. Dear God. *Dear* God. *Feverishly*: Mother! Send Ekart away! Oh, Mary! The sky's so damned near. Almost touch it. My heart's thumping. One. Two. Three. Four.

Whimpers, then all of a sudden, loudly: I can't. I won't. It's stifling here. *Quite distinctly:* It must be clear outside. I want to. *Raising himself with difficulty.* Baal, I want to go out. *Sharply:* I'm not a rat. *He tumbles off the bed, and falls.* Hell. Dear God! As far as the door! *He crawls to the threshold.* Stars . . . hm. *He crawls out.*

In the 1922 version the five invocations of God and one of Mary are replaced by the three invocations of 'Dear Baal'.

Other scenes:—

Seven further scenes were cut or telescoped with others when Brecht revised the play in 1919. Two of these represent a loss to the narrative: 9, which shows Baal arrested on Corpus Christi day because he is drunkenly outraged by the cutting of branches for the procession, and scene 11, where a theatre review which he has written is rejected by the manager of his newspaper, and the editor then sacks him. The main points of the other five scenes (which elaborate the affairs with Emmy and Johanna, show him being visited in prison by his mother, and later forcing an unnamed girl to sell herself for him) are incorporated in or anticipated by other changes.

There are three new long scenes in the 1919 revision, and five others of which two appear in this version only. The long ones are [10] the scene over the body of the dead woodcutter Teddy, [13] the Bolleboll–Gougou scene, and [9] Baal's pretence of buying bulls. The two scenes subsequently cut are scene 8, immediately following the first Sophie scene, where the barman Nigger John offers Baal (in a top hat) a job in his cabaret; and scene 19, preceding the 'Death in the Forest' scene, where Baal, Ekart and a new girl called Anna try to get a night's lodging. A man opens his window and says that Anna can come in his room and the others sleep in the hay.

ANNA: I'm so frightened. I don't want to be alone.
BAAL: You won't be alone.

The man says he can offer them soup with milk and fresh bread. 'The young lady gets the cream, hahaha.'

ANNA: I must do whatever you want, but I'm sure it's not right.
BAAL: Nonsense. Warmth is right and soup is right. Get on in! You've been a burden so far; now you can make yourself useful.

The other new scenes are [12], where Baal and Ekart abandon the pregnant Sophie; an early version of [11], with Baal and Ekart in a hut in the winter; and the very short [14], in the undergrowth by the river, where Baal says, 'I don't care for women any longer . . .'

In the 1922 text the position of all these new scenes is changed relatively to the basic framework. Four more are added, of which [4 ii], where the two sisters visit Baal's room, is the most substantial. [5] with the drunk tramp restores the point of one of the scenes cut in 1919. [16] is the scene with Ekart's pale red-haired girl, now very much part of the present. [19] is Baal's brief passage across the stage '10° East of Greenwich'. Nine scenes are cut, including the two 1919 additions mentioned above and the detached (quarrel at the dance) episode of [17]. The others are two scenes with Baal's mother, who is thus eliminated from the play (one, originally scene 4, showing her reprimanding her son for his drunkenness, the other preceding the last tavern scene and showing her on her deathbed); a scene following the cabaret episode, with Baal arrested by the police in a café; and the next scene after that, with Baal in prison being reasoned with by a clergyman:

CLERGYMAN: You're sinking deeper all the time.
BAAL: Thanks to my immense weight. But I enjoy it. I'm going down. Aren't I? But I'm doing all right, aren't I? Am I going off course? Am I a coward? Am I trying to stave off the consequences? Am I scared of you? Death and I are friends. Hardship's my whore. I'm humbler than you.
CLERGYMAN: You're too light to go under. You cheerful bankrupt.
BAAL: Sometimes I'm like a diver whose cables and breathing tubes have been cut, going for a walk all alone in the depths.
CLERGYMAN: Nothing is so terrible as loneliness. Nobody is alone with us. We are all brothers.
BAAL: Being alone has so far been my strength. I don't want a second man in my skin . . .

Finally, two short scenes are deleted near the end of the play: one with a moralizing Baal interrupting lovers on a park bench, the other between [20] and [21], where Baal, on the run at night, tries vainly to get a peasant girl to walk with him.

'LIFE STORY OF THE MAN BAAL' (1926)

This later typescript is published in the second of Dieter Schmidt's volumes, and is subtitled 'Dramatic Biography by Bertolt Brecht. (Stage adaptation of "Baal".)' It consists of the nine basic scenes in shortened and largely rewritten form, plus [12] and [19], and a new short scene only found in this version (scene 9 below). All except scene 1 are given titles. Some of the names are spelt differently. The play begins with seven verses of the Hymn (verses 1, 2, 4, and the last four) sung by Baal, who then leaves the stage.

Scene 1. Room with dining table.

Enter Mäch, Emilie Mäch, Johannes Schmidt, Dr Piller, Baal.

MÄCH *while Baal stands eating at the buffet:* I think I may claim to have been the first to foresee your path to those heights of fame for which born geniuses are predestined. Genius has always suffered persecution; as it listens in its unworldly way to higher voices it is brought down to the cold realities of the world. I would like to think that my salon had been the first to welcome you, before the distinction of the Kleist Prize snatches you away from us. Will you have a glass of wine? . . .

Johannes says that Baal sings his poems to the taxi-drivers.

MÄCH: Fantastic.
EMILIE:

With cynical penury of airy poems
Of an orange-flavoured bitterness
Chilled on ice, black Malayan
Hair over the eyes! O opium smoke! . . .
Is that really by you?

JOHANNES: That's Herr Baal's. They generally give him three glasses of kirsch for each song. And one glass for a look at the special instrument he invented, which he says posterity will know as Baal's original tin-stringed banjo.
MÄCH: Fantastic.
JOHANNES: It's in a café at a goods station.
EMILIE: I suppose you've read a great deal?
MÄCH: Just let him eat in peace for the moment. Let him recover. Art's hard work too, you know. Help yourself to brandy, Hennessy, it's all there.

EMILIE: You live in a garage?

BAAL: 64a Holzstrasse.

MÄCH: Fantastic. Weren't you a mechanic?

EMILIE:

> In wind-crazed huts of light paper
> O you bitterness and gaiety of the world
> When the moon, that soft white animal
> Falls out of colder skies.

Apart from one remark of Baal's, who announces: 'In the year 1904 Joseph Mäch gives Baal a light for his cigar,' the last two-thirds of the scene are close to our version from after the last remark of the Young Lady (on p. 8) to the end. Then the Servant is cut (as in 1922) and, after Johannes has asked if he may visit Baal, Emilie says: 'I don't know. I like him. He needs looking after.' Then a new closing speech from Baal:

> It's raining. At the time of the Flood they all went into the ark. All the animals, by agreement. The only time the creatures of this world have ever agreed about anything. They really all did come. But the ichthyosaurus didn't. Everybody said he should get on board, but he was very busy just then. Noah himself warned him the Flood was coming. But he quietly said, 'I don't believe it'. He was universally unpopular when he drowned. Ah yes, they all said, the ichthyosaurus won't be coming. He was the oldest beast of them all, well qualified by his great experience to say whether such a thing as a Flood was or was not feasible. It's very possible that if a similar situation ever arises I shan't get on board either.

Baal's Unhesitating Abuse of Divine Gifts.

Scene 2. Garage.

The tone is drier, but essentially the scene is a condensed version of the Baal–Johannes scene as we have it, except that it ends with Baal saying not 'you should avoid it' but 'I think you should bring her to me'.

Baal Abuses his Power over a Woman.

Scene 3. 'Pub.'

Baal, Eckart, a tart. Taxi-drivers at the bar.

ECKART: I'm on the move. I've had just about enough of this town. Last night I slept with this lady and realized that I'm too grown up for that sort of thing. My advice is to hang all ovaries on the hook once and for all. I'm for freedom of movement till one's forty-five. Plato says the same if I'm not mistaken.

BAAL: Where are you going?

ECKART: The South of France, I think. Apart from anything else they seem to have a different type of town there. The plan is different, to start with, because there's enough light and that guarantees order. Are you coming?

BAAL: Got any money?

ECKART: Up to a point.

BAAL: Enough for a train?

ECKART: Enough for feet.

BAAL: When are you off?

ECKART: Today. I'm leaving this pub at eleven-thirty.

BAAL: How come?

ECKART: I've got a photo of Marseilles. Three dingy ellipses. Are you coming?

BAAL: Possibly. I don't know yet.

A version of the scene as we have it then begins, with Baal's account of Mäch's party and then Johannes's entrance. Johanna, however, is now fifteen: two years younger. It is not specified what ballad Baal sings. Eckart having already made his appeal does not make it again, but before singing Baal says:

Today, my friends, I was made an offer which no doubt has erotic motives. Kirsch, Luise. The man in question is about to move off. He's just smoking his last cigar and drinking his last kirsch. I'm probably going to say 'not yet'. Drink up, Emilie. Obviously I'm in the market for counter-offers. I imagine that poses a problem for you, Emilie.

EMILIE: I don't know what's the matter with you today . . .

After the driver Horgauer has kissed Emilie the ending is wholly changed. The taxi-drivers applaud and Johanna tells Baal he should be ashamed of himself, as in our version. Then Emilie tells Johanna:

> Don't pay any attention to me. I've been criticized for not having enough temperament for this kind of place. But perhaps I've shown that my dirtiness has been underestimated.

ECKART: Bill!

BAAL: Emmi, you haven't paid. You can relax. It's over now. Forget it.

ECKART: I'm going.

BAAL: Where?

ECKART: South of France. Are you coming too?

BAAL: Can't you put it off?

ECKART: No, I don't want to do that. Are you coming or not?

BAAL: No.

64a Holzstrasse

Scene 4. Garage.

A condensed conflation of scenes [4 i] and [4 ii]. The tone of Baal's dialogue with Johanna is drier. She has no remorse, and is only concerned about getting dressed. The Porter's Wife irrupts after Baal's 'Give me a kiss', and berates him in much the same shocked words as the landlady of [4 ii]. Then back to the finish of [4 i], with Baal saying:

> Off home with you! Tell Johnny Schmidt we just came in for five minutes because it was raining.

JOHANNA: Tell Johnny Schmidt it was raining. *Exit*.

BAAL: Johanna! There she goes.

– and no music.

Two Years later: Baal Discovers a (to him) New Kind of Love

Scene 5. Garage.

On the wall a nude drawing of a woman. Baal arrives with Miss Barger.

BAAL: My workshop.

BARGER: Excuse me, but I'm going back down.

BAAL: You can't just do that.

BARGER: They'll find me here. There was a man who followed us when you came up and spoke to me outside.

BAAL: Nobody'll find you here.

BARGER: Out there you told me you were a photographer.

BAAL: That's what I said out there, wasn't it?

BARGER: Then I'm going.

BAAL: There was something particular I wanted to ask you.

BARGER: No.

BAAL: What are you scared of all of a sudden?

BARGER: I'm not the least bit scared.

BAAL: Oh. That's a drawing I did to help make matters clear. If you don't like it we'll take it down. But you see, I know you inside and out; there's no mystery. There! *He scratches out the drawing with his knife.*

BARGER: Holy mother of God! *Screams.*

BAAL: What are you screaming about? Don't make such a noise. They'll hear you next door. Is it the knife? *Picks up a bottle.* Nothing left in there. No air left either. As for the meat! The meat's pathetic. It's not meat at all, just skin and a couple of fibres. I don't call that meat. Altogether this planet's a washout. A piece of impertinence. All fixed up for visitors. With mountains. But there aren't any mountains. That's what the valleys are for. Stuff the one into the other and the stupid planet's flat again. There, now you've stopped.

BARGER: Shall I stay with you?

BAAL: What?

BARGER: Your drawing's very ugly. But you look discontented. Me too. When I was fourteen the butcher next door wouldn't even let me sweep the snow off his pavement because I was too ugly. Lately men have taken to turning round and looking at me in the street; what I've got won't last long; I think I ought to make use of it. I don't think it has to be a man in a smart hat. But it's no good having something that isn't made use of.

BAAL: Now could that surprising way of talking be because she's scared of death?

BARGER: Scared of death? Have you had ideas of that sort?

BAAL: Don't get up. You don't suit. *Smokes.* Get your voice in operation again. It was a great moment. I'm abandoning hope. Seven years in this room, eighteen months' conscious abstention from food, washing out my mind with unadulterated consumption of alcohol. Never in my life having done the least little thing, I'm on the verge of entering new territory. This place of mine is all worn out. Mostly by systematic overestimation of everything, I suppose. I can see them saying that at the time of my death table and wall had been utterly worn away. And I still have to resolve the permanent problem of my life: the devising of an evil deed.

BARGER: It isn't easy, but I'm sure I can understand you if I really try.

BAAL: I give up. You talk now. Nobody shall say I neglected anything. You've got a woman's face. In your case one could perhaps cause seven pounds of disaster, where with most women one can't even cause two. How old are you?

BARGER: Twenty-four in June.

BAAL: How many men have you had in your life?

Barger says nothing.

BAAL: Then you've got that behind you. Any relatives?

BARGER: Yes, a mother.

BAAL: Is she old?

BARGER: She's sixty.

BAAL: Then she's got used to evil.

BARGER: They oughtn't to blame me. I can't support myself.

BAAL: You'll learn.

BARGER: You're asking an awful lot. You're so ugly it's terrifying. What's your name?

BAAL: Baal.

Baal Earns Money for the Last Time.

Scene 6. The Prickly Pear nightclub.

This is scene [7], still the 'Small, swinish café', with the difference that the parts of the Soubrette and her accompanist have been considerably written up, that the text of Baal's song is not given, and that when Baal escapes through the lavatory window it is (according to the accompanist) to go to the Black Forest, where a postcard from Eckart at the beginning of the scene has asked him to join him.

Baal Abandons the Mother of his Unborn Child.

Scene 7. Flat land, sky, and evening.

This is approximately [12], but without reference to Baal's taking Eckart's women, or having been in prison, and without the two men's wrestling at the end of the scene. It is all shorter, and it appears to come as a surprise to Baal that Sophie is pregnant:

BAAL: Pregnant? That's the last straw. What do you think you're up to? And now I suppose I'll have you hanging round my neck?

ECKART: On principle I don't interfere in your exceedingly shabby human relationships. But at least when a third party is present they should be conducted with some semblance of fairness.

BAAL: Are you going to abandon me on her account? That'd be just like you. She can clear out. She's going downhill. I'm as patient as a lamb. But I can't change my skin.

SOPHIE: You see, Baal, I didn't need to tell you before. It's been slower than I thought, mostly because you didn't like me all that much. I'm in the fourth month.

ECKART: She's showing some vestige of common sense. Once again: I refuse to let my feelings get involved, but I'll wait here till it's all settled.

Sophie then starts begging them to stay, for an hour, for half an hour. She tells Baal: 'Oh yes, it's a beautiful evening, and you like it. But you won't like it when you have to die without another soul there.' 'Yes, I will,' says Baal. And as Sophie shouts that they are degenerate beasts Baal tells Eckart, 'I absolutely insist that you and I leave now.'

In the Years 1907–10 We Find Baal and Eckart Tramping across South Germany.

Scene 8. Countryside. Morning. Wind.

Baal – Eckart

BAAL: The wind's getting up again. It's the only thing you get free in this country, but all it does now is touch my skin. It isn't strong enough for my ears these days. Your fugue hasn't made much progress either.

ECKART: The sounds my fugue is based on are no worse than most. As for the mathematics of it, it's more mathematical than the wind. The landscape keeps getting more mathematical. It's humanity's only prospect. There's already a corrugated iron barn over there; tomorrow there'll be a steel-framed building. The big cities are spreading their standardized limbs across the old landscape. Between all those tall buildings the wind will be measurable.

BAAL: We're the last people to see the flat plain. In forty-nine years the word 'forest' won't be needed. Wood will cease to be used. Mankind will disappear too, if it comes to that. But to stick to our own lifetime, by the time your big cities are built you'll be delirious. Instead of those tall constructions you'll see rats.

ECKART: By then it will take entire typhoons to make you hear the slightest noise.

BAAL: My friend, I want to live without a skin. You're really an evil man. Both of us are. Unfortunately. Here's a poem I've written.

He then reads 'The Drowned Girl', as in [15], after which:

ECKART: You don't seem to have lost much of your power.

BAAL: Everything there is to say about life on this planet could be expressed in a single sentence of average length. That sentence I shall some time or other formulate, certainly before I die.

Scene 9. Countryside.

Night. Baal asleep. Eckart looking at him.

ECKART: This man Baal worries me. He's not light enough any longer. I'm an objective kind of person. It would be simple enough to pick up a piece of chalk and establish the graph of his life on all the house walls. When I think about it, the only thing that keeps me is the fact that his character's if anything getting harder. All the same, I'm the last man to want to witness the enfeeblement that's bound to accompany his decline and death. I'm not a vindictive character. Just lately he's been keeping a very sharp eye on me. It's difficult to tell if he's genuinely asleep now, for instance. There are no fields left for him to graze down. It's starting to rain again; I'd better cover him up.

In the Year 1911 Baal Succumbs to his Predestined Disposition to Murder.

Scene 10. 'Pub.'

Autumn evening. Eckart, Emilie Mäch, and Johann Schmidt in black.

This is essentially [18], with the difference that the waitress is Sophie and that Emilie is present, with a good deal to say. Watzmann is cut, his verse about 'When the hatred and venom' from the 1919 version being now hummed by Emilie. There are no other verses apart from those of the 'Ballad of the Adventurers' sung by Baal.

It starts with Johann asking, 'When's Baal coming?' Then Eckart:

> It's become increasingly clear to me in these last few years that great times are in store for us. The countryside is going to ruin. I've seen photographs of buildings on Manhattan Island which indicate a vast power in the human race. Having reached a high point of insensitivity, mankind is setting to work to create an age of happiness. The years in question will be limited in number; what matters is to be there. For a few weeks I've felt myself becoming increasingly restless.
>
> EMILIE: When's Baal coming?

They discuss who has any money to pay for drinks. Emilie's husband has died. They discuss Baal, before his entrance, somewhat as in [18]. Emilie, who says she has 'come to see the golden boy eight years later ... You know, I'd feel there was something missing if he didn't somehow or other go completely to pieces,' asks Eckart if he is abandoning him. Eckart says: 'Yes, it's already written on my face. It's obvious to everybody. Only he doesn't realize it yet. Although I keep telling him. As I did today,' then breaks off as Baal arrives.

The first exchanges are much as in [18], but Baal then asks the waitress, 'Is that you, Sophie?' Johann answers:

> Yes, that's her all right. How are you? I'm doing very nicely. It's a very good atmosphere here. Beer.
>
> SOPHIE: Beer.

After Eckart's outburst, where he says he is going back to the forests, Baal says 'Are you off again? I don't believe it, you know. I feel perfectly well myself.' Eckart then tells the story of the man who thought he was well, as told by the Beggar in the Bolleboll–

Gougou scene [13], up to the final 'Did he get well?' (here asked by Baal). 'No.'

Johann(es) makes none of his long melancholy speeches, but when he for the second time says, 'It really is a very good atmosphere here,' he adds, 'Like in the old days.' Emilie thereupon hums her verse, and Baal turns to Eckart:

> That girl Johanna Schreiber was with us then.
>
> EMILIE: Oh, the one who killed herself. She's still stuck in a culvert somewhere. They never found her. He's got a wife now, and a nice little coal-merchant's business.
>
> JOHANN: Brandy.
>
> SOPHIE: Brandy.
>
> EMILIE: Have I altered much? I wasn't too bad after you'd finished with me. I don't imagine you're pleased to hear that. For a time I couldn't take any drinks that hadn't been mixed eight times over. My late husband got me off wood-alcohol by hitting me.
>
> BAAL: Nothing doing.
>
> EMILIE: Give me a cigar.
>
> SOPHIE: Cigar.
>
> EMILIE: Give me the strongest schnaps; it's all right. And I'll go to bed with any of you that knows his business. Technique: that's what I'm interested in. What are you looking at now?

She claims to have drunk more than any of them. Baal replies: 'You were never drunk, you had amazing control of yourself, you never were worth anything. That girl back there, for instance, who was very close to me once, is absolutely used up. She was a first-class phenomenon on this planet.' As Emilie weeps, Baal sits by her and makes a formal declaration:

> ... If you for your part still have some inclination towards my body, then I, being unaccustomed ever in my life to let any sort of offer go by, would now like to say this to you: my outward circumstances will make me incline towards you in six years at the most, by which time you will have achieved a total age of forty years.

He smashes the light and sings, and Eckart's murder follows much as in [18].

Baal on the Run. 10 Degrees East of Greenwich.

Scene 11.

Almost identical with [9].

Baal Dies Wretchedly among Woodcutters in the Year 1912.

Scene 12. Night, rain, woodcutters playing cards.

Baal on a dirty bed.

This is considerably cut, but otherwise very close to [21]. The main difference is as the last woodcutter is leaving, after wiping Baal's forehead. Baal calls him closer and says:

> . . . I agree. [Ich bin einverstanden.]
> MAN: What with?
> BAAL: With everything.
> MAN: But it's all over now.
> BAAL: That was excellent.
> MAN: Off we go, then.
> BAAL: Hey, give me the book.
> MAN: But you haven't any light.

In Baal's final speech there is no 'Dear God' and no 'Dear Baal'. He calls for Eckart, not for his mother, and his last words are 'It's better in the doorway. Man! Trunks. Wind. Leaves. Stars. Hm.'

DRUMS IN THE NIGHT

BALLAD OF THE DEAD SOLDIER
(Sung by Glubb at the beginning of Act 4)

And when the war reached its fifth spring
with no hint of a pause for breath
the soldier did the obvious thing
and died a hero's death.

The war, it appeared, was far from done.
The Kaiser said, 'It's a crime.
To think my soldier's dead and gone
before the proper time.'

The summer spread over the makeshift graves.
The soldier lay ignored
until one night there came an official army medical board.

The board went out to the cemetery
with consecrated spade
and dug up what was left of him
and put him on parade.

The doctors sorted out what they'd found
and kept what they thought would serve
and made their report: 'He's physically sound.
He's simply lost his nerve.'

Straightway they took the soldier off.
The night was soft and warm.
You could tip your helmet back and see
the stars they see at home.

They filled him up with a fiery schnaps
to bring him back to life
then shoved two nurses into his arms
and his half-naked wife.

The soldier was stinking with decay
so a priest goes on before
to give him incense on his way
that he may stink no more.

In front the band with oom-pah-pah
intones a rousing march.
The soldier does like the handbook says
and flicks his legs from his arse.

Their arms about him, keeping pace
two kind first-aid men go
in case he falls in the shit on his face
for that would never do.

They paint his shroud with the black-white-red
of the old imperial flag
with so much colour it covers up
that bloody spattered rag.

Up front a gent in a morning suit
and stuffed-out shirt marched too:
a German determined to do his dut-
y as Germans always do.

So see them now as, oom-pah-pah
along the roads they go
and the soldier goes whirling along with them
like a flake in the driving snow.

The dogs cry out and the horses prance.
The rats squeal on the land.

They're damned if they're going to belong to France:
it's more than flesh can stand.

And when they pass through a village all
the women are moved to tears.
The party salutes; the moon shines full.
The whole lot give three cheers.

With oom-pah-pah and cheerio
and wife and dog and priest
and, among them all, the soldier himself
like some poor drunken beast.

And when they pass through a village perhaps
it happens he disappears
for such a crowd comes to join the chaps
with oompah and three cheers. . . .

In all that dancing, yelling crowd
he disappears from view.
You can only see him from overhead
which only stars can do.

The stars won't always be up there.
The dawn is turning red.
But the soldier goes off to a hero's death
just like the handbook said.

In memory of Christian Grumbeis, infantryman, born on
11 April 1897, died in Holy Week 1918 at Karasin (Southern
Russia). Peace to his ashes! He could take it.

[Appendix to the 1922 edition. Now in the 'Hauspostille' section
of Brecht's collected poems, dated 1918, less the dedicatory note
and under the title 'Legend of the Dead Soldier'.]

NOTE FOR THE STAGE

At Caspar Neher's suggestion this play was performed in Munich with the following scenery. Pasteboard screens some six feet high represented the walls of the rooms, with the big city painted in childish style behind them. Every time Kragler appeared the moon glowed red a few seconds beforehand. Sounds were thinly hinted. In the last act the Marseillaise was performed on a gramophone. The third act can be left out if it fails to work fluently and musically and to liven up the tempo. It is a good idea to put up one or two posters in the auditorium bearing phrases such as 'Stop that romantic staring'.

[GW *Stücke*, p. 70. In all previous editions the words 'At Caspar Neher's suggestion' were absent and a second phrase 'Everybody is top man in his own skin' included at the end.]

NOTE TO THE SCRIPT OF THE BERLIN PRODUCTION

A small stage, consisting of wood and pasteboard. Thin flats, only partly painted. Doors, windows, walls all have a makeshift air. Similarly, although the great revolutionary operation steadily grows in power offstage it makes only a thin, ghostlike effect in the auditorium. The persons nevertheless must be extremely real and the acting naïve. The auditorium contains posters with phrases from the play such as 'Everybody is top man in his own skin' and 'The eye of the Lord maketh the cattle fat' and 'Stop that romantic staring'.

[Unpublished. Brecht Archive typescript no. 2122 and 1569. This production was in December 1922.]

PREFACE TO 'DRUMS IN THE NIGHT'

I

Conversation with George Grosz

What the bourgeoisie hold against proletarians is their bad complexion. I fancy that what made you, George Grosz, an enemy of the bourgeois was their physiognomy. It's fairly common knowledge that war is currently being waged between the proletariat and the bourgeoisie. To judge by the arguments on both sides it isn't a war that depends on divergences of taste; but those arguments are deceptive and unconvincing, and above all, nobody ever pays them the slightest attention. The bourgeoisie commit injustices, but then injustices are committed on all sides. You and I, George Grosz, are against injustice (like everybody else). But we would be less against it if it could be committed by the proletariat. I mean to say: that can't be the injustice that 'forced you to take up your brushes'. And if it were, then you'd be a counter-revolutionary, and I would shoot you and erect you a monument. I don't believe, Grosz, that overwhelming compassion for the exploited or anger against the exploiter one day filled you with an irresistible desire to get something about this down on paper. I think drawing was something you enjoyed, and people's physiognomies so many pretexts for it. I imagine you becoming aware one day of a sudden overwhelming love for a particular type of face as a marvellous opportunity for you to amuse yourself. It was *The Face of the Ruling Class* [*Das Gesicht der herrschenden Klasse*, one of Grosz's early albums]. I'm not underrating your enjoyment of protest, which was what no doubt moved you to expose as swine the very people who saw themselves as the élite of the human race – and necessarily had to be since none but an élite could be permitted such swinish behaviour. In the Protestant sense there wasn't any truth worth revealing in reducing a proletarian type to his basic pattern. Proletarians have no call to be other than they are. In the immense effort it costs them just to keep alive they spontaneously adopted their most genuine basic form. Any kind of frills were out of the question. In appearing better than he really was, that type of bourgeois was doing business, but proletarians don't do business at all. Art nowadays is in the same position as you: the type you adore as subject-matter you are bound to detest as a member of the public. Politically you regard the bourgeoisie as your enemy not because you are a proletarian but because you are an artist. Your political position (which unlike you I treat as secondary, you see,) is a position in relation to the public, not in relation to your subject-matter. I have gone through the same process as you, just as seriously though with nothing like the same success. Let me refer you to a play of mine which greatly displeased those who share your political opinions: the little comedy called *Drums in the Night*.

2

Drums in the Night's success with the bourgeoisie

This play was performed on some fifty bourgeois stages. Its success, which was considerable, simply proved that I had come to the wrong address. I was totally dissatisfied: why, I could not immediately say. I just had an uncomfortable sensation. I had a vague idea that the people who were so wildly anxious to shake my hand were just the lot I would have liked to hit on the head, not in this play perhaps but in general. My condition was like that of a man who has fired a gun at people he dislikes, and finds these same people coming and giving three cheers for him: inadvertently he has been firing off loaves of bread. When I then consulted the papers to find out what had happened I found that the chief element of my success lay in the furious attacks launched by the aesthetically reactionary press. So there were still those who complained of the loaves!

The whole thing was an aesthetic business of which I understood nothing. In any other period I might have been able to understand something about it, but at this particular moment, with New York being built and Moscow being destroyed, and both processes seeming likely to concern the whole world, aesthetics were wholly irrelevant. The bourgeois theatre, equally incapable of performing the oldest plays or the most modern, imagined that its continued existence was merely a question of styles. Like a foundering ship, the sinking theatre concerned itself with the possibly very difficult but basically unimportant question whether it was better to sink to the left or to the right. And the crew criticized the band, which in its confusion kept on playing 'Nearer, my God, to Thee', meaning the God who is on the side of the big battalions. To avoid dreadful misunderstandings I should point out that this image for the decline of the theatre may perhaps be inappropriate, for the reason that the theatre was a lot more expensive than an old steamship and worth a lot less, and that those who went down in her by no means suffered any loss but quite the reverse. Moreover, a brief bout of introspection was enough to convince audience and artists alike that the theatre was bound to go under; and those shrieks of desperation were paid for by the theatres out of what they made by selling advertising space in the programmes.

I have always regarded myself as a man who, given a few drinks and cigars, can equip himself to turn out a literary work such as careful reflection will lead him to think desirable. The only thing is that I'm not sure what will happen if I give my abilities their head. *Drums in the Night* is an admirable instance of the weakness of the human will. I wrote it to make money. But although, amazingly enough, I really did make money I would be deceiving you if I said that my pains had been rewarded with success. A number of people managed to hand me money for them; but I managed to write a political play.

3

The love story

In view of the fact that my choice of subject for the play was decided on speculative and financial grounds, it is perhaps of public interest that I should specifically have decided that a love story was called for. Writing this play was a really serious business undertaking, which was precisely what made me able to understand the needs of the paying public. (The experiences embodied in the play, in other words, were avarice and writing.) I was accordingly quite ready to supply the love story, but what I found interesting about it above all was of course the property aspect. The character of Kragler, who struck me as a typical hero of our time, reduced it to that. He wanted a particular woman, and the only course open to him psychologically if he didn't get her was that of a man who fails to get a house that he used to, or wishes to, possess. The causes of his desire struck me as not worth going into. I didn't in fact make the woman particularly desirable. She commands a certain run-of-the-mill sensuality, which can hardly be termed strong since it gets satisfied without further ado, and indeed without reference to the object or partner. The entire sexual motivation remains makeshift and ordinary. You or I would call it innocuous. It is not that powerful, almost revolutionary call for physical satisfaction which arises when a woman needs somebody to sleep with her and has to put up with whatever man she can get. To Anna Balicke a man is not an article for use but a cheap luxury. In bourgeois society the erotic sphere is exhausted. Literature reflects this by the fact that sex no longer gives rise to associations. In fact, the strongest erotic life nowadays is probably to be found in that primitive literature (which occurs in the form of certain notoriously efficacious words and) which ordinary people wield with naïve virtuosity. Clearly the significance of their refusal to use vulgar words in front of women is that such words can be relied upon to be thoroughly effective.

Today the tragic potentialities of a love relationship consist in the couple's failing to find a room. Unfortunately, it is difficult to find out whether today's conditions also applied yesterday, as one can hardly ask one's father about his sex life. But at least today one can clearly establish the attraction of vulgar words relating to sex and its organs. Enjoyment of dirty words largely depends on their guaranteed obscenity. Indeed, there are times when enjoyment of sex depends on its guaranteed obscenity. This romantic factor comes into play when Miss Balicke lusts after Kragler's obscene ignominiousness. The bourgeoisie will see it as a triumph of the ideal. In my view not even such depressing considerations as these will deprive the love story in question of its charm.

It may also be that real sexual enjoyment is now only to be got from venereal diseases. Here is a dumping-ground for our feelings where there is still some activity going on. One of these venereal diseases is pregnancy. Murk, whose rootlessness is due to the woman's indifference – a very common pestilence that can truly be compared with those in the Bible – goes and infects her with a child. His conduct is moral: in occupying her troubled mind he improves his economic standing. But morality is there to prevent miscalculations. And the woman behaves immorally. She thinks she will get more from that atmosphere of obscene sexuality: from lying with Kragler when in a pregnant condition.

4

1918: The Kraglers' Revolution

When the play proved successful what succeeded was the love story and the use of drums offstage. (At the same time I'm prepared to admit that a certain fresh and personal quality and a fairly unrestrained penchant for putting things in a poetical way counted in my favour.) My interest in the revolution whose job it was to serve as background was about as great as the interest felt in Vesuvius by a man who wants to boil a kettle on it. Moreover, my kettle seemed to me a very large affair compared with the volcano in question. It truly wasn't my fault that the play ended up by giving something like a picture of the first German revolution and, even more, a picture of this particular revolutionary.

This revolution followed after a war which originated in a nervous breakdown on the part of the diplomats and was finished off by the military. The bourgeoisie waged it with particular force. Wars have been waged before now for sillier reasons than the annexation of the coal and iron-ore districts of Briey. That famous dagger which the proletariat thrust into the army's back (the legend of which went on . . . buzzing a long while in people's heads) would, if successful, have struck a region the army had long since abandoned; defeated, it was withdrawing. That was where the Kraglers came in. They made a revolution because their country, which some of them hadn't seen for four years, had changed. The Kraglers were rigidly conservative. Thanks to the sudden disappearance from all government positions of that part of the bourgeoisie which was aware that it was the bourgeoisie, the part which wasn't (i.e. the Social Democrats) was put in the embarrassing situation of having to fill them. These men were revolutionaries in the sense that miners in an insecure pit are mining engineers. The problem for the Kraglers was how to become bourgeois. Most people treated them as revolutionaries, and on the stage indeed I found that Kragler gave a very revolutionary impression. Above all, he gave the impression of being a proletarian. Of course the military had been proletarianized. Their complexion was not what it used to be. Factories had always been like barracks, and now it could be seen that they had similar effects. For a while the true revolutionaries could deprecate the play, since they took Kragler to be a proletarian and had learnt what good heroes such proletarians make. They could also oppose it on the grounds that they took Kragler to be a bourgeois and didn't want a hero like that. For there wasn't any doubt about his being a hero. Today, however, they could no longer deny that it is a thoroughly political play. An object-lesson such as one seldom gets. What they had before them was that disastrous type of Social Democrat, and in his heroic incarnation at that. It was difficult to identify him as a bourgeois, either on the stage or in real life. The revolution had undeniably been lost. This was the type that had made it. What mattered most was to learn how to identify him. He had made it, and here he was. Here, in an ordinary romantic love story with no particular depth to it, was this Social Democrat, this fake proletarian, this catastrophic revolutionary who sabotaged the revolution, who was more bitterly fought by Lenin than the bourgeois proper, and who so evaded even Lenin's grasp that before the Russian revolution it was scarcely possible to identify him to the masses so that they could be warned. This, then, was Kragler, this revolutionary whom sympathy converted back into a property-owner, who wept and nagged and, as soon as he got what he had been lacking, went home. As for the proletarians, they were not shown the play.

[GW *Schriften zum Theater* 3, p. 960 ff.
Written after Brecht's move to Berlin.]

NOTES OF CONVERSATIONS ABOUT 'DRUMS IN THE NIGHT'

BRECHT: Ten years since I wrote it. The whole business pretty strange to me now. What I saw was important. Possibly a lot there that I failed to see. Total impression a wrong one. Kragler = drama of the individual. But impossible to depict the German revolution as drama of the individual. I see him coming back after the war. He finds home devastated, no place for him. One's shown what happened to the fellow. But not shown, e.g. that the fellow is first-rate material; not shown him in any situation where the revolution can make use of him; not shown how the revolution fails to do this. The way Lenin would have seen him: out of reach for four years, but submitted to increasing revolutionary tension. If he

would have ratted none the less, then play bad. That isn't
what happens, though.

PISCATOR: That would make sense if there'd been nobody
capable of showing. But you had Liebknecht, Luxemburg ...
When the troops came back from the war the line was all of a
sudden: 'Take part in the Workers' and Soldiers' Councils!'
Play needs changes. The man was a prisoner. Doesn't alter
the position. Battle for the newspaper offices. Everyone knew
the proletarian slogans. Only a half-wit could avoid them.
Can Kragler remain so ignorant and apart? Then he's an
individual case, not a typical worker. Didn't act as a blackleg
either. No feeling either for or against the revolution ...
That's as close as one can get to him. There lies the tragedy,
but it didn't originate with Kragler. The tragedy about
Kragler ...

BRECHT: He's not tragic.

PISCATOR: The world around him's supposed to seem
tragic. The tragedy is that the German revolution is a failure,
that people aren't faced with a challenge.

BRECHT: Tragic or not tragic, from the point of view of
the revolution it's wrong that no approach was made to the
man.

PISCATOR: Establish the crux. The man turns up as an ex-
prisoner. Chance is the decisive factor in the situation. He's
always having to circumvent chance incidents.

STERNBERG: The 1918 revolution must be present in the
background. I'd say that, now we've got a militant red
organization, the German Communist Party, we're too apt to
project everything back to the 1918 period, which is something Brecht has instinctively avoided doing. The slogan
'Convert the war into a civil war!' only dates from the
beginning of the revolution. This was one thing in Russia,
where they already started trying to convert a war into a civil
war in 1905, and another in Germany, where social democracy
was a force. (New number of *Klassenkampf* today: Ebert
wanted to save the monarchy as late as 9 November: the
leader of social democracy!) That's how things were in 1918

when the troops came home. So and so many million workers were then in the same sociological situation. They had the same programme as the majority Socialists: let's hope we get in. There must have been a tremendous preponderance of pacifist forces to detach a worker from the revolution.

BRECHT: Needs every possible force to get his girl back.

STERNBERG: The girl's running away isn't an occasion for making a revolution. But suppose you were a German worker who had been slung into the war and badly misused and had heard one side's slogans, then you would have to be a lot more positive in your attitude to the revolution. In the days of the Spartacists there were 8 million workers coming back from the war and 2 per cent who joined in.

PISCATOR: Projecting back is something we do with Shakespeare as well as with Brecht. Seeing things in a present-day light.

BRECHT: But not modernizing a 1918 play.

PISCATOR: You mustn't forget, though, that you're now seeing what you failed to see then. Today's angle on the subject is a new one. Not a question of seeing further; that's not possible. The new viewpoints are different and must be brought into use too. Piscator came back to Berlin at the beginning of January. Factories all striking, workers all parading with enormous signs along Unter den Linden. More workers coming the other way with signs saying 'Liebknecht, Luxemburg', both groups grabbing each other's signs. Fighting, till somebody shoots. All the workers on the streets. Everywhere small parties of people arguing.

BRECHT: Make him just a historian. Kragler was part of the general movement. Hearing different advice from all directions, 'You must save the revolution – You must carry on the revolution – You must pull back, reconstruct – Bourgeois republic's the pattern now – etc.' He is simply raw material. And on the third day? He goes home. He counts how much money he's got in his pocket, and goes home.

PISCATOR: That'd be an exceptionally calculated reaction.

BRECHT: An Ebert man, who really does reckon that private life's more important.

PISCATOR: In that case the line has got to be drawn very clearly. He must connect up with the subject if he's to be dramatic. As it stands, the play is felt poetically. Brecht saw the man splitting the movement rather than the movement itself. Brecht today is looking back at the revolution scientifically; in those days he was a poet.

BRECHT: All the same, Kragler does notice one or two things. He's been told he must go along, he's faced with the choice of going along, he doesn't go along, he has an extremely bad conscience, he feels he's a swine, that it's a cheap drama. It ends with him saying, 'I'm a swine, and the swine's going home.'

STERNBERG: That's the crux. Piscator's right.

BRECHT: He turns against the revolution, rejects it; he's for romanticism. (The Russian revolution classic, the German not.)

PISCATOR: You may say I look at the revolution romantically, but Liebknecht and Luxemburg didn't.

STERNBERG: What he said agrees with Piscator's view. He's a chance instance. Finds the revolution romantic.

BRECHT: Bunk, according to a lot of people.

[. . .]

PISCATOR: What are they sitting at home for? Kragler because he realizes the revolution's bunk; many others because they're disillusioned.

BRECHT: They're still Kragler. All those you saw, Kraglers. The only kind who weren't Kraglers, the genuine revolutionaries around Rosa Luxemburg and Karl Liebknecht, were the chaps with their eyes open, and they weren't typical. Typical were types like Kragler. He was my revolutionary.

STERNBERG: This is where you need [. . .] film to show how they came to be the majority.

BRECHT: And to get their way.

[. . .]

STERNBERG: I can picture Kragler today sitting in the KPD, a proper communist. A simple type. He's no longer typical today. He's once again subject to the law of decreasing wages, no longer views the revolution as bunk. A type who has undergone a change.

BRECHT: In effect: a man sits there, in this year of grace 1928, talking about 1918. Not at all the same conversation as in 1918. (What with all conversation becoming increasingly political.) In those days he thought about nothing but the woman.

PISCATOR: It's still an isolated case of one individual's drama. Observed by somebody who had nothing to do with the movement.

BRECHT: One can't say that. He'd just as much to do as those million others.

STERNBERG: We're taking one man and showing what they were all like in 1918.

[. . .]

PISCATOR: Why does the play have to be performed?

BRECHT: To show why these people went home, why the revolution came to nothing. Historical enlightenment. The stumbling block was a type who really existed.

PISCATOR: In the hope of showing how revolution can lead to something.

[*Schriften zum Theater* 2, p. 272 ff, shortened as indicated. Not in GW. This conversation, dated 18 November 1928, was followed by another six days later.]

ON LOOKING THROUGH MY FIRST PLAYS (i)

Of all my early plays the comedy *Drums in the Night* is the most double-edged. Here was a case where revolting against a contemptible literary convention almost amounted to contempt for a great social revolt. A 'normal' (i.e. conventional), approach to this story about the returning soldier who joins the revolution because his girl has got engaged to somebody else would either have given the girl back to him or have denied her to him for good; either way it would have left him taking part in the revolution. In *Drums in the Night* Kragler, the soldier, gets his girl back, albeit 'damaged', and puts the revolution behind him. It seems just about the shabbiest possible solution, particularly as there is a faint suspicion of approval on the part of the author.

Today I realize that my contradictory spirit – I'm suppressing my wish to insert the word 'youthful' as I hope I still have it at my disposal in full strength – led me close to the limits of absurdity.

The 'human predicament' drama of those days, with its unrealistic pseudo-solutions, was uncongenial to the student of science. It set up a highly improbable and undoubtedly ineffectual collective of 'good' people who were supposed to put a final stop to war – that complicated phenomenon whose roots lie deep in the social fabric – chiefly by moral condemnation. I knew next to nothing definite about the Russian revolution, but my own modest experience as a medical orderly in the winter of 1918 was enough to make me think that a totally new and different permanent force had entered the arena: the revolutionary proletariat.

It seems that my knowledge was not enough to make me realize the full seriousness of the proletarian rising in the winter of 1918–19, only to show me how unseriously my obstreperous 'hero' took part in it. The initiative in this fight was taken by the proletarians; he cashed in. They didn't have to lose property in order to make them rebel; he got restitution. They were prepared to look after his interests; he betrayed theirs. They were the tragic figures, he the comic. All this, I realized on reading the play, had been perfectly evident to me, but I could not manage to make the audience see the revolution any differently from my 'hero' Kragler, and he saw it as something romantic. The technique of alienation was not yet open to me.

Reading Acts 3, 4, and 5 of *Drums in the Night* I felt such dissatisfaction that I thought of suppressing the play. The only thing that stopped me erecting a small funeral pyre was the feeling that literature is part of history, and that history ought not to be falsified, also a sense that my present opinions and capacities would be of less value without some knowledge of my previous ones – that is, presuming that there has been any improvement. Nor is suppression enough; what's false must be set right.

Admittedly I could not do much. The character of Kragler, the soldier, the petit-bourgeois, I couldn't touch. My comparative approval of his conduct had also to be preserved. Anyway, even the workers always find it easier to understand the petit-bourgeois who defends his own interests (however sordid these may be, and even if he is defending them against the workers) than the man who joins them for romantic reasons or out of a sense of guilt. However, I cautiously reinforced the other side. I gave the publican Glubb a nephew, a young worker who fell as a revolutionary during the November fighting. Though he could only be glimpsed in outline, somewhat filled in, however, thanks to the publican's scruples, this worker provided a kind of counterpart to the soldier Kragler.

The reader or spectator has then to be relied on to change his attitude to the play's hero, unassisted by appropriate alienations, from sympathy to a certain antipathy.

[From 'Bei Durchsicht meiner ersten Stücke' in GW *Schriften zum Theater*, pp. 945–7. Dated March 1954.]

Editorial Note on the Text

The original version of this play was written in the spring of 1919 and entitled *Spartakus*; no script of it has so far been found. The Brecht Archive has only the typescript of the version used for the Deutsches Theater production of December 1922, three months after the Munich première. The earliest known text is that published by Drei-Masken Verlag in Munich in 1922, which was also reissued twice by Propyläen-Verlag (i.e. Ullstein) in Berlin during the second half of the 1920s. Brecht used it for the first volume of his collected *Stücke* in 1953, with the extensive revisions outlined in his own retrospective note. This revised text was printed, with minor amendments, in the *Gesammelte Werke* of 1967 and is the basis of the present translation.

Three main versions are thus accessible: the 1922 publication, the script of December 1922, and the final text of 1953. The first describes the play as a 'Drama', the other two simply as a 'Play'. In the second the prostitute Augusta is for some reason called Carmen, though Augusta remains a nickname. At some earlier point the Bar in Act 4 seems to have been called 'The Red Grape' (or 'Raisin'): hence the nickname given to one of the waiter brothers in the final version. The confusion in the timing of the action (which is said to take place in November, though the Spartacist revolt and the battle for the Berlin newspaper offices actually occurred in January) was not cleared up till 1967, when a note appeared in GW saying, 'The action of the play now takes place in January 1919.' The most serious divergences between the different versions however occur in Acts 3, 4, and 5, and they represent a seemingly permanent dissatisfaction on Brecht's part with the second half of the play.

This is already on record in his diaries of 1920, even before our earliest version. 'I have rewritten the beginning of Act 3 of *Drums*,' he noted on 3 August, 'and the second (optional) ending to Act 4. . . . I've done four versions of Act 4 and three of Act 5. I've now got two endings, one comic, one tragic.' A little later he is 'dictating *Drums in the Night*. The third act is in the main good; the fourth a bastard, an abortion. . . .' Twenty-five diary pages later he is still at it:

nagging away at *Drums in the Night*. I'm drilling rock, and the drills are breaking. It's terribly hard to make this fourth act follow grandly and simply after the first three, at the same time carrying on the external tension of the third, which works pretty well, and bringing the internal transformation (in 15 minutes) forcefully home. What's more, the play's strong, healthy, untragic ending, which it had from the outset and for the sake of which it was written, is the only possible ending; anything else is too easy a way out, a weakly synthetic concession to romanticism. Here is a man apparently at an emotional climax, making a complete volteface; he tosses all pathos aside, tells his followers and admirers to stuff it, then goes home with the woman for whose sake he got involved in this extremely dangerous mess. Bed as final curtain. To hell with ideas, to hell with duty!

The contrast between this view of the play and the author's verdicts of 1928 and 1954 needs no stressing. Moreover, even by 1922 he had become less certain of the effectiveness of the third act, which seems to have gone badly at the première.

The detailed notes that follow show what passages Brecht cut or changed when he reviewed the 1922 text in the early 1950s. One or two minor amendments apart, the whole of the 1922 edition can be reconstructed from it. The script used by the Deutsches Theater is different yet again, particularly where Acts 4 and 5 are concerned. This would be too complicated to analyse in full, but an account of the more substantial changes follows the extracts from the 1922 edition. It will be found to shed light on one or two obscurities, notably the characters of Glubb and Laar.

VARIANT MATERIAL FROM THE 1922 PUBLISHED TEXT

The figures correspond to the annotations marked in the play. A figure in the play shows where a passage or phrase has been *cut* from the 1922 text. Figures with small arrows show the beginning and end of a passage or phrase which Brecht *rewrote* in the 1950s. In each case the original is given below. There were also a very few entirely new *additions*, which are marked by arrows without figures.

Where the 1922 text ends with a different punctuation mark from that shown in the play the next word should be correspondingly amended to start with a capital or lower-case letter, whichever is required.

A few very minor amendments have been overlooked for the sake of simplicity.

ACT 1
1 It looks as if the revolutionaries are confining their action to the suburbs.

ACT 2
2 *Then an ever-louder sound of stamping feet outside. Shouting. Whistling. Singing. Drumming. The stamping and shouting are prolonged.*
3 and whistling into the cafés.
4 And got drums out in the street?

ACT 3
5 Street Leading to the Slums
6 wife . . .
7 Oh god, there's sleep. There's schnaps. There's tobacco.
8 tobacco
9 down.
  MARIE: They'll be swimming in schnaps down there tonight.
10 THE ONE: They're drumming pretty hard.
  THE OTHER: Hell! In our district!
11 THE ONE: Feeling dizzy?
  THE OTHER: Haven't you got a slow puncture?
  THE ONE: You're getting smelly already.
12 slums
13 Now it's drunk, but once it had buttoned boots and could do what it wanted with a tart on the dance-floor. Still, it's cold now, I'd say, and has no very clear idea what to do. And shouldn't be left lying about.
14 Is it that sack of booze?
15 and that will be him who is frightened out of his wits. I've known him since he was a boy.
  MANKE: To the dogs and to Glubb's schnaps parlour, that's where he'll go. If he's lucky he'll be put up against a wall.
  BABUSCH: He'll choose the schnaps parlour. Or else he'll whistle them all up and when you hear a din towards dawn at the newspapers and there's something drumming in the night: there he goes!
16 MURK: Don't you see me?
  ANNA: Yes.

17 MURK *sobering up:* The linen has been bought and the flat is rented. And where do you want to go?

MANKE: Hear the rabble singing? Where does she want to go? We say: to the little filthy houses, that's where. You know, where one slithers on all the sick on the staircase. To the tumbledown black attics the wind whistles through.

ANNA: That's where I want to go.

MANKE: We're not beaten. The old beds with the rain coming in on them, and how's anyone to keep warm, the wind whistles through. Perhaps it's worse there. You go there! One disappears there. Those are the houses they are drumming in now. Stuffed full of sacks like this one, with no shirt on, and everything takes twenty or thirty years, the last years on this earth, they've never counted and yet your soul feels more at home there than anywhere else.

MURK: Father and Mother are fixing the wedding.

18 waited four years.

MURK: Who has no clean shirt on his body . . .

MANKE: And his skin is like a crocodile-hide!

MURK: Whom you failed to recognize, the way he looked.

MANKE: But the lily was still in her hand when he came.

ANNA: He is come who has

19 slums.

20 To the slums, the darkness, the nothingness?

ANNA: Yes. Into nothingness.

MURK: Nothing but a drunk man's dreams. Nothing but a woman's magazine story. Nothing but a snow of yesteryear.

ANNA: Nothing else . . .

MANKE: That's it: nothing else! She knows now: it's for nothing!

MURK:

21 What about the 'lily'? What about when no breath of wind gets to you and you're frightened out of your wits?

22 MURK: We packed him off. Bag and baggage.

ANNA: And they

23 was, packed off good and proper.

ANNA: And he was finished.

24 He's drunk.

25 Into the wind and I'm so drunk. Can't see my own hands, and she leaves me!

BABUSCH: Now I begin to get it, man. So that's the fish we're frying. That's the end of the Ride of the Valkyries now, my boy. The whole fishy ghost story's starting to turn horribly serious.

26 to the slums.

27 Take it home, do something for your immortal soul.

28 MANKE *drags Murk to his feet, spreads both his arms widely once more, says grandly:* The slums are

ACT 4

29 THE SCHNAPS DANCE

30 BABUSCH *at the window:* Has a man in artillery uniform been here?

GLUBB *pouring schnaps:* No, not here.

BABUSCH *over his shoulder:* He hasn't been here.

GLUBB: Is one supposed to be coming?

Babusch shrugs his shoulders.

GLUBB: Shall I tell him anything?

BABUSCH *looks at Anna, who shakes her head:* No, we'll come back.

Exeunt both.

MANKE: When they grab something it's schnaps, when they share something it's a bed, and when they produce something it's babies. My god, my god. When they had some schnaps in them, dear man, with those pale faces and trembling knees – *he imitates it* – and their nose in the air where it was raining, raining bullets, dear man. And a gun in the hand and a sticky feeling at the tips of the fingers, my boy!

BULLTROTTER: Freedom! Space! Air!

31 Marseillaise

32 , you bourgeois!

BULLTROTTER *throws a newspaper at him:* Where there's a horse there's horseshit. *They throw papers at one another.* Freedom!

MANKE:

33 So that's the sort you are?

34 BULLTROTTER: Riots! Strike! Revolution!

35 BULLTROTTER: But what's that wind?

36 BULLTROTTER: That's fine. He's got an artillery tunic on.

MANKE: A funny sort of casing. Are you laying an egg, then?

37 , turning up with the guns like that?

38 MANKE *goes across to him:* Well, what have you been up to, my boy? I know the type. A row in a bar, eh?

(AUGUSTA *continues:*)

39 MARIE: They took away his beloved he had waited four years
for. They drove to the Piccadilly Bar; he trotted the whole
way to the Piccadilly Bar behind the cab.

THE DRUNK MAN: Like a calf? What a story.

AUGUSTA: A love story?

KRAGLER: None that I know.

BULLTROTTER: Where do you belong? Belong to him?

MARIE: I just ran along with him.

MANKE: What are you running like a calf for?

40 THE DRUNK MAN: Is there a story?

BULLTROTTER: What do you mean, story?

THE DRUNK MAN: Or is it a gospel, perhaps? Give him some
schnaps, let him smoke and then he can tell it. *The door is
shut. Kragler stands against the wall. The others smoke and stare at
his mouth. Glubb wipes glasses.*

THE DRUNK MAN: Keep that door shut. It's only the
wind, brother, but there's wood between. There's wood
between.

KRAGLER *boasting, with sour humour:* I was in Africa ... The
sun's hot there. We shot up wogs, boy, and ... so on. We
were making roads too. We'd gone down there in cattle
trucks.

41 KRAGLER: Ah, Africa. *Silence.* The sun shrivelled your head up
like a dried fig, our brains were like figs, we shot up the
wogs, always in the belly, and worked on the roads and I'd
got a fly in my head, my friends, and no brains left and they
hit me on the head a lot.

BULLTROTTER: That's a true-life story. Well told. Drink up.
What came before that?

KRAGLER: Before that? I lay in a hole full of mud. Like a
corpse in polluted water. We pumped water out. We stared
at the time. It never moved. Then we stared at the sky, a
patch like an umbrella, dark as a puddle always, but anyway
we had the dropsy because the trench was always full. *He
drinks.*

42 AUGUSTA: About Africa! About Africa!

KRAGLER: Well, it never moved, nothing for us to do but
stink. We defended our homes, our native soil and the other
thing, and I defended the lot, the sky and the earth and the
water and – the lot.

MARIE: Andy! They call him Andy.

KRAGLER: Andy! They call me Andy. They used to call me

Andy. Thick green trees in the air, that's something I've seen. But not those four years.

GLUBB: You didn't see them, what of it?

KRAGLER: I defended and now and again somebody fell and I'd got a fly in my head, a fly, and that was my wife, only she wasn't that yet, she was innocent *drinks* and then came Africa.

BULLTROTTER *smiling broadly:* And the tarts down there, what were the tarts like?

KRAGLER: It was like an island. No letters, and chilly nights. *Opening his eyes.* All you people need do is chase cats off a wall! *Drinks.*

MARIE: How long did it last, how long?

KRAGLER: Three years. Three years, that's more than a thousand days. They held us under water, you see, like kittens in a bucket, they don't want to die. *Counting on his fingers.* I could have died the second day, or the tenth, or in twenty days, or in forty days ... But there was Anna, standing dawn after dawn behind the barracks, among the dogs.

THE DRUNK MAN: Didn't you desert?

KRAGLER *calmer:* The third time I deserted it went well, and I sang when it became too tough, and it went well and there I was. *He sits down, speaks more and more slowly and laboriously, drinks a lot; now he makes a break and says quite calmly:* You mustn't think I was sort of mean and imagined she went to the barracks in the morning and that was all she did. I'd worked out a plan how she was to get accustomed to me once more, because I'd become a ghost. That's a fact. *He drinks. Sound of wind. The drunk man groans with the suspense.*

KRAGLER *calmly:* She wasn't at home when I came.

GLUBB: No, that she wasn't. Truly not.

BULLTROTTER: Well, then?

THE DRUNK MAN: Had she gone? Where was she?

KRAGLER: The schnaps was drunk and the wogs were dead and the umbrella had been rolled up and the fly, the fly had flown off. *Stares ahead.* I defended him. He sent schnaps for the cattle and he sent the umbrella, and he let the fly live so we shouldn't be bored. *Points with his finger as if he could see him.* And now he's going round in the sun, the other fellow. And now he's lying in bed, and you take off your hat when he arrives and he takes the skin off your back and my wife's lying in his bed.

BULLTROTTER *with the paper:* Somebody stole her, eh?

GLUBB: They stole my bicycle.

MANKE *passes his hand across his throat:* I'll say you're patient, mate!

AUGUSTA: Didn't you strangle her like a cat?

MARIE: They went off with her. He just trotted along after.

KRAGLER *drinks:* So I went quite cold when I heard that, and my mind was a blank. And even now my pulse is normal when I think about it; feel for yourselves. *Stretches his hand out, drinks with the other one.* I looked for her and she knew me too, even though my face was once like milk and blood and she said something to me. Give me another glass.

THE DRUNK MAN: Go on. What did she say?

KRAGLER: Yes, she said. *He drinks.* It's all over. *Silence. He is still absent-mindedly feeling his pulse.*

GLUBB: Oh, you'll forget in time.

THE DRUNK MAN: What did you do then?

KRAGLER: Booze away, I'm going. Keep it up, I'm getting out. Jig and drink and drop dead at the right moment. *He is getting noisy.* Me for instance, Africa's in my blood, a nasty malady. A fly in my head, a horsefly, dance up, give me schnaps, they don't know the half of it. Let's have a tune, they're going to know.

MANKE: It's bad, what you've been through. Drink all you like, mate.

BULLTROTTER: Booze yourself silly. He's got a feeling like a corpse, he'll live longer than himself. Last week we had a story from Merseburg . . .

THE DRUNKEN MAN: Is she still alive? *He has started the nickelodeon.* Not possible.

KRAGLER *hums the tune, seizes Augusta, jogs round with her:* March, march, double march!

43 KRAGLER *who is being given schnaps by Augusta upstage:* Is it a relief? Is he paper, isn't he made of flesh? Console yourself, brother, just say: Not possible. Can you hear, brother Schnaps-vat, can you hear the wind? Hop, sister prostitute! Hop, brother Red! I say unto you, you mustn't wait. What is a swine before the Lord? Nothing. Drink yourselves silly, nothing to do with the swine, then you won't notice.

GLUBB: What are you shouting like that for?

KRAGLER: Who's paying here? Who's responsible for the music here? There's always music, isn't there? I've got the

fly! I just need schnaps and it'll drown itself. Can we do
away with the army or God? Can we do away with suffering
and the torments the devil has learnt from the human race?
No, we can't do away with them, but we can drink. You can
drink schnaps and sleep even on paving-stones. They that
sleep, please note, shall find everything of service to them;
that's in the catechism, it must be true.

44 Don't let in the ghosts. They are frozen.

45 Did you say injustice, brother Red? What sort of word is that?
Injustice! Make yourselves at home on our planet, it's cold
here and rather dark, Red, and no time for injustice, the world's
too old for the millennium and schnaps is cheaper and heaven
has been let, my friends. *Goes upstage humming, puts money in the
nickelodeon, which still plays quick short pieces only.*

BULLTROTTER *has been drinking quietly:* What's one to say to
that? Cuffs! Cuffs!

MANKE *gets up:* But your wife's looking for you, man.

KRAGLER *dancing on his own:* Trot! Trot! Double march! *Hums.*
A dog went to the kitchen to find a bone to chew.

MANKE *smoking:* He's dancing around with his horsefly now.

AUGUSTA: Do you like that tobacco?

GLUBB: Look here, all you may do is drink schnaps.

MANKE: We're smoking as well.

THE DRUNK MAN: You're the revolutionary all right. We
know you and your speeches. They poured your schnaps
down the lavatory, you were selling schnaps.

GLUBB *still busy with the glasses, coldly:* I'd more under the floor-
boards. And it's not because the schnaps went but because
of the human hands pouring it down the lavatory.

KRAGLER *blinking and as if he were waking up:* Anna! Anna!

BULLTROTTER *crows:* Cuffs! You ought to have pinched some
cuffs, mate.

GLUBB: I was standing in the yard, it was night-time. It was
just raining, I looked around, then I suppose it struck me.
And now I'm for drinking and I sing.

KRAGLER:
The cook picked up his chopper
And cut that dog in two.

MARIE: What can we do? We're nobodies. A lot of them say:

46 MANKE: Your wife's certainly looking for you, man.

THE DRUNK MAN *has climbed up on the table and is looking out into
the night at the city:* Drink, will you?

47 LAAR: There was a fellow who just happened to have some
money on him, see.

48 beast?

Laar goes off at the back.

GLUBB *to Kragler, who is much calmer:* Just drink! There are a
few people drumming outside and now they've even begun
to shoot. One can hear it quite clearly. If one's prepared to
shut up for a moment. They're shooting for you. Yes,
heaven and hell are making a revolution, man, and you
shouldn't even be drinking schnaps. You've suffered a slight
injustice. Say yes and stomach it.

49 *Places a glass behind him, calmly:* To the machine-guns with you!

SOME: To the newspaper offices!

GLUBB: Yes, you'll have to publish a paper.

KRAGLER: It's pretty far to the Piccadilly Bar.

MANKE *with a cigar between his teeth, takes his coat off:* If it's too
far, there's no need for anyone to let himself be trodden
on.

GLUBB *sees the man stand there in shirtsleeves:* Go on, put clean
shirts on your decaying skins so nobody will notice them!
Are stories just fodder? God alive, a slight injustice! Eat
salad and drink kirsch! *Starts up the nickelodeon.* Yes, you
people are a bit drowned in brandy, you've been a bit
pushed about by rifle-butts,

50 AUGUSTA: You cowards let us starve, then say Amen. A glass
of schnaps! *Tumult, consternation.* Look at me. I'm no good
and I've not had it good. Just look at me. I'm called Augusta.

GLUBB: And you've got syphilis.

NEWSPAPER WOMAN *in the background:* Papers!

51 State of siege! Revolution!

BULLTROTTER: Give us a paper. That's something for us.

NEWSPAPER WOMAN *shrilly:*

52 *Bends down.* Is it a joke? To the barricades with the ghost!
Stands firmly, draws a deep breath. A clean end is better than
schnaps. It's not a joke. Better disappear than sleep.

BULLTROTTER *leaps on the table:*

53 *Glubb shuts the cupboard full of glasses, dries his hands.*

MANKE: Let's go, Augusta. Do or die.

BULLTROTTER: And how about your distillery, schnaps-
seller?

GLUBB: The rats'll take it over.

KRAGLER *on a chair, tinkering with the lamp, a prehistoric survival:* They're whistling again, my friends. On top in the morning or like drowned kittens in the roadway.

THE OTHERS *shout:* On top in the morning, Andy!

KRAGLER *puts out the light:* Or like drowned kittens!

MANKE: Forward, Augusta!

54 KRAGLER *gets down:* I'm a corpse, you're welcome to it. *Angrily.* This way with you, over the top with you, to the newspaper offices with us. *The others follow him.*

THE DRUNK MAN *following behind:* Wash me, Lord, that I may become white! Wash me that I may become white as snow!

ACT 5

55 They stormed the barracks a bit after two.

ANNA: He won't come now.

BABUSCH: Now they're marching to the newspaper offices. Yes,

56 BABUSCH: The last time, somewhere round four, it looked to me as if he'd gone down, he was swimming powerfully but didn't surface.

ANNA:

57 ANNA: How far gone the year is, and how red the moon. Like in one's sleep. I sit here on a stone, and the red moon, and the year's far gone.

BABUSCH: They're drumming again down there.

58 The streets wake up wherever they go. Fever falls through the roofs. The houses become restless.

59 It's fever,

60 Shouldn't you go, though?

61 I've forgotten it now. I suppose it's hopeless.

62 wife

63 GLUBB: She's earth too, my lad; have a look from down there.

64 THE ONE: They've got into the newspaper buildings.

THE OTHER: Artillery's being brought up.

THE ONE: Things will change now.

THE OTHER: They're far too slow, far too few.

THE ONE: Far more are on the way.

THE OTHER: Far too late.

They have passed, but behind them are many marching past to the newspaper buildings.

65 Is his hand still in his trouser pocket?

66 They're marching, they're screaming, they're waving.

67 your lack of hair may be due to the unflattering light.

68 Your fingers are black too: show us.

69 I've known you for just four hours.

70 ANNA: Is it seven?

KRAGLER: Come over to me, Anna.

71 ANNA: So gracious, are you?

GLUBB: Wouldn't you rather have a Scotch?

KRAGLER: Over here to me.

ANNA: Is it because of the catechism?

KRAGLER: Anna.

AUGUSTA: Aren't you a soldier, love?

ANNA: Are you whistling me again?

GLUBB: You must milk a cow while it's still warm.

MANKE: In your army tunic, man?

KRAGLER: My voice is gone with the shouting but my knife's still there, you!

Glubb places himself in front of Anna, the tall shadows of the marchers in the background fall across the buildings, and snatches of the Marseillaise are borne on the wind.

GLUBB: Yes, she looks like sicked-up milk, it's not very pleasant.

72 and it was the same with smoking a cigar. Which was a pity.

Kragler is silent.

GLUBB: Won't you come along for a bit, brother gunner?

Kragler is silent.

MANKE: What's he staring for in that queer way? Is he laying another egg?

73 ANNA: You can go, Andy, go on.

AUGUSTA: Now watch him light his pipe again.

ANNA: Go on, go on, I don't want to see you again, you've got a black face, go away, I'm glad.

74 *Kragler shakes his head.*

Augusta gives a horse-laugh.

GLUBB: The Eternal Feminine is drawing him upwards.

KRAGLER *looking at her:* Come, Anna.

GLUBB: Couldn't you just step into the water and have a bath?

KRAGLER: I'm all cold.

AUGUSTA *upstage:* Only a few left now, they're hurrying, they're disappearing in no time. Oh, the newspapers, come on to the newspapers!

GLUBB *to Anna:* Can't *you* get this wild beast down to the newspaper buildings?

75 Everybody is top man in his own skin.

76 GLUBB: So you've no sympathy for these people?

KRAGLER: God help me, stone me, no. What kind of face is that, Anna? Have I got to defend myself to you too? They poured your kirsch down the lavatory, but I've got my woman back. Anna, come.

GLUBB: They could give me six kirsch distilleries, I'd spit in their face because of the kirsch, I'd rip out their bowels because of the kirsch, I'd burn down their houses because of two barrels of kirsch, and smoke as I did it.

KRAGLER: Anna! *To Glubb:* Look! You'll go to the wall and smoke as you do it. I see you against the wall before dawn, can't you see how grey and glassy he looks as he stands against the wall? Can't you smell it in him? What's to become of you all, go home!
Augusta laughs.

GLUBB: Oh, they'll get little wounds in their throat or their chest, all very tidy, they'll get labels with numbers stuck on them when they're stiff, not like drowned kittens, more like victims of a slight injustice.

KRAGLER: Drop it.

77 What'll that do to your chest?

GLUBB *looks coldly at him:* The rats'll take it over.
Across the bridge comes a dolled-up woman.

AUGUSTA: You come from down by the newspaper offices?

THE WOMAN: Yes, down that way.

MANKE: Are they fighting there, how's it going?

THE WOMAN: Nobody knows.

AUGUSTA: Have they taken the newspaper buildings yet, then?

THE WOMAN *raises her arm, there is a distant screaming:* Is that the artilleryman the Friedrichstadt people have been waiting for?

AUGUSTA: Oh, have they been waiting?

THE WOMAN: Yes, there'll be a lot of dead men today. *Exit hurriedly.*

AUGUSTA: You hear, they're going into the attack!

KRAGLER: Anna.

AUGUSTA: Would it be too much bother for the gentleman?

KRAGLER *to Anna:* What are you looking like that for, damn it?

78 Devil!

79 That's the attack going in.

80 And I love you.
81 Now they're being blown open like fishes.
82 the moon's fading out, and
83 The night blows away like black smoke.
84 The Half-Dead Suitor
85 A Man Works his Passage; The Thorn in the Flesh or A Tiger at Dawn.
86 *But the man goes to the woman and goes home.*
87 It gets cold, so early in the year.
88 *Like a little flag, the first red appears in the smoky grey dawn sky above.*

THE DEUTSCHES THEATER ACTING VERSION

A copy of the Deutsches Theater's typescript is in the Brecht-Archive in Berlin. It is annotated in pencil (not by Brecht) with a full cast list, a sketch plan of the stage arrangement for Act 1 and other production details, and was presumably used for the production of 20 December 1922. This was directed by Otto Falckenberg, who had also directed the Munich première three months earlier. Kragler was played by Alexander Granach, Glubb by Heinrich George, Babusch by Paul Graetz, Anna by Blandine Ebinger.

The introductory note, which differs from that to the 1922 edition, has been given above on p. 394. The Piccadilly Bar becomes the Grünes Haus (though at one point it has been changed back in pencil). Augusta becomes Carmen; she is sometimes alluded to as Augusta, and then objects, presumably because the name is not fancy enough. Kragler on his first entry is described as 'a short, thick-set man', and there is no reference to his old blue uniform. Otherwise the main changes in the first two acts are confined to cuts.

There is also a long cut at the start of Act 3, which now begins with Anna's entry. The stage direction for this begins: *Clouds racing by. The street runs from upstage left to downstage right. From the left come* . . . The street leads over a bridge, not along a barrack wall. The rest of the act is virtually unchanged.

Act 4 starts thus:

Glubb, a pale desiccated individual with a little red goatee, sings 'The Ballad of the Dead Soldier' to guitar accompaniment. Two drunks – a farmer and a sinister man, both drunk – stare at his fingers. Manke the waiter, a tall fellow, is dancing with Carmen, a blowsy creature. A small square man called Bulltrotter is reading the paper. The drunks keep on laughing.

BULLTROTTER: When the landlord's drunk and singing like a primadonna, rattling the glasses, then everything's cockeyed. Look at that tart dancing with a shark like that between her legs: how the hell is a fellow to digest his paper? You see your arse through it. A god-forsaken bar in the back of beyond, where the waiter shuffles round the dance-floor looking like a shark and the landlord serves him when he isn't singing hymns.

BULLTROTTER *putting his feet on the table:* The revolution's on the way! Freedom's here!

GLUBB: You're spoiling my fake marbling. *Goes on singing.*

THE DRUNK MAN *to Laar:* Scum and Lazarus. I'm scum, you're Lazarus. Heaven, arseholes and bits of string. None of them know a bloody thing.

MANKE: When they grab something it's schnaps, when they share something it's a bed, and when they produce something it's babies. Augusta, come across my knee and pour some brandy into me!

BULLTROTTER: That's all talk. Pure grand opera. Where are you saying it? In a schnaps bar.

MANKE: Where there's a horse there's horse-shit; that's the way, Augusta.

CARMEN: Make up your mind. It's Carmen, or you can dance by yourself. Vulgar beast!

MANKE: Ah yes, Augusta, they're practising the Marseillaise, in four parts with tremolo. The bourgeois. Well done, landlord.

THE DRUNK MAN: The bourgeois. *Coming forward:* The bourgeois is a necessity, just like the Gents. If it weren't for those two institutions public life would be simply immoral.

BULLTROTTER: Change the record. Shut up, landlord! I saw the fellows earlier. And they've got a look in their eye, mates, or rather landlord, just like before going over the top. You know what I mean?

MANKE: I've a notion. When they had some schnaps in them, dear man, with those pale faces in the air where it was raining, raining bullets, dear man. And guns in their hands and a sticky feeling at the tips of the fingers, my boy!

BULLTROTTER: That's how they look, that's how they looked just now, just a minute or two ago.

It then continues much as before up to Kragler's entrance, which is slightly different in that the rumble of guns is not heard, and no reference is made to his artillery tunic. His account of his experiences in Africa is also very much as in the 1922 edition (see notes 38–40 above), up to where the nickelodeon plays and he begins dancing with Carmen/Augusta. Then comes an expanded version of Laar's cryptic remarks about the fir trees, (which in both other texts are put later):

GLUBB: Quiet: the farmer's got something to say, the stone is going to speak. Watch out! He's always opening his mouth; now he's made it.

LAAR: But I had land and animals and a wood, simply fir trees, little fir trees.

GLUBB *excitedly watching him:* Listen to the stone speaking, he's speaking now.

LAAR: Nowadays I'm drunk all the time. There was a fellow who just happened to have some money on him, see?
Silence. Kragler sits by the nickelodeon, which has stopped playing. Carmen has her arm round him.

BULLTROTTER: And you sold, you beast?

LAAR: Yes, I did. I didn't want to deliver, and I thought . . . I thought I'd sell instead. It's just a lot of paper, and I handed over my land and my animals, I did, for paper and some schnaps in my gullet. The wife and kids are living like pigs. I live here. We're peaceable folk and we get on; the music plays and the schnaps flows and we say, 'Yes, yes, Amen.' A small schnaps, please.

GLUBB: A small schnaps, please!

MANKE: Can't you get your land back?

GLUBB:
They'll have the whole damn lot –
Wife, land and all you've got.
Let them swallow it . . . etc.

BULLTROTTER: What a world!

CARMEN: It isn't possible.

THE DRUNK MAN: Looks as though it is, mate, so close your eyes. Close your hand, mate.

GLUBB: Isn't it possible? Isn't he flesh and blood? Is he just paper? . . .

Glubb's song 'They'll have the whole damn lot' recurs below. (The songs or jingles in the other two texts are omitted.) Glubb also has more to say about his particular motive for joining the revolutionaries. After The Drunk Man's remark in the 1922 edition (note 45 above), he says:

> Don't insult me. Don't insult anyone, mate. Yes, they poured my schnaps away, just two little barrels; I'd more under the floorboards but it went down the drain because of a regulation on a bit of paper. Mind my words. Since that day I have[n't] slept properly, not because the schnaps went but because of the human hands that poured it down the gutter. Because that's the moment I decided the world was all wrong.

Needless to say there is no hint of this (not even by the Drunk Man) in the 1953 text, where Glubb is relatively silent. Glubb is also given a verse speech, more or less in lieu of his two longer speeches (48 and 49 above). He *climbs on a chair:*

> You who have drowned in schnaps –
> You whose skin is covered in rashes –
> You whom they thrust back with bayonets –
> You whom they gave guns and swords to and turned into
>   murderers –
> You who have always been beaten and spat upon –
> You who were never loved
> Come here and see, your hour is here
> And you shall enter into the kingdom!

Then, as the bullets whistle and the woman selling newspapers appears calling her headlines about the Spartacists, it is he rather than Kragler who leads them all into the street:

> GLUBB: Just keep calm. Come along, all of you, link arms. Join all the others and face up to the soldiers and just let them shoot. And the story will be told wherever there are people who have forgotten their own . . .

These changes in the character and weight of the role persist throughout the next act, and may of course be connected with the powerful talents of Heinrich George, the actor in question. There is none of the disillusioned cynicism of the other versions.

In Act 5 the opening stage direction is again changed:

A street corner in the slums. Autumn night. Big red moon. Left, the low pale wall of a house. In the right background a wide wooden bridge, rising towards the rear. Sitting on a stone, left, Anna, who is still wearing her light-coloured dress. Babusch is walking up and down. The wind is blowing. Distant shots and shouting are heard. Rapid tempo.

The start of the act is basically as in the other two versions, though it is somewhat expanded both before and after Kragler's entry. Then, when Anna has told him she is expecting a child his next stage direction (*Sways . . . as if trying out walking*) is made to run on:

Then turns and looks round at Anna. Anna sits on the stone and looks up at him with as loving a look as she can muster, while he groans and shuts his eyes and draws a deep breath. Manke and the drunk man approach from the bridge. Glubb squats there, waiting. Behind them Marie slowly comes nearer.

Kragler's attack on Anna with clods of earth is again expanded, mainly with additional rhetoric that represents no change of substance. An extra stage direction describes the scene as the men hold Kragler down and Babusch crosses the battlefield (p. 110):

At this point Marie is standing protectively in front of Anna, with her arms round her. Glubb has stood up by the bridge. Laar is sitting in the roadway, picking dirt out of his hair. Manke is holding Kragler by the collar . . .

Babusch's ensuing speech is likewise expanded, and concludes:

It isn't a vast idea. The nights are chilly in November. You're out to liberate the world, by all means do so, it's an excellent thing; but tell the woman that you want no part of her. Tell her straight to go home if she can. Don't give us any purple passages, no more speeches, it's a small and perfectly simple human situation.

The emphasis on the 'idea' is peculiar to this version. The two Men are cut, with their conversation about how the attack on the newspaper offices is going. Then from Carmen/Augusta's appeal to Kragler to come down there (p. 110), to his final refusal with the speech beginning 'Fling stones at me,' (p. 112) there is an entirely new section, enlarging on the 'idea'. Thus:

BABUSCH: Say yes or no. Or else you're a coward.
GLUBB: Tell her, Andy. Try to think what you want. Don't tell her all that quickly. It's as well to say yes or no. Have you got your idea inside you? It needn't be in the catechism. Tell her. She'll go away, she's not bad-looking.

THE DRUNK MAN: I'll marry her, let's have her. Because none of them know a bloody thing.

BABUSCH: They don't. Know a thing, I mean. That's to say men don't. Dogs do.

GLUBB: Don't listen to him, Andy. Watch the woman. He's making fun, he has rotten teeth. Watch the woman. Andy! Have you still got your idea? You have to sense it in your throat.

MANKE: What nonsense are you talking? He said, 'To the newspaper buildings'; he's going to the newspaper buildings. Why is he hanging around with his hands in his pockets, trying to get out of it? Come along!

CARMEN *on the bridge:* They're coming! Stop quarrelling. They're coming, lots of them, the streets are black with them, as if they'd gone rotten.

BABUSCH: *He's* got one, Kragler, I'm quite sure. I know the story of his schnaps. But you haven't, though you did have. You've got a gullet full of phrases.

GLUBB: Andy, it's only the devil, but best say yes or no.
The others start concentrating on events offstage, where it seems that masses of people are approaching with drumming and shouts.

BABUSCH: Don't let them make a hero of you, Kragler. If it's what you want it isn't so tragic. Do whatever you really want. Everybody is top man in his own skin.
[There is a blank space in the typescript here.]

MANKE *over his shoulder:* Why doesn't he say something? Has he fallen on his face?

CARMEN: More and more of them are coming, and the whole lot's going to the newspaper offices. Do come along! Isn't it settled?

GLUBB *somewhat hoarsely:* And I'd like to know why you don't say something too. Are you so feeble? It's irritating, your not saying anything. Here we are, charging through the streets like bulls and finding nothing, and you're not with us. God has tossed you your woman, half torn to pieces and with a body full of strange fruit, all you need do is step over her; are you stuck? I tell you, if you're pure a hundred women won't be able to touch you. They're less than an idea, they only mislead you. The swine poured my schnaps in the gutter; it made my head go queer, and no wonder. They can give me a hundred schnaps factories instead of those two small barrels of mine, and I'll still spit in their faces for the schnaps that was

washed away and will never come back. I'll tear out their guts
for that schnaps. I'll burn down their houses for that schnaps
that went down the drain. I'm telling you, Andy, the idea is
what matters.

KRAGLER *angry and obstinate*: No, it isn't.

BABUSCH: Bravo! No, it isn't! When a woman's going to
pieces it isn't the idea that matters.

GLUBB: Well? Do you want to stay back here?

*Offstage crowds are marching by. The wind brings snatches of the
Marseillaise and military band music.*

Kragler is silent.

In all this concluding section of the play Anna now gets given
nothing to say, nor is there any mention of Kragler's knife as in the
1922 edition. His 'fling stones at me' speech ends 'It's a waste of
time, believe me, it's nickelodeon stuff and you're all drunk and
that way you're going to hell.'

GLUBB: Andy, it's not a waste of time. God forbid that you
found it one. There's a thin red flame shooting sharply out of
the human breast and scorching the world.

KRAGLER: What for?

GLUBB: At the innermost heart of the world, racing at the speed
of our planet – a man blown like a leaf, lonely, ice-cold, and
without a home, a man who goes on strike and the world falls
apart.

BABUSCH: Don't be bamboozled; he's got a pigeon's egg in
his head. His talk is all newspaper articles, his ideas are grand
opera. Go to bed. Don't be drunk. Mind the cold wind – it's
November 9th – and go home.

KRAGLER: I was drunk. I'm sober now. It's a waste of
time.

GLUBB: Heaven and hell are full of revolution, and you are
going to bed! Smash your head against the bridge! Jump in
the water and float with the ice; but don't go home!

BABUSCH: You've no coat and it's freezing, Andy. November
nights are cold, and it's nearly morning. Four years is a long
time. Take your woman with you.

GLUBB: Let her lie, let the woman lie. Let her lie where she's
lying on the stones. She's like grass in the wind, she's not
there any more and she doesn't know where she belongs. In
four times four years her face will have faded, and we'll all be
dead by then and wondering where to go next.

BULLTROTTER: The whole lot have gone past, pretty well. We're last, and you're still hanging back.

CARMEN: They're last, and they're still hanging back.

GLUBB: And we're hanging back. He'll never let her lie, the world will roll on, and they'll let the schnaps go down the gutter and nothing'll ever change. O Andy, come with us. We're setting off into the dark, into our most crucial hour. Don't abandon us. What can we do with the schnaps in our heads if there are so few of us? What will the beast do if we're beaten? I've known you for only four hours, yet in that time whole skies full of stars have floated away and kingdoms have surrendered. I've known you for four ages; oh, don't disappoint me.

Silence.

Why do I have to stand here at a street corner in the dark after all those years, so they can shoot me tomorrow? Wrestling with you for your soul, and my hands not strong enough? Look: none of these people are any help to me.

KRAGLER *calmly:* We all know a lot of unfortunates go under, and if it's in our power we give a hand. But I'm nearly done for myself and must fight for dear life. My girl's with child.

GLUBB: Is that all you have to say?

CARMEN: Coward! Coward! He's shaking like a jelly because he heard shots. He isn't coming with us, you bet, he's going to take cover. In her body, which has already got something in it.

KRAGLER *calmly:* Don't you think it takes rather more to go home now and tell the hyenas 'I want no part of it', and say to the sharks as they swim round under the red moon hunting for corpses 'I've got some procreating to do'? More than to run along after you lot yelling something I don't believe in?

THE DRUNK MAN: Look at the old blood-orange! Sh! Quiet! Don't shoot, look at the sky!

KRAGLER: Go home too. All one has to do is what one wants. Because one mustn't do what the others want. And I want to go home. That's all I wanted. I ought to know. *Very calm.* I can't go on. *Silence.*

GLUBB: I don't know what to say to you. There's nothing in my mouth that would fit you.

KRAGLER: They poured your schnaps into the shit, brandy-seller, and they turned your farm into paper, Laar. But I've got my woman back.

After Glubb's 'So you've no sympathy for these people', etc.
(p. 420) (his following remarks having been transposed as above)
they move more or less straight on as in the 1922 edition to
Carmen/Augusta's 'Then that was all lies, Africa and so on?' and
to an extended version of Manke's 'The gentleman was bellowing
like a stockbroker'. Right up to the attack on Anna by Laar and
Manke (p. 113) the only substantial differences lie in Anna's silence
and the absence of any clue as to how the fighting is going. This
is given only when the shooting starts after Glubb has extricated
Anna. The final section which follows is a good deal longer, but
the changes are unimportant until everybody begins moving to the
bridge. Then:

> GLUBB: If he wants to go, let him. Don't stop him. Let him get
> into bed, we're fighting for him. Let them all do as they want,
> don't press them. He shouted for us, he went with us. There
> are so many of us, allow him to feel tired. We've got the room,
> we can accommodate lots of them. Admit him too, he still
> belongs to us.
>
> KRAGLER *laughs raucously:* You people almost drowned at first
> with weeping at my story, and now you want to drag me down
> to the newspapers to get shot. Just because you've stuffed
> your heads with newspapers and novelettes, because you can't
> get grand opera out of your system. I barely managed to get
> my own wife; am I now supposed to liberate all yours? Free
> my neck so I can hang a hurdy-gurdy round it? And I simply
> washed my shirt in your tears. Ha ha ha ha! My flesh is to rot in
> the gutter so that your idea can come out on top! Are you drunk?
>
> CARMEN: What nonsense is he talking? Come on! They've
> retreated. We'll still be in time for the attack!
>
> BULLTROTTER: It's about time, damn you!
>
> GLUBB *with simplicity and grandeur:* Tonight everybody must be
> out on the street. Tonight it will happen. Come with me, we
> must stick together now. Take each other by the hand and
> run for all you're worth. That's the way!
>
> *They run up the slope and vanish over the bridge. Glubb can still be
> heard, singing:*

> They'll have the whole damn lot –
> Wife, land and all you've got.
> Let them swallow it,
> They'll get no benefit
> The kingdom must be ours.

BABUSCH *flaps along after him:* There'll be heavy gunfire over Berlin in a quarter of an hour's time.
Exit across the bridge.

KRAGLER *piqued:* All right, go off to your newspaper buildings. Do yourselves in! If you won't let a man help you.
He throws dirt after them. Anna tries to come to him, but he thrusts her off and doesn't look her in the eyes.

ANNA: Andy! *She has sat down.* I must go home, Andy. I'm not going to have one. I'm not going to have a baby.

Kragler's long last speech, which follows, is basically the same as in the other two versions, including the anomalous mention of 'so early in the year'. Among the passages added are 'The shouting and that red moon they hoisted over the newspaper buildings: all of it's to swindle the people!', and

Am I a baritone? Ha ha ha! Were you aiming to wash your dirty faces with tears once again? Did you want a swollen pregnant body floating down to the weir under the red moon? Was I myself to die in the newspaper buildings for you? Every evening? Did you want to have a good cry? Well, I'm going to bed. Would you like to help them? Rip the phrases from their throats! *Drumbeat.* Wash your own shirt! *Drumbeat.* Hang, hang yourselves if you don't get ahead!

Finally, in lieu of 'Very drunken and infantile' comes 'You can all stuff it. I'm the lover.'

IN THE JUNGLE OF CITIES

(1) The play is set in an unreal, chilly Chicago. Shlink wears a long dirty yellow costume down to his ankles, picturesquely blackened hair, and a black tuft on his chin.

George Garga is like A. Rimbaud in appearance. He is essentially a German translation into American from the French.

(2) Towards the end of *Jungle*

Everything performed in front of a cyclorama. At the back all the actors not immediately involved sit in a dusty light, following the script. When Jane Garga dies she drops hers, and so on.

(3) A play

Chicago

The timber dealer Shlink, a Malay (Wegener's type), fights a war of annihilation with the younger George Garga (Granach's type), during the course of which both reveal their most extreme human characteristics. By means of an appearance of passivity the man Shlink slashes through the ties binding young George Garga to the world round him and makes him fight a desperate war of liberation against the steadily thickening jungle of Shlink's intrigues against him. Shlink's timber business and Garga's family are among those annihilated. Increasingly isolated, more and more tightly entangled, the two go into the woods to fight it out. In the final conflict, which is fought with utter dedication, George Garga regains solid ground; he breaks off the fight (which was the man Shlink's final sensation) and takes over his timber business in the great city of Chicago.

The events dealt with are concrete ones; the fight for the timber business, the family, a marriage, the fight for personal freedom. There are not many characters, no walking-on parts.

[From Bertolt Brecht: *Im Dickicht der Städte*. Erstfassung und Materialien. Edited by Gisela E. Bahr. Suhrkamp, Frankfurt, 1968, pp. 134, 136-7. Paul Wegener and Alexander Granach were prominent German actors of the time.]

PROGRAMME NOTE TO THE 1922 TEXT

The judicial proceedings to clarify the *Jane Garga murder mystery* led to the unmasking of one of those *sinister affairs in Chinatown* in Chicago which are so irresponsibly exploited by the press. A *Malayan timber merchant's fishing expedition* in a lending library, the almost total *ruination* of an immigrant *family* of French descent, the *mysterious lynching of the Malay*.

The play before you provides a possibly somewhat rough piece of theatrical carpentry whose raw material would certainly interest a wider public. There are a fair number of gaps in it. It omits even points which the proceedings cleared up, such as the *Malayan murderer's crimes*, thanks to which he regained possession of his *timber business donated to the Salvation Army*, and which characterized his flight into the yellow swamps with George Garga as an act of fear of the *lynch law of the respectable population*. Others remained obscure, and will no doubt always remain so. The *fate of Mae Garga*, her whereabouts, her motives for abandoning a family she had cared for for many years, have never been cleared up.

The present stage text is primarily intended to make theatrical material of *certain remarkable incidents* whose originals in real life appear to have taken place in the gloomy September of 1914 in *Chicago's Chinatown*, and whose consequences will no doubt be recalled from the newspapers. Accordingly only extracts are given of the few conversations that concern us here (for this unusual and most horrific story reposes only on a small number of conversations, whose substance was difficult and expensive to get at). They consist, making allowance for some clarifications and *improbabilities* such as are *inevitable* to the drama and for a perhaps over-*romantic embroidery* of the events due to stage requirements, simply in the most important sentences uttered here at a specific point on the globe's surface at specific moments in *the history of mankind*.

[Ibid., pp. 9–10. Brecht instructed that the italicized words should be shouted from behind the curtain before the start of the play, in imitation of newspaper sellers' cries.]

SYNOPSIS *(incomplete)*

i. A Malay called C. Shlink appears in the life of George Garga and for no known reason starts a fight. He tries Garga out to establish his fighting qualities, then starts by annihilating his economic existence.

ii. George Garga fights back.

iii. Shlink gives up his property so as to fight on equal terms. He thereby arouses the interest of Marie Garga, his enemy's sister.

iv. Garga abandons his family so as not to be hampered in the fight. Shlink moves into the vacant space.

v. Garga has vanished. Shlink has summoned up his reserves.

vi. Garga reappears, determined to exploit Shlink's fighting mood to further his own and his sister's objectives.

vii. Shlink is ready to follow out Garga's instructions.

viii. Garga tries to dig in behind his family. This results in the Garga family's total liquidation. Garga himself disappears provisionally into prison, but not unprovided with weapons.

[Ibid., p. 137, with the suggested date 1923–4.]

A STATEMENT

At one or two points in my play *Jungle* a character quotes verses by Rimbaud and Verlaine. In the script these passages are marked as quotations by means of inverted commas. Apparently the stage has no technique by which to express quotation marks. If it had, then a considerable number of other favourite works would become possibly more palatable for literary scholars but pretty intolerable for the audience. In view of the difficulty of their craft, those currently concerned with the manufacture of plays are unlikely, I fear, to have time either now or in the next ten years to sit back and think about such matters. Interested parties from the world of scholarship are accordingly invited to ring back in eleven years or so. (It can be divulged here and now that if the drama is to progress at all it will progress surely and serenely over the dead bodies of the scholars.)

['Eine Feststellung', from GW *Schriften zum Theater*, p. 969. This appeared in the *Berliner Börsen-Courier* of 4 November 1924, after an article by Herwarth Walden in *Die Republik* of 31 October complaining of Brecht's borrowings. There were statements under the same heading by the Rimbaud translator Hans Jacob, siding with Walden, and by Herbert Ihering, pooh-poohing such revelations.]

PROLOGUE TO 'JUNGLE'

What was new was a type of man who conducted a fight without enmity but with hitherto unheard of (i.e. undepicted) methods, together with his attitude to the family, to marriage, to his fellow-humans in general, and much else – probably too much. That wasn't, however, what people regard as new. The sort of thing they regard as new is the machine, in other words something they can use without having made it or being able to understand it. In literature the last thing to strike them as new is the idea, say, that a husband ought not to treat his wife as a doll, or that marriage is dangerous, or that a cart-driver can be just as tragic as a more highly placed individual, indeed more so in that he doesn't know his way around so well.

To those with this culinary outlook, formal novelty lies

exclusively in the packaging. Since we were served up in the oldest possible packaging we were not new enough. 'Valencia' with jazz is new. It's not particularly new without. Jazz itself is of course new.

['Neu und alt' from GW *Schriften zum Theater*, p. 67. ?About 1926.]

PROGRAMME NOTE FOR THE HEIDELBERG PRODUCTION

Visiting the play *In the Jungle of Cities* has turned out to be such a difficult proposition that only the most courageous theatres have been prepared to tackle it. Indeed nobody should be surprised if the audience rejects the play entirely. The play rests on certain assumptions, which is always troublesome, which is why the general run of the drama avoids it. The following notes about these assumptions will be of little or no help.

2

The behaviour of our contemporaries, as frequently though by no means fully expressed in the newspapers, is no longer to be explained by old motives (largely borrowed from literature). An increasing number of police reports attribute no 'motive' to the criminal. That being so, it ought not to surprise you if the newer plays show certain types of person in certain situations behaving differently from what you expected, or if your guesses as to the motives for a particular piece of behaviour turn out to be wrong. *This is a world, and a kind of drama, where the philosopher can pick his way better than the psychologist.*

3

In the theatre as elsewhere, the bourgeoisie, having wasted a hundred years staging fights between men merely over women, is not going to have much time left for fights over more serious matters before it finds itself forced, in the theatre as elsewhere, to concentrate on the most serious of all contemporary fights, the class struggle. An idealized fight such as can be seen in the play *In the Jungle of Cities* is at present only to be found in the theatre. For the real thing you will have to wait fifty years.

4

In the meantime I am sure you see that I still need to defend the simple basic conception of the play *In the Jungle of Cities*. This is that pure sport might involve two men in a fight which transforms them and their economic circumstances to the point of unrecognizability. The passion for sport is here being classed with all the other passions already at the theatre's disposal. No doubt it will take at least five decades of continuous practice in at least two continents before this passion is put on an emotional par with those great and tragic passions liable to produce triumphs and catastrophes on the grand scale. What I mean is: there are catastrophes today whose motive is sport even though it cannot be recognized as such. Besides this continuous practice there will have to be an end to those other, less pure motives for fighting which still preponderate, such as the urge to own women or means of production or objects of exploitation: motives, in short, that *can* come to an end since they can simply be organized away.

5

The territory used for fighting in this play is probably unfamiliar. For the territory so used consists in certain complexes of ideas such as a young man like George Garga holds about the family, about marriage or about his own honour. His opponent uses these complexes of ideas in order to damage him. Moreover, each combatant stimulates such thoughts in the other as must destroy him; he shoots burning arrows into his head. I can't explain this way of fighting more clearly than that.

6

My choice of an American setting is not, as has frequently been suggested, the result of a romantic disposition. I could just as well have picked Berlin, except that then the audience, instead of saying, 'That character's acting strangely, strikingly, peculiarly,' would simply have said 'It's a very exceptional Berliner who behaves like that.' Using a background (American) which naturally suited my characters, covering them rather than showing them up, seemed the easiest way of drawing attention to the odd behaviour of widely representative contemporary human types. In a German setting these same types would have been romantic; they would have contrasted with their setting, not with a romantic audience. In practical terms I would be satisfied if theatres projected America photographically on the backcloth and were content to imply Shlink's Asiatic origin by means of a plain yellow make-up, generally allowing him to behave like an Asiatic, in other words like a European. That would keep at least *one* major mystery out of the play.

['Für das Programmheft der Heidelberger Aufführung', 24 July 1928, from GW *Schriften zum Theater*, p. 969.]

ON LOOKING THROUGH MY FIRST PLAYS (iii)

My memories of writing the play *In the Jungle of Cities* are far from clear, but at least I remember the desires and ideas with which I was seized. One factor was my having seen a production of Schiller's *The Robbers*: one of those bad performances whose very poverty emphasizes the outlines of a good play, so that the writer's high aims are brought out by the failure to fulfil them. In *The Robbers* there is a most furious, destructive and desperate fight over a bourgeois inheritance, using partly non-bourgeois means. What interested me about this fight was its fury, and because it was a time (the early 1920s) when I appreciated sport, and boxing in particular, as one of the 'great mythical diversions of the giant cities on the other side

of the herring pond' I wanted my new play to show the con-
clusion of a 'fight for fighting's sake', a fight with no origin
other than the pleasure of fighting and no object except to
decide who is 'the best man'. I ought to add that at that time I
had in mind a strange historical conception, a history of mankind seen through incidents on the mass scale and of specific
historical significance, a history of continually new and different modes of behaviour, observable here and there on our
planet.

My play was meant to deal with this pure enjoyment of
fighting. Even while working on the first draft I noticed how
singularly difficult it was to bring about a meaningful fight –
which meant, according to the views which I then held, a
fight that proved something – and keep it going. Gradually it
turned into a play about the difficulty of bringing such a
fight about. The main characters had recourse to one measure
after another in their effort to come to grips. As their battle-
ground they chose the family of one of the fighters, his place
of work, and so on and so forth. The other fighter's property
was likewise 'thrown in' – and with that I was unconsciously
moving very close to the real struggle which was then taking
place, though only idealized by me: the class struggle. In the
end it dawned on the fighters that their fight was mere
shadow-boxing; even as enemies they could not make contact. A vague realization emerged: that under advanced
capitalism fighting for fighting's sake is only a wild distortion
of competition for competition's sake. The play's dialectic is
of a purely idealistic kind.

At the same time one or two seemingly quite formal wishes
were involved. In Berlin I had seen Jessner's production of
Othello with Fritz Kortner and Hofer at the then State
Theatre on the Gendarmenmarkt, and had been impressed by
one of its technical aspects: the lighting. Jessner had used
intersecting spotlights to create a peculiar dusty light which
strongly emphasized the figures; they moved about in it like
figures by Rembrandt. Other impressions also played a part:
my reading of Rimbaud's *Une saison en enfer* and of J. V. Jen-

sen's Chicago novel *The Wheel*. Also the reading of a collection of letters whose name I forget; they had a chilly, conclusive tone almost like that of a will. The influence of the outskirts of Augsburg should also be mentioned. I often used to go to the annual autumn *Plärrer*, a fair with sideshows on the so-called Small Parade Ground, with music from a number of roundabouts and with panoramas showing such naïve art as 'The Shooting of the Anarchist Ferrer in Madrid' or 'Nero Watching while Rome Burns' or 'The Lions of Bavaria Storming the Earthworks at Düppel' or 'Flight of Charles the Bold after the Battle of Murten'. I remember Charles the Bold's horse. He had huge scared eyes, as if aware of the historical situation. I wrote the play very largely out of doors while walking. An alley of Spanish chestnuts ran parallel with the old city moat past my father's house; beyond it were the wall and the remnants of the fortifications. The chestnuts were shedding their yellow leaves. The paper I wrote on was thin typing paper, folded in four to fit inside my leather notebook. I made concoctions of words like strong drinks, entire scenes out of words whose texture and colour were specifically designed to make an impression on the senses. Cherry-stone, revolver, trouserpocket, paper god: concoctions of that kind. At the same time I was of course working on the story, on the characters, on my views of human conduct and its effectiveness. I may be slightly overstressing the formal side, but I wanted to show what a complex business such writing is and how one thing merges into the other: how the shape arises from the material and in turn moulds it. Both before and later I worked in a different way and on different principles, and the resulting plays were simpler and more materialistic, but there too a considerable formal element was absorbed by the material as they took shape.

[From 'Bei Durchsicht meiner ersten Stücke' in GW *Schriften zum Theater*, pp. 949–50. Dated March 1954. Brecht reviewed a production of *The Robbers* at the Augsburg municipal theatre on 23 October 1920. Leopold Jessner's Berlin production of *Othello* with Fritz Kortner, Johanna Hofer, Albert Steinrück and Rudolf Forster had its première on 11 November 1921; it must have been one of the first plays that he saw in Berlin. For a note on Brecht's debt to Rimbaud and Jensen, see p. 450 below. The collection of letters, so Dr Reinhold Grimm has suggested, may be a volume called *Knabenbriefe* edited by Charlotte Westermann and published in Düsseldorf in 1908.]

Editorial Note on the Text

This is based, with grateful acknowledgements, on the texts and information given in the volume of 'materials' edited by Gisela E. Bahr under the title *Im Dickicht der Städte. Erstfassung und Materialien*, and published by Suhrkamp-Verlag in 1968 ('edition suhrkamp' number 246). References in the text are to the notes on The Play's Literary Ancestry, which follow on p. 450.

A diary note of 4 September 1921 shows Brecht just before his visit to Berlin wondering why 'nobody has yet described the big city as a jungle'.

> Where are its heroes, its colonisers, its victims? The hostility of the big city, its malignant stony consistency, its babylonian confusion of language: in short, its poetry has not yet been created.

As he was then fresh from reading Jensen's *The Wheel* and Sinclair's *The Jungle*, both of which are set in Chicago, this cannot be taken too literally, but it relates none the less to the first draft of the play, on which he embarked about that time.

In the Jungle, as it was then called, had its première on 9 May 1923. The typescript (of which two versions exist in the Brecht Archive) had by then already been considerably modified, to judge from the evidence of the two heavily amended scripts used by the director Erich Engel (and left by him to the East German Academy of Arts) and of the printed programme. Thus there are sixteen scenes in the typescript, but the programme says it is a 'Drama in 10 Scenes'. It evidently began with the shouted headlines from the Programme Note (p. 432 above), and lasted over three hours. At the first Berlin performance, which took place on 29 October 1924 at the Deutsches Theater, again under Engel's direction, it was renamed *Jungle*, with the subtitle 'Decline of a Family' and prefaced by the present prologue. Essentially, however, it seems to have been a cut version of the same play.

The revised *In the Jungle of Cities*, virtually in its final form, was published by Ullstein (Propyläen-Verlag) in spring 1927, and given its first performance under Carl Ebert's direction in Darmstadt that

December. There are eleven scenes (though misnumbering makes it look as if there were only ten); their titles have been made apparently more precise, with exact dates and times; stage and lighting directions are less atmospheric; some names and characters are altered, notably those of Skinny and Manky; there are fewer references to the jungle and more to the fight; a generally more urban, American, technological flavour is given, not least by the illustrations at the end of the book, which show 'typical cities and people of the first decades of the century'. There are also some major alterations in the story: Jane's murder is dispensed with; the illegal reselling of Shlink's timber is new, and the lynchers who come for him in the end are no longer individuals he has wronged but citizens responding to a denunciation made by Garga before he goes to gaol and left smouldering under Shlink like a kind of time-bomb.

In the 1950s a few very small changes were made when the play was republished in Brecht's collected *Stücke*. Among them are the substitution of 'Schönes' (or 'beautiful') for Manky's odd English term of endearment 'Nice', and the cutting of the dedication to Brecht's first wife Marianne.

The following is a scene by scene comparison of the typescript (corrected version) of *In the Jungle* (1922) and the published text of *In the Jungle of Cities* (1927). Arabic scene numbers refer to the former, Roman to the latter.

1. *Lending Library*. (Fairly close to I.)

Described as '*Brown. Wet tobacco leaves. Soapy-green sliding windows, steps. Low. Lots of paper*'. Shlink (who had originally been conceived of as Chinese) wears a '*long dirty yellow soutane*'. According to Engel's script he 'speaks quickly, but with large slow gestures, never giving anything away. Broad, powerful back.' Moti Gui, who was renamed Skinny in the 1927 text, 'has a rather asthmatic snuffle. Rhythmic speech due to pauses for breath. Half-breed, run down, agog for sensations.' Worm, who then had no other name, is 'bald, syphilitic. Saddle-shaped nose, wide-set eyes. Genial.' Baboon, likewise, 'A pimp. Dressed in greasy black. Occasionally imitates Shlink.'

The references to Jensen and Rimbaud early in the scene are new in 1927. In 1922 Garga at one point recommends 'Noa! Noa! A good, first rate book, written in blood on leather . . .' and Brecht evidently considered inserting a quotation from this work of Gauguin's to follow Shlink's first reference to Tahiti.

By 1927 pounds had become dollars and schnaps whisky. Garga's references to prostitution and Shlink's declaration that he is opening the fight against him and will shake his foundations are all new.

2. *In the Quarry*. (Cut.)

This dialogue between Garga and The Green Man is given in full at the end of the present notes. It was cut from the 1927 version, and probably also from the two earlier productions as, although it is in Engel's and Erwin Faber's (the Munich Garga)'s scripts, The Green Man is not named on the 1923 programme.

3. *Shlink's office*. (Cut and slightly transposed to form II.)

Described as 'Brown, like an open sluice-gate'. In lieu of the opening exchange with Worm, Shlink soliloquizes:

> Smooth, round, full, that's me. It's all so little effort, it all comes easy to me. How easily I digest! *Silence*. For ten years there's been no difficulty in living like this. Comfortable, well dug in, avoiding any kind of friction. Now I've begun to take easiness for granted, and I'm fed up with everything.

Marie enters in white. As Garga puts on his new linen behind the screen he exclaims 'White linen! That means adventures. White muslin. For daydreaming about horses in.' He makes his remark about Shlink having stripped his skin (now on p. 128) immediately after emerging from behind the screen, thus establishing the relation between the two leit-motivs of *skin* and *linen*.

The resale of Broost and Co's timber is all new in 1927. In the 1922 text the sacking of Moti Gui (= Skinny) is more elaborate. Baboon is not in this scene at all (nor are his remarks re Papua and 'the chick'), so when Shlink tells Marie 'he loves you' he is referring to Moti Gui – altogether a more pathetic and less comic character in this version. He tries to woo Marie by telling her that she gives off a smell like a horse; hence Garga's remark at the end of the scene, which remains, a little bafflingly, in the 1927 text. In a sub-episode labelled 'The Auction' and cut in the second of Engel's scripts Marie is inspected 'like a horse' and has been put up for auction when the Salvation Army arrive. Her closing lines to the scene are new.

4. *The Family Sacrificed*. (III is much the same, but plus the episode with Worm and subsequent references to it.)

The setting is an '*attic with light-coloured wallpaper. Ivory people.*

Dark circular table. John, Mae, Mankyboddle seated around it.' Mankyboddle, sometimes called Manky for short in this version, is
altogether more prominent and more emphatically an old sea dog
than in 1927. A very early note referring to Marie's suitor as
'(Kutteldaddeldu)' suggests that both name and character may
derive from Joachim Ringelnatz's comic seaman of that name.

More is made in 1922 of the tension between the Garga parents,
also of George Garga's drinking. 'This is a city,' says John before
George's entrance, 'people live in holes like this; my brother ran
around in the jungle – the deserter. George has got his blood.' It is
new in 1927 that George should bring money and hand it to Mae.
The episode with Worm is already in two of the 1923 stage scripts.

In one of these when John and Manky reappear before Shlink's
entrance they sing a verse of the 'Ballad of the Woman and the
Soldier' (subsequently used in *Mother Courage*). In the other they
sing 'Fifteen men on the dead man's chest' from *Treasure Island*.
It is suggested that they did so in the Munich production.

5. *In the Coal Yards*. (Replaced by IV 'Chinese Hotel', which was
evidently written for the 1923 production.)

In the first half Marie, who has been bringing food to Shlink as
he heaves coal, declares her love for him and is rejected. The second
is a long battle of words between him and Garga, ending with the
latter's refusal to go to Tahiti. In the background 'the thunder of
awakening Chicago'.

The 1923 'Chinese Hotel' scene is largely the same as in the 1927
text, the chief addition in the latter being Baboon's opening
remarks about Shlink's activities.

6. *In the Sack*. (Cut and partly rewritten to form V, the second
Chinese Hotel scene.)

'Schnaps saloon in the Coal Bar. Divided by sacking, though
not completely.' The division is in effect as in V. Garga is lying on
the bed 'psalmodizing'; Manky is sitting drinking in the saloon.
There are even more Rimbaud quotations or imitations than in
1927, and an introductory episode where Worm and Moti Gui/
Skinny report to Garga, and the latter humiliates Moti Gui by
throwing a coin into the washing-up water and getting him to fish
it out with his teeth. In the 1927 text Skinny is not in this scene.

Marie and Garga have more to say about their parents' plight.
Shlink announces that he has bought back his house. Garga tells
Shlink that he is beginning to feel at home in his skin; then when

he tries to cadge a drink Shlink says he can't buy his skin with money. The general gist of the scene remains the same, though it is new in 1927 that Shlink should hand over the proceeds of the Broost timber sale and then be treated as 'overdrawn'.

7. *Mankyboddle's Attic.* (Cut from 1927 text.)

'*Greenish wallpaper.*' A short scene between Manky and Marie. Her desperate efforts to love him have been too much for both. She denounces him and goes out, leaving him muttering, 'Nice! Christ, what a hysterical cow you are! Nice!'

Manky is rum-sodden and nautical in this scene. Thus:

MARIE: You puff away at your cigar and lie in bed with your clothes on. Why don't you take your pants off?

MANKY: I got the habit on the *Anaqueen*, see?

The scene is in Engel's script, but has evidently not been worked on and is deleted from the list of scenes there.

8. *At the Gargas'.* (Telescoped with scene 10 to form VII.)

'*Attic. Sacking. Whitewash. Circular table. Midday meal.*' About five-sixths of the scene are cut in the 1927 version, and there is a good deal of cutting already in the 1923 stage scripts. About a third of scene 10 (q.v.) is tacked on to what remains.

The evidence of prosperity in the Gargas' room – the new clothes and furniture and John's opening speech – is absent from the 1922 version, which begins with a desultory mealtime conversation in which Manky is prominent. He also plays the accordion, and later joins John in singing verses taken (unacknowledgedly) from Kipling's *The Light That Failed*:

There were three friends that buried the fourth,
The mould in his mouth and the dust in his eyes,
And they went south and east and north –
The strong man fights but the sick man dies.

There were three friends that spoke of the dead –
The strong man fights and the sick man dies –
'And would he were here with us now,' they said –
'The sun in our face and the wind in our eyes.'

In 1927 Manky is named in the opening stage direction, but has nothing to say.

Between Shlink's entry and Jane's description of the wedding about 130 lines are cut. Shlink announces that Marie has left

Manky, then the landlord appears demanding the rent and complaining of the accordion. Shlink produces the title deeds to some southern cotton fields and hands them to Garga, thus saving the family. A reference by Garga to the 'chalky light' is changed in 1927 to 'a cold light'.

The mention of the Broost timber swindle and of Garga's intention to go to gaol is new in 1927. The scene ends with Mae's disappearance and the entry of the waiter with John's farewell drink.

9. *Coppice.* (VI.)

'*Low trees with faded brown leaves. Whiteish mist.*' Taken over almost unchanged in 1927, but transposed to precede the foregoing scene. The word 'jungle' is used instead of 'bushes' where Shlink speaks of Marie being like a [crazy] bitch.

10. *Garga's Attic.* (Telescoped with 8 to form VII.)

'*Yellow wallpaper. Watercolour. Evening drips down the panes like dishwater.*' Most of the rest of VII after the waiter's exit is from the beginning of this scene: i.e. Marie's attempt to give John Garga money. Garga's reappearance, however, and his writing of the note to the newspaper (the police in 1927) are new.

In 1922 Shlink arrives after Marie's exit, and accuses Garga of raising money in a bar on his cottonfield deeds. In fact Jane was responsible, but Garga is prepared to take the blame and go to prison. He threatens Shlink with a knife; Shlink challenges him to plunge it into his breast.

11. *Bar.* (Transposed and cut to form IX.)

Scene VIII in the 1927 text is entirely new. IX, called 'Bar in Chinatown' in 1927, was rechristened, as we now have it, in the 1953 *Stücke* volume. In 1922 the setting is not described. The characters named include The Yellow Gentleman (not listed in the 1923 programme) – he tells the G. Wishu story – and Moti Gui (Skinny). Worm is not in this scene.

After the Wishu story the Snub-nosed Man asks, 'Do you believe in God?'

THE YELLOW GENTLEMAN: No. By no means. Not in any sense. Absolutely not. I'm an anti-semite.

Otherwise, apart from the absence of Baboon's opening remarks (new in 1927), the beginning of the scene up to Garga's entrance is much as in the final version. Garga, however, appears alone, without witnesses. The arrangement of his dialogues with Jane and with Marie is rather different, though their substance is much the same. Jane, on going off with Baboon, leaves the possibility of returning to Garga open. The Salvation Army man's attempted suicide is put at the end of the scene.

Garga's speech about the fight, the ring and the knock-out is new in 1927. Shlink's entrance at the end of IX is taken over in very shortened form from scene 12 below.

12. *Garga's Attic.* (A few lines taken into IX; otherwise cut.)

'*Night. Flying shouts from below. The partition seems to be rocking. A ship.*' Three-quarters of the scene is Shlink and Garga. Garga looks out of the window and sees 'Black linen hanging on the balcony. No wind.' Shlink thinks the shouting is getting louder.

> GARGA: They're looking for you. *Silence.* They're going to lynch us. They might ... They might lynch us. They've been lynching today. Niggers strung up like like dirty linen. I heard on the Milwaukee Bridge that they were looking for you, – you.

Shlink again calls it 'the white howling'. (*His* lynching party, however, is only organized in scene 14.)

They leave together to go 'down to the marshes'. Then Jane and Baboon appear and occupy the rest of the scene. She is drunk, and he makes her write a note to Garga saying she is coming to him.

13. *In the Jungle.* (Telescoped with scenes 14 and 15, with a good deal of transposition, to form X.)

'*Brown. Golden.*' The scene is confined to Shlink and Garga, who begin by speaking of their enmity, somewhat as at the start of X but at greater length. Shlink then gives Garga Jane's note.

In Engel's stage scripts the scene is cut and partly incorporated in 15.

14. *Bar in the Jungle.* (Almost entirely cut.)

No description of setting. Characters are The Bear, The Chair, The Ape, The Preacher, joined shortly by Garga and Moti Gui. The first three are not listed in the 1923 programme, but the stage scripts suggests that Chair and Ape are identical with Worm and Baboon.

Bear reads in his paper that a woman's body has been found in the marshes. Garga on entering speaks of his enmity with the Malay. Asked if it is a business matter he says, 'A physical affair. You must help me, because we've all been moulded from the same earth. Is this our country or not?'

THE OTHERS: It's our country! He shall hang! They're our trees!

Garga works them up into a lynching party. 'Are you free?' he calls after them. 'Come down into the dark arena. Your knife in your hand, bare in the cold blackness. ... Are you free? Your mistress, freedom, is sailing on the ships!'

15. *Hut in the Jungle*. (See 13. Most of X derives from this scene.)
Again Shlink and Garga talking about their fight. 'Yes,' says Shlink. 'You wanted it to end, but I wanted a fight, Garga.' He offers to lend him a horse to escape on. Then shows him the books of the timber business, where Garga finds as the final entry: 'Twenty pounds for strangling Jane Garga in the yellow swamps.' Garga's speech on p. 173 beginning 'Shlink, I've been listening to you now for three weeks' is new in the 1927 edition, which also adds Garga's 'New York' after Shlink's 'Tahiti?', thus altering the direction of Garga's Rimbaud quotation. The words 'in the eyes of God' are cut where Garga, just before his exit, says that it is not important to be the stronger man.

Marie enters in black gauze. '*A whiteish light appears around her.*' Shlink's auto-obituary ('I, Wang Yen', etc.) on taking the poison is new in 1927. In 1922 the lynching party (the five characters of scene 14) propose to rape Marie, and drag her off.

16. *Shlink's Office*. (Largely rewritten as XI.)
In 1922 John says '... march! Against the jungle' merely, 'of the city!' being added in 1927. Garga is off to the south to till the soil, not to New York. The play ends with a longer speech by Garga, finishing up: 'It was the best time. The chaos is used up: it dismissed me without a blessing. Maybe work will be a consolation. It's certainly very late. I feel abandoned.' Then Moti Gui's voice, off: 'East wind!' Garga remains alone, grinning.

2
In the Quarry

White chalk slope. Morning. The rumbling of the Pacific trains, off. People shouting.

George Garga. The Green Man.

GARGA *ragged, in shirt and trousers, hands in pockets:* An average morning. Anything strike you, sir?

GREEN MAN: Let's go and have another drink.

GARGA: What's that noise?

GREEN MAN: The trains to Illinois.

GARGA: Yes. As usual.

GREEN MAN: Aren't you working in a shop any longer, sir?

GARGA: It's my time off.

GREEN MAN: Let's have a drink.

GARGA: No, no.

GREEN MAN: How's the seamstress?

Garga whistles.

GREEN MAN: Is she off too?

GARGA: The clouds! Like soiled swans! Do you enjoy having a boot put in your face?

GREEN MAN: No.

GARGA: What can one do about it?

The Green Man pulls out a pistol.

GARGA *takes it:* We'll have a drink afterwards. It's not pleasant having a boot put in one's face.

GREEN MAN: What's he really after?

GARGA *shrugs his shoulders:* One fine morning he spat a little cherry stone in my eye.

GREEN MAN: Unknown?

GARGA: Never saw him before.

GREEN MAN: Careful. Cold blood.

Sound of trains rumbling by above.

That's the Pacific–New York. Will he want to dig his heels in?

GARGA: Surely.

GREEN MAN: . . . Have reckoned with you?

GARGA: I turned up out of the blue.

GREEN MAN: Having a drink is undoubtedly better. Sleeping with women. Smoking.

GARGA: Baring your teeth isn't bad.

GREEN MAN: If you've got good ones.

The Play's Literary Ancestry

A NOTE BY GERHARD NELLHAUS

At the start of the opening scene Brecht acknowledges, in the order of their importance, the two writers who particularly influenced his play. They were the Danish novelist Johannes Vilhelm Jensen (1875–1950) and the French poet Arthur Rimbaud (1854–91). In the note on pp. 438–9 he specifies the works from which, directly and indirectly, he had drawn: the novel *Hjulet* (*The Wheel*) and the prose poem *Une saison en enfer*. He knew both in the German: the former in a translation by Mens published in 1908 under the title *Das Rad*, and Rimbaud's writings in translations by K. L. Ammer (Karl Klammer) and Adolf Christian.

Of the two, the influence of *The Wheel* was the greater in every way: background and plot, characterizations, imagery, illustrations of which are given in the notes below (which are based on the German edition published by S. Fischer in 1921, since *Hjulet* has not been published in English). It is in the main the story of 'a fight between two human beings, two different types of nervous organism, a relentless fight which could only end with the extermination of one of them, because one was fighting blind and with all the strength of his basic appetite while for the other it was a question of life or death' (German edition, pp. 107–8). This was the continuation of a fight that had begun in a novel *Madam d'Ora*, which Jensen had written a year earlier, in 1904. In it the lay-preacher Evanston, a self-styled superman, destroyed the renowned scientist Edmund Hall by accusing him of his own murder of one Elly Johnson in London. But later in New York, Evanston is defeated by the young journalist, Lee, in a boxing match, 'an encounter . . . which [Evanston] could not possibly forget . . . [He] came to love Lee . . . to long for [him], to long for [him] from the moment when [Lee] with a blow of his fist shut [Evanston's] eyes' (p. 182). Now Evanston, alias Cancer, has come to Chicago, for this was the hub of the world's wheel, 'a grand international centre . . . the centre of the most materialistic philosophy in the world' (p. 165). Here Evanston starts out in a hole in the wall as a revivalist and becomes the prophet of a mass movement which he hopes to turn into a new religion. For it, Evanston wants Lee to write the new Bible because he knows

Lee's 'God is in Chicago' as well, since he has read Lee's tract proclaiming Americans as the lost people of God who in America have the opportunity of creating the vital civilization Europe might have become had the Gothic and not the Gallic influence won out.

Evanston's 'spiritual rape' of Lee consists not only of stealing the would-be poet's views of life, but of seeking to possess him physically, of alienating him from his fiancée, of charging him with a murder – just as he had done Hall – in an anonymous letter. Evanston can do this because he has studied this 'naïve young man' and knows that he is 'both a coward and full of self-importance', a 'sentimentalist' who, 'not being much for women', is 'still pure' and yet is engaged to the daughter of Chicago's richest man. A general strike organized by Cancer against the latter fails when Lee kills Evanston, this 'long extinct type who existed outside of society', in order to redeem 'his city and all his own kind'. After fleeing Chicago, first to Japan and then around the world, Lee returns to his pregnant fiancée and, learning of her father's death, quite 'sensibly' takes over the business.

By contrast, the relationship between Verlaine and Rimbaud now occupied Brecht less than it had done in *Baal*. He was more concerned with Rimbaud's literary manner, his 'concoction of words'. The Rimbaud quotations put into the mouth of Garga are often somewhat free; hence the original French is given below wherever possible for comparison. Though in Brecht's 'Statement' of 1924 (p. 433 above) he claimed also to have been quoting Verlaine, no lines comparable in style or content have been found.

1. Evanston in *The Wheel* (p. 84) says that 'it happens to be a female's pleasure to have her ears boxed by as malicious and dirty a baboon as possible'.

2. Rimbaud, *Une saison en enfer*: 'Je suis une bête, un nègre. Mais je puis être sauvé. Vous êtes de faux nègres, vous, maniaques, féroces, avares. Marchand, tu es nègre; magistrat, tu es nègre; général, tu es nègre; empereur, vieille démangeaison, tu es nègre: tu as bu d'une liqueur non taxée, de la fabrique de Satan. – Ce peuple est inspiré par la fièvre et le cancer . . . Je ne comprends pas les lois; je n'ai pas le sens moral, je suis une brute: vous vous trompez.'

3. 'Stormy the night and the sea runs high' is a line from a sentimental and trashy song 'Asleep in the Deep', for which, according to information supplied by Dr Kurt Opitz, Adolf Martel wrote

the text (about 1890) and H. W. Petrie the music (1897). It was very popular at the turn of the century, and Brecht heard it often as a child, so that it became for him the quintessence of *Kitsch*. He referred to it in *Drums in the Night* (p. 86 above), in scene 13 of *Mahagonny*, in chapter 14 of *The Threepenny Novel* and in an unfinished essay of the 1950s on popular poetry ('Wo ich gelernt habe') where he noted that it contained 'one quatrain of great beauty'.

4. In *The Wheel* (p. 162) Lee says of Evanston, 'What was one to do about a man whose nerves hardly reached his skin?'

5. Cf. *The Wheel*, p. 221: 'In all the streets people began to move about, all the faithful early risers in the city, people like himself, whom he had always fully comprehended, whether they were driving in their waggons or were striding off with their tools, or were half-running along the sidewalk, a mountain of fresh newspapers on their shoulders.' There is a similar echo in Shen Teh's speech in scene 4 of *The Good Person of Szechwan*.

6. 'L'époux infernal' is the subheading of the first 'Délire' in *Une saison en enfer*, where the virgin exclaims, 'Je suis esclave de l'Epoux infernal, celui qui a perdu les vierges folles.'

7. Rimbaud: 'J'aimai le désert, les vergers brûlés, les boutiques fanées, les boissons tiédies.'

8. No such passage was found in Rimbaud, but perhaps Brecht was inspired by Rimbaud's lines: 'Je suis veuve... J'étais veuve . . .' in the first 'Délire' above.

9. In *The Wheel*, too, Evanston reproaches Lee for drinking.

10. 'Une souffle ouvre les brèches opératiques dans les cloisons' are the opening words of 'Nocturne Vulgaire' in *Les Illuminations*.

11. These are said to have been the dying words of Frederick the Great.

12. In *The Wheel* Lee refuses Evanston's love because he finds him so unappealing, because he 'knew instinctively that Evanston was an old man' (p. 168), 'a worm of the past' (p. 245), who fought 'with the powers of an ape and mostly with the corruption of age' (p. 297).

13. This key speech echoes both Rimbaud's 'J'enviais la félicité des bêtes' and many passages from *The Wheel*. Note Evanston's remark (p. 216) that 'the only thing real in this world is sensual lust . . . the only proof I have of being alive is that I die of pleasure'. And several times Jensen describes how Evanston confronts Lee 'like a beast of prey, baring his teeth' (p. 163), and how 'they faced each other like two wild animals' (p. 280).

14. Towards the end of their fight, Lee in *The Wheel* complains of his adversary's 'endless babbling' (p. 293).

15. Rimbaud, *Une saison en enfer*: 'Je reviendrai, avec des membres de fer, la peau sombre, l'oeil furieux; sur mon masque, on me jugera d'une race forte. J'aurai de l'or: je serai oisif et brutal. Les femmes soignent ces féroces infirmes retour des pays chauds. Je serai mêlé aux affaires politiques. Sauvé.'

16. The final scene recalls what happens at the end of *The Wheel* when Lee decides to devote himself to his dead father-in-law's business: 'The everyday had returned with its chances and ways, the everyday and the old taste for work.'

EDWARD II

ON LOOKING THROUGH MY FIRST PLAYS (iv)

Adapting Marlowe's *Edward the Second* was a job which I undertook in collaboration with Lion Feuchtwanger because I had to do a production at the Munich Kammerspiele. Today it is hard for me to come to terms with it. We wanted to make possible a production which would break with the Shakespearean tradition common to German theatres: that lumpy monumental style beloved of middle-class philistines. I am reprinting it without any changes. The reader may find something to interest him in the narrative methods of the Elizabethans and in the emergence of a new stage language.

[From 'Bei Durchsicht meiner ersten Stücke'. Foreword to *Stücke I*, all editions except the first. Dated March 1954.]

Editorial Note on the Text

No manuscript, typescript or prompt copy of the play has yet
come to the notice of the Brecht Archive. Nor did Brecht write any
formal notes to it. The version which he decided to print unchanged in the collected *Stücke* was that published by Kiepenheuer
in 1924, the year of the play's original production. (There were, in
fact, some very slight editorial changes, probably not by Brecht
himself.)

The version of Marlowe's play which Brecht and Feuchtwanger
used was a German translation by Alfred Walter Heymel, originally published by Insel-Verlag (Leipzig) before the First World
War. It has been reprinted by Dr Reinhold Grimm in the Edition
Suhrkamp volume *Leben Eduards des Zweiten von England. Vorlage,
Texte und Materialien* (Frankfurt, 1968). Miss Louise Laboulle has
calculated that they took over about one-sixth of Marlowe's
lines, but even where they did so they often changed Heymel's
wording.

In the same volume there is a reprint of the extract originally
published in the Munich literary magazine *Der neue Merkur* in
February 1924, on the eve of the première. This only goes up to
the end of Anne's scene with Mortimer after the (imaginary) Battle
of Killingworth (p. 221), but already contains one or two major
differences from the final version. In particular it follows Marlowe
in having Edward sign the decree banishing Gaveston when the
Archbishop threatens to 'discharge these peers / Of duty and
allegiance due to thee'. Edward then persuades Anne to seduce
Mortimer as best she can (part of the dialogue was later brought
forward to the catapult-showing scene) to have the decree re-
scinded. Gaveston, as in Marlowe, returns from Ireland and is
assaulted by the peers. In the final version, of course, Edward
refuses to sign, and the battle immediately follows (after a hypo-
thetical gap of nine years).

Other differences include the swapping round of the catapult
scene with that where Mortimer is discovered alone with his books,
and the omission of Gaveston's monologue when writing his will.
In the opening scene a few lines are left of Gaveston's best-known
speech from the original ('I must have wanton poets . . .'), which is

entirely missing from the final version. Lancaster's comment on Edward's love for Gaveston is also perhaps worth recording: 'Goddam!' he says. 'That's what I call passion.'

The magazine called the play a 'History by Bertolt Brecht', without mentioning either Feuchtwanger or Marlowe. Feuchtwanger's name was also apparently missing from the programme of the first Berlin production at the end of the same year, and the exact nature and extent of his contribution cannot as yet be judged. Brecht's own note 'I wrote this play with Lion Feuchtwanger. Bertolt Brecht' should be set against the corresponding note three years later to the published version of Feuchtwanger's *Kalkutta. 4 Mai*: 'I wrote this play with Bertolt Brecht. Lion Feuchtwanger.' (Strictly speaking this was a joint revision, made in 1925, of a play written by Feuchtwanger in 1915.) No trace has been found of the revised text of 1926 referred to in an undated note (p. 141 of the volume *Im Dickicht der Städte. Erstfassung und Materialien* in the Edition Suhrkamp series: not included in GW). The relevant passage goes:

> Thus in *Edward* (second version, summer 1926), I have tried to sketch that great sombre beast which felt the first shock-waves of a mighty global disaster threatening the individual like premonitions of an earthquake. I have shown his primitive and desperate measures, his terrible and anachronistically isolated finish. In those years the last of the saurians loomed up before the eyes of posterity, heralding the Flood.

It is the same idea as in scene 1 of the 1926 revision of *Baal*.